Routledge Revivals

Turkish Nationalism and Western Civilization

Turkish Nationalism and Western Civilization (1959) presents Ziya Gökalp's synthesis of nationalism, Islam and Western civilization in a developmental and systematic way. More than as a sociologist, poet, man of public affairs, or ideological slogan-maker, Ziya Gökalp (1876–1924) deserves the attention of social practitioners and scientists for his insight into the problems of accommodating non-Western cultures and Western civilization progressively and creatively.

Turkish Nationalism and Western Civilization
Selected Essays of Ziya Gökalp

Ziya Gökalp

Translated and Edited with An Introduction by Niyazi Berkes

First published in 1959
by George Allen & Unwin Ltd

This edition first published in 2025 by Routledge
4 Park Square, Milton Park, Abingdon, Oxon, OX14 4RN

and by Routledge
605 Third Avenue, New York, NY 10017

Routledge is an imprint of the Taylor & Francis Group, an informa business

© 1959 Niyazi Berkes

All rights reserved. No part of this book may be reprinted or reproduced or utilised in any form or by any electronic, mechanical, or other means, now known or hereafter invented, including photocopying and recording, or in any information storage or retrieval system, without permission in writing from the publishers.

Publisher's Note
The publisher has gone to great lengths to ensure the quality of this reprint but points out that some imperfections in the original copies may be apparent.

Disclaimer
The publisher has made every effort to trace copyright holders and welcomes correspondence from those they have been unable to contact.

A Library of Congress record exists under LCCN: a 60001297

ISBN: 978-1-032-99669-1 (hbk)
ISBN: 978-1-003-60539-3 (ebk)
ISBN: 978-1-032-99670-7 (pbk)

Book DOI 10.4324/9781003605393

TURKISH NATIONALISM AND WESTERN CIVILIZATION

SELECTED ESSAYS OF ZIYA GÖKALP

Translated and Edited
with an Introduction by
NIYAZI BERKES
*Institute of Islamic Studies
McGill University*

Ruskin House
GEORGE ALLEN AND UNWIN LTD
MUSEUM STREET LONDON

FIRST PUBLISHED IN 1959

This book is copyright under the Berne Convention. Apart from any fair dealing for the purposes of private study, research, criticism or review, as permitted under the Copyright Act, 1956, no portion may be reproduced by any process without written permission. Inquiry should be made to the publishers.

© *Niyazi Berkes*, 1959

PRINTED IN GREAT BRITAIN
in 11 point Fournier type
BY HAZELL WATSON AND VINEY LTD
AYLESBURY AND SLOUGH

PREFACE

THE purpose of this volume is to provide the English reader with samples of the writings of Ziya Gökalp (1876–1924), the Turkish thinker, regarding Turkish nationalism and its meaning in terms of Islam and Western civilization. It must be emphasized, therefore, that the present volume is not a complete edition of Gökalp's writings.

Gökalp's writings can be classified roughly into three groups: (*a*) literary works, (*b*) writings on folklore, history, and sociology, and (*c*) prose writings dealing with cultural matters in short essay form.

The first and second categories are left entirely outside the framework of the present work. In excluding these, I believed that the Western reader would lose very little. Gökalp's poetry was devoid of art and was extremely didactic. He seems to have written poems as a hobby and never posed as a poet. He used poetry, however, to popularize his ideas in the form of rhymed slogans. This, I believe, helped to popularize some of his ideas, but, on the whole, was a factor in causing his ideas to be understood partially or inadequately. Another of his aims seems to have been to develop a modern literature which would develop into the writing of religious hymns as well as folk stories for children, but, unfortunately, his lack of artistic genius made this attempt almost a complete failure in so far as art went.

The second category of his writings have been excluded because of their length and technical nature. Among them must be mentioned his *Türk Medeniyeti Tarihi (The History of the Turkish Civilization)*, of which only the first volume appeared, then posthumously.

The present volume has been compiled from his essays. Again, it is not a complete collection of this type of his writings. It contains selections which I found to express Gökalp's often repeated basic ideas best, to demonstrate the changes that took place in his formulations, and to show inconsistencies or contradictions in his ideas.

This volume will be found lacking by some readers because it includes nothing specific to one issue. Gökalp was believed to have been the prophet of Pan-Turanism. The belief was widespread and was shared by me when I began making an assortment of articles for translation. Upon completing a first selection, I found, to my surprise, that I had not included a single essay dealing directly or exclusively with Pan-Turanism. On reviewing Gökalp's works, I found, to my

8   PREFACE

greater amazement, that he wrote only two short essays on this subject ('Türk Milleti ve Turan', *Türk Yurdu*, Vol. VI, No. 62 (1914), pp. 2053–8, and 'Turan Nedir?', *Yeni Mecmua*, No. 37, February 1918, pp. 82–3), neither of which were representative specimens of his writing, neither of which contained any theoretical formulations of his ideology, and neither of which contained a formulation of the Pan-Turanian ideology itself. To be sure, these essays favoured the idea, but they were not of a nature to be written by a prophet of a movement. Furthermore, Gökalp ceased even to mention the word 'Turan' in his poetry after 1915, when he developed his theory of nationality (F. A. Tansel, *Ziya Gökalp Külliyatı*, Vol. I (Ankara, 1952), p. xv), and he dismissed the idea after 1918 as one which 'may only serve to inspire the too imaginative poets' (cf. the second article mentioned above, p. 82). The present work, therefore, contains neither of Gökalp's two essays impinging upon Pan-Turanism; neither would add to our knowledge of the ideology itself or to our understanding of Gökalp's system of ideas.

Both chronological sequence and topical interrelationships were kept in view in arranging the selected articles. In other words, the essays were arranged in a chronological order modified by the second criterion. Fortunately, this scheme has not created much difficulty, as Gökalp's writings underwent a logical development with time. Hence, only a few essays had to be introduced out of their chronological order —to provide the reader with certain background information.

The majority of the essays have been reproduced in their entirety. Brief excerpts from a few have been included. Some omissions have been made from otherwise complete essays when (*a*) statements were repeated, (*b*) the author digressed in order to clarify some points for his Turkish readers, or (*c*) the author repeated ideas elaborated in other included essays. Short additions, within brackets, have been made in order to complete a sentence or to make it more readily understandable to the English reader.

The sources from which the selections have been taken are given in the footnotes in their original Turkish, transliterated into the modern characters. The English titles are not always literal or exact translations of the originals in order (*a*) to adapt, without making too great deviations, the titles to English usage, and (*b*) to give a more coherent appearance to the Table of Contents with a view towards facilitating an understanding of the intellectual content of the volume.

PREFACE   9

Despite efforts to do otherwise, it has been necessary to use many Turkish or Turkified words in the text. (A glossary of the Turkish and Arabic words retained in the translation is appended.) Words which have been anglicized—such as Ottoman, sultan, and caliph—have been used in their English forms. Words derived from the Arabic but used in Turkish in their Turkified forms have been rendered according to the present-day Turkish spelling. Where relevant, the Arabic equivalents of these words are given within brackets. In cases where Gökalp used Arabic words in their original rather than in their Turkified forms, these have been rendered according to their Arabic transliterations. (The following letters in the modern Turkish alphabet are pronounced as indicated: c, English j; ç, English ch; ğ, almost the English y; ö, German ö; ü, German ü; ş, English sh; and ı, the actual sound value given to the English tion in addition or ton in carton.)

The translation is neither strictly literal nor fully adapted to the English literary style. I have sought to solve some of the problems posed by the fact that certain figures of speech are amenable to direct translation, while others are not by following a middle course. I believe that in taking some liberties with the text I have remained true to the *meaning* of the original, or at least have not rendered the material in a way contrary to the original. It was hoped that by not seeking to achieve a fully polished English rendition the reader would get some feeling for the style of thinking and writing of a non-English-speaking writer.

In concluding this Preface, I should like to express my gratitude to those who have made the appearance of this work possible. I wish to thank the Faculty of Graduate Studies, McGill University, for a grant towards the preparation of the translation. I am particularly indebted to Professor Wilfred Cantwell Smith, the Director of the Institute of Islamic Studies, McGill University, for his constant and generous encouragement. My thanks are due also to Dr Howard A. Reed and Professor F. Rahman, both colleagues at McGill during the preparation of the volume, for their help and encouragement. I am grateful to Mrs Nora Grosheintz-Laval and Miss Judy Speier for reading, correcting, and typing the text. I thank the editors of the *Middle East Journal* for permission to reproduce the following Introduction which appeared originally as an article in that journal (*Middle East Journal*, Vol. VIII, No. 4, Autumn 1954).

PREFACE

Finally, I want to express my gratitude to my brother, Enver Berkes, who, as always, did not fail to give me all the necessary support in obtaining materials for this work. To him this volume is affectionately dedicated.

Montreal, January 1958   NIYAZI BERKES

CONTENTS

PREFACE	page 7
TRANSLATOR'S INTRODUCTION	13

PART I

I. AUTOBIOGRAPHICAL

My Father's Testament	35
My Teacher's Testament	37
The Testament of My Spiritual Guide	39
My Nationality	43

II. THE PHILOSOPHY OF VALUES AND IDEALS

The Philosophy of Today	46
The Philosophy of Idealism of Ibn Al-'Arabi	50
New Life and New Values	55
Historical Materialism and Sociological Idealism	60
The Nature of Ideals	66

III. THE IDEAL OF NATIONALISM

Three Currents of Thought	71
Nation and Fatherland	76
The Ideal of Nationalism	79
National Language	82

PART II

IV. CULTURE AND CIVILIZATION

Civilization of the People	89
Tradition and Formalism	92
Community and Society	97
Culture and Civilization	104

PART III

V. THE EVOLUTION OF SOCIETY

The Scientific Study of Communities	113
Classification of Social Species	123
A Note on the Terms 'Society' and 'Community'	125
The Rise of the Nations	126
What is a Nation?	134
Villages and the Commune	138
Is Turkey a Modern Nation?	142
The Turkish Renaissance and Literature	144

12   CONTENTS

VI. SOCIAL VALUES AND INSTITUTIONS

Value Judgments	148
Moral Values and Society	149
Mores	152
Manifestations of the National Ethos	156
The Methods of Cultural Sociology	171

VII. RELIGION, EDUCATION, AND FAMILY

Social Functions of Religion	184
Islamic Jurisprudence and Sociology	193
The Social Sources of Islamic Jurisprudence	196
Religion and Law	199
State and Religion	202
Islam and Modern Civilization	214
The Caliphate	223
The Nature of Islamic Education	233
National Education	235
Modern Family and National Culture	247
Foundations of the Turkish Family	252

PART IV

VIII. NEW ORIENTATIONS

Towards the People	259
Towards Genius	262
Revolution and Conservatism	265
Towards Western Civilization	268
Towards Modern Science	279
Culture and Refinement	280

IX. THE PROGRAMME OF TURKISM

What is Turkism? – A Recapitulation	284
The Aim of the Turkists	289
The Turkist Programme Language	290
Literature and Music	298
Religion	301
Morality	302
Law	304
Politics	305
Economy	306

TRANSLATOR'S NOTES	314
GLOSSARY	323
INDEX	328

TRANSLATOR'S INTRODUCTION

THIRTY-FOUR years after his death, Ziya Gökalp still stands as the most original and influential among the Turkish writers of the twentieth century.* Born in 1876, he died at the age of forty-nine on October 25, 1924. He produced his basic writings between 1911 and 1918 and between 1922 and 1924. He initiated in the first period a new approach to the discussion of the fundamental problems which had become acute in Turkey following the restoration of the constitutional régime in 1908. He continued along the same lines in the second period, although many of his ideas had materialized already with the establishment of a nationalist régime in Anatolia under Atatürk.

The recurrent theme in Gökalp's writings was the question of how the Turks should adopt Western civilization, and how this effort should be harmonized with the Turks' two historic traditions, i.e. their Turkish and Islamic backgrounds; or, in other words, what the Turks as a nation and Islam as their religion would look like under the conditions of contemporary civilization. Raising this question was not on Gökalp's initiative. There had been others in Turkey who had anticipated or influenced him, as we shall note below; but his uniqueness lay in the fact that he was able to discuss this question in terms of a coherent, although too schematic, intellectual framework, analyse all of its ramifications, and draw certain conclusions, setting them up as formulae for a cultural policy.

This he did first amidst the throes of the declining Ottoman Empire, and then at the rather nebulous stage of the rise of a new nationalist régime, both of which, of course, conditioned his work to a great extent in form and content, in its merits as well as in its shortcomings. However, the downfall of the Ottoman Empire, following its defeat in World War I, prepared a more favourable ground for the materialization of his ideas. Although he died in the early phase of Atatürk's drastic reforms, one will find in Gökalp's writings the ideas behind the main trends of these reforms. His ideas with regard to the particulars

* The best account of Gökalp's life and works to date is to be found in Uriel Heyd, *Foundations of Turkish Nationalism* (London, 1950). The reader will find there, p. 174, a selected list of books and articles on Gökalp.

14 TURKISH NATIONALISM AND WESTERN CIVILIZATION

of the Islamic reform suffered most during the ensuing period of drastic secularism. However, I believe that if he had lived longer he would have been able to reconcile himself to the Atatürk policy because his ideas on the caliphacy were already at variance with the logical consequences of his Westernist nationalism, being rather fanciful utopias designed to find a basis of internationality to Turkish nationalism. Furthermore, we know that the constitutional clauses on secularism and the freedom of conscience and thinking were from his pen, as he was a member of the committee which prepared the new constitution in 1924. Probably it would have been more difficult for him to reconcile himself with the radical purist language-reform policy followed by Atatürk. Nevertheless, he remains as the best intellectual formulator of the main trends of the Turkish Republic: Westernism, democracy, political and economic national independence, and secularism. Although in actual practice there have been deviations from some of his contentions, it is still his style of thinking with regard to the basic issues which has intellectually dominated the modern reforms in Turkey.

The practical orientation of Gökalp's ideas and their close association with political action during the years preceding and following World War I have led many critics to blame him for Turkey's political misfortunes. But in spite of this ideological association, he always remained outside of politics and lived as a teacher and writer. He never assumed any responsible public office and never aimed at any political or personal gain. He lived almost in privation. He had none of the aptitudes of the man of action. He was extremely shy and introversive. At the same time, he had an exceptional charismatic power over the youth of Turkey and even over the politicians of the Party of Union and Progress. He was the type of intellectual not infrequently found in the East: a spiritual guide, an inspirer, a *mürşid*, as he was called in Turkey. He had marked Sufi inclinations, and the influence of *tasawwuf* always remained conspicuous in his thinking. This helps to explain a paradoxical situation with regard to his position today. In spite of his enormous influence during his lifetime and the prestige he still holds, his writings, with the exception of some scattered publications, are to a large extent unknown and unread. Certain slogans and catchwords which he popularized have remained in the memories and on the lips of the people. Some of his ideas are completely forgotten or have become distorted; a few which he clearly rejected are still ascribed to him. Socialistically inclined étatists, extremist racists, Westernists, and

TRANSLATOR'S INTRODUCTION

liberals saw him in different ways. His solidarism, or syndicalism, and his caliphate utopia are completely forgotten. Only a fraction of his writings have been printed in the Latin script, these repeatedly. Until now, no edition of his complete writings has appeared* and not even a complete and reliable bibliography of his writings exists.†

One of the reasons for this situation is, of course, the change in the Turkish alphabet. There are, however, other reasons to account for it. One of these, perhaps, is the fact that he published most of his prose writings in periodical reviews, or even in daily newspapers, in the form of short essays. Even the few books published in his lifetime, with the exception of one or two, were collections of his essays. Some of the reviews or newspapers to which he contributed are not easily available today—they were short-lived, and few copies still exist.

Another factor was that Gökalp's most active period of writing corresponded to the most unstable and critical periods of Turkish history, unfavourable to continuous, careful, and detailed book writing. For this reason, as he confessed himself, he never had time to write comprehensive studies to elaborate his historical, sociological, or philosophical ideas. And, finally, there is a social-psychological fact to be remembered in this connection. In periods of upheaval, trans- formation, and confusion, ideas which win mass appeal tend to become myths. Under such circumstances, people miss the fine distinctions a thinker makes in his concepts, the precise and subtle definitions he gives of his terms, and tend instead to make stereotypes. Thus, for example, even today many people fail to understand Gökalp's insistence on a distinction between culture and civilization or between race and nationality; and one wonders how an anti-Western jingoism or a doctrine of racism has come to be derived from his writings.

Gökalp himself, however, was very systematic in the use of his terminology. On this matter he was perhaps too mechanistic and arbitrary. He used to pigeonhole his facts and put labels on them, and then proceed with his discussion by manipulating these symbols. In doing this, he had little regard for existing terms or even for the facts

---

* The Turkish Historical Society recently announced the publication of his complete writings. So far, however, only the first volume has appeared, containing his poems and tales: *Ziya Gökalp Külliyatı*, Vol. 1, *Şiirler ve Halk Masalları*, edited by Fevziye A. Tansel (Türk Tarih Kurumu Yayınlarından, Seri II, No. 18 (Ankara, 1952).

† The best bibliography so far published is Cavit Orhan Tütengil, *Ziya Gökalp Hakkında bir Bibliyografya Denemesi* (Istanbul Üniversitesi Iktisat Fakültesi Yayınların- dan, No. 13 (Istanbul, 1949).

16 TURKISH NATIONALISM AND WESTERN CIVILIZATION

themselves. He either used his symbol-terms in the meanings he ascribed for them, or else invented new ones which were unknown until then. This, too, has been one of the reasons for the confusion in the exact meanings of his symbol-terms. He felt he had to do this because, in order to find his solutions, he had to revolutionize the sociological and political language of the Turkey of his time. Those who fail to see his ultimate aims usually tend to miss the exact meanings of his terms as well, and to turn them into mystified fetishes.

Bearing in mind these points about Gökalp's personality, influence, language, and symbols, we shall discuss first the general intellectual situation before him and the problems he faced, then how he approached these and how he treated them anew in terms of his early philosophical outlook, and finally the general conclusions which he proposed as a programme of action with regard to the economic, political, religious, legal, and cultural problems of Turkey.

II

The beginnings of the major problems with which Gökalp dealt are to be found in the first half of the nineteenth century, in the Tanzimat period of Turkish history. They came about mainly as a result of attempts to reorganize the political, legal, and administrative structure of the Ottoman Empire. Turkey, it is true, had already been touched by the impact of the West. There had been signs in the eighteenth century that, in spite of resistance, the idea of Turkey's having to adapt herself to the requirements of European civilization gained ground continuously.* But neither in political organization, nor in social life or in the cultural and intellectual spheres, can we find any substantial change in the older Ottoman system, which was then in a state of corruption and disorganization. In the political field sultanism still reigned as a political-military-fiscal system of the Ottomans. Its two pillars, the benefice system of the Sipahis and the Janissary organization, still remained, although only in an entirely degenerate form. Why the vast and efficient military, agrarian, and administrative organization of the Ottomans was disrupted before the effective modern European economic and political impact started in the nineteenth century is a question still almost untouched today but beyond

* This is discussed in detail in the writer's forthcoming study of the history of reform in Turkey.

TRANSLATOR'S INTRODUCTION 17

the scope of this essay. Suffice it to say here, however, that these factors were not much different in nature from those which had given rise to modern European economic and political institutions. Our present concern is to note that in the eighteenth century—in spite of such novelties as the introduction of the printing press—intellectual life in Turkey was still under the domination of the *medrese*, the medieval colleges, and was thoroughly scholastic. Likewise, literature and art were in a state of a rigid formalism and conventionalism.

It was only at the beginning of the nineteenth century that the feeling of dissatisfaction which had run through the eighteenth century turned into a decision to introduce Western methods. The first radical step was the destruction of the Janissary system, together with a fight against feudalization, which was taking the place of the previous benefice system. For the first time in Ottoman history it had become necessary to destroy an important institution in order to introduce new ones, in a manner somewhat reminiscent of Peter the Great's reforms in Russia a century earlier. The Tanzimat edicts of 1839 and 1856 were but official confirmation of this movement; henceforth it became an established policy to abolish old institutions which were found to be incompatible with corresponding modern institutions and to found new ones on the European models.

Two factors, however, led to the unsatisfactory application of this idea. To follow this principle would necessitate ultimately a radical change in the ruling institution itself, which was the only force to put the policy into practice. In other words, a despotic monarchy had to democratize itself—a situation observed also in Russian history. The second factor was the inevitable economic and political consequences of the contact of a medieval society with the full-grown European expansionist economy and politics. Under the pressure of the difficulties arising mainly from these two factors, the leaders of the Tanzimat reforms failed to pursue wholeheartedly their programme of modernization, as well as to understand the full scope and nature of the social transformation in which they were involved. This hesitancy inevitably led to imitation, opportunism, and inconsistencies. One of the consequences was the creation of a series of dichotomies in almost every field of life. In politics, in administration, in the legal and juridical system, in education, in intellectual life, two sets of institutions, two sets of ideas, two loyalties—one to the old and the other to the new—stood side by side.

T.N.W.C.—2

18 TURKISH NATIONALISM AND WESTERN CIVILIZATION

The man who diagnosed the morbid nature of this situation and recognized it as a major obstacle to progress towards the establishment of a modern state was Namık Kemal (1840–88). He attempted to show the original, or rather idealized, forms of the religious, moral, and legal institutions which were associated with Islam, and the original, or idealized, forms of the political institutions of the old Ottoman tradition at the time of its prime; and, at the same time, those aspects of civilization of the West which had given progress, prosperity, and superiority to the European nations. By his discussion of these three elements, he arrived at the conclusion that there were no basic contradictions among them. Islam, according to him, would provide the moral and legal bases of society; the Ottoman tradition of statecraft, together with its multinational and multireligious cosmopolitan policy of toleration, would be the political framework of the Ottoman (not Turkish) state; and Western civilization would furnish the material and practical methods and techniques to enable this system to survive in the contemporary world of power and economic progress.

In this way Namık Kemal distinguished the areas of the three elements in the life of the nineteenth-century Turks. For him, the most important factor in the failure of the Tanzimat was the mental confusion with regard to these three elements. Thus, for example, the *sheriat*, the Islamic law, was dropped in order to take codes from France, while European methods in techniques of education, government, science, economy, and agriculture were not introduced. By their naïve wish to modernize the state, the men of the Tanzimat reforms unnecessarily undertook economic and political obligations towards European powers which robbed the Ottoman state of all independence and integrity. They did not apply any of the principles of modern democratic régimes in their administration. But neither the old Ottoman political institutions nor Muslim law were in reality incompatible with democracy and progress or with modern science. The main reasons why they were thought to be so were, first, the fact that all of these traditions had lost their original functions, and second, that the imposing penetration of European imperialism prevented their smooth adaptation.

The course of events at first ran counter to Namık Kemal's ideas and led to their repudiation. Following the constitutional revolution of 1908, however, they were almost completely revived, but in a different atmosphere. Under the previous suppressive régime the attempt at reconciliation among the elements that Namık Kemal had discussed gave rise to three ideological movements, each of which capitalized one of the three elements at the expense of the others. Thus reactionary Islamic groups, zealous to defend Islam against the increasing criticisms of the missionaries and the new group of European orientalists and thinkers, like Renan, provided the support for Sultan Abdul Hamid's pan-Islamic policy. Over against them, the secular intelligentsia—now increased in number because of the new secular educational institutions and enlightened through increasing contacts with European literature and thought—stood up as protagonists of the idea of Westernism. In addition to these, there arose a small, weak group interested in an entirely new concept: Turkishness. Stimulated by the political, economic, and literary awakening of the Turkish-speaking peoples under Russian rule in the nineteenth century, by the new interest of certain romantically inspired European writers (such as Léon Cahun), by the increasing effect of the movement 'towards the people' initiated by Namık Kemal's teacher, Shinasi, and of its interest in the basic Turkish language and past, and, finally, by the nationalist movements of the non-Muslim and non-Turkish communities of the Ottoman Empire, together with those of certain European pan-movements, such as pan-Slavism and pan-Germanism, a group of writers shifted the attention which the Islamists paid to the Islamic past of the Muslim-Turkish Ottomans to the ethnic past of the Turks themselves.*

However, the Islamists and Westernists, as well as those interested in the Turkish masses and culture, were all Ottomanists at heart so far as political problems were concerned. Even the Young Turks, who were active in foreign countries beyond reach of the suppressive régime, were not clear on these issues. Only gradually and through discussion in party conventions, or through communications and publishing, did they come to ask the question: For what are we fighting? For a new sultan? For a new constitutional Ottoman state which would guarantee the rights and privileges of the non-Muslim and non-Turkish communities of the empire? All of the Westernist Ottomanists were highly shocked when they were confronted with the nationalist demands of the representatives of these communities. For obvious

---

* For a recent account of the rise and development of nationalist historiography in Turkey, see the admirable article by Bernard Lewis, 'History-writing and National Revival in Turkey', *Middle Eastern Affairs*, Vol. 4 (June-July 1953), pp. 218 ff.

20 TURKISH NATIONALISM AND WESTERN CIVILIZATION

reasons, none of them could admit nationalism either for their non-Muslim and non-Turkish colleagues or for themselves.

During these pre-revolutionary years of discussion and intellectual confusion, only one voice reflected the views of the new nationalist group on a political level. That was Yusuf Akçura (1876–1933), who, in turn, was inspired by Hüseyinzade Ali, a doctor from the Caucasus.* He discussed Turkism as a pan-Turanian movement in comparison with the pan-Islamist and pan-Ottomanist policies. Akçura pointed out that the concern of the Islamists and the Ottomanists was primarily to maintain the integrity of the Ottoman Empire and to create an international block against European aggression. He proposed another pan-idea which was equally grandiose, but perhaps more effective and more modern as well as more useful to the Turks.

III

Ziya Gökalp was a young small-town student. He was idealistic and had an intense patriotic zeal. But he had none of the opportunities of the Turkist scholars of Istanbul or the pan-Turanist ambitions of the sophisticated and experienced exiles in Europe. When he came to Istanbul in 1896, from Diyarbakır, his home town in south-eastern Anatolia, the concepts of Ottomanism, pan-Islamism, and pan-Turkism were under discussion among the intellectuals. The fact that he wrote poetry which reflected the influence of Namık Kemal, the utopian Islamist, and of Tevfik Fikret, the Westernist humanist, plus Sufism, shows that he was struggling and wavering between the three trends. He was fighting within himself the battle that intellectuals and politicians were raging on other levels. His temperament, his environment in his home town, and his education brought three forces together to struggle against each other: mysticism, theology, and the natural sciences. Later, these took a more intellectualized garb in the terminology of his writings as Turkish culture, Islam, and contemporary civilization.

In spite of his obscurity before 1908, Gökalp quickly became known, at least within a small circle, in the years following the constitutional revolution. He is then found in Salonika associated with the Party of Union and Progress, around which was a group of young intellectuals who longed for a new life without knowing, however,

* See Heyd, *op. cit.*, p. 107.

TRANSLATOR'S INTRODUCTION

what it was they wanted or how it would be realized. It was a time when Turkey had to exert enormous effort to recover not only from the effects of corruption, tyranny, and economic bankruptcy, but also from moral and intellectual confusion; indeed, a complete reconstruction of Turkey was considered by most intellectuals to be of the utmost urgency. An intense patriotism, in reaction against the nationalist movements among the non-Muslim and non-Turkish peoples of the decadent empire, provided the emotional background.

Gökalp readily came to the conclusion that a mere political change meant nothing unless it was followed by a social and cultural revolution. But the intellectuals, as well as the politicians, were still hopelessly divided in their opinions as to the proper basis for social reconstruction. After the revolution, the conservatives among them boldly urged a reversion to the *sheriat* of the Islamic *ümmet*. On the other hand, the liberals–those who more staunchly supported the idea of Westernization—could say nothing but that everything existing was 'irrational' and everything coming from Europe was 'rational'. Only vaguely did they hope for a secular basis of reintegration. And, finally, there were the Turkists who longed for the romantic ideal of racial or ethnic unity of the Turks and preached a return to the pre-Islamic past.

Gökalp found some truth in each but agreed fully with none. He rather followed Namik Kemal's middle road: that only the material civilization of Europe should be taken and not its non-material aspects. Namık Kemal had been forced to pay a high price for this conviction as he failed to see the incompatibility between the demands of modern civilization and those of Turkey's traditional institutions. However, in developing this conviction, Gökalp did not follow Namık Kemal's track, but proceeded with an approach which signified the shift from Tanzimat rationalism, inspired by the eighteenth-century thinkers of the European Enlightenment, to the romantic thinking of the nineteenth century. He believed that both Islamists and Westernists based their ideas on individual reason, and that the individual and his reason could not be criteria for social reconstruction as they led either to conservatism or to utopianism, both of which were blind to realities. The new reconstruction would proceed not from the reason of individuals but from the reason of society. No one can restore or revive a dead institution at will, or import new ones, on order, from Europe. In terms of an idealistic philosophy, he accepted the transcendental reality of society, identifying it with the nation in a way reminiscent of the

22 TURKISH NATIONALISM AND WESTERN CIVILIZATION

German Romanticists or the Russian Slavophils and Populists. He believed that it is the people, or the nation, which is the final and unerring criterion of what is desirable or undesirable, what is to be taken and what rejected. Whatever the 'collective conscience' of the people accepts is 'normal'; whatever it rejects is 'pathological'. As the ultimate reality of contemporary society is the nation, and as national ideals are ultimate forces orienting the behaviour of the individuals, so the most urgent task for the Turks consisted of awakening as a nation in order to adapt themselves to the conditions of contemporary civilization. He transformed the Turkism of the purist pan-Turkists from a mere political concept into a cultural one.

Having an unlimited faith in sociology as the supreme positive science,* Gökalp felt that it was the primary task of this science to determine what the Turkish people already possessed or lacked to be a modern nation.

IV

To investigate this question, Gökalp began by describing what he believed to be the basic malady of the then existing cultural situation in Turkey. This consisted of a diagnosis of the dichotomies in every field of Turkey's social life. On the one hand were the people with

---

* Gökalp knew the ideas of the major schools of European sociology of the late nineteenth century. He found most congenial to his own thinking Emile Durkheim's conception of sociology, its methods, divisions, etc., as well as its philosophical basis. His belief in Durkheim's sociology as *the* science of society led some critics to the conviction that Gökalp merely imitated Durkheim. It is true that he did not deviate from a Durkheimian understanding of sociology. This was not fortuitous, because, like Durkheim, Gökalp too was a student of philosophy trying to develop a philosophy of values and of action from a reconciliation between positivism and idealism, which he attempted before he became acquainted with Durkheim's writings. In developing his sociological analyses of the cultural problems of Turkey, he proceeded with this philosophy, which he later called sociological idealism, and utilized data, sources, concepts, and methods not alike to those found with Durkheim. His discussion of culture and civilization and his views on nation and nationalism—which, I believe, constitute the core of his social philosophy—are entirely lacking in Durkheim (see Heyd, *op. cit.*, p. 66). On these points he is nearer to some of the German sociologists, such as Tönnies (*ibid.*, pp. 67 ff.) and Alfred Weber, and even reminds us of some ideas expressed in W. G. Sumner's *Folkways*. No direct influence of these sociologists, however, has been established so far. It seems to this writer that Gökalp developed his ideas on the above-mentioned points quite independently, although they were one possible logical consequence of Namık Kemal's distinction of the two aspects of Western civilization. For a brief account of the various sociological ideas current in Turkey before and after Gökalp, see the writer's article, 'Sociology in Turkey', *American Journal of Sociology*, Vol. 2 (September 1936), pp. 238–46.

TRANSLATOR'S INTRODUCTION 23

their intimate, informal institutions, their religion, their art, and their thinking; on the other was the official organization with its formal, artificial institutions, all borrowed from the civilizations of the East and the West: its *fiķh*, its *divan* literature, its hodgepodge of unintelligible language, and all its imitations of the superficialities of French civilization. None of these latter had taken root among the people; they remained not only alien but even irreconcilable. To Gökalp, the reason for this anomalous situation was a lack of adjustment between the two essential but distinct aspects of social life—*civilization* and *culture*.

The concepts of culture and civilization thus occupied a major position in his thinking, yet they puzzled many of his critics who tried to see wherein lay the importance of making a sharp distinction between the two. If his analyses are taken as a whole, however, these two concepts do not represent antithetical and mutually exclusive entities, but rather two closely related and complementary traits of social reality. Briefly stated, civilization refers to modes of action composed of the 'traditions' which are created by different ethnic groups and transmitted from one to another. Culture, on the other hand, is composed of the 'mores' of a particular nation and, consequently, is unique and *sui generis*. The 'traditions' are rational forms of behaviour imposed upon individuals by their common civilization, while 'mores' represent the specific value judgments, or ethos, of a particular nation. Culture constitutes a system whose elements have an integral connection with one another on the basis of a peculiar logic which constitutes the ethos; civilization, on the other hand, is a product of detachment from that logic. Civilizational elements assume meaning and function in the life of men only when they enter into the service of culture. Without a cultural basis, civilization becomes merely a matter of mechanical imitation; it never penetrates into the inner life of a people and never gives fruit of any kind.

That was exactly what had happened in Turkey and perhaps in other Muslim nations, where civilization had come to be a mere skeleton corroding and annihilating all cultural flesh and blood of the social body. When a new civilization presented itself from the West, this lifeless skeleton lost all meaning and creativity. With this addition of the impact of Western civilization, the situation presented a threefold difficulty to thinking minds, but the question was basically the same dichotomy between civilization and culture.

24 TURKISH NATIONALISM AND WESTERN CIVILIZATION

The remedy, according to Gökalp, lay in discovering the basic social unit which is the source of cultural values. To him, that source was the form of society which he called 'nation'. The nation, he furthermore believed, is that independent social unit which is at the basis of modern (Western) civilization. In other words, modern Western civilization is the international product of several peoples who have reached the stage of nationhood in the course of social evolution. Turkey was in turmoil because it was in the process of transformation from a theocratic (*ümmet*) civilization to a civilization based on modern nationality, the full nature of which was still unknown. In order to prove these points, it was necessary for him to establish the sociological reality of the 'nation' in terms of social evolution, trace its historical formation, analyse its elements, and, finally, develop a method of cultural criticism with a view to discovering the roots of maladjustments and the means of their amelioration.

Gökalp's ideas all revolved around his understanding of 'nation', and undoubtedly this constitutes his major contribution to Turkish thought. The word *millet*, which now stands for 'nation', at that time simply meant a religious community. Even Namık Kemal, who for the first time awakened a national consciousness among his people, failed in his Islamic utopianism to see the unreality of such a concept of nation within the framework of contemporary civilization. Gökalp set about giving the Turks a new definition, and in this he surpassed in success his predecessors as well as his contemporaries. He mobilized all his energies to demolish the theocratic conception of nationality. It was his mission to demonstrate that the average Turk, who at that time used to identify himself as a Muslim member of the Ottoman 'nation', was confusing nation with two other sociological entities. One was *ümmet*, an international religious community, and the other was a political organization comprising in itself several nationalities as well as religious communities. In addition, Gökalp pointed out, with the rise of Westernism and pan-Turkism, 'nation' came to be confused with two other concepts: with race or ethnic family, and with contemporary international civilization. The true nation could be identified with neither of these.

To Gökalp, the social process is visible only in the historical development of nations from primitive societies to the societies of contemporary Western civilization. In the course of this evolution every society develops a specific culture. There is no continuous process of evolution

TRANSLATOR'S INTRODUCTION

of the totality of human society. Societies may, however, be grouped by species. Interdependence, factual relations, and similarities between societies of the same species lead to the formation of intersociety groupings or 'civilization circles', but, according to Gökalp, these are 'communities' rather than 'societies'. From a sociological point of view, they remain weak and loose formations because they lack common binding cultural values. Only civilizational links tie them together, whereas societies, or nations, follow characteristic life attitudes and an immanent development.

However, throughout the social evolution from the primitive segmental type of society to present-day organic society, the confines of the nation have widened, chiefly through a civilizational process. Thus, the modern nation is a new type. The primary factor in its formation is neither race or ethnic unity nor a symbiotic coexistence with other nations within a political, religious internationality, or a civilization circle. The modern nation is a community in a unique complex of cultural values, on the one hand, and a society based on organic solidarity, division of labour, and functional differentiation, on the other. The ethnic societies which have emerged as modern nations went through a sort of period of captivity within international politico-religious civilizations and, as a result of the disintegration of these civilizations, have come out as entirely new formations with the development of the processes of secularization and democratization. Nations never come into existence out of nothing, as we see in all the vain attempts at creating artificial nationalities. They must have an ethnic basis, must undergo a process of transformation within supranational formations, and must experience the revival of national consciousness under great events. Although nations turn to their ethnic past during their revival and think that they are continuations of it, they are no longer the same ethnic units and cannot return to archaic conditions. Neither can a modern nation carry on the hang-overs of its imperial or theocratic civilization. It is a homogenized product of various racial, ethnic, and religious elements welded to one another by historical catastrophes, and is no longer reducible to its elements. In this new form of nation, all hang-overs from the tribal or theocratic civilizational elements become 'pathological'. Only cultural remains are normal, because it is only these that are alive and capable of giving cohesion and orientation to the life of the nation.

The modern nation is an independent cultural unit within the confines of contemporary civilization. However, the two stand in rather precarious relation to each other. As in the past ethnic societies were swallowed by larger civilizational groups, so modern nations have to remain in the orbit of contemporary civilization. Would this lead to merging in a larger international society? Gökalp was sceptical of the expectations to that effect and dismissed them as utopias. Only civilizational organizations might arise in the future, and of their effectiveness he was not fully convinced. Like many of his contemporaries, he did not attach much value to the high-sounding international ideals of contemporary civilization. For Gökalp, only nations had social reality as cultural units.

However, Gökalp's main concern was not the future problems of modern nations within the contemporary civilizational internationality, but rather the immediate problems of Turkey *vis-à-vis* Western civilization. His purpose in dealing with the relations between culture and civilization was to explore the difficulty of producing adjustment and harmony between the two, especially when a culture was trying to extricate itself from one circle of civilization in order to enter another. Disharmony was the tragic situation in the case of Turkey, that which differentiated it from the modern nations arising out of the folds of European Christianity. The Turks inherited from their past their ethnic culture, which had withstood the enormous impact of a highly developed Eastern civilization and had thus proved its power of survival. Only the unity engendered by this culture remained as a refuge for the Turks from the dangers of extinction in the past as well as at present. They also inherited a political system and a religion from the internationality of the East; both, however, were now confronted with a civilization before which they were in a process of collapse. The Turks obviously could not cease to be Turks, nor would they desire to do so; neither could they extricate themselves from their religion by the power of reason or enlightenment, since it had taken deep roots in the culture of the people even though its *fikh* and its *medrese* had never succeeded in doing so. But as a nation they had to adapt themselves to contemporary secular Western civilization, since the civilization to which they belonged in the past was neither secular nor adaptable to modern nationality. This was the problem of cultural criticism which Gökalp finally aimed at solving.

V

Gökalp's distinctions and definitions had been aimed at a clearer discussion of this problem. He believed that he had formulated the outlines of a branch of sociology which we might call a sociology of culture, a normative discipline based on the general positive science of sociology. By applying the principles of his sociology of culture, he came to the conclusion that the three factors represented by the three ideologies (Islamism, Westernism, and Turkism) were not, in reality, incompatible with one another, provided that the areas of the national social life to which they referred were viewed from correct angles. Then would it be seen that they are even complementary to each other *within the framework of the modern nation.*

The Islamists were wrong because they did not see the reality of the nation as distinct from the theocratic *ümmet.* They insisted on the restoration of, or return to, the *sheriat,* which was, in fact, nothing but a civilizational crystallization of law fitted to an *ümmet.* They failed to distinguish the universally valid truths in Islam from those aspects which were only socially and temporally relevant, and therefore identified the first with the second. They identified religion with law and ritual, as would be normal within the framework of a theocratic *ümmet.* Thus, they failed to see Islam as having a universal message for the pious, good man, and a moral, ethical character. That is why one found religious fanaticism and moral laxity side by side. They made Islam something concerned with only the technicalities and intricacies of the observance of ritual and legal rules, and inevitably stood against everything new because they identified life with rules. They wanted to maintain the same rigidity, nay, even to tighten it, in the face of the increasing pace of progress under contemporary conditions, and as a result came to clash more violently with the needs of the nation. Here lay the source of the idea that Islam and contemporary civilization are incompatible—the basic conviction of the Westernists.

But the latter were wrong in their convictions, too. Gökalp contemptuously called them the zealots of Europeanism, as he called the former the zealots of *fikh*ism. In spite of the undeniably great service performed by the Europeanist leaders of the Tanzimat reforms, they were wrong because they did not take care to proceed in terms of a cultural framework. They were like automatons in what they did, devoid of meaningful objectives. They were under the illusion of certain civilizational fictions, for example, as they desperately tried to convince the people that the Ottoman community was a nation. Their political system had nothing to do with the political structure of modern democratic nations. They thought that an autocratic and theocratic system would be modernized when partially modified by a half-hearted Europeanization which allowed all meaningless superficialities and formalities to enter full sway.

Viewed from the right angle Westernization was not only compatible with Turkey's national culture, but was even indispensable to its flourishing. A full-fledged national culture could come into existence only when its raw material, still on an ethnic and folk level, was worked with the fresh techniques of a civilization to which many nations had contributed. Similarly, there was no incompatibility between Western civilization and Islam. In order to defend this latter thesis, Gökalp had to refute two contentions of the Islamists which were shared by many Europeans and were a constant sore point and dilemma for the Westernists: he rejected the idea that Islam was a civilization and that Western civilization was synonymous with Christianity. It is true, he said, that religions have developed civilizational forms, but it is equally true that they have given cultural content to the ethos of nations. Civilization is basically free from value judgments; it is a matter of factual reality. And, furthermore, contemporary civilization, arising out of the victory of the rational mind and positive science over civilizational Christianity, is destined to become more secular as it encompasses Muslims, like the Turks, and non-Muslims-non-Christians, like the Japanese. Therefore, the acceptance of contemporary Western civilization has nothing to do with either nationality or faith. The confusion on this point is due to a confusing of culture with civilization.

There emerges in connection with the problem of the relationship between culture and civilization an interesting question which we would expect Gökalp to discuss. To what extent were the cultural and the religious backgrounds of the Turkish nationality receptive and stimulating to contemporary Western civilization? Many Europeanists of his time thought that they were not. Gökalp, on the other hand, wanted to demonstrate the contrary. In order to prove that Turkish culture was not only favourable but even conducive to the requirements of modern civilization, he preferred to resort to dubious history rather than to examine the present existing institutions of the people.

TRANSLATOR'S INTRODUCTION 29

Apparently he felt it necessary to discover the original ethnic basis of Turkish culture. But the infancy of the Turkological studies of his time, his questionable competence in the field compared to the authority of such present-day scholars as Fuad Köprülü, the insufficient character of the materials he used, and his too-evident bias in using these materials, cast shadows on the credibility of his findings or at least on his methods. However that may be, Gökalp's conclusions were entirely new and fascinating to his contemporaries. With bold generalizations he proclaimed that the basic Turkish cultural traits were not those salient features of the so-called Oriental institutions which were regarded as contrary to modern civilization and had long been associated with the Turks, such as polygamy, the seclusion of women and their low status, fatalism, and asceticism. Neither was that sickly Oriental music or that fearful conception of a transcendental God Turkish at all. These were imposed upon the Islamized Turks, chiefly through the infiltration of the civilizational traditions of the Near East into the *fikh* books, into the *medrese* teaching, and into the *enderun* (palace) etiquette and the *divan* art. They never got a hold over the Turkish ethos. They had a place only among the de-Turkified and 'civilized' Ottoman intelligentsia.

The same features were also traditionally attributed to Islam. But to Gökalp they were not inherent in Islam, as he found their origins elsewhere. Certain elements of Arab and, secondarily, Persian culture had crept into the *sheriat*. When cultural elements of a certain social species of a particular time became common civilizational elements, they tried to impose themselves as value judgments on the national ethos by book, law, court, or state. But, in spite of the sanctioning of these institutions, certain tribal customs, such as *lex talionis*, or polygamy, remained only in the *fikh* books and never became universal institutions of Turkish culture.

The only customs or habits or ideas existing among the Turkish people which were not compatible with modern civilization, Gökalp believed, were those which remained as survivals or fossils of such dead institutions and were, therefore, easy to eradicate. He always urged the men of reform not to be frightened by them since they were vestigial structures in the social body, to be cut out with one stroke without damaging the life of the nation—provided it was nourished by fresh cultural and civilizational nutrients. (Atatürk, in his iconoclastic decisions, later proved him to be right.)

Gökalp tried to find yardsticks to judge the genuinely basic culture traits and thus to distinguish, in terms of his understanding of good and bad, the normal from the pathological, i.e. those elements which were incompatible with modern conditions. As mentioned earlier, he found one in the pre-Islamic origins. He accepted, as a second rule, the ethos of the nation as expressed by the Great Man, the genius, the hero, and the sage. These men, with their exceptional power of insight and intuition and utmost sincerity, were the real representatives of the national ethos as well as the mainsprings of progress. It is absurd, he believed, to take the opinion or behaviour of the average man as a criterion of action. Thirdly there were the works of the anonymous collectivity. The people learned humanity, goodness, and meaning in life not from the dead books of the doctors of law or the artificial, unnatural literature of the courts. Their hearts and imaginations for centuries had been nurtured not by these, but by their own humble religious experiences in their mystic fraternities and by their aesthetic experiences in their rich folklore. These institutions of the people, which constitute a virgin and fertile soil for the creation of a modern culture, should be studied, learned, and cultivated by the elite of the nation, who are the bearers of modern civilization and the builders of the future modern national culture. Their cravings to create will be satisfied, not by blind imitation or parrotlike repetition of the cultural products of the nations of Western civilization, but by refining this store of raw material through the knowledge, techniques, and skills which they acquire from modern civilization.

VI

This was, in short, the message which Gökalp brought from his cultural analyses to the leaders of Turkish national reconstruction. His programme shows that his original three-fold treatment, in the final analysis, amounted to a two-fold directive: towards the culture of the people and towards contemporary civilization. Uncover culture in order to reach civilization. Base on a secure foundation in order to achieve progress.

What were the tangible effects of his teachings? By taking the nation and the people as the ultimate cultural, political, and economic unit, he paved the way to a view of Turkey as a nation, as a national state, and ultimately as a democracy. By differentiating Turkey from a

TRANSLATOR'S INTRODUCTION 31

theocratic conception of the *ümmet*, he prepared the Turks for a secular view of religion, culture, and civilization. Stressing the possibility of incorporating Western civilization on a Turkish cultural foundation, he prepared the way for a dynamic policy. He also initiated a new historical and sociological interest in the pre-Islamic past of the Turks and in the history of the actual institutions of Islam in contrast to Islam as conceived within the theoretical framework of the *sheriat*. He stimulated a vigorous and passionate interest in folk culture. If his own researches on history, folklore, and sociology have little value compared to the works of Turkish and foreign scholars of our time, this does not at all minimize his significance as a pathfinder and explorer. If some of his ideas are almost forgotten in present-day Turkey, and if some of them, quite new in his time, seem merely commonplace today, it is because they have become facts. All this shows the depth of his influence and the scope of his vision.

We see, therefore, that Gökalp was not a philosopher, although there was a philosophy at the base of his social thinking. He was also neither a sociologist nor an historian in any real sense. Equally influential as a talker, lecturer, professor, and man of public affairs, Gökalp consecrated his writings as well as his teachings to giving a new orientation to the thinking of a people which was, as he believed, in a stage of transition from one civilization to another and to pointing up new goals for the achievement of this transformation. Whatever his shortcomings as a philosopher or sociologist, he will remain in Turkish history as a genuine thinker who had exceptional insight into existing problems and a vision of a brighter future.

NIYAZI BERKES

PART I

CHAPTER I

AUTOBIOGRAPHICAL

MY FATHER'S TESTAMENT[1]

I HAD just entered the fourteenth winter of my life. I was the laziest student in the military high school. I had, however, an inborn aptitude for mathematics and a passionate inclination toward poetry and literature. The courses in mathematics did not prevent me from being a lazy student because I could solve the problems and prove the theorems with ease. And since I read books of poetry and literature with great delight, I was never tired of them. As to other subjects, I disliked and hated them, for, in accordance with the pedagogical methods of the time, they required a great deal of rote learning.

My father was not like the other fathers of those days, but a man who was able to combine within himself both piety and free-thinking. He had freed himself of all kinds of superstitious beliefs, old and new. Like all timid and introspective persons, he had an inborn insight into matters of the spirit. Once, a friend of his who had heard about my tearful reading of books like *Shah Ismail* and *Kerem the Lover*, advised him to keep me away from these books of the folk minstrels and to induce me to read serious books in their stead. 'A child', my father replied, 'should read only what he understands and enjoys. If you impose books on a child, and if he is not interested in them, he may hate them.' In fact, it was because I was allowed to read what I enjoyed that I was able to progress from the books of the minstrels to works of drama and short story, and then to pure poetry and great novels, reading at last works of history, science, and philosophy.

Although my father left me free to read what I wanted, he did not miss any opportunity—at critical psychological moments—to impress me deeply enough to evoke new interests in my soul. One evening when I had come home from school I found him very sad and unhappy. 'Come here', he said as soon as he saw me, 'I have some sad news to tell you. You will certainly weep and mourn. Today will be a day of great sorrow for you and for your friends, because your greatest

36 TURKISH NATIONALISM AND WESTERN CIVILIZATION

teacher and the greatest man of this nation, Namık Kemal, has died!'[2]

I was acquainted with the works of Namık Kemal, even with his unpublished and forbidden works, but I did not know that he was a great teacher and a great man. My father told me, in a sad voice, the story of his struggles, his ideals, the injustices he suffered, the heroic resistance he showed, and finally he said: 'And now, you will be a follower of this man. You also will be a patriot like him, and a lover of freedom as he was.'

The moment chosen to impress me, and the manner in which it was done, could not have been better. My father's words were so inspiring that they created in my soul an entirely new strength—the strength of an idealism of which I had not been aware until then. From that moment on, my thinking was that of a conscious lover of freedom and of an awakened patriot. I began to become alive to the ideals of liberty, fatherland, and nation above everything else. My soul had been suddenly changed by a creative *élan*.

But let me come to my main point. As I said, I was just beginning my fourteenth year. One day my father was talking with one of his friends who was telling him something about my great ambition for learning. He said that if I were sent to Europe to study, the country would gain a man of learning. My father said: 'The youth sent to Europe to study learn only European sciences, but remain ignorant of our own national learning. Those who attend the *medreses*[3] may learn something about our religious and national learning, if they happen to have good teachers, but they remain ignorant of the European sciences. I believe that for us the most useful teachers will be those who know the truths which are most immediately necessary for us. And these truths cannot be discovered by the European sciences, nor do they exist now in our national learning in a real sense. Our youth must study carefully French, on the one hand, and Arabic and Persian, on the other. They must come to a position where they can master both Western and Eastern learning. And then they must discover the great truths which our nation needs, by comparing and combining Western and Eastern learning. This is the way I want to educate Ziya, if I can only live long enough to see to it.'

My poor father did not live for even a year after the time he said these words. He could not realize his plans. But his words remained engraved on my soul in distinct letters, as a sacred testament.

I have never forgotten and will never forget them as long as I live.

AUTOBIOGRAPHICAL

His words had initiated a great change in my life. Till that time I lacked any critical sense in my reading, entertaining a boundless trust in authors. Books and authors had tremendous influence and authority over me. Now, before my eyes, the words of my father dethroned the libraries of the East and the West at one stroke, and gave unlimited freedom and independence to my own mind and intelligence.

Furthermore, they invited me, as a member of the whole body of youth, to the fulfilment of a long and very difficult task.

MY TEACHER'S TESTAMENT[4]

In the college we had begun to study natural sciences on the one hand and theology on the other. These two opposite currents, one charged with the positive and the other with the negative electric power over morality, do not long fail to strike shafts of scepticism instead of sparks of truth as they collide in a spiritual void. Thus, positive truths and ideals began to vie within my soul with an intensity increasing every day. My heart could not remain content while seeing Man—virtuous and heroic, the only source of my inspirations—turned into a Machine, devoid of will and freedom, and made only of Matter, low, base, servile—sterile.

My greatest desire was to know whether my people—threatened by a thousand dangers and yet unaware of them because of the narcotics of Tyranny—would be able to save themselves by some miraculous effort. What I needed was a philosophy of hope, a theory of salvation. If Man was nothing but a Machine, if he lacked the miraculous power to raise himself above Nature, then my people would not be able to survive. And Humanity, too, would be destined always to flounder in the wilderness.

Neither theology nor mysticism could give me this philosophy of hope and this theory of salvation. They were unable to penetrate into the ideals of modern life. I wanted to see Humanity, Man, elevated; my people and my land freed. But within my head was living a hidden personality weighing all my judgments with only mathematical measures, evaluating with logical standards, refusing to accept any judgment without subjecting it to the touchstones of facts and experience. That was my reason. It was a rebel, struggling to break my hopes and choke my illusions. My sole support at that time was escapism, by which I could more or less maintain an equilibrium in my soul.

38 TURKISH NATIONALISM AND WESTERN CIVILIZATION

But one day a line from my own pen took even this support from me:

What is the use of evading the Truth?

It was during these days that a teacher—a philosopher—was appointed to our school to teach us natural history. Besides being acquainted with European philosophy and French literature, this man had also studied the modern period of Turkish literature. He was an odd man, a physician who yet did not believe in medicine. 'There is no positive truth in medicine,' he used to say, 'excepting Epsom salts.' He was a Greek, and yet a friend of the Turks. Or at least, we used to think he was.

Dr Yorgi had come to our Eastern provinces as an army doctor after his graduation from the [Turkish] Medical School. He had travelled many years from town to town and had seen many places. He lived in solitude. How did he spend his leisure time? By doing one thing only: reading! Maybe it was his constant reading that had made Dr Yorgi a learned man, a philosopher.

When Dr Yorgi came to the school, he used to read daily the compositions we wrote as class assignments for our teacher of literature. This was the most intense period of my internal crises. The bitterness of my conflicts was intensely reflected in my compositions irrespective of the subjects our teacher assigned. Dr Yorgi apparently found a smell of philosophizing in my troubled reasonings. Whenever he came to our classroom he used to talk about my compositions. I listened with great attention, each word opening new horizons to me. . . .

It is not necessary that I now describe at length the crises I was going through. Suffice it to say that they led me finally to attempt suicide, and to insomnia which continued for several years and left me almost a skeleton. I did not have any organic disease, nor had I any social discomfort. The source of my trouble was my thoughts. I used to believe that if I were able to reach what I then called the Great Truth, I would be relieved from all pain. But where could I find it? When I was writing a revolutionary poem, another line flowed suddenly from my pen pointing out where I should seek:

The honour of the Nation is today entrusted to us.*

The Great Truth, then, was nothing but ideals. And the highest

---

* This poem was published two years later in *Istikbál*, edited by Ali Şefkati in London.

AUTOBIOGRAPHICAL

ideals were those of nationality and liberty. I described the power of
the ideal of freedom on the human soul in the following stanza:

> The passion of life had shackled me
> Until I broke its chains; I was free!
> But now Being has caught my soul
> In its ubiquitous chains of steel
> I am free, and being free
> I am enslaved by Freedom's passion.

I had come to Istanbul to fight for the cause of these ideals. At that
time there was a secret organization[5] there, formed by the students of
the Medical School. I began to work with them.

After a while, Dr Yorgi too came to Istanbul. One day, Abdullah
Haşim, one of my former classmates, proposed that we pay a visit to
the Doctor. He knew his house in Moda. We went there together. Our
former teacher talked about the recent movements in Istanbul. 'The
Turkish youth', he said, 'want a political revolution, the foundation
of a constitutional régime. This is a praiseworthy movement. However,' he added, 'a revolution cannot be achieved by imitation. A
revolution in Turkey must suit the social life and the national spirit of
the Turkish people. The Constitution must emerge from the soul of
the Turkish nation. It must fit into its national structure. Otherwise a
revolution may do harm rather than good to the country. To make a
good constitution, you have to study, first of all, the psychology and
sociology of the Turkish people. You know the revolutionaries, more
or less, I presume. Have they made these studies? Do they base their
programme on them? Are they, in short, prepared in a scientific spirit
for the fight they are initiating?'

We were unable to answer these questions. As a matter of fact, they
were asked not in order to be answered, but rather to tell something.
He knew very well that the studies he had in mind were not what
either of us was doing. Certainly he wanted only to give a final lesson
to his two former students, to leave them a philosophical testament.

I never forgot my teacher's testament, as I always remembered that
of my father. From that day on I set out to study the fundamentals of
psychology and sociology in order to understand the Turkish nation.

THE TESTAMENT OF MY SPIRITUAL GUIDE[6]

In the year 1900 I spent ten months in Taşkışla prison. These ten
months, during which I lived in solitude in the clothing depot of a

40 TURKISH NATIONALISM AND WESTERN CIVILIZATION

dormitory full of soldiers, delivered me for ever from my psychological depressions. From Taşkışla I was moved to Mehterhane, and then to the police gaol.

There I met a revolutionary whose name was Naim Bey. This old man, who belonged to a distinguished family of Istanbul, was imprisoned, as was I, in the building of the police general headquarters, for political reasons. During the time I stayed there, I used to listen to the words of this enlightened old man, full of idealism, hope, and inspiration. On the day of my departure, he took me to a corner and said: 'As Peter the Great had a testament to his nation, I too have a message to leave to the youth of my nation. For some years I have been telling it to every young man I have met. If only one among them could fulfil my testament, it would be enough for me to rest peacefully in my grave until eternity. I am convinced that one day freedom will surely come to my country, though I do not know how it will be attained. Perhaps when the present ruler dies, the one to succeed him will restore the Constitution to please the people. I am old and I do not hope to see that day. But I am sure you will live to see it.

'You must know that the first constitutional régime, in whatever way it might be achieved, will not be a genuine one. It is not enough for it to be wanted and established by a few persons. To be real it has to be understood by the people. Today, however, our people are in a deep slumber. Can a sleeping people understand the value of freedom? The first constitutional régime, therefore, cannot live long. The doors of the Parliament will be closed once more. We can understand how this will happen by comparing it with similar events which have taken place in Europe and by looking at the state of affairs in our own country.

'I visualize the situation in my imagination thus: as there will be no moral control over the people, the deputies will soon start a race for spoils; newspapers will start blackmailing; the extremists will attack even the most vigorous traditions. This will naturally distress supporters of the constitutional régime. Some people, on the other hand, will start Pan-Islamic organizations and campaigns. The British, becoming suspicious of these organizations and propaganda, will put pressure upon the Palace to suspend the Parliament. The Court, already realizing that its influence is diminishing under the democratic opinions expressed in speeches and in the press, will readily give way to this pressure, and, hiring one or two papers, will start a wild campaign

AUTOBIOGRAPHICAL

against the constitutional régime. And then one morning we shall read the Holy Decree declaring that the Parliament has been suspended until a more suitable moment comes for reopening it. Such will be the fate of the first parliamentary administration. I can see it now in detail. If you had lived through my experiences, you too would be able to visualize it.

'And yet you should not be discouraged by this quick ending. It could not have been a genuine parliamentary régime.

'The most important thing, however, is to maintain the freedom of the press. And my testament will be only on this point. I said that the nation is in deep slumber. The people will awaken only when they themselves are aware of their own aims and goals. But if there is no free and independent press, how will they ever be brought to this realization?

'In order to do this, however, our own thinkers should know these ends first. Today they do not have any definite and clear notion of them. The danger frightening me most is the absence of thinking minds who will be ready at the coming of the constitutional period. If such people do not exist, what is the use of having a free press? It is this worry that is guiding me to leave a message to the youth. You will have ten more years till the day freedom comes. The youth must spend these years reading, thinking, and searching day and night. You must discover where the salvation of this nation lies. Which ideals and beliefs should be inculcated in our people? Which ideals will waken them, will move and lead them in the new direction? Which principles can elevate them towards civilization? You must discover all these fundamentals in order to have a clear scheme by which to lead the nation, or you may be lost when the day of freedom comes. You ought to know what to do and say. In preparing your course in this way, you must take over the leadership of a paper or a review as soon as the press gets its freedom. You must publish your guiding principles untiringly, principles which will bring the new ideals and new orientations before the people. I say untiringly because this initial freedom will not last long, since it will not be a genuine one. Freedom of the press will also be of short duration. Therefore, you must write as much as possible; you must incise every vital wound, every grievance of the people, as quickly as possible, so as to get the maximum benefit from this short period. The opportunity is elusive like a bird, it slips out of your hands quickly. In such periods you cannot move slowly and cautiously, for

42   TURKISH NATIONALISM AND WESTERN CIVILIZATION

if you do hesitate to write what you think, it will remain unwritten for ever.

'But you must not believe that whatever you have written will be read and will lead to anything. Not at all. Maybe it will never be read at that time of emotion, struggle, and anarchy. Or it might be read but not understood. The most necessary thing, however, is not that your message should be read and understood immediately. What we most urgently need is to have the ideas that will express our national aspirations printed. A printed idea can never be destroyed. Once it becomes printed and published, do not worry any longer. Let Tyranny come again, a thousand times more powerful if it wishes. Let the press be put under chains much heavier than before. Let all papers and reviews printed in the days of freedom be declared noxious and forbidden. It doesn't matter. On the contrary, the more suppressive the tyranny becomes, the stronger the reaction to it will be, the more rapid the awakening. People are more eager to read writings once they have been declared subversive. Just as we today read subversive materials braving all dangers, so will it be in the days of the future Tyranny. They will be sought for impulsively, and pass from hand to hand. If the ideals shown are valid, if the principles proposed useful, these writings certainly will awaken the people and invite them to take their fate into their own hands. It is only when the people have been awakened that they can win freedom by their own efforts, the kind of freedom they will find indispensable to their own existence.

'This last constitutional régime will become thus a genuine one and it will give permanent freedom to the people, to the press. These are what I want to convey to the youth of my people as my last wish.'

Time has proved how right he was! After the Armistice, Tyranny came again and dispersed the Parliament. Several writers, journalists, and thinkers were exiled to Malta, and an end was put to the freedom of the press. As calamities are greater stimuli than great ideas, this made the people shake themselves and save their honour and independence. A hero, a genius[7] led the people to great victories. If these extraordinary events had not taken place, the predictions of the old revolutionary might never have materialized.

When he had finished speaking, he asked me to promise to commit myself to the truth he had shown me. I made him my Spiritual Guide (*pír*), as he had revealed to me the right path to the goals for which I should consecrate myself.

AUTOBIOGRAPHICAL 43

MY NATIONALITY[8]

... A person's nationality cannot be determined arbitrarily. It is a matter to be solved scientifically. When, in my youth, I went for the first time to Istanbul to study, I was forced to make this scientific inquiry for myself because there, in accordance with a bad habit which had survived of old, people from the Black Sea coast were called Lazes, those from Syria and Iraq, Arabs, and those from Rumeli [Turkish territories in the Balkan peninsula], Albanians; all those who belonged, like myself, to the Eastern Anatolian provinces were called Kurds. Up until that time I had considered myself a Turk. This feeling of mine, however, was not based on any scientific knowledge. In order to discover the truth, I began to study the Turks and the Kurds.

Above all, I began with language. In the city of Diyarbekir the people know some Kurdish although their mother tongue is Turkish. This bilingualism can be explained in either of two ways: either the Turkish spoken in Diyarbekir was the Turkish of the Kurds or the Kurdish spoken there was the Kurdish of the Turks. My linguistic studies have shown that the Turkish spoken in Diyarbekir was nothing but a natural language extending from Baghdad to Adana, to Baku and to Tabriz—the Azerī dialect peculiar to Akkoyunlu and Karakoyunlu Turks. There is nothing artificial in this language, and, therefore, it is not a language corrupted by the Kurds. (The fact that the Diyarbekir dialect is the Azerī dialect also disproved the thesis that the urban population spoke Turkish under the force of the Ottoman government, because if it were so the dialect spoken in the cities would be the Ottoman dialect.) On the other hand, the Kurdish spoken by the people of Diyarbekir, consisting of a limited number of words, is, as I discovered, different from the pure Kurdish spoken in villages. Kurdish, although related to Persian, does not resemble it at all in syntax. In Kurdish there are masculine and feminine genders as well as case-endings as in Arabic and Latin, whereas none of these exists in Persian. Therefore, Kurdish is a more complex and mixed language than Turkish. As the Turks were not accustomed to masculine or feminine genders, nor to case-endings, it would inevitably be difficult for them to understand these peculiarities in Kurdish. In reality, that has been the case, and the people of Diyarbekir have invented an artificial Kurdish by discarding these rules of Kurdish and fitting the Kurdish

44 TURKISH NATIONALISM AND WESTERN CIVILIZATION

grammar to Turkish syntax. It is entirely correct to call this Kurdish the Kurdish of the Turks.

This fact, very important from a linguistic point of view, is the most significant evidence in proving that the people of Diyarbekir are Turks. Furthermore, the people of Diyarbekir use this language only when they speak to Kurds. Among themselves they speak Turkish. The vocabulary of this artificial Kurdish, which the people of Diyarbekir do not master very well, is also very limited. For this reason, they fill in the gaps with Turkish words. As a matter of fact, the Kurdish known by most of them consists of a few simple words, such as 'come' or 'go'.

I found another proof of the Turkishness of the people of Diyarbekir in their division into religious sects. The bulk of the population are of the Hanafī rite like all Turks; whereas the Kurds are Shāfiʿīs in general. These two characteristics are peculiar not only to the inhabitants of Diyarbekir but also to those of all the eastern and southern provinces. . . .

Besides these differences, there are other important differences such as those relating to cultural matters like clothing, eating, building, and furniture.

These evidences demonstrated to me that the inhabitants of Diyarbekir are Turks. I have learned also that I am racially a Turk, since the two grandfathers of my father came a few generations ago from Chermik, which is a Turkish area.

However, I would not hesitate to believe that I am a Turk even if I had discovered that my grandfathers came from the Kurdish or Arab areas; because I learned through my sociological studies that nationality is based solely on upbringing. I believe that my researches have solved an exceedingly important question, not only for myself but also for all the people of the eastern and southern provinces, urban as well as rural, whose population has so far remained Turkish.

The inhabitants of Diyarbekir[9] have been Turks since the times of the Seljuks, of Benaloğulları and of Artıkoğulları. Later, with the coming of the Khwārizm Turks, Akkoyunlu and Karakoyunlu Turks, the area became more extensively Turkified. Even if this historical information, the *divans* of scores of poets, inscriptions on mosques and city walls did not exist, the language, customs, and traditions of the people would sufficiently testify to their Turkishness. The culture found in Diyarbekir is Turkish culture at its richest. The folklore materials we have collected clearly prove this. In addition to the fact that the old inhabitants of Diyarbekir were Turks, all of those who came from this tribe or that district and settled there a few generations ago are Turks in that they were raised in the Turkish culture and spoke the Turkish language from infancy.

CHAPTER II

THE PHILOSOPHY OF VALUES AND IDEALS

THE PHILOSOPHY OF TODAY[1]

IN the past, philosophy was regarded as the mother of all sciences. It was believed to have given birth to the sciences and other disciplines. But when positive sciences born of observation and experimentation began to establish themselves, philosophy gave up its maternal duty and became instead the policeman of the sciences. The young sciences, in their zeal to extend their realms, were transgressing their boundaries and were trespassing on the neighbouring domains. To maintain an accord between these quarrelling neighbours, it was necessary to demarcate the area of each carefully and to put them all under the administration of the same laws. Philosophy thus finally succeeded in unifying the various sciences under one science by realizing this task of reconciliation and unification. But the solidary system of sciences which came into existence through this co-ordination began to clamour for independence. It wanted to gain autonomy by freeing itself from the tutelage of philosophy!

When philosophy thus lost its authority in the field of science, it was forced to retire to a domain far beyond the realm of science. Upon the advice of a great reformer, the young sciences had chased metaphysics from their precincts. When the sciences had established a united front among themselves, there remained beyond their frontiers only the mysterious ghosts of metaphysics.

As the two watchful eyes of science, observation and experimentation, could not see these ghosts clearly, the field beyond the frontier seemed always to be a mysterious and unknowable land of darkness. Philosophy, driven out of its estate of science to the realm of darkness, was respectfully welcomed by metaphysics. The latter entrusted to this fertile mother the task of enlightening and ordering its dark realm. Mindful of the would-be attacks of science, philosophy, to feel itself on a sure ground, also accepted the guidance of observation and experimentation.

PHILOSOPHY OF VALUES AND IDEALS

As the data of science are external phenomena, known through the senses, science had always relied on observation and experimentation as the only sources of knowledge of the external world. As the data of metaphysics, on the other hand, are internal experiences known only through *consciousness*,[2] metaphysics relied only on introspection and internal experiences. But since it was not forgetful of the truths which science had discovered, it always avoided arriving at conclusions contrary to those of science. Science had studied the external appearance of nature, and attempted to reduce all qualitative properties to a single quantitative property of motion. As qualities are primary and not irreducible to each other, science had succeeded only in reducing the quantitative aspects of these qualities to the quantity of motion. Science saw every phenomenon as a mechanism; it measured, weighed, and calculated all inorganic, organic, and superorganic factors.

Philosophy had assigned the inside of nature to metaphysics as its subject-matter. The outside of nature consisted of observable phenomena. The visibility of phenomena requires the observation of an observer. In other words, there must be observing beings as well as that which is to be observed. Science dealt with the things observed, but as long as the inside nature of the observing beings remained unknowable, the reality of the observed thing could not be totally grasped. Who would deal then with the observer? As this aspect of existence belongs to the inside of nature, this task obviously belongs to metaphysics. Thus, metaphysics started its job with the analysis of mind.

Science had scrutinized the material nature of man in every detail. Its branches, such as anatomy, histology, physiology, pathology, and anthropology, always dealt with the outside of man; that is, with those aspects which could be observed with the naked eye or by microscope. His bones, his flesh, his blood-vessels, and nerves, the most minute corners of his brain—the structure and functions of each were studied. It was found that all were nothing but mechanisms, and that man was nothing but a machine with a consciousness. But there was one point still to be explained. Why did this machine have a consciousness while all other machines worked without one? When science was busy in the fields of physics and chemistry, it had not encountered any phenomena associated with consciousness. Thus when it attempted to apply the laws it had derived from the study of the phenomena without consciousness to the organism of man, it came face to face with a

48 TURKISH NATIONALISM AND WESTERN CIVILIZATION

shock with the phenomena of consciousness. What was the origin of this consciousness which was also called 'conscience'? Did it also originate as a product of some chemical process?

Metaphysics made this question, to which science failed to give an answer, its own starting-point. It accepted the consciousness or conscience as the first development, as the first emergence of Being. Seeing, thinking, understanding—all imply an observer, a thinking person, an understanding person, on the one hand, and the things to be seen, to be thought of, to be understood, on the other; thus two kinds of being are implied. The first was called the 'subject' and the second the 'object'. In fact, that which exists is not the thing seen, thought, or understood, but the subject which sees, thinks, and understands. The subject which sees, thinks, and understands is nothing but the consciousness or conscience, and the things observed are nothing but the impressions of consciousness. If we liken consciousness to a mirror endowed with the capacity to understand, the things observed become nothing but the reflections in this mirror. As consciousness projects these reflections back to the outer world and puts them into space, we accept the reflections as the things themselves. Just as a mirror which is supposed to have the quality of consciousness might mistake the images appearing on its own surface as the real objects, we also suffer from a similar illusion. Just as the surface of the mirror is a pseudo-space, we too see the impressions in an imaginary distance.

Metaphysics did not content itself with saying that objects are nothing but reflections in the mirror of consciousness; it searched also for the reflectors of these reflections, the original sources of these shadows. It believed that these reflectors or originals were themselves also subjects or consciousnesses. Therefore, all existence consisted of more or less dim, more or less distinct, consciousnesses occupying different positions in the scheme of evolution. Consciousness sees the consciousness [in others] as matter, but sees itself as consciousness. As science studied observed phenomena, it became materialistic; but as metaphysics took observed beings as observed beings, it became spiritualistic. Science studied objective phenomena, metaphysics subjective phenomena. As objective phenomena consisted of quantities, science could not go beyond the quantity and failed to explain the quality. As quality consists of the subjective elements of sensation, metaphysics studied the quality and found the essential nature of being in these different irreducible manifestations. Science had affirmed observed

PHILOSOPHY OF VALUES AND IDEALS 49

phenomena, metaphysics disclosed the nature of the observer and the observed.

Science discovered determinism in physics and the laws of natural selection and evolution. Metaphysics disclosed spiritual determinism, spiritual selection, and evolution. It proved that quality, like quantity, can be a factor in determinism, selection, and evolution.

When metaphysics had acquired a positivistic character based on observation and experiment, it did not need philosophy any more, and said to it: 'You may go, I can take care of myself'. Philosophy remained homeless. The realm of observed beings was taken over by science, the realm of the observer by metaphysics. Where should this aged explorer find a new, an unoccupied, and unknown continent for itself?

Yet, there was an entirely unknown virgin land for philosophy! Like Christopher Columbus, it discovered the America of the world of the intellect. It is not sorry for its loss of the realm of the observed to science and the realm of the observer to metaphysics, because the realm of 'things desired' is now providing it with a ground far richer in potentialities for fighting. Philosophy wanted to like what it thought and to think what it liked. Neither the generalizations reached by science nor the qualitative essences discovered by metaphysics had ever satisfied the aspirations of its heart. It wanted always to reach the essence of the beautiful and the sublime. The new field presented to philosophy the treasure of the *world of values*.

Value is not something static like quantity, nor is it something incapable of evolution like quality. It acquires a desired perfection, and it is subject to evaluation. It may not have an objective existence, but its existence in the mind is sufficient, because metaphysics has proved that the mind, too, has a reality of its own. And again the discoveries of psychology and metaphysics have shown that this existence does not consist of an inert being, but is an active power. This force definitely shows its effects in the external world. Values are nothing but *idées-forces*. They appear at first to be of an intellectual nature, then acquire a psychological character, and at last become an external reality, on condition that they correspond to what is possible in the actual situation. Thus, when philosophy wants to evaluate and create new values, it has to take real and actual trends into account. The aspirations to perfection pointing to the ends in the evolution of external and internal reality are *ideals*. Ends having no basis in the evolutionary process, and born out of the speculative desires of the

50 TURKISH NATIONALISM AND WESTERN CIVILIZATION

person are nothing but fictions. Thus, to provide a positive basis for the values to be created, philosophy must not contradict science and metaphysics, but must value only those ideals which will be in harmony with them.

Philosophy, conscious of these conditions, began to attach value to aspirations after perfection, and to serve a creative function. It offered sublime and pure quiddities existing in the mind and yet realizable in the objective world—things which the noble heart could find neither in material truths nor in spiritual quiddities. Philosophy has proved that man is able not only to see but also to effect. It has proved that man has a creative power and a faculty for perfection. It now became a new rising sun for our hopes. It gave rise to the contention that a super-man can emerge from man, that a life higher than mortal life can be experienced.

This is the state of the philosophy of today. At first it was believed that philosophy could be reconciled with science and that it consisted of logic. Then it began to roam over the territory of metaphysics, and turned into a general theory of aesthetics. Now philosophy has found its proper domain. It has begun its own work—that of evaluating the political, legal, and moral values that regulate our social life, and of creating the new values that will elevate humanity. The philosophy of today, therefore, is a theory of ethics. Once it searched the laws of thought, the intimate details of sensibility, and now it is searching for the sublime ends of the Will. Its present method is not inductive and analytical, but normative and creative.

THE PHILOSOPHY OF IDEALISM OF IBN AL-'ARABI[3]

Among Muslim thinkers, the one who is closest to present-day philosophy is Muhyi'l-dīn Ibn al-'Arabī.[4] He was an innovator who gave rational expression to the intuitive states which the *Sūfīs* reached through *dhawk* (direct experience).

It is erroneous to equate sufism with that school of thought called mysticism in Western philosophy. Sufism corresponds, in its general meaning, to idealism. Among the sufis there were those who represented different forms of idealism, and among them there were those who were mystics. The term *tasawwuf* is a general term covering various doctrines which did not ascribe a real existence to the world of sensibles. Some of the idealists reduced reality to ideas, some to sense-experiences,

PHILOSOPHY OF VALUES AND IDEALS 51

and some to will. In sufi doctrine these corresponded to what the sufis themselves called stations (*makam*). When the sufi denied the real existence of the world of sensibles, he formulated his idea by saying: 'The realm of existence is of the order of idea' ('*innamā al-kawnu khayālun*'). Those who remained at this stage of knowledge and did not go beyond were idealists.

But as the sufi was a seeker after perfection, he could not remain at a fixed station. He sought for continuous progress, continuous elevation. Thus, when he discovered that the idea is a reproduction reflected from outside on consciousness, and that the objects which we perceive have an external source and become coloured by the sensibility of our consciousness, he summarized this discovery in the saying: 'The colour of the water is the colour of its container' ('*lawn al-mā'i lawnn inā'ihī*'). Those who remained at this station were sensationalists.

Sense experiences are the acts of expansion and of contraction, which are the results of satisfaction and thwarting of the will. The will is the most absolute, the most real part of the being which, not content with existing perfections, strives to perceive and construct those perfections which ought to exist. Muhyi'l-dīn calls these perfections inherent in things which ought to exist, the 'eternal essences' ('*a'yān-i-thābita*). These real goals of the will which are real existents are the real motives and factors of universal evolution, of the universal apogee of perfection. He formulated this great truth by saying: 'The decree of divine providence on things takes place only according to the nature of those things' ('*mā hakama al-kadā 'ala al-ākhyā'i illā bihā*').

The three stages through which idealism passed in the history of modern Western philosophy exactly correspond to these three 'stations' of the sufis formulated in the above three Arabic sentences. When Berkeley believed that the things which we perceive consists of our sensations, he had just repeated the sufi's saying: 'The realm of existence is of the order of idea'. Thus, Berkeley's doctrine of phenomenalism was the first step for the sufis. And when Kant declared that our perceptions do not consist of objective forms, he only explained the insight formulated in the saying: 'The colour of the water is the colour of its container'. Thus, philosophy of criticism corresponded to the second 'station' of the sufis. And, finally when recent philosophers such as Alfred Fouillée, Guyeau, Nietzsche, William James declared that ideals are nothing but *idées-forces*, or that hope, will, belief are forces leading to highest and purest happiness by creating new values, they

52 TURKISH NATIONALISM AND WESTERN CIVILIZATION

did nothing but interpret the sufi dictum: 'The decree of divine providence on things takes place only according to the nature of those things.' It seems, therefore, that upon a closer examination we can find the philosophy of values of today in the rich treasures of *tasawwuf*.

Muhyi'l-dīn Ibn al-'Arabī had taken the *hadith*, which says: 'I am what My worshipper thinks (*ẓann*) of Me, so let his thought be good' (*'ana 'inda ẓanni 'abdī falyaẓunna bī (kh)ayr^{an}'*) as the torchlight of his doctrine and illuminated reality under its light. 'Opinion' (*ẓann*) is an *idée-force*, which is a factor and a motive in our life and conduct as our good opinions are useful forces which regulate our life, and the bad ones are those harmful forces ruling our life.

Psychological facts, which we call opinion, ideal, belief, are not mere passive ideas and ineffective representations. In them, creative and destructive forces, positive or negative values, are inherent. Everybody carries an ideal perfection in his thinking, opinion, and beliefs. He moves upwards towards these ideal perfections through the creative force of his ideas, opinions, and beliefs. He follows the evolutionary path of a universal zenith, sets out towards an ideal perfection. Therefore, the past, present, and future states of the person are transitory and momentary shadows. If there is something unchanging, it is the ideal perfection which is the end of evolution. Muhyi'l-dīn al-'Arabī called this ideal perfection 'eternal essence', which corresponds to our term 'ideal'. He did not ascribe an external existence to these eternal essences or unchanging patterns. When he said: 'The eternal essences have not smelled the smell of existence' (*'al-a'yānu al-(th)ābitatu mā (sh)ammat rā'ihata' l-wujūdi'*), he meant that they had only a mental existence. However, he regarded these quiddities which exist only in the mind without having an external existence as the sole factors of nature. The decree of divine providence on things takes place only according to the nature of things in themselves. For him, divine providence does nothing but put into execution the decisions of the eternal essences just like a constitutional monarch. In a poem that he wrote as from the mouth of the eternal essences, he said: 'If He did not exist and if we did not exist, that which exists would not have existed' (*'falaw lāhu wa law lānā / lamā kāna' lla(dh)ī kanā'*). Thus, he clearly stated that in nature divine providence and eternal essences are the sole factors. In the same poem, in the line reading: 'The things which He manifests in us and gives us have only been given to Him by us' (*'fa ātaynāhu mā yubdihi fīnā wa ātānā'*), he shows that the legislating power is in the eternal

PHILOSOPHY OF VALUES AND IDEALS

essences and the executive power lies in the hands of the divine providence. The couplet saying:

> God is servant and the servant is God
> Would that I knew who is the compelled [or compelling] one*

expresses the same idea.

Eternal essences are not confined only to human beings. As matter is the manifestation of spirit, everything consists of spirit more or less consciously. Spirit is the real being and matter is its manifestation. As everything is spirit, in all inorganic, organic, supra-organic things there are eternal essences immanent in them. He calls matter and the extension which is the ultimate reality of matter *kursi* (the seat of God), and calls that universal spirit which forms the dimension of this infinite extension, *'arsh* (the Throne of God). And he finds the mystery of God's ascending to the throne in the Absolute Perfection which leads things to a universal zenith by showing a goal of perfection as eternal essences for every particle of this universal spirit. He calls the world of eternal essences the 'supernal plenum'.

> 'Ponder upon the lines of nature
> Because they are messages to you from the supernal realm.'†

In other words, what we see are rough copies of eternal essences. Everything is a perfection in embryo. Wherever you look, you will see that hidden perfection which is the aim of evolution. The objects which we see are the words, lines, and pages of the Book of Universe on which are written poems not adequately expressed because of the insufficiency of the words. However, if you read them carefully you can discover the hidden meanings behind these verbal imitations (symbols). These pages are like letters sent to you from the supernal realm.

After having explained that the eternal essences or ideals are basic factors in cosmic perfection, that everything aims at a goal of perfection, and that all being aims at absolute perfection, he states that each of these eternal essences or ideal perfections has received a divine name. As things are manifestations of eternal essences, the latter are also the manifestations of divine names. According to him, the God whom we

---

* Fa'l-rabbu 'abd^un wa'l-'abdu rabb^un;
  Yā layta sha'rī man al-mukallaf [mukallif].
† Ta'ammal [?] suṭura'l-kā'ināti, fa 'innahā
  Min al-mala' al-a'lā ilayka rasā'ilū.

54 TURKISH NATIONALISM AND WESTERN CIVILIZATION

can reach is as He is believed by us; we can never reach the Absolute God. The God whom prophets and saints reached is only the believed-in God. Even prophets and saints did not reach the Absolute God. However, we can approach the Absolute God even if we cannot reach Him. In order to do this, it is necessary to reach the believed-in gods of inanimate things, plants, animals, men, and all existence, and thus unite them into the Absolute One. He expressed this idea in the following couplet:

> The people have various kinds of beliefs in God
> And I testify all that they believe.*

Those who thought that Muhyi'l-dīn was a pantheist were mistaken. To consider existents as the manifestation of the eternal essences, and the eternal essences as the place of manifestation of divine names, does not mean believing in pantheism. The eternal essence of any thing existent is the manifestation of the believed-in God. Every individual analyses the concept of God which transcends our capacity to conceive it in accordance with its own being. When Junaid of Baghdad was asked about the knowledge of God, he answered: 'The colour of water is the colour of its container.' This truth, which some people tried to call anthropomorphism or sociomorphism, was expressed by a sufi poet in the following way:

> Those who would look at Thy beautiful face
> When observing from a distance
> Would see their own face in Thine—
> In their position lies the difference of features.

Muhyi'l-dīn did not ascribe a material existence to the eternal essences. The names which are described by these eternal essences and the Absolute, the One named by these names is naturally free from any material existence and contingency. However, he did not, as Plato and Kant did, ascribe a transcendental existence to the eternal essences. He disclosed this when he said: 'The eternal essences have not smelled the smell of existence'. For him, eternal essences have an immanent existence. They are latent and immanent and hidden in the will which is the deepest element of the being. Primeval chaos is nothing but a hidden treasure of the zenith of perfection.

* 'Aḳada'l-khalāiḳu fī'l-ilāhi 'aḳā'id^{an}
Wa ana shahidtu jamī'a mā 'taḳadū.

PHILOSOPHY OF VALUES AND IDEALS

Being has three manifestations—as 'divine seat', 'divine throne', and as 'the Merciful'. The degree of coarseness and rarefaction in this series is proportional to the ratio of coarseness between matter and spirit, between spirit and ideal. 'Praise be to God whose self is refined which He called truth and whose self is coarse which He called creation' (*'al-ḥamdu li' llāhi' lla(dh)i laṭu fa nafsuhu fasammāhu ḥakk^{an} wa ka(th)ufa nafsuhū fa sammāhu khalq^{an}'*), states that the state of coarseness of being is Creation and the state of rarefaction is Truth. Coarseness is the state of deficiency of being, and rarefaction is the hidden perfection immanent in the constitution of this deficiency. But the natural motion of things is to approach this unattainable end. Universal praise and glorification of God is nothing but this course of evolution. Muhyi'l-dīn tells that the power which manifests the things is just an exercise of these things for perfection, and that every existent is nothing but a deficient and rough copy of Absolute Perfection, when he says: 'Glory be to God who created things, being Himself their essences' (*'subḥān' alla(dh)ī aẓhara'l a(sh) yā'a fahuwa a'yānuhā'*).

We conclude from this that although philosophy has undergone great developments during the last few centuries, its spirit has remained unchanged. Ghazzalī had anticipated Descartes's methodical doubt. Berkeley's and Kant's philosophies were also anticipated. Muhyi'l-dīn al-'Arabi had shown long before Alfred Fouillée that ideals are creative factors in evolution, and had laid the grounds of present-day philosophy. The spirit of his philosophy is telling us human beings:

> You are the vice-gerent of true Being,
> All the Universe is under your sway;
> That which is conceived in your heart
> —the preserved tablet—is just what is predestined.[*]

NEW LIFE AND NEW VALUES[5]

We have achieved the political revolution;[6] now we are confronted with yet another task: to prepare for the social revolution!

The political revolution was easy to realize because it meant merely applying the machinery of the constitutional régime to government. The social revolution cannot be attained by a mere mechanical action.

---

[*] Zât-i hakkın halifesisin sen,
Bütün ekvân sana musahhardır;
Levh-i mahfûz olan zamîrinde
Mutasavver olan mukadderdir.

56 TURKISH NATIONALISM AND WESTERN CIVILIZATION

It will be difficult to achieve because it must be the product of a long process of organic evolution.

In order to put the political revolution into practice, it was enough to disseminate certain *idées-forces*, such as liberty, equality, and fraternity which symbolize the spirit of the constitutional régime. The social revolution, on the other hand, is dependent upon the growth and consummation of certain *sentiments-forces*. Acceptance or rejection of the ideas is within the power of reason. The sentiments, on the other hand, cannot evolve easily because they are the products of social habits developed in the course of several centuries. Hence the social revolution is a most difficult and a most time-consuming struggle, for which we have to mobilize all our forces from now on.

There are non-Muslims among us. As they have remained outside active political life, they have been occupied primarily with economic activities. Since our governments had left all [religious] communities to organize themselves [under their religious leaders], their organizations became the bases of their social enterprises, and in this way our non-Muslim compatriots have been able to develop a special aptitude in economic enterprises.

When all of us realized the inevitability of a social revolution following the political one, our non-Muslim compatriots had already attained a more favourable position in the economic and social spheres of life. Political preoccupations had forced the Muslims, however, to remain very weak in respect to economic and social activities.

What does a social revolution mean? It means simply the creation of a New Life by discarding an older one. The concept of life has very general connotations. It covers the economic, domestic, aesthetic, philosophical, moral, legal, and political spheres of living. A New Life means, obviously, a new form of economy, a new form of family-life, new aesthetic standards, a new morality, a new conception of law, and a new political system. Changing the old life is possible only when a new way of living is created, with its economic, domestic, aesthetic, philosophical, legal, and political features.

It is obvious also that the factors which determine the orientation of a mode of living are the human values which it fosters. As the old mode of living had its own specific economic ethics, it had also its specific domestic, aesthetic, philosophical, moral, legal, and political values. To attempt the creation of a New Life necessitates the discovery and the fostering of genuine values with respect to each sphere of life.

PHILOSOPHY OF VALUES AND IDEALS

When the youth will have taken the New Life as their goal, they will be in fact in search of these genuine values. To understand the New Life presupposes a knowledge of these values. Are they known?

You will be mistaken if you think that we are in a position to give a definite answer to this question. You should, above all, remember that a value can be appreciated only when it is known. And it is generally accepted only when it is appreciated, for it is only then that it begins to reign in our life. To know them now means, therefore, that they are actually dominating our conduct. If this is so, then, why should we need a new way of life and its values?—we would then believe that our present values of living are the most valid ones, and there is no need for a new way of life.

But we do not approve of the old life and the old values. We strive for the new ones. There are then some values, which we not only are not living up to but which we are not even in a position to know. But, you will ask, what is meant by that mysterious life which we are not experiencing and which we have not even imagined until now? And what is the use of thinking about the unknown values which will make up that life?

This objection seems to be logical but not psychological. It is undeniable that the real factors in the evolution of humanity are ideals. Ideals are those vague and unknown ends which have driven human beings only through the attraction of their vagueness, by the mystery of their ambiguity, and have led them towards progress. Sometimes they have even led mankind to unexpected and unforeseen achievements. Here are two examples: Those who were in pursuit of alchemy finally discovered chemistry; those delving into astrology emerged with astronomy. The Crusaders wanted to capture the Holy Land, but instead they captured Arab civilization. Vague goals like socialism and feminism have contributed to progress and social justice and freedom. It is true that some of their protagonists had clearly defined their objectives and had constructed utopias in their minds. But today we see clearly that the movements of socialism or feminism themselves are not advancing towards the exact realization of these utopias. While they progressed, they got farther and farther away from the utopian paradises which the theoreticians had constructed in their imaginations.

The followers of the New Life will not entertain such utopias, will not go forward towards preconceived goals with preconceived programmes as the utopians did in following their fictions. The New Life

58 TURKISH NATIONALISM AND WESTERN CIVILIZATION

is a movement, but not a definite and a straight-line movement. We cannot ascertain and predict the ends to which it will lead us and the consequences which it will bring forth.

The New Life has no pre-defined goal and no programme, but it does have a disciplined method. A programme necessitates a prophetic prevision of the future idea before it is realized. The method is not so haughty. It does not propose unattainable goals. Sciences have methods but not programmes, because they do not determine in advance what truths they are going to discover. They only follow their own disciplined methods, and the truths emerge slowly in the course of their investigation.

What will be the method of the followers of the New Life? First of all, they have made a division of labour among themselves. The values relating to each sphere of life are going to be studied by various research workers in special monographic works. None will ever attempt to put forth his own opinions as the final truths of the New Life. The new values that will be agreed upon, and even those which by then have been implemented, will have only tentative validity and be subject to evolutionary selection. In fact, to claim no final truths will be the most important principle of the followers of the New Life.

Researches in connection with the New Life will be based on the most recent practices and philosophical views, and will avoid all kinds of arbitrary speculation. They will be written in book form by our young intellectuals, whom we shall ask to write on the subjects in which they have specialized. Everyone's contentions will be respected. The 'Outlines' on the values of the New Life will be published in cheap booklets; and although the values proposed in them will be nothing more than mere incomplete sketches of the genuine values, they will certainly gain acclaim and wide acceptance.

Let us explain the method of the New Life a little further. *Tout par la science et pour l'humanité,'* said Dr Isnard. The followers of the New Life believe that humanity today is exemplified in the nation, and thus the phrase is restated to read in the following form: 'Every advance through science and for the fatherland'. The first duty of the followers of the New Life is to work for the strengthening and elevation of the Ottomans by means of literature, science, and philosophy. The New Life is not a cosmopolitan but a national life.

I had pointed out before that our non-Muslim compatriots are ahead of us with respect to experience in economic enterprises and matters of

PHILOSOPHY OF VALUES AND IDEALS 59

social organization. Let me now describe another aspect of their favourable position: they were not in need of a painful search for a New Life. For them the civilization of Europe, like the ready-made suits sold in department stores, was easily available for wear. The majority of the Greeks, Armenians, and Bulgarians living among us have readily accepted the manners and habits of European civilization. Because of the existence of certain conditions peculiar to our life, we Muslims could not imitate the ready-made norms of Europe and its standardized ways of living. For us, it was necessary to have them made to order, like tailored suits, to fit our own body. Our non-Muslim compatriots were in a position to take European standards as their models as soon as they discarded their old ways of living. But, since we belong to a different *ümmet* [religion][7] we did not reproduce these models, believing that we should create a new mode of civilization from our own understanding. It is this belief which has given birth to our New Life.

The New Life will be created, not copied. Our new values will be economic, domestic, aesthetic, philosophic, moral, legal, and political values born out of the soul of the Ottomans. To create their own civilization, the Ottomans themselves have to work out a new form of family life, new aesthetic standards, a new philosophy, a new morality, a new understanding of law, and a new political organization. Only through the knowledge of these national values will the national civilization of the Ottomans inspire the praise of the Europeans.

I have already pointed out the more favourable position of our non-Muslim compatriots with respect to economic and social conditions. This observation, however, does not tell the whole truth. They are in a more favourable position only with regard to economics and social living. Because we are going to benefit from the achievements of modern science and philosophy in our search for a New Life, the methods we shall follow in every aspect of life will be more up-to-date. Thus, for example, we shall not waste time on small crafts, but will immediately introduce modern industry. We shall have the most modern merchant marine to master the seas. Our social life will not be based on the communal principle, but will be founded on the principles of the solidarity and fellowship of free wills. We shall benefit from the most recent discoveries and theories in every field of civilization. Our non-Muslim compatriots are only anxious imitators of European life. We, as I have explained, should create a new synthesis. We certainly shall seek, discover, and appropriate the genuine values. The belief that they

60 TURKISH NATIONALISM AND WESTERN CIVILIZATION

are in a more favourable position as compared to ours seems therefore nothing more than a pseudo-truth. The New Life will expose the real nature of this belief, which represents us always in dim and them in bright lights. It will show also that the foundations of European civilization are worn, sick, and rotten, that they are destined to fall and disintegrate. We shall create a genuine civilization, a Turkish civilization, which will follow the growth of a New Life. The Turkish race has not been degenerated like some other races by alcohol and debauchery. Turkish blood has remained rejuvenated and hardened like steel with the glories of the battlefield. The Turkish intelligence is not worn out, its sentiments are not effeminate, its will is not weakened. The conquest of the future is promised to Turkish resolution.[8]

HISTORICAL MATERIALISM AND SOCIOLOGICAL IDEALISM[9]

Among the sociological schools trying to interpret social phenomena, there are two schools of thought which are close to each other in one respect but divergent in another. I mean historical materialism and sociological idealism. The first is represented by Karl Marx and the second by Émile Durkheim.

At first glance, these two schools appear to be quite close to each other, because both admit as a principle that social facts are produced by certain natural causes, and that social facts are subject to natural laws just as are physical, biological, and psychological facts. In other words, both accept the principle of determinism in social science.

From this point on, however, the two begin to diverge. Marx claimed a kind of monopoly for a single determining factor; for him the privilege of being the determining cause belongs only to the economic factor among other social facts. The remaining social facts, such as religious, moral, aesthetic, political, linguistic, and intellectual facts, cannot by any means be the causes of other social facts, but can be only the products of [economic] causes. Therefore, for Marx all social facts other than the economic facts are epi-phenomena. If a social fact is an epi-phenomenon, it cannot exercise any effect upon other facts, just as the shadow of a person obviously does not produce any effect upon the action of the person. Just like the shadow, it merely follows. For Marx, only economic facts are genuine realities. The rest are neither realities nor phenomena, but simply the products and shadows of economic facts. In terms of this view, Marx would interpret, for example, the origin of religions, the differentiation of religious sects, the rise of the ascetic orders or of mystic fraternities, the Reformation, the separation of the State from the Church, as well as the rise, growth, and decline of certain moral, legal, political, aesthetic, linguistic, and intellectual traditions and ideals, mainly by the changes which take place in the techniques of production.

According to the sociological school of Durkheim, such a single-factor interpretation is wrong. Economic facts do not hold any particular privilege against other social facts. In the same way as economic institutions are facts and realities, other social institutions . . . are natural facts and realities. To regard them as epi-phenomena, as shadows of realities, is missing the objective reality. As there are no shadow-facts in physics, chemistry, or biology, why should they exist in sociology? It is true that in the past some psychologists, such as Maudsley, called 'consciousness' an epi-phenomenon, and claimed that it exercised no effect on psychic phenomena. Recent psychologists, such as Alfred Fouillée, Theodule Ribot, William James, Harald Höffding, Henri Bergson, Pierre Janet, Alfred Binet, and Paulhan, have definitely rejected this theory, so that the term epi-phenomenon is no longer used in psychology.

To believe that only economic facts constitute reality in the social realm is similar to the belief that only the facts of the gastric and digestive functions are the real facts among all other physiological functions, and that the latter are nothing but unreal and ineffective shadows of the first. No physiologist can accept such a view.

Marx fell into another error when he extended this single-factor view from theory to practice. For him, the common people [the proletariat] consists only of the working class, and this class will abolish all other classes. But the common people means all; that is, the sum total of all classes accepted to be equal before the law. It is true that the imperialistic, aristocratic, and feudal classes who refuse to be equal with all are to be excluded from the common people. Equally, those among the bourgeoisie and the intellectuals who claim special privileges for themselves are also cut off from the people. But everyone who admits the equality of all before the law belongs to the common body of the people, regardless of the class to which he might belong.

In Durkheim's sociology, economic facts are capable of affecting other social facts, as all other social facts may be the causal factors of economic facts. Thus, this sociological school does not deny the

62 TURKISH NATIONALISM AND WESTERN CIVILIZATION

significance and importance of economic facts. Durkheim himself has shown that economic factors have an increasing importance in modern society, in which economic life is even the basis of the social structure. He has shown that social solidarity in primitive societies is a 'mechanical solidarity' based on *la conscience collective*. He called these societies 'segmentary' because they are composed of similar segments such as family, clan, phratry, and tribe. In complex societies there is, in addition to 'mechanical solidarity', an 'organic solidarity'. Thus, he called them 'organic societies'. Division of labour is the basis of the economic life of these societies. Religious, political, scientific, aesthetic, and economic groupings in modern societies are occupational and professional groups arising out of the division of labour. We see, thus, that Durkheim has given to the economic factor the recognition that it deserves.

However, it is true that Durkheim also reduced all social facts to a single factor; that is, to 'collective representations'. What he meant by this term may be explained by examples rather than by a definition. There were, for instance, working men in Turkey before the 1908 revolution, but there was no working-class consciousness in the mind of these men, no realization of 'we are the working class'. As long as this consciousness did not exist, a class of workers did not exist. And again, before the same revolution, there were Turks, but there was no idea 'we are the Turkish nation' in the collective consciousness of that people; in other words, there was no Turkish nation at that time. It follows that a group is not a 'social' group so long as its existence has not been felt in the common consciousness of individuals. In the same way, an originally Turkish word is not Turkish, and hence is not a social fact as long as it is not alive in the linguistic consciousness of the Turkish people. Similarly, a custom originally a part of the customary law (*töre*) of the Turks is not a social institution, is not an element in the moral life of the Turks, so long as it remains forgotten in the consciousness of the Turkish people.

These examples show that social facts exist only when and if they are experienced as conscious realizations in the collective consciousness of the groups to which they belong. Now, these conscious realizations in the collective consciousness are called 'collective representations'.

Collective representations are not ineffective epi-phenomena in social life, as Marx would believe. On the contrary, all spheres of our social life are shaped by them. As soon as such representations as 'we

PHILOSOPHY OF VALUES AND IDEALS 63

belong to the Turkish nation', 'we are of the *ümmet* of Islam', 'we are a part of Western civilization', become distinct representations in the common consciousness of the Turks of Turkey, every aspect of our social life will begin to change. The more we say 'we are of the Turkish nation', the more we shall be able to show originality and personality in terms of the Turkish taste and values in language, in art, in morality, in law, and even in religion and philosophy. As we say 'we are of the *ümmet* of Islam', we shall behave in accordance with the belief that the Kur'an is our sacred book, Muhammad our sacred prophet, the *Ka'ba* our sacred place, and Islam our sacred religion. As we say 'we are of Western civilization', we shall behave as do the European peoples in science, philosophy, techniques, and in all other aspects of civilization.

Collective representations do not consist only of group concepts. Myths, tales, legends, proverbs, beliefs; moral, legal, economic, and technical rules; and even scientific and philosophical views are all collective representations. Even rituals and practices which are not based on a faith or a theory are collective representations because people do them after they have conceived them mentally.

Individual ideas are the private ideas of persons. Collective representations, on the other hand, are mental patterns which are common to the members of a society, and which are consciously realized in the collective consciousness. Individual ideas exercise no effect upon society. But when they become collective representations based on a social force, they are factors of great importance in social life. The thoughts of a saviour, of a man with great charismatic power,[10] sooner or later become common ideas of the masses. Individual ideas of this nature have always been influential in social life. When a nation produces a great personality who actually proves his genius, the heroic and self-sacrificing power of his great deeds achieves great changes easily through his power to create collective representations. Today we have such an inspiring genius. As a single person he is capable of realizing great changes which ordinary persons and even men of great learning or skill are utterly powerless to achieve, and he does this by a single word, speech, or appeal to the people.

Collective representations gain their utmost power and prestige by enveloping themselves with a halo of ecstasy during times of excitement and fermentation. Then collective representations are called 'ideals'. They become the source of genuine revolutions only when they become ideals. The idea of Turkism was merely a representation,

64 TURKISH NATIONALISM AND WESTERN CIVILIZATION

shared only by a part of the youth. The forces which spread it to the entire nation and made it into a national ideal were the disasters following the Tripolitanian and Balkan wars, and the single person who transformed it into a national policy and made it a reality was Gazi Mustafa Kemal.

As we have seen in the foregoing examples, Durkheim explained idealism in sociological terms as the product of collective social behaviour. For him, all social phenomena consist of ideals or, their lesser equivalents, collective representations. Collective representations are more or less charged with value judgments. We evaluate social institutions as sacred, good, beautiful, or true. Evaluation by such adjectives shows that institutions are not free from the attachments of sentiments or emotions. We regard an object as 'sacred' whenever we feel a religious attachment to that object; we call something 'good' for which we experience a moral feeling; we call something 'beautiful' which stimulates an aesthetic emotion; we believe something is 'true' when we have a rational attachment to it. In other words, all collective representations express our ideals.

Although collective representations or ideals are the causes of social phenomena, they themselves are dependent upon certain social causes for their rise, growth, decline, and disappearance. These consist of the changes taking place in the social structure. According to Durkheim, the primary causes of social phenomena are those of social morphology such as the degree of density, and of conflict or homogeneity of population, and the stage of development of the division of labour. The rise of the Turkist movement has also been socially conditioned. Here, too, we find the two views, of historical materialism and sociological idealism, conflicting. According to the first, the Turkist movement is the product of economic factors, and according to the second, it is the result of those changes taking place in social ideals which were caused by certain changes in the social structure.

There were two main religious communities in Turkey—one the Muslims under the Caliphate, and the other the Christians under the Greek Orthodox Church. If religion had maintained its previous hold with the same intensity, these religious communities would not have disintegrated. With the increase in social density in the cities, the social division of labour expanded and gave rise to occupational groups which, in turn, gave rise to the occupational consciousness. Thus the collective consciousness of the Muslim and Christian communities

PHILOSOPHY OF VALUES AND IDEALS

began to weaken. This weakening led to the disintegration of the communal solidarity which was based on religious collective consciousness. Newspapers and schools, literature and poetry, replaced the unintelligible *ümmet* and Church language with the vernacular of the people. Collective representations of both communities changed. In the past men accepted their religious communities as social organisms of which they themselves were an indispensable part; now they have begun to see their own language groups as the basic social organism and themselves as indispensable parts of it. The disintegration of the religious community and its replacement by language groups took place in the end. The separation first of the Armenians and then of the Vlachians, Serbians, Bulgarians, and even of the Greeks from the community of the Byzantine Church, and the establishment of Exarchates by some of these peoples, are telling evidences of our argument. The fact that the separation of these language groups from the political collectivity, called the Ottoman Commonwealth, took place only after the religious separation shows that the real factor was purely cultural rather than political.

Nationalities consisting of language and culture groups did exist in the past, but were restricted by religious and political imperialisms to the confines of imperium and Church. When the chains of these political and religious communities broke, the groups imprisoned within them began their struggles for liberation. Nationalist movements in Turkey thus started first as movements of religious autonomy, and then as movements of political autonomy and independence. The movement started in a similar fashion among the Muslims. The Toscan Albanians, who were the backbone of Albanian nationalism (*Bashkim*), had long ago dissented from the Muslim community by accepting Bektashism. They wanted first to use their national languages in order to enjoy the new institutions of the modern age such as the school, press, literature, and poetry. To revive their language they needed a script, and accepted the Latin script, which shows that the Toscans at that time broke from the religious community. They put cultural solidarity into the place of the weakened religious solidarity.

Among the Arabs and Kurds, too, nationalism started as a cultural movement. Political and economic forms of nationalism followed as second and third stages. We know that Turkish nationalism also started as a cultural movement. One of its early fathers was the founder of our oldest university, and the other that of our military schools. If the

T.N.W.C.—5

66 TURKISH NATIONALISM AND WESTERN CIVILIZATION

medrese had been powerful enough, the university could not have been founded. As long as the Janissaries, the armed forces of the *medrese*, could survive, [modern] military schools could not have been founded. As a result of the social division of labour, the strength of the religious communal solidarity among the Turks declined. The foundation of the Academy and the University, and the attempts towards the reorganization of the military schools towards the end of Abdul Aziz's reign, were the products of this religious decline. Ahmed Vefik and Süleyman Pasha, as heads of these modern institutions, realized the need to revitalize the nation by a linguistic, cultural, and historical spirit, since it had lost its orientation with the disintegration of the community of the *ümmet* and of the Sultanate. They also saw how necessary it was to educate the youth according to the ideals of this new spirit. The purist movement and the new language movement, which followed it twenty years later, show that language and culture were the chief factors in the rise of Turkish nationalism.

It is true that towards the end of the Turkist period, ideas of national economy were born as well. But the men who initiated them were neither economists nor business men, but the leaders of cultural Turkism who were in search of legal, educational, and even philosophical manifestations of nationalism. The idea of national economy was born from a purely disinterested idealism and began to be applied, in an entirely theoretical way, to the economic conditions of the country, to legal conditions and technological forms current in agriculture, industry, and commerce. Our national economists would be in a position to distinguish between 'normal' and 'pathological' and prescribe remedies to ameliorate economic conditions, only after having surveyed our economic life.[11] Unfortunately, the [1st] World War stopped these scientific studies and led in practice to the rise of various policies. National economy is not something to be exploited for speculative purposes, but a school of economy, founded by Friedrich List in Germany. Durkheim's comment on List's work on national economy was: 'This is the first book on economy written objectively and based on facts.' National economy does not produce the national ideal, but is itself a product of it.

THE NATURE OF IDEALS[12]

Germination of a seed takes place in two phases: the first is the act of impregnation, which is a matter of a moment; the second is the

PHILOSOPHY OF VALUES AND IDEALS 67

period of growth, which is a matter of time. The first phase is the creative event for the seed. Without impregnation it cannot grow into an organism.

The same phases may be observed in the creative activity of a poet or in the thinking of a philosopher. The inspiration of a poet requires the germination of his imagination. Revelation of an intuition to a thinker is nothing but the germination of a mind. It is only after germination that the imagination of a poet and the mind of a thinker conceive, and sooner or later give birth to, a literary or philosophical product.

A people without a national character is comparable to the seed before it becomes a living organism. It may be likened further to the imagination of a poet or to the mind of a thinker. Nations, too, need to pass through the stages of germination and growth. When a nation experiences a great disaster or when it is confronted with grave danger, individual personality disappears and becomes immersed in society. In such times it is only the national personality which lives in the soul of the individual. All souls feel nothing but the great desire to see the continuation of the national personality. In time of crisis a person does not worry about his own liberties, but thinks only of the survival of national independence. Now, this sacred thought, fused with cherished sentiments, we call *Ideal*, and the time of crisis the period of germination of the ideals.

Ideals are always created in such critical moments. They are born in hearts in communion—hearts unified by national disasters which create one single heart. In their period of growth, they flourish into institutions which are new in all their ramifications. The Germanic ideal was born in this manner, in the face of the great calamities which arose when Napoleonic armies humiliated Prussia. Even Fichte, who until then would have said: 'My people is nothing but mankind—my fatherland the entire world',[13] felt to his bones that he was a German. Nipponism was the product of the dangerous and humiliating pressures put on the Japanese by the United States and Europe. When the French nation was endangered by the possibility of British invasion, the consciousness of the nation was ignited by a crazy peasant girl, of whom it made a saviour. The bondage of the children of Israel in Egypt was followed by the rise of Moses. The suppression of conquered peoples under Roman rule gave rise to Christianity. The rise of Islam took place when Arabia was threatened by political and religious invasion from three directions.

68 TURKISH NATIONALISM AND WESTERN CIVILIZATION

When a nation faces danger, individuals cannot save it. The nation itself becomes its own saviour. At these times, the individual is enchanted by the spell of a supra-mundane spirit; his will becomes silent; a general will becomes the only 'I' in every consciousness. The nation then appears to its members as a divine or collective ideal, and invites them to a promised victory or to a heralded paradise. It is the nation that creates self-sacrificing fighters out of egoists and danger-seeking heroes out of cowards. It is the nation that gives intelligence to the dull, diligence to the lazy, and zeal to the indifferent.

When the time of disaster and crisis has passed away, the fire of the ideals is not extinguished in their hearts; it continues to motivate the people constantly, as if it were a spring inside them. As the ovum gets the vital impulse necessary for its growth from seminal germination, so the institutions of the nation get their evolutionary direction from its ideals. The lore (*irfan*) and the civilization (*medeniyet*) peculiar to a nation come into existence only in this manner.[14] Genuine ideals, born out of the emotional outbursts of the national soul which invades the soul of the individual in times of crisis, are the true creators of the future. No one has any material instrument at his disposal to discover the future of a nation, and the ideals are the only moral instruments by which it may be foreseen.

Once a nation creates its own ideals, it never turns its face towards a dark future; on the contrary, a promised land, a heralded Garden of Eden, unfolds itself, day by day, in an ever-clearer and more inviting prospect. Nations without ideals think that they are doomed to catastrophies; nations with ideals, on the other hand, are destined for resurrection even if they are politically dead. A nation with a resurrecting and creative ideal never dies.

Psychologists have argued over whether or not there is a power of will to overcome our desires. But they have searched in vain for the answer because there are equally cogent arguments for and against its existence. Those members of a nation who have an ideal may have this will, but those who belong to a nation without it do not. Great sacrifices, extraordinary renunciations, which are the indications of a strong will, are seen only at times of great events. In the beginnings of the French Revolution, nobles renounced their rights during a meeting of great enthusiasm. Under the impact of the national fervour created by the war of 1870, the smaller German states renounced their independent sovereignty and accepted Prussia as their sovereign state.

PHILOSOPHY OF VALUES AND IDEALS 69

Again, at the time when Japan had to decide either to live decently or to die with honour, the Shogun willingly renounced its sovereignty and the nobility its fiefs, and the Mikado, renouncing his absolute rights, proclaimed the sovereignty of the people. The old fatalist philosophy which explained this will by supra-individual power was right because the power which creates and directs the will is ideals. Men think that the inspirations of national grace are their own wills; they do not seem to realize that this will emanates from the soul of the nation.

The ideals manifest their power in two forms: by the power of popular appeal and by that of sanction. The power exercised by popular appeal ensues from the direct manifestation of the ideals in the souls of the people. When men are under the spell of the ideals, their souls are filled with an intense enthusiasm. They plunge into an exalted, zealous, extravagant state of mind. At these moments, their only response is an experience of holiness. Their exalted spirits believe in the sanctity of their ideals, and condemn everything that is contrary to them. They not only sacrifice their lives, interests, and happiness for the sake of them, but they want to worship and glorify those who cultivate them; they want to destroy, burn, or tear up those things or persons who seem to be against them. The ideals, by the power of their popular magnetism, almost make somnambulists of men, leading them to superhuman deeds by the enthusiasm which they kindle in their souls.

The sanctioning power of the ideals is a natural consequence of their power of appeal. Even those who at the beginning are not profoundly affected by the spell-binding power of the ideals soon experience it indirectly. They realize that any action congruent or incongruent with the ideals will be met with the reactions of others who have been directly captivated by them. This reaction of approval or disapproval by those who believe is the sanctioning power of the ideals which, because of their undetermined form, first exert themselves by means of public opinion, but soon become legal norms. Appeal is the property of the 'beauty' (*iamāl*) and sanction that of the 'majesty' (*jalāl*) of the Ideal.

Through these two powers the ideals merge all individuals into a united, homogeneous, moral oneness. Children experience impersonal sensations; it is only when they become aware of the 'I' that the personality, which until then had experienced only vague sensations of existence, suddenly comes into being. A nation realizes its ideals in the same way as the child becomes conscious of his 'I'. National crisis, the experience of calamity, is a 'social Gabriel' which breathes the spirit of nationality, a feeling of family unity into a dispersed people. Once infused with this spirit, a nation awakens to its identity, its origin, its destination, and its historical mission, and sets about pursuing them.

Postscript: This discussion shows that the ideals are actually experienced by a nation in the times of great events in its past. They are neither utopias never experienced, nor goals to be reached at some future time. The ideals are the educators of the present, the creators of the future, and the realities of the past. They are mental outbursts which derive from the past and push the nation towards the future. As the term 'ideal' [in European languages] is derived from the word 'idea', so I use the word '*mefkûre*', derived from the word '*fikr*' to denote it [in Turkish].

CHAPTER III

♣

THE IDEAL OF NATIONALISM

THREE CURRENTS OF THOUGHT[1]

IN our country there are three currents of thought. When we study their history, we see that in the beginning our thinkers realized the need for modernization. The current of thought in that direction, which originated during the reign of Selim III [1789–1807], was followed later by another—the movement towards Islamization. The third, the movement of Turkism, has come forth only recently.

Because the idea of modernization has always been a main theme, it has no particular exponent. Every journal or paper has been an exponent of it in one way or another. Of the doctrine of Islamization, the chief organ is *Sırat-ı Müstakim* ([later] *Sebil-ür Reşat*); and of the school of Turkism, *Türk Yurdu*. We can easily see that all of these trends have been the expression of certain real needs.

Gabriel Tarde tells us that the idea of nationalism has been the product of the newspaper, and gives the following explanation: the newspaper has given a common consciousness to those who speak the same language by uniting them into a 'public'. In addition to this influence, which has been made rather unconsciously and unwillingly, the newspaper which has spurred the feelings of honour and sacrifice in the masses, merely to increase its circulation, has consequently aroused a consciousness of national traditions and of cherished ideals. The sentiment of nationality once it arises amongst the masses spreads easily over neighbouring peoples. Once awakened, it leads to revivals in moral life, in language, in literature, and in economic and political life by reinforcing the feelings of solidarity, sacrifice, and struggle among its supporters. Naturally the idea of nationality spreads quickly when emulated by neighbouring peoples, especially if they also have the press appealing to the masses in the vernacular.

The ideal of nationalism appeared [in the Ottoman Empire] first among the non-Muslims, then among the Albanians and Arabs, and finally among the Turks. The fact that it appeared last among the

72 TURKISH NATIONALISM AND WESTERN CIVILIZATION

Turks was not accidental: the Ottoman state was formed by the Turks themselves. The state is a nation already established (*nation de fait*), whereas the ideal of nationalism meant the nucleus of a nationality based on will (*nation de volonté*). With intuitive cautiousness, the Turks were reluctant, in the beginning, to endanger a reality for the sake of an ideal. Thus, Turkish thinkers believed not in Turkism but in Ottomanism.

When the movement of modernization started, the supporters of the *Tanẓimat*[2] reforms believed that it would be possible to create a nation based on will out of an existing 'nation' composed of several nationalities and religions; and they thus attempted to give a new meaning, devoid of any colour of nationality, to the older term 'Ottoman', which had a certain historical meaning. Painful experiences proved that this new meaning of 'Ottoman' had been welcomed by no one save the originators of the term. Inventing this new conception was not only useless but also detrimental, for it gave rise to harmful consequences for the state and the nationalities—and especially for the Turks themselves.

Today the West as well as the East shows unmistakably that our age is the Age of Nations. The most powerful force over the mind of this age is the ideal of nationalism. States, which have to govern on the basis of national consciousness, are doomed to failure if they ignore the existence of this important social factor. If our statesmen and party leaders do not hold this ideal, they cannot establish a spiritual leadership over the communities and the peoples constituting the Ottoman state. The experiences of the last four years have shown that the Turks who, in order to maintain understanding between the nationalities [under the Ottoman rule], denied Turkism and proclaimed Ottomanism have, at last, realized bitterly what kind of a conciliation the nationalities would accept. A people moved by the sentiment of nationality can be ruled only by men who have the idea of nationalism in themselves.

The Turks' avoidance of the idea of nationalism was not only harmful for the state and irritating to the diverse nationalities, but it was fatal for the Turks themselves. When the Turks identified the nation and the state with the already existing nation and state, they failed to see that their social and economic existence was deteriorating. When economic and social ascendancy passed into the hands of the [non-Muslim] communities, the Turks did not realize that they were losing

THE IDEAL OF NATIONALISM 73

everything. They believed that they were the only class constituting the Ottoman nation, and did not pay attention to the fact that they were excluded from certain classes, especially from those that constituted the most important strata of their age. They were not bothered by seeing the existence of economic and occupational classes of which they were not a part, from which they were excluded. As a consequence, they ceased to constitute the masses of people even in Anatolia. They were merely government officials and farmers. Farmers and animal breeders live only on the creative powers of nature, and are not themselves creative powers. Government officials also are not actively productive. The growth and development of the mental faculties, of will and character, are the products of active occupations as in industry and manufacturing, and of practical arts like trade and the liberal professions. It is because of this that it is almost impossible to create a national organization out of a people composed solely of farmers and civil servants. Our incompetence in administration, our difficulties in strategy and logistics, which led to the Balkan disaster, are all due to this state of affairs. The non-existence of efficient government in our country is mainly due to the non-existence of economic [commercial and industrial] classes among the Turks. Wherever the government is based on economic classes, there an efficient government exists. Business men, artisans, and traders want an efficient government for their own interests. Wherever the government is based on the class of state functionaries, it is always inefficient because those who are dismissed from government service always have their eye on government jobs, and those who are in the administration always have an eye on higher posts, and both are for ever discontent with the existing government.

As the non-existence of the ideal of nationalism among the Turks resulted in the lack of any national economy, so the same factor has been an obstacle to the development of a national language and to the appearance of national patterns in fine arts. And, again, because the ideal of nationalism was not present Turkish morality remained only a personal and familial morality. The notions of solidarity, patriotism, and heroism did not transcend the confines of the family, the village, and the town. As the ideal of *ümmet* [religion] was too large and the ideal of the family too narrow, the Turkish soul remained a stranger to the sort of life and to the intensive moral feelings that should be the bases of sacrifice and altruism. The disintegration seen in our economic,

74 TURKISH NATIONALISM AND WESTERN CIVILIZATION

religious, and political institutions is the consequence of this state of affairs.

Turkish nationalism is not contrary to the interests of the Ottoman state; in fact, it is its most important support. As in all young movements, there are some extremists among those who uphold Turkish nationalism, mainly among a portion of the youth, who have caused certain misunderstandings to arise. In fact, Turkism is the real support of Islam and of the Ottoman state, and is against cosmopolitanism.

Tarde had also shown that the idea of internationalism is a product of the book. Since the newspaper appeals to the sentiments of the masses, it uses the vernacular, the living language. Books, on the other hand, appeal to the abstract thinking of the scholar and the scientist, and are dependent upon neologisms rather than the living word. Scientific and philosophical terms, as a rule, do not grow out of the vernacular of the people, which is natural and living, but are artificial constructs, lifeless words. The natural words of the vernacular carry vital and emotional meanings, and as such are not suited to abstract and conceptual usage. For this reason, every nation has borrowed its neologisms from its religious language. European nations have derived their scientific terminology from the Greek in which the Gospels were written and, as Latin became auxiliary to Greek in the Church, the Germanic and Slavonic languages also inherited much from the Latin. Islamic peoples derived their neologisms mainly from Arabic and, secondarily, from Persian. Even today, when we translate contemporary scientific works [of the West] into our language, we coin Arabic and Persian words for the Greek and Latin terms [therein]. The earliest books were the Scriptures. As ethics, law, literature, science, and philosophy were developed out of religion as separate branches, books began to be written about them as well.

It follows, then, that as the newspaper helped the rise of the ideal of nationalism by expressing the social and local sentiments of the masses in a colourful way, so the book has been instrumental in the creation of the idea of internationalism, or those aspects of life commonly shared by various nations, by formulating, in an abstract and exact style, the principles, rules, and formulae of civilization whose foundation of knowledge and science originated in religion.

It is not true that the sentiment of internationalism prevailed among men during the earlier stages of history. It is true, however, that there was a sentiment of internationalism during the European Middle Ages.

THE IDEAL OF NATIONALISM

But if we analyse this sentiment, we see that the international love and solidarity of that period was confined only to Christian peoples, and international law likewise pertained only to the rights of the Christian states. The Balkan wars demonstrated to us that even today the European conscience is nothing but a Christian conscience. If we analyse the conscience of the Turk, we shall see that he agrees, for instance, to wed his daughter to an Arab, to an Albanian, to a Kurd, or to a Circassian, but not to a Finn or to a Hungarian. He will not wed her to a Buddhist Mongolian or a Shamanist Tunguz unless he embraces Islam. During the Tripolitanian and Balkan wars, those who shared the griefs of the Turks and gave freely of their moral support were not Hungarians, Mongols, or Manchurians, but Muslims of China, of India, of Java, and of the Sudan, whose names we do not even know. It is because of this that the Turks regard themselves as one of the Muslim nations, although they belong to the Ural-Altai group from the linguistic point of view.

Anthropologically, human beings of the same anatomical types constitute a race, but sociologically the nations that belong to the same civilization constitute an 'internationality'. When the Turks, as an ethnic people, joined Islamic civilization, the Turkish language assumed an Islamic character with the introduction of the Arab script and terms.

Thus, the factor that creates the spirit of internationality, and hence civilization, is the book. Consequently, there is no incompatibility between Turkish nationalism and Islam, since one is nationality and the other is internationality. When Turkish thinkers entertained the idea of Ottoman nationality composed of different religious communities, they did not feel the necessity of Islamization, but as soon as the ideal of Turkism arose, the need for Islamization made itself felt.

However, as nationality is the creation of the newspaper and internationality the creation of the book, modernity is the product of technology. Those peoples are 'contemporary' who make and use all those machines made and used by the peoples most advanced in the techniques of the age. For us today modernization [being contemporary with modern civilization] means to make and use the battleships, cars, and aeroplanes that the Europeans are making and using. But this does not mean being like them only in form and in living. When we see ourselves no longer in need of importing manufactured goods and

76 TURKISH NATIONALISM AND WESTERN CIVILIZATION

buying knowledge from Europe, then we can speak of being contemporary with it.

As there is no contradiction between the ideals of Turkism and Islamism, there is none between these and the ideal of modernism. The idea of modernity necessitates only the acceptance of the theoretical and practical sciences and techniques from Europe. There are certain moral needs which will be sought in religion and nationality, as there were in Europe, but these cannot be imported from the West as if they were machines and techniques.

It seems, therefore, that we should accept the three ideals at the same time by determining the respective fields of operation of each. To put it in a better way, we have to create 'an up-to-date Muslim Turkism', realizing that each of the three ideals is an aspect of the same need taken from a different angle.

Contemporary civilization, which has been coming into existence for some time through the development of modern machines and techniques, is in the process of creating a new internationality. A true internationality based on science is taking the place of the internationality based on religion. The participation of Japan, on the one hand, and of Turkey, on the other, in Western civilization is giving a secular character to European internationality, as we shall show later; and thus the area of the *ümmet* is differentiating itself from the area of internationality increasingly.

In short, the Turkish nation today belongs to the Ural-Altai group of peoples, to the Islamic *ümmet*, and to Western internationality.

NATION AND FATHERLAND[3]

... Currently discussed in the press are three concepts dealing with social questions that need definition: Turkism, Islamism, and Ottomanism. These concepts cannot convey any meaning unless they become symbols of certain social facts and unless they derive their value from social reality. Without this understanding, they will not yield any fruitful result, even if people continue to quarrel over them for years to come.

When we look at social realities, we cannot fail to see that an Islamic *ümmet*, an Ottoman state (*devlet*), a Turkish or an Arab nation (*millet*) do exist. However, if this statement corresponds to any reality, the term '*ümmet*' must denote the totality of those people who profess the same religion, the 'state' all those who are administered under the same government, and the 'nation' all those who speak the same language. The statement will be valid and will correspond to reality only if the above definitions are accepted. It seems, then, that those who do not accept this statement deny it, not because its meaning does not correspond to reality, but because they do not believe that these words are suitable for denoting the respective meanings.

The Islamists say that the word 'nation' [*millet*; Arabic *milla*] denotes what we cover by the word '*ümmet*'. The term '*milla*', they say, means 'sect' in Arabic. The perfection of a language means the existence of a meaning for every word and a word for every meaning, and also the existence of words expressing several meanings. Even if we ourselves do not do this, the language itself will. It is for this reason that the current [Turkish] language uses the word '*ümmet*' for those who belong to the same religion, and the word '*millet*' for those who speak the same language. As the majority of the people uses them with these specific meanings, we too must accept them. There is no use creating difficulties on questions of terminology.

The Ottomanists, on the other hand, believe that the 'state' and the 'nation' are synonymous. To them, the sum total of the citizens of a state constitutes a nation. This might be true, if we disregarded reality and took only the logical relation between the concepts into account. As a matter of fact, to have a state composed of peoples who speak the same language, or to make only those peoples who speak the same language an independent state, seems more natural and most desirable. But are existing states formed that way? If not, then how is it justifiable to disregard that which *is* existing and to believe that what *ought to* exist is really existing?

The Turkists, on the other hand, criticizing the theses of these groups, come to the following conclusions: (*a*) the *ümmet* and the nation are different things; (*b*) the nation and the state are also not the same. One may object to these conclusions, but only in so far as they do not correspond to sociological realities, and not by insisting that these realities should not be so. We must fit our concepts to the realities and not the realities to our own concepts!

However, the external realities of the concepts of *ümmet*, nation, and state are not altogether independent of each other. The relation between the *ümmet* and the nation is a relation between the general and the particular. The *ümmet* is a whole which comprises several nations

78 TURKISH NATIONALISM AND WESTERN CIVILIZATION

belonging to the same religion. Individuals actually constituting a nation are not the only members of a nation. All those who may speak that language in the future will also be members of that nation. Thus, for example, the Pomaks [Bulgarian Muslims] now speaking Bulgarian and the Cretan Muslims now speaking Greek may learn Turkish in the future and cease to be Bulgarian- or Greek-speaking peoples. This means that nationality is not determined by language alone but also by religion.

There is a more or less similar relation between the terms 'nation' and 'state'. For example, the Ottoman state is a Muslim state—that is, it is formed of Muslim nations. Two great nations, the Turks and the Arabs, by their numbers as well as by their culture and learning, served as the bases of the Ottoman state in such a way that the Ottoman state might even be called a Turkish-Arab state. It should also be remembered that the Turkish and Arab nations are not confined only to those who live within the Ottoman territories. Those who speak the same languages but live under foreign rule also belong to these nations.

About the concept of 'fatherland'. It means a sacred piece of land for whose sake people shed their blood. Why is it that all other lands are not sacred, but only that which is called fatherland? And how does it happen that those who believe this way do not hesitate to sacrifice their lives, their families, their most beloved ones? Evidently not because of any utilitarian value. The sacredness is certainly derived from something sacred. But what can that sacred thing be?

Is it the state? We have already seen that the state is not a power existing by itself. The state derives its power from the nation and from the *ümmet*: *sharaf al-makān bil-makīn* ['the glory of the residence is with the resident']! Thus, there are only two things which are sacred: the nation and the *ümmet*. As the objects of reverence are two, their symbols or the homelands which are the seats of these two sacred objects should also be two: the homeland of the *ümmet* and the homeland of the nation.

There is, in fact, a homeland of Islam which is the beloved land of all Muslims. The other one is the national home which, for Turks, is what we call *Turan*.[4] The Ottoman territories are that portion of Islamdom which have remained independent. A portion of these is the home of the Turks, and is at the same time a portion of *Turan*. Another portion of them is the homeland of the Arabs, which is again a part of the great Arab fatherland.

THE IDEAL OF NATIONALISM 79

The fact that the Turks have a special love for the home of the Turks, *Turan*, does not necessitate that they forget the Ottoman land which is a small Muslim homeland, or the great land of all Muslims. For national, political, and international[5] ideals are different things and all are sacred ideals.

THE IDEAL OF NATIONALISM[6]

Youth is asking: 'If we believe that ideals are the product of historical disturbance and social crises, will it not then be necessary to assume that another ideal, one which may be born from the impulse of different circumstances, will succeed the ideal of nationalism? Will not, for example, the idea of socialism supercede the sentiment of nationality in the near or distant future?'

My answer to this question is as follows. Essentially an ideal is the actualization of the existence of a social group by its members. The rays of the sun do not have the power to burn unless they are intensified through a lens. Similarly, the group is unable by itself to manifest its 'sacredness' unless it reaches a state of social combustion. This sacredness, even before it has reached consciousness, exists in an unconscious state in the psychological unity of the social group. So far it has remained a hidden treasure (*al-kanẓ al-makhfî*), with all its halo of sanctity. The function of the crowd situation is to make this reality manifest to the members of the group by transforming the latter amorphous existence into a clear-cut form. Social agitation becomes a source of ideals by its capacity to transform the group, which until now has been in a loose state, into a compact body. The emergence of an ideal means its rise from the subconscious to the conscious level.

Before the rise of the ideals of Ottomanism, Islamism, and Turkism, the Ottoman state, the Islamic *ümmet*, and the Turkish nationality all existed. The working class existed in a scattered state before the ideal of socialism was born, the latter emerging as a consequence of the concentration of workers, which itself was a result of the development of large-scale industry in Europe.

Therefore, a social group must have an existence, an organized form and institutions, in order to assert its existence in the consciousness of its members in a crowd situation. Its institutions, political, religious, or linguistic, must certainly have an existence. No crowd situation or condition of social agitation can create a group from nothing. Not only

80 TURKISH NATIONALISM AND WESTERN CIVILIZATION

do ideals not emerge from a crowd situation that has no organizational basis, but such a crowd is itself inconceivable. Only something which exists in a state of laxity may be transformed into a state of solidity.

It follows from what has been said that any major social emergence taking place in the future must have its basis in already existing conditions. In order for an ideal to arise in the future, it must spring from the intensification of one of the existing groups. Therefore, a great ideal should be born out of the intensification of only that group which, in addition to being the richest and most powerfully organized, is in a position to bring together and assimilate all other groups in its own organization.

Which, then, is this inclusive group? Among the existing ones it is the language group—that is, the nationality group—which is most capable of fulfilling such a function.

First, those who speak the same language are usually descendants of the same stock, and thus a nation also means an ethnic unity. . . . Secondly, language is the carrier of ideas and sentiments, the transmitter of customs and tradition; hence, those who speak the same language share the same aspirations, the same consciousness, and the same mentality. Individuals thus sharing common and homogeneous sentiments are also naturally prone to profess the same faith. It is because of this that language groups in many cases are of the same religion. Even if in the beginning certain conditions interfered somewhat with this religious homogeneity, historical events show that peoples of the same language groups do tend to embrace the same faith. Thus, the Latins have been inclined to Roman Catholicism, the Germanic peoples to Protestantism, and the Slavonic peoples to Eastern Orthodoxy. Of the Ural-Altai group, the Mongols adopted Buddhism, the Manchurians Confucianism, and the Finno-Ugrians Christianity. Various sections of the Turks, in the beginning, had accepted Buddhism, Manichaeism, Judaism, and Christianity; but with the conversion of the majority to Islam, all became Muslims with the exception of the Shamanist Yakuts, who constitute only some two hundred thousand people. The main reason why the latter remained outside Islam is that their home lies far out of the Turkish lands. They will either embrace Islam and remain Turks or become Russified by accepting Christianity.

As language plays a part in deciding religious affiliation, so religion plays a part in determining membership in a nationality. The Protestant French became Germanized when they were expelled from France

THE IDEAL OF NATIONALISM

and settled in Germany. The Turkish aristocracy of the old Bulgars became Slavicized following their conversion to Christianity. And today, the non-Turkish Muslims migrating to Turkey in a scattered way are becoming Turkified because of their religious affiliation. We may conclude, therefore, that there is a close relationship between linguistic and religious association.

Thirdly, when universal military service and sovereignty of the people were introduced, national defence ceased to be the monopoly of a trained and privileged *sipahi* order, and administration of the government was no longer the privilege of a ruling class directly responsible only to the ruler. The peasants who previously had no arms except their ploughs, and the townsfolk who were used to staying at home, now became soldiers; the people, who had no notion of administration, came to the point where they could control the government. It became necessary to instil in them a sense of patriotism and to teach them how to assume the responsibilities of voting. When the needs of adult and universal education became apparent, conflicts arose among the different ethnic groups in the state over the question of which language should be spoken in the schools. The government began to insist on the dissemination of an official language, but each ethnic group demanded that its own language become the main channel of education and instruction. Thus, in the last century it came to be realized that confining the state and the country to a single language was no longer possible, and, as in the case of Austria-Hungary, the state adopted two main languages. Today in Europe only those states which are based on a single-language group are believed to have a future. Every national group is demonstrating the kind of future to which it aspires by voicing its wishes for a national home, with or without an historical basis.

Today all of us realize that the idea of a state or homeland supposedly common to diverse nationalities, is nothing but a mere concept, devoid of any zeal, enthusiasm, and devotion. Just as it is inconceivable for more than one person to win the love of one individual, so there can be no real common home and fatherland for diverse peoples. A state that is not based on a united spirit can be only a common source of subsistence and nothing more. A land that is not the home of a nation is like a public kitchen where everyone merely feeds himself.

The institutions of state and fatherland achieve permanent life only when based on a national ideal, but they are destined to fall if they are

82 TURKISH NATIONALISM AND WESTERN CIVILIZATION

based only on individual interests. Men without ideals are egoistic, self-seeking, pessimistic, faithless, and cowardly; they are lost souls. A state must be founded on national ideals, a country has to be the home of a nationality if it is to have permanent existence.

We see, therefore, that the concept of the language group encompasses the concept of state as well as that of national home. Smaller units, such as family, class, corporation, village, tribe, and religious community, exist within the confines of the national unit. The family is composed of individuals of the same faith. They speak the language of a single nation. Other groups share a common religion and language. They are all, therefore, but smaller, constituent organs of the nation.

In short, all ideals connected with the ethnic unit (*kavm*), religion, state, national home, family, class, corporation, etc., are auxiliary to the national ideals. As long as social evolution substitutes intellectual and sentimental for material factors, the value and effectiveness of the national language as a means of expressing these ideals will increase, and in this way the sentiment of nationality will become a permanent ideal.

It is true that, as large-scale industry grows in Turkey, the ideal of socialism will arise here too. But this ideal is destined to remain auxiliary to the national ideal, as have all other secondary ideals. Although socialism in Europe is constantly gaining strength, we see clearly that it gives way to the national ideal in times of war. Not only during political wars, but even in economic competition, class ideals are subordinated to national ideals.

Furthermore, we can easily detect that the substance of all aspects of social life—such as religion, morality, law, politics, economics, science, and fine arts—is language. Any increase in the importance of these spheres of social life means an increase in the importance of language. Language is the basis of social life, the texture of morality, the substratum of culture and civilization. All future social movements —with respect to any group or activity—will always solidify language groups directly or indirectly, and out of every crisis the ideal of nationalism will effervesce, each time more powerful and with increasing vitality.

NATIONAL LANGUAGE[7]

Just as physical bodies have length, width, and depth, so the social consciousness also has three dimensions—nationality, religion, and

THE IDEAL OF NATIONALISM 83

modernity. I propose to test the validity of this observation first with regard to language, which is the best mirror of social consciousness.

The Turkish language has been in a process of growth for the last fifty or sixty years. As the lights of modern civilization penetrate our country, every day our eyes see new products, our minds think in new concepts. Since the new objects and ideas cannot remain unnamed, our language becomes richer by the addition of several new words every day. We also make translations from the papers and books of the leading nations of our century. In this way, several new concepts which formerly did not exist in our store of knowledge require the creation of new words in our speech.

Thus, the more our language meets the advanced languages, the more it tends to imitate them word by word. It sometimes imitates in form newly coined [Western] words, as we see in the case of words such as *hurdebīn* (microscope) or *dûrbîn* (telescope), or *şehkâr* (masterpiece), or *mefkûre* (ideal). Sometimes it coins new words by imitating meanings, as we see in the case of words such as *tayyare* (aeroplane), *tekâmül* (evolution), *meşrûtiyet* (constitutionalism), and *bediiyat* (aesthetics).

This tendency suggests the following points for consideration: a day will come when the Turkish language will have all the words corresponding to those that exist in French, English, or German. As speech is an expression of subjective thinking, there grows a language expressing the concepts of our century, to which every national tongue must adapt itself. Until the Turkish language fulfils this requirement, it will not be a modern language—a language fully evolved from the point of view of the needs of our time.

The new words entering our language are of three kinds: (1) foreign words; (2) words derived from Arabic and Persian, or those which were coined from these languages; (3) and those derived or coined from the original Turkish.

The words of the first category enter the language through smuggling. The taste of the language tends to reject these words, and replace them either by Arabic (in the case of scientific terminology) or by Persian words (in the case of general vocabulary). This feature of rejecting foreign words by putting Arabic or Persian roots in their places is peculiar not to Turkish only. All Muslim languages show the same tendency. These languages, which have something in common in so far as the religious terms or the scientific terms derived from religion are concerned, have to maintain this unity in connection with

84 TURKISH NATIONALISM AND WESTERN CIVILIZATION

the derivation of new expressions. If, for example, the Turks living in Russia derive their terms from Russian, those in China from Chinese, and if we do it from the French, the Turkish of these peoples will vary from one to the other. But if we take these terms from Arabic or Persian, or from Turkish, they will be more uniform. The terminologies used in the languages spoken in Christendom (*ümmet*) were basically derived from Greek and Latin. The Muslim languages are threatened by the loss of unity in their religious-community (*ümmet*) background by borrowing these terminologies.

However, Muslim languages will not fulfil their duties with respect to this question of religious-community (*ümmet*) background merely by deriving their terminologies from Arabic or Persian. If each one derives its terms from different roots, the desired unity is still not going to be obtained and the religious-community basis of the language will not be maintained. It is for this reason that we [Turks] have to build our terms by adopting those which have already been accepted by other Muslim peoples, or those likely to be accepted by them. To realize this aim, it is necessary to organize societies for introducing new terms into the languages of the Muslim peoples. These organizations must sponsor meetings from time to time to discuss the problems of terminology. When the terms to be used in Muslim languages are decided upon systematically through such meetings, it will be possible to say that our language has completed its growth from a religious point of view, that is, that it has become thoroughly Islamized.

Once our language acquires a dictionary of terminology common to the *ümmet* of Islam, it should avoid any further borrowing from Arabic and Persian. Arabic and Persian words introduced into Turkish have not been confined only to terminology. Several unnecessary words of the vernacular have also been taken from these two languages. Furthermore, the influence of these tongues has not been confined to the mere transmission of words. Certain Arabic and Persian rules of grammar have also entered into Turkish in such a way that Turkish grammar has become a compound of the grammar and syntax of the three languages.

As it is imperative to modernize our language from the point of view of enriching it with new concepts, and to Islamize it from the point of view of unity in matters of terminology, it is equally necessary to Turkify it from the point of view of grammar, syntax, and spelling.

THE IDEAL OF NATIONALISM

Every word in our language, with the exception of scientific terms, must be in Turkish if possible, and, if not possible, at least Turkified. Arabic and Persian rules of grammar should be expelled entirely. We should say, for example, not *şuarâ-yı cedîde* but *yeni şairler*; not *edebiyât-ı Türkiyye*, but *Türk edebiyatı*; not *tabiîyyet* but *tabiîlik*; not *serbestî* but *serbestlik*; not *mûciz bir muharrir* but *icazlı bir muharrir*; not *mûciz bir ifade* but *icazli bir ifade*. However, it is not enough to restrict Turkification only to vocabulary (*lûgat*). If possible, it would be even better to create all terms from Turkish roots; but if this is not possible, it is preferable to derive them from the Arabic and Persian roots rather than from French or Russian. In any case, it is necessary to make the terms as well as the vocabulary common, if not among all Muslims, at least among the Turks; in other words, all Turks should have a common literary and scientific language. We must not forget, therefore, that when we Turkify our language, we have to develop towards a common Turkish which will be understood by all brothers-in-race.

To summarize, the new concepts are the expression of the modern age, the terms used are the expression of religious-community and the vernacular form, the expression of the nation. Unless Turkish becomes a sensitive reflection of the three aspects of our social consciousness, we cannot speak of a well-established and fully developed language.

PART II

CHAPTER IV

CULTURE AND CIVILIZATION

♣

CIVILIZATION OF THE PEOPLE[1]

I

EVERY nation has two civilizations. One is its formal civilization, the other is the civilization of the people. Sociology, which studies civilization in general, should have a branch to study this folk civilization. The field which comprises this traditional, unwritten, and oral civilization is folklore.

In other nations not much disparity may be seen between the two civilizations. Among the Turks, however, it strikes the eye immediately. Among them there is the language, the literature, the morality, the law, the economics, the organizations of the folk which are entirely different from those which are formal. The reason for this dichotomy lies in the fact that the Turks have borrowed the institutions of foreign peoples and produced an artificial civilization out of them, instead of creating their own by developing their own institutions. In ancient times their spirit inspired them with certain healthy feelings and prevented them from creating such disparities. They believed in their nobility and used to call others *tat*s to distinguish them from themselves. They used to distinguish those among themselves who had imitated other peoples as *sart*s. They distinguished their own civilization which they called *uygarlik*. Their traditions were called *töre*, their laws were called *tüzük*, and their constitution was called *yasa*. As a nation they called themselves *budun*, a word derived from *bütün* [whole], as they believed themselves as free as the whole world. They called their deity the God of Turks, and believed that it took care of their welfare alone, as we see in the Gültekin [Orkhon] inscriptions.

In spite of this idealism inspired by their ethos, the official leaders of the Turkish people forgot national traditions for the sake of their court life. They believed in the superiority of the *tat* and imitated them, and thus the official élite of the Turks headed towards the abyss of

90 TURKISH NATIONALISM AND WESTERN CIVILIZATION

*sart*ness. Fortunately, the folk élite preserved their oral traditions and saved the nation from total extinction. When Mehmed Bey of Karaman had put Prince Giyas-ud-din on the Seljuk throne, he immediately forbade the use of Persian as the official language and of Greek as the cultural language, replacing them with Turkish. This explains why the Greeks of Karaman of today know no language other than Turkish.

Ottoman Turks were able to found a powerful empire within a short span of time only because the government was in the hands of the folk élite. There were three practical schools, the Palace School (*Enderun*), the School of Pages (*Acemi Oğlan*), and the Vezir Households (*Paşa Dairesi*), in which, not the written lore of the Arabs or Persians, but the oral lore of the Uygur Turks—the products of their political and social experiences—was used (and not taught!). Pashas like Lala Şahin, Ferhat, Özdemiroğlu Osman had been trained in accordance with this folk-lore, the Turkish *yasa*, which was not written in books but lived in memory. The scholars and poets trained in the official *medrese*s did nothing but praise in their *kaside*s these superhuman, and for them ignorant, heroes. It was when government passed from the hands of this folk élite (the men of the sword) to the men trained in the *medrese*s (the men of the school) that the Ottoman power lost its centre of gravity and headed downwards.

It seems, therefore, that the factors responsible for our rise should be sought in the folk civilization, and those factors responsible for our decline sought in our formal institutions. It should not be forgotten that when so deep a disparity exists between the oral traditions and the written learning of a nation, formal civilization draws the minds of the people to itself and produces an anaemic condition. In other nations there is an uninterrupted exchange of ideas and sentiments between the people and the official élite. Since this connection between the two ceased to exist among the Turks, neither a national consciousness among the official men of learning nor a methodical discipline and refinement in the lore of the people would have been possible. As a result of this condition, the Turkish people continuously declined and became denationalized. This point should be investigated in a study of Turkish folklore. . . .

II

For those who expect everything from the government, that is, from official organization, government is the mind and the people the

CULTURE AND CIVILIZATION

matter. We believe that the opposite is true: the people certainly are the spirit, and the government the matter of a nation.

Government consists of certain formal bodies, such as the cabinet, the parliament, the army, the civil service, local councils, official schools, and institutions. They are tied together in every respect by strict rules and laws. The status of their functionaries is determined by unchanging regulations. Formal rules put seniority before efficiency, office before intelligence. As government bodies are run by inflexible rules, they fail to adapt themselves to the needs of the dynamics of social and political life. They are like the organic mechanisms of our bodies or like certain machines connected and geared to each other.

The whole which we call the people, on the other hand, is composed of informal groups[2]—such as family, village, tribe, artisan guilds and corporations, associations, political parties, religion and language groups. These bodies are not ruled by formal laws, but by living and growing traditions whose roots are in the past and whose branches are growing towards the future. There are no hierarchies in them to check the growth of intelligence and aptitude, unless they too degenerate by becoming formalized into official bodies.

To show that folk organizations constitute the spirit of a nation, it is enough to indicate that it is the informal group which is the real motivating force behind the formal mechanical bodies. For example, in the machinery of government the most important bodies are parliament and cabinet, behind which, as everybody knows, is the force of political parties. Political parties are nothing but fellowships or people's institutions. Local government councils are also directed by local parties or bodies of citizenry, economic corporations, spiritual councils, voluntary aid associations. . . .

If we ask who is profiting from the organizations of government which dominate all the sources of our country's wealth, we find that it is those who have their own economic communities. The Muslim-Turkish population, unfortunately, does not get even a small share from this wealth because it lacks this kind of organization.

These examples are enough to show us that it is the organization of a community which motivates formal machinery. Therefore, we must realize how futile it is to rely only on government bodies and neglect the organizations of the people. We must become not only a nation with a body but also a nation with a spirit.

During the foundation of the Ottoman state, our institutions were

92 TURKISH NATIONALISM AND WESTERN CIVILIZATION

of the nature of confraternities. Young minds used to enter these confraternities and acquire status ranging from *timar*-holding to grand vizirate according to their talents. The *levend* confraternities used to produce men like Barbarossa and Turgut Reis, who could conquer lands with their corsair ships. Janissary corps, *sipahi*s, West [African] confraternities, *Kölemen*s of Egypt and Baghdad were all organized as confraternities. They had their own traditions, spiritual guides, and peculiar sense of solidarity.

Transformation of these organizations into formal institutions marks the senility of a nation. From the time when folk organizations began to be official institutions in our history, Ottoman power began to decline. Non-Muslim peoples, on the other hand, rejuvenated themselves by reviving their folk organizations. Church organizations, community schools, companies, trade organizations, [Macedonian revolutionary] committees were centres of struggle, and finally, from these centres, nations and states came into existence by gaining independence from the Ottoman Empire. These independent small states formed their official institutions, but they always retained their spirit of confraternity. Thus they have succeeded in developing themselves as nations with *ésprit de corps*. We, on the other hand, continued in our decline and disintegration, because our spirit was numbed.

Nations are not like biological organisms. Biological organisms, once aged, never rejuvenate. Nations can rejuvenate themselves by reviving their national folk organizations. Some believe that a young nation can emerge only after a resurrection. In other words, they believe that a people can rebuild its institutions only after its government has collapsed. We are not of this opinion. We believe that such a miracle, if it is to be realized by a natural process, can be achieved by an *élan vital*.

TRADITION AND FORMALISM[3]

When we look at any aspect of our social life, we can observe two conflicting attitudes: radicalism and conservatism. These two attitudes represent two ways of thinking that are usually thought to conflict with each other, whereas, in fact, both are based on the same principle: formalism.

The conservative tends to see an existing social convention as an unchangeable truth, and regards any attempt to revise it as blasphemy.

CULTURE AND CIVILIZATION

The radical, on the other hand, makes the rationalizing of a convention an absolute formula, and regards those who do not accept it as reactionaries. Neither ever attempts to question the origin and growth of the old or of the new, or the way in which norms adapt themselves to different environments at different times. Both believe that the *rule*, or convention, is something above time and space, that it exists by itself. For both a rule is not merely the product of a stage, an intermediary stage, in the evolution of a society. To them it is an eternal truth or principle, definite and fixed in an objective reality above time and space.

As the repeated observance of rules establishes habits, aged persons usually tend to be conservative. Youth, on the other hand, tends to attribute the causes of the progress of the advanced nations, shining with the wonders of modern civilization, only to the validity of the rules that these advanced nations apply; thus they tend simply to imitate them and align themselves with the radicals.

A rule—whether it is a rule of fashion, of manners, or of etiquette; whether it is a rule with regard to matters of belief or opinion; whether it is a rule of sacred or secular law—always has a certain character that seems to inhibit people from taking it as something transitory or as a part of a development. However, as soon as a rule is taken in this way, as a fixed and inflexible entity, it assumes the character of a lifeless skeleton, whereas the essence of life is a creative evolution. Only lifeless things are outside of creative evolution. The formalist then mistakes the effect for the cause. The *rule* is only the temporary product of a process. The formalist, however, tends to think of the rule as the cause of the process, and thus, as the cause is known to him, he does not care to study the process itself.

As one section of the people of this mentality regards the *rule* as an absolute monarch, another part of the same bent of mind puts all blame on the wretched rule whenever it is realized that its application is useless. Then the radical immediately raises his voice to hush the conservative. For him the thing to be done is very simple: depose the Old Rule and put a new one in its place! But the sovereignty of the New Rule does not last very long because during the period of its application new incongruities soon arise. Then the custodians of habit raise their heads and order the imitationists to withdraw from the scene.

Now, this is what happens to us all the time! Study the past of the

94 TURKISH NATIONALISM AND WESTERN CIVILIZATION

Turks, and you will find that they have always lived their history in a variety of disconnected stages. Our institutions have been like the treasury of invading conquerors, becoming suddenly full with the booty of victory, but destined to be suddenly empty again because its sources are not within the national culture. Instead of making our institutions living traditions born out of an evolutionary process by maintaining their historical continuity, we tend to take from every country institutions devoid of any history and tradition and to discard our own traditions.

The British are a people without rules, but we find in them the best example of a tradition whose historical continuity and evolutionary significance is well known. We Turks, on the other hand, are formalists, and yet we lack traditions. We do not trace the historical continuity of our Turkish and Islamic traditions, and we do not study the origins of the advancements which characterize our age. We think that we need merely the results. Our Turkish and Islamic past, after successive ebbs and flows, has left us with only the precipitates in the form of certain practical and ritualistic rules. European civilization seems to us only a collection of certain theoretical and practical formulae. One part of us is content just to use the precipitations while the other wants simply to loot imported formulae.

The rule, whether it is habitual or imitative, is always devoid of creativity and growth because discrete imitations are not reconcilable with each other and are without foundations. Each of them, being an independent and absolutely separate entity, remains as it is. It does not create its own future. Tradition, on the other hand, means creativity and progress. This is so because tradition has a past which knits the discrete moments to one another, and an historical movement which pushes forward as a motivating force. Thus it always creates new developments, new orientations. Tradition is something growing and creating by itself, and, moreover, giving life to the borrowed innovations grafted on itself in such a way that the foreign elements do not dry out and become rotten, as happens in ordinary imitation.

Bergson tells us that the mind of the individual is the sum total of his habits. The memories of a nation, likewise embodied in its traditions and its habits, are the product of its rules. Thus, tradition constitutes the spirit of a nation, the social rules its body. One represents the meaning, the other the words. The traditionalist nation lives in the freedom of history, the formalist in the bondage of geography. During

CULTURE AND CIVILIZATION   95

the Balkan wars, the Bulgarians were inspired by their fiery traditions; we were inspired by our cold rules. The result was the victory of history over geography.

It follows, then, that both conservatism and radicalism, both of which so far have had a following among us, are blind roads. Our New Life should avoid both. We must, first of all, know the traditions and the historical growth of the institutions peculiar to the Turks. Turkish literature, for example, begins neither with Âşık Paşa nor with Nevaî. We must look for the sources of our literature on the stone engravings or deer skins, on the one hand, and in the folk poems, folk tales, and epics, on the other. Our national language must be based on Turkish grammar. Our national literature must take its themes, its symbols, from Turkish social life, from Turkish social organization, and from Turkish mythology and epics. We must discard foreign rules from our grammar, foreign metre from our poetry, foreign symbolism from our literature. We must realize that the periods of foreign invasion since the beginnings of our linguistic and literary traditions have been transitory and pathological periods for these. We must revive the history of Turkish law by studying Turkish folkways, *mores*, and tribal laws. As we find Turkish architecture and painting in the artistic works of the age of *ümmet*, so we must discover Turkish music as well as Turkish poetry in the oral traditions of the folk. The Turks will find their Turkish Ideal still surviving in the life of their words, proverbs, folk-tales, and folk epics. It is their duty to collect them from the scattered remains, and to discover the ethnic pre-history hidden in them.

Yet, at the same time the Turks have to study the traditions and the history of our Islamic institutions. They have to know the history of Islamic theology, mysticism, and jurisprudence. When the development of these institutions and the manner in which they have accommodated themselves to manifold circumstances in terms of time and space become clear, then it will be evident which elements of contemporary civilization will be adopted and how they will develop in the future.

Tradition not only establishes continuity and harmony between the forms that an institution assumes at various times, but also shows how all of them are derived from the same origin, thus serving to cement them together. Durkheim believed that institutions such as those of law, morality, politics, logic, aesthetics, and economics are all derived

96 TURKISH NATIONALISM AND WESTERN CIVILIZATION

from religion. These branches gain a living force and a dynamic life only by deriving their roots from a religious origin. As tradition requires continuity and harmony, it becomes necessary to find the connection between the pre-history of the Turk and the metaphysics of religion, and by so doing to develop an Islamic-Turkish philosophy of history. And, thirdly, it is necessary for us to study the historical development, the conditioning social circumstances, and applications of technology and science, and the methods and philosophies of our age in order to use them.

The history of civilization shows that whenever industry develops in a country, the sciences develop as well. Science is born out of industry, and aims at regulating and organizing it. Among us, however, the study of science is not a means but an end. Our scientists only talk about science, they do not see its applications. In this way, there is among us neither science nor scientist in the true sense. Science is born of technology as philosophy develops out of methods [of science]. The philosopher is not a man who merely puts together and organizes the discrete truths that others have discovered. The real philosopher is one who knows the methods of seeking the truth and actually applies them. Today we can no longer regard philosophy as the sum total of a series of truths already established. Philosophy consists of the methods that are continuously discovering and modifying these truths. Therefore, it is clear also that we do not have philosophy and philosophers in the real sense.

It is, therefore, necessary for us to direct our development towards a nation based on history and tradition, on the one hand, and to develop a science actually based on technology, on the other. Furthermore, we must create a philosophy that is fed continuously by [scientific] methods. When we have merged and combined the science, philosophy, and technology of our age with our national and religious traditions in the manner that we have discussed so far, we shall be able to create a contemporary Islamic-Turkish civilization. And it is only when we have reached the promised land which the spirit of the people calls 'Red Apple' (*Kızıl Elma*) that we shall be free in culture and independent in civilization in their true sense.

CULTURE AND CIVILIZATION

COMMUNITY AND SOCIETY[4]

I

The reason why students of sociology arrive at conclusions so divergent from one another is that some of them view social life in culture-groups (communities), while others observe it in terms of civilization-groups (societies). This divergence in viewpoint is seen first of all in the definitions of the 'social fact'. Gabriel Tarde, for example, defined a social fact as that which consists of 'invention', made by individuals and socialized through 'imitation'. Durkheim, on the other hand, opposed Tarde's view on the grounds that a fact is not social simply because it becomes common through imitation. He believed that a fact becomes common through imitation simply because it is social. Durkheim believed that the facts that belong to the realm of the individual are those which present themselves to the individual as a purely internal constraint such as pain, thirst, or sleep. The social facts, on the other hand, are those that present themselves to the individual as external constraint; for example, religious beliefs, moral duties, legal rules, political and social ideals.

These definitions show that Durkheim found social life in culture-groups, whereas Tarde found it in civilization-groups.

The individual needs mentioned above, and the sensations such as seeing, hearing, smelling, tasting, and feeling which are called individual facts, are, in reality, biological phenomena of the human species. It is erroneous to call them individual facts.

The ideas which are called social facts and excluded from the first category may also be divided into two categories: subjective and objective facts. Beliefs, moral duties, aesthetic feelings, and ideals are, in general, of a subjective nature and are the accepted norms of a certain culture-group. Scientific truths, hygienic or economic rules, practical arts pertaining to public works, techniques of commerce and of agriculture are all of an objective nature and are the accepted norms of the civilization-groups. The constraint exercised over the individual by the representations of the culture-group is called 'power of sanction', and the external validity of the concepts of civilization, 'objectivity'. If we do not observe the rules of hygiene, we lose our health as a natural consequence of our disobedience to the laws of biological nature. When we neglect the rules of economy, we suffer as an inevit-

98 TURKISH NATIONALISM AND WESTERN CIVILIZATION

able consequence of our disregard of the laws of economy. When we do not observe the directions of religious, or moral, or aesthetic ideals, then moral punishments of the courts of conscience or the conscience of the courts strike us. The punishments of common taste are expressed in the form of ridicule. All of these are natural and inevitable consequences. These punishments are a result of the fact that these rules are the accepted values sanctioned by the conscience of the culture-group.

The facts of culture produce in the individual the faculty of conscience,* which is charged with the task of evaluation and classification of the normative concepts or values; the facts of civilization produce the faculty of reasoning charged with the task of analysis and synthesis of empirical concepts or objective truths. *The individual in culture* has to appropriate to himself the commands of the social conscience as cherished ideals and norms of conduct; *the individual in civilization* has to think in terms of the logical framework of the social intellect.

Scientific concepts, technical knowledge, and the tools of economic production in a civilization pass from people to people by imitation or by exchange. A civilization first appears as a local civilization, but soon expands itself over lands and continents, and, finally, over the whole of mankind. It is only in this sense that the sociologists like Tarde or Karl Marx or Edmond Demolins were right. But if humanity were composed only of a civilization-group made up of individuals, it would be possible to attribute the diffusion of the social facts to imitation, or to believe that only technology is an important factor in social life. Humanity is, however, not a civilization-group composed of independent individuals. Individuals are incorporated into several culture-groups such as family, clan, commune, corporation, class, ethnic unit, Church (*ümmet*), and state.

If we are allowed to take an analogy from the physical world, we may say that the aggregation of the social atoms is not merely the product of a physical mixture but rather that a process of chemical synthesis, so to speak, combines these atoms to form compound particles, which constitute new units. Similarly, in biology, the cells, with the exception of unicellular organisms, produce organisms in a variety of forms and qualities, and their existence is dependent upon these compound ('social') organisms.

---

* In French the term *conscience* is used differently in psychology and sociology. We shall use the word 'consciousness' (*şuur*) for its psychological meaning and 'conscience' (*vicdan*) for its sociological meaning.

CULTURE AND CIVILIZATION 99

Since the processes of assimilation and integration within society restrict the scope of free contacts, the processes of imitation and exchange necessitated by the life of a civilization do not take place smoothly. States, for example, restrict the freedom of economic exchange by levying high tariffs in order to protect their internal industries. Ethnic groups (*kavm*) want to prevent the intrusion of foreign words into their languages in order to preserve linguistic purity. In their efforts to maintain the national character of literature, they try to take their topics and themes from their folklore and reject classical literature which has a universal character. Peoples who belong to a certain religion (*ümmet*) attribute the sanctity and inviolability of man only to those who share their own religious beliefs (as the Europeans have always done, especially during the Balkan wars) by making religion the basis of international law and morality. The family creates a united in-group against outsiders with respect to livelihood and property by establishing ties between husband and wife, between parents and children, and among children. A tribe transforms a handful of herdsmen into a commune, a village, or a town; a corporation, the members of a trade into a sect; a church, the members of a faith into a kind of family, closed against outsiders. Men living in civilization-groups share at the same time the ethos peculiar to each one of these culture-groups.

Durkheim has been regarded as the most penetrating sociologist because he realized the importance of those groups that play the role of natural joints in the social organism. The components of the ethos of a culture are in constant conflict with the reason and logic of the society. The individual may sometimes fail to think in logical terms when he becomes too much the slave of his conscience, and sometimes may choke the dictates of his conscience by subordinating them to his reason. This duel between conscience and reason, between culture and civilization, is not necessarily unavoidable. The function of the conscience is to evaluate the values that are upheld by society; the role of reason is to codify the objective truths. The first answers the question 'why live?' saying 'for the sake of the ideals'; while the second answers the question 'how live?' by saying 'in a rational way'. The first controls and guides our will by its normative judgments, while the second guides our practical reason by its empirical judgments. In short, one gives us the ends and the other the means.

The aim of education and of politics as conceived by Edmond

100 TURKISH NATIONALISM AND WESTERN CIVILIZATION

Demolins is, we might say, to transform men of culture into men of civilization, because this writer attributes the superiority of the Anglo-Saxons to their individualism (in our terms, to their civilization), and the inferiority of the Eastern nations to their collectivism (in our terms, to their culture). To attribute the progress or the decline of nations to a single factor such as this is not a scientific procedure. Besides, the claim that the Anglo-Saxons are of an individualistic and not of a collectivistic type is, in itself, untenable. It is true that the Anglo-Saxons do not put the state above the individual as do we, but is the state the only culture-group? The local administrations, the national sects, the organizations of nobility, which are all culture-groups, are more prominent in England than anywhere else. Their racialism is also an indication of their emphasis on culture. The point is that in England these organizations did not prevent the growth of civilization, in spite of their strength and vitality.

Just as an unnatural conflict between culture and civilization may take place, there may also be contradictions, of a pathological nature, between the values of the sub-groups within the whole culture-group. Thus, family sentiments may sometimes weaken national solidarity by being too extreme and narrow. Religious zeal may take such a form as to exclude all ethnic allegiances. Sometimes the sentiment of nationalism may tend to destroy the feelings for a common homeland and state. Class consciousness in Europe gives rise to the feeling of enmity against the fatherland and military service. It is the duty of the sociologist to convert this unnatural state of warfare to a peaceful condition by dis-covering the natural hierarchy between the social sub-groups. Thus, when the situation demands, the family should subordinate itself to the trade corporation, the corporation to the state, and all of them to the Church (*ümmet*), or to the language group (the nation); and it should be remembered that the nation, which is above all other social groups, is a language group, and that internationality is a civilization-group.

A civilization-group originates in a way similar to that of a market group. In a market-place, the tailor, the shoemaker, the baker, and the milliner act only for their own interests. From the pursuit of their interests arises a common interest. In the same way, several nations within a civilization-group make a division of labour, each one creat-ing an original culture for itself. Just as out of the diversity of individual capacities there arises a local division of labour, so from the diversity

CULTURE AND CIVILIZATION 101

of national aptitudes a cultural division of labour comes into existence. At first the peoples that are in proximity to each other initiate commercial, intellectual, and technological relations with each other, and then the area of these relations grows wider and wider. From ancient times, the peoples of the Mediterranean basin were exchanging goods, knowledge, and tools with each other. The discovery of the Cape Route and of the New World, the invention of printing, the opening of the Suez Canal, the construction of railways, and telegraph and postal services increased the contacts between these nations and gave them a universal character.

Culture-groups, on the other hand, began as clans whose members regarded themselves as descendants of a common ancestor. The earliest culture-group, then, was a religious and linguistic group. As this spiritual unit lived entirely a religious life, it was an entirely religious group in the beginning. From this group, which had contained in its fold all the seeds of the latter patterns of groupings, successively originated the family, the phratry, the tribe, the village, the town, the classes, corporations, communes, and, at last, ethnic groups, the Church (*ümmet*) and the state. Therefore, the law regulating the life of the culture-groups is the differentiation and multiplication of the primitive groups from an undifferentiated and multi-functioning unit to a state in which special groups come into existence to perform specific functions.

It follows from these observations that modernization means the acquisition and equal sharing of the sciences and technical arts which contemporary civilization is continuously perfecting. To share a common human life in a civilization-group is not detrimental to the existence of the family or state, nor to the integrity of religion or the nation. We Turks have to work to create a Turkish-Islamic culture by fully appropriating to ourselves the mentality of contemporary civilization and its sciences.

II[6]

. . . In present-day civilization there is no genuine sentiment of humanity transcending the confines of religion. The events of our time show eloquently that there are as many internationalities and humanities as religions. For a European, humanity is nothing but Christendom. It is true that there are principles of justice and right, brotherhood and kindness in the West, but their application extends only as

102 TURKISH NATIONALISM AND WESTERN CIVILIZATION

far as the boundaries of the Christian religion. And, again, it is true that there is morality, philosophy, and civilization in the West, but on all of them there is the implicit or explicit stamp of the Cross.

It is evident that certain things not coloured by Christianity are not lacking entirely in Europe. Science, technology, and industry are universal and common to all humanity as they are not the products of 'community' but of 'society'. We as Muslims, under the guidance of our own style of social life, divide European civilization into two levels, and accept the 'civilization of society' because it is common [to humanity]. As to the other level, which belongs to the 'community', we are trying to build a civilization of our own out of our own 'community' life, by profiting from the methods of the former [international civilization]. In reaction to the treatment we received [from Europe], the sentiments of an Islamic internationality and humanity are rising in our consciousness. . . . .

In spite of the growth of several ideals, it is still religion that exercises the most powerful force over the minds. . . . We know how powerful a factor religion still is in countries like the United States and Switzerland which are most free from medieval political institutions. We have seen a religious revival recently even in France which had declared war against the Church. As it is evident that religious consciousness has a lasting life, there remains only one means by which to attain the unity of mankind, and that is through the creation of a world faith (*bayn al-'umam*) which would be the product of conciliation and *rapprochement* among [existing] religions. Only in this way may a humane community be created to eradicate the misunderstandings between religions, and only then will real equality of nations, universal justice and kindness, brotherhood and solidarity be realized. Until the rise of such a new ideal, a religious internationality which is a partial humanity will inevitably rule men's souls, in the East as well as in the West.

By the term Turkish-Islamic civilization, we mean a 'community' civilization. There can be a 'society' civilization common to all Ottoman 'communities'. This Ottoman civilization will consist of a local manifestation of the universal 'society' civilization.

The separation between religion and state is a goal sought by all civilized nations. Not only politics, but even ethics, law, and philosophy have freed themselves from their previous dependence on religion and have gradually won their autonomy. In spite of the separation of these

CULTURE AND CIVILIZATION 103

areas of social life, religion has not lost its appeal to the heart. On the contrary, religion has begun to fulfil its function more effectively as it has demarcated its private domain. . . .

Islam has not been a power in our country simply because it could not perform its private function independently within the framework of the state. If you want to understand the power of the religion of Islam, you must study it in India, in Egypt, in Java and China, and in the Turkish lands that are under the rule of Russia. Then you will see that the attachment of religion to the state in our country has not been to its advantage, but rather to the extreme detriment of religion. The reason for this can be seen easily. The state is a legal machinery; it tends to legalize and formalize any social force upon which it touches. It is because of this fact that Islam started to lose its vitality from the moment it began to be fused with the political organization and began to be formalized as a system of law closed against all *ijtihād*. The religion that the state recognizes officially today and the *sharī'a* which it formally holds is nothing but the *fiķh*. But the *fiķh* did not exist until one and a half centuries after the *Hijra*. Until that time religion and *sharī'a* consisted of the Kur'an and *Sunna*. The state today officially recognizes only one *sharī'a*, that of the Hanafī school. Thus, a sect that has only a scholastic value is held prior to religion which is the main thing. The situation is different in those places where Islam is independent. As religion is understood to be a religious life in these countries, the *sharī'a* finds its sources only in the Book [the Kur'an] and *Sunna*, on the one hand, and in social life, on the other, and is increasingly becoming a social *sharī'a*. . . .[7]

If we accept the existence of a social reality as distinct from physical reality, we cannot put religion and the *ümmet*—that is, the community of religion—outside this social reality. Like all other ideals and values, these too have an existence in the social consciousness which is sanctioned by the power of their social appeal. . . .

It then follows that we do not hold the monistic view in sociology. People cannot live with only one ideal. As the ideal of nationality is imperative, the ideals of inter-community life, of international life, and inter-religious life are equally needed. With respect to ideals, we are pluralist. Our national ideal will be Turkishness, our international ideal will be Islam. We also favour the ideal of Ottoman unity of the [religious] communities and the ideal of humanity among the great religions, to the extent that we see the same applied to us.

CULTURE AND CIVILIZATION[8]

There are areas of convergence and divergence between culture and civilization. Convergence is due to the fact that both culture and civilization cover religious, moral, legal, intellectual, aesthetic, economic, linguistic, and technological spheres of social life. It is the sum total of these eight major spheres of social life that constitutes both culture and civilization. In this sense, culture and civilization overlap and appear to be identical.

But there are also certain differences between culture and civilization. First, culture is national, civilization is international. Culture is composed of the integrated system of religious, moral, legal, intellectual, aesthetic, linguistic, economic, and technological spheres of life of a certain nation. Civilization, on the other hand, is the sum total of social institutions shared in common by several nations that have attained the same level of development. Western civilization, for example, is a civilization shared by the European nations living on the continents of Europe and America. Within this civilization, however, there are English, German, French, etc., cultures, which are different and independent of each other.

Secondly, civilization is created by men's conscious actions and is a rational product. Our knowledge, theories, and techniques with regard to religion, law, ethics, fine arts, economy, science, philosophy, and language are all conscious and rational products of individuals. The sum total of these products within a certain area of attainment constitutes a distinct type of civilization.

The elements that constitute a culture, on the other hand, are not creations of conscious individual actions. They are not created artificially. Just as plants and animals grow naturally, so the elements of a culture rise and grow spontaneously. Language, for example, is not made individually and rationally. We cannot change the words of a language, and put new ones, invented arbitrarily, in their places. We cannot change the grammatical rules which have grown by themselves. The rules and the words of a language change, but they change by themselves. We are just spectators of these changes. Individuals can introduce certain terms into a language. But these words can only become a part of the language when they are appropriated by specialized groups as specific terms. Even then, they remain the property of only a certain group. It is only when they are accepted by the people

CULTURE AND CIVILIZATION 105

that they become a part of everyday language. The acceptance or rejection of a new term by a people does not depend upon the will of its originators. Thousands of new words have been introduced into old Ottoman Turkish since Shinasi's[9] time, but only a small number of them have been accepted by a certain group, and only a very few have been accepted by the general public.

Thus, we find a good illustration of the meaning of culture in the words of a language, and a good illustration of the meaning of civilization in the invention of terms. Words are social institutions, while terms are individual products. A term invented by a certain person may be accepted immediately by the public, but this general acceptance is not due to its inventor; it is due to an unseen trend of society which is not consciously known to its members.

Until fifteen years ago there were two Turkish languages current in this country. One was official and was used exclusively for writing. This was called Ottoman. The other was the language of the common people. It was known, in a derogatory sense, as Turkish. It was believed to be the 'slang' of the common people. In fact, it was the real and natural language of the nation. The Ottoman language was nothing but an artificial mixture of the grammar, syntax, and vocabulary of Turkish, Arabic, and Persian. Turkish developed naturally. It was the language of our own culture. Ottoman was a language consciously and rationally made by certain individuals. Only a few Turkish verbs or prepositions found their way into this mixture of languages. There was only a small fraction of our culture in it. It was the language of the civilization of the Ottomans.

Similarly, two metric systems existed in poetry. The metric forms of folk poetry were not consciously cultivated. Common men wrote their lyric poems without any knowledge of metre. Their poems were the result of inspiration and creativity, and not of imitation and artificial methods. Thus, like the Turkish language, this metric form was also a part of Turkish culture. The metre used by the Ottoman poets, on the other hand, was copied from Persian poetry. These poets were imitative and followed certain strict rules. Their prosody did not penetrate to the people. They studied Persian literature and adopted its rules of prosody. Persian literature never became a part of our literature. Among the Persians, even the peasants composed poems in the *aruz* metre, and thus it was a part of Persian culture.

Again, two systems of music existed side by side. One was Turkish

106 TURKISH NATIONALISM AND WESTERN CIVILIZATION

music which arose spontaneously from the people. The other, Ottoman music, was originally adapted by Fārābī from Byzantium. Turkish music was a product of inspiration, not an imitation of foreign music forms. Ottoman music was imitative, and was nothing but a matter of technique. One was the music of culture, the other of civilization.

Civilization is the sum total of the concepts and techniques developed according to certain methods and transmitted from nation to nation. Culture, on the other hand, is composed of sentiments which cannot be developed artificially and cannot be transmitted from nation to nation. Ottoman music consisted of a technique based on certain rules; Turkish music consisted of melodies bound not by stereotyped rules, methods, and techniques, but by a sincere expression of the emotions of the people. . . .

We find the same dichotomy in literature. Turkish literature consisted of proverbs, riddles, tales, ballads, epics, adventure stories, chants, hymns, humorous anecdotes, and folk plays. . . . Ottoman literature, on the other hand, consisted of short stories and novels— instead of anonymous tales—and imitative *gazels* or *sonnets*, instead of folk ballads and epics. Every Ottoman poet had his counterpart, in the past, in Persia, and, more recently, in France. Even Fuzulî and Nedîm[10] are not exceptional. Thus, none of them had any originality. They were all imitators. Their works were the products of intellectual craftsmanship, not of aesthetic inspiration. . . .

The same dichotomy is found in the field of morality. It may be said that Turkish morality and Ottoman morality are diametrically opposed to each other. Mahmud of Kashgar[11] described the Turks briefly in his *Divan-i Lûgat* as people devoid of pretension and presumption, unaware of the heroism in their heroic acts. Jāḥiẓ[12] described them in exactly the same terms. Amongst the Ottomans, on the other hand, boasting in old poets, and presumptuousness and pretentiousness in the newer ones were normal. The writers and poets of the *Servet-i Fünûn* school of literature,[13] which represented the most outstanding period of Ottoman literature, were mostly sceptical, pessimistic, despairing, sickly spirits.

Even among the scholars, this dichotomy existed. The traditional title of the Ottoman scholars was official *ulema*, while the educated men of Anatolia were called the *ulema* of the people. The first had ranks and titles, but were ignorant. The second had practical wisdom, but lacked any official status. . . .

CULTURE AND CIVILIZATION

The political and military successes of the earlier Ottoman period were due to uneducated and illiterate pashas who rose from the rank and file. But when affairs of state were entrusted to men like Rağıp Pasha and the extravagant Ibrahim Pasha, who had attained high positions in Ottoman intellectual circles, decay set in.

These dichotomies, however, were confined to intellectual activities. As menial work was left to the common people, the privileged classes remained aloof from all technical skills. Consequently, we find only one artistry—people's artistry—in the practical arts: architecture, calligraphy, engraving, book-binding, gilding, joinery, iron-work. dyeing, carpet-making, weaving, painting, and manuscript illuminating, Thus, these arts, which attained a high aesthetic level, may be called genuine Turkish arts. They were a part of Turkish culture, not of Ottoman civilization. . . .

What is the reason for the existence of this strange dichotomy which is peculiar to our country? Why was there such opposition between the two patterns—the Turkish and Ottoman—existing side by side in this country? Why is everything in the Turkish pattern so beautiful and everything in the Ottoman pattern so ugly? Because the Ottoman pattern took an imperialistic course, which was harmful to the culture and life of the Turks. It became cosmopolitan and put class interests above national interests. The more the Ottoman Empire expanded through conquest, the deeper became the dividing line between the two classes of ruler and ruled. The Ottoman class were the ruling cosmopolitans and the Turkish class their ruled Turkish subjects. The two classes hated each other. The Ottomans regarded themselves as the ruling nation and looked down on their Turkish subjects as a subjugated nation. The Ottoman called the Turk 'the stupid Turk', while the Turks fled from their villages when an Ottoman official visited them. The appearance of the Red Heads[14] among the Turks can be explained by this disparity. . . .

The Ottoman élite were known as the *havas* [*khavāṣ*], while the Turkish élite were humble minstrels, poets, and dervishes. Thus there were two groups of élites. The first represented, and was supported by, the court. Their poets and musicians received gifts, grants, and salaries from the court. The artists of the people lived on the offerings of the people. The official *ulema*, as government dignitaries, received high salaries or benefices. The religious leaders of the Turkish people, *imām*s and *baba*s, were supported by the people. The artisans, the

108 TURKISH NATIONALISM AND WESTERN CIVILIZATION

guild-masters and guild-elders, who were the leaders of the people in the fine arts as well as in the practical arts, were always recruited from amongst the lower classes and always remained Turks.

We see, therefore, that culture is composed mainly of emotional elements, while civilization is composed of ideas; this is another difference between the two. Emotions are not conscious and rational products of men. A nation cannot imitate the religious, moral, or aesthetic feelings of another nation. For example, in the pre-Islamic Turkish religion, the sky-god (*Gök-Tanrı*) was a god of reward and did not have the power to punish. There was a lesser god of punishment, called *Erlik-Han*. Because the Turks regarded God as beautiful, they loved Him and were not terrified by Him. The emphasis on the Love of God among the Islamized Turks was a continuation of this old tradition. Fear of God among the Turks is very rare. The experiences of preachers show that sermons emphasizing beauty and goodness gain larger attendances, while preachers who talk of hell and its demons find few listeners. In the religious practices of the ancient Turks there were aesthetic and moral rituals but no asceticism. Consequently, the Turks, after Islamization, maintained a strong and sincere piety, but remained free from ascetic and fanatic practices. The works of Yunus Emre[15] are sufficient evidence of this fact. The importance that the Turks attach to the singing of hymns and the *Mevlid* [Birthday Poem] in the mosques, and to the performance of poetry and music in the *tekke*s, is an expression of the aestheticism in the practice of their religion. . . . The aesthetic characteristics which distinguish Turkish art are simplicity, gracefulness, and originality. These are found in their tiles, rugs, architecture, calligraphy, and in their religious morality.

This shows that there is an intimate affinity, an internal unity, between the different aspects of a culture. . . . But it is erroneous to believe that there is the same harmony between the elements of a civilization.

The civilization of the Ottomans was a mixture of institutions borrowed from the Turkish, Persian, and Arab cultures, from the religion of Islam, from the Eastern and, more recently, Western civilizations. These institutions were never really integrated and never produced a harmonious system. A civilization becomes a harmonious unity only when it is incorporated into the national culture. Civilization in England is welded into English culture, hence there is a consistency between the civilization and culture of the British.

CULTURE AND CIVILIZATION 109

Another relation between culture and civilization is this: in its earliest stages each nation had only its own culture. From the growth of a nation's culture stems its political development and the institution of the state. Although civilization arises out of culture, it borrows freely from the civilization of neighbouring peoples. But . . . the overgrowth of civilization [at the expense of culture] results in the disintegration of culture and produces culturally degenerate nations.

Finally, we note the following difference between culture and civilization: when a conflict occurs between a nation strong in culture but weak in civilization and one which is culturally disrupted but superior in civilization, the former always wins. When the ancient Egyptians developed their civilization, their culture declined. The rising Persian state, though backward in civilization, was culturally strong and defeated Egypt. After a few centuries civilization developed in Iran—and, consequently, its culture declined. The Iranians were defeated by the Greeks whose culture was as yet intact. As Greek culture declined, both the Greeks and Iranians were defeated by the uncivilized but culturally vigorous Macedonians. The same cause accounts for the defeat of the Macedonians who, when they lost their culture, were overthrown by the Parthian and Sasani dynasties in the East and the Romans in the West. Finally, the Arabs, who knew nothing of civilization but had a strong cultural background, defeated both Sasanis and Romans. In turn, the Arabs too lost their culture as their civilization developed. They relinquished political supremacy to the Seljuk Turks, who had newly come from Turkestan with their traditional customs as their national culture. The power of Turkish national culture was the only force that enabled the Turks to remain independent up until the time when they expelled the British and the French from the Dardanelles and, after the Armistice, defeated the Greeks and Armenians and, indirectly, the British who had armed and financed them. . . .

PART III

CHAPTER V

THE EVOLUTION OF SOCIETY

THE SCIENTIFIC STUDY OF COMMUNITIES[1]

I

In order to study an ethnic community scientifically, one has to study, not how it should be in the future but what it was in the past and is at present. To propose measures to be taken in order to remove the factors that arrest the social evolution of a people, or in order to facilitate the evolution of society in accordance with a certain ideal of orientation, is not the business of [pure] science but the task of applied science. Science does not operate with practical aims in mind. The art of social amelioration has to proceed by hasty judgments because of the pressure of practical needs. Science, on the other hand, cannot sacrifice truth for practical considerations, and thus has to proceed with patience and freedom and avoid the haste imposed by practical interests. Scientists know, however, that the results of scientific researches are immediately utilized and applied by the social arts. It may even be said that the spiritual incentive leading the scientist to work patiently is his anticipation that his disinterested researches will one day benefit his own people or the whole of mankind. Without such an ideal, the scientist would not consecrate his life to such an arduous task. In spite of this, he must never forget that practical results are not the ultimate aim of science but are only the necessary consequences of it. Just as art exists exclusively for art's sake, so science exists only for the sake of science. . . .

To study a community scientifically, however, this disregard for immediate practical ends is not enough. Our own community is for us a cherished being to which we are attached with deepest sentiment. To be biased in favour of our own community or the communities which are of the same religion or race, or which are allied with us against our enemies, is not something that is within our own will. It is especially difficult to rid ourselves of all bias in our feelings for our

114 TURKISH NATIONALISM AND WESTERN CIVILIZATION

own people. Our greatest duty to our people is, however, to know it as it is. We must diagnose the ills from which our people suffer and discover their remedies. . . .

In order to study our own community scientifically, therefore, it is not enough to disentangle ourselves from immediate, practical concerns; we need also to free ourselves from the cherished feelings of our conscience. The feelings from which we should free ourselves should not be, however, only those of an optimistic nature; we have to liberate ourselves also from all pessimistic sentiments. Certain persons who have not been educated in their own country tend to hold unjustifiably pessimistic opinions of their own people. To be biased either optimistically or pessimistically is equally detrimental to scientific studies. To pursue scientific studies, one has to free oneself from all sentiment and proceed with pure reason.*

But to work scientifically, to maintain a disinterested approach, freedom from practical considerations and from national or anti-national bias is not enough. The objective of the scientist will be attained neither by pure objectivity nor by [pure] rationality. Reason implies two things: first, it means a totality of hierarchically classified concepts independent of ourselves. To think in terms of this pre-established hierarchy cannot be the sole basis of scientific research because to think in this way means to restrict the objective reality to a frame-work of preconceived concepts. The function of reason is to rearrange and reclassify the concepts of our intellect in accordance with objective reality. For doing this, the ability to think creatively is indispensable; it is, in fact, the second function of reason. Reason, from the point of view of science, should be understood in this sense. To think in terms of mechanical, pre-established reason is deductive procedure; that is, to proceed from concepts already existing in the mind towards the objective reality. To think in terms of the creative and living reason means to observe objective reality and to derive concepts from this observation—a procedure which we call induction. The scientific investigator should rid himself of all the concepts that

---

* As national problems are generally problems with an emotional content, my statement about objectivity in the study of communities may, at first sight, seem strange. But it will be understood that what I mean is to disentangle the researcher from his sentiments, but not to claim that the phenomena to be studied sociologically are not emotional facts. Facts relating to national life are emotional. The sociologist should study the sentiments, the emotions, and the ambitions of a nation, but should never be confused by his own personal and private feelings about them.

THE EVOLUTION OF SOCIETY

he has acquired in various ways about the people whom he is going to observe. He should follow Descartes's methodical and temporary scepticism, and should doubt all traditional concepts current among the people and even the scientific investigations carried on before him. He should proceed directly to the facts, avoiding all pre-existing, scientific constructions. He should try to observe inductively the particular and concrete facts which constitute objective reality, and proceed step by step towards more general and more abstract concepts.

It is true that this procedure also will lead ultimately to a hierarchically classified system of concepts. But concepts derived from such a procedure constitute condensed statements of objective reality, while the preconceptions existing before the observation of objective reality are nothing but traditional conceptions which come down from the various stages of the past and survive only as sentimental or habitual residues. The new concepts derived from scientific procedure may seem paradoxical compared to these traditional conceptions or to the mechanical reason which is constituted by the systematization of such conceptions. As Durkheim stated, science is not in search of paradox, but if it arrives at such a paradox through its own investigation, it will not reject it. If science had to arrive at nothing but commonplace knowledge, why should it carry on all these painstaking researches?

We may conclude, therefore, that there are three main methodological prerequisites to scientific research: (a) the procedure should be carried out with theoretical and not practical objectives in mind; (b) it should not be emotional but rational; and (c) it should not be deductive but inductive. In short, it should not be subjective but objective.

II

Objectivity is dependent upon the realization of these three conditions. However, even objectivity is not sufficient. There is a further and an important condition: the object of scientific inquiry should constitute an independent reality. Thus, if a community is not an independently existing reality it cannot be the object of scientific inquiry. The objective existence of the community depends, first, upon the objective existence of a social reality and, secondly, upon the objectification of this reality in what we call community. Those who view the community as nothing but an aggregate of individual organisms or of individual psyches deny the objective reality of the com-

116 TURKISH NATIONALISM AND WESTERN CIVILIZATION

munity. In order to recognize the peculiar existence of the community, it is necessary to recognize the existence of a social reality independent of biological and psychological realities. In this sense the community will mean nothing but that form of the social reality which has become a real organism through association in language and custom.

We may state the same idea in another way: the existence of a science demands a corresponding reality. As there are physical, biological, and psychological realities, physical sciences, biology, and psychology exist. Is community the subject-matter of any of these sciences? Or shall we assume the existence of a social reality and make the community the subject-matter of a science which will deal with it? There is no doubt that the community cannot be the subject-matter of the physical sciences. A community is composed of human individuals who have a biological and psychological nature. Biology deals with these individual organisms and psychology with their individual psychic lives. But the community is a reality which is completely different from both of the former. Thus, for this reality we need a special science. As community belongs to the category of the social, the science to study it is the science which deals with social reality; that is, sociology.

When we accept that the community is an independent social reality, we must seek the causes of all the phenomena relating to this reality only among social factors. As a matter of fact, for the existence of a science the mere existence of an independent reality does not suffice. This reality should, at the same time, be subject to the principle of determinism; in other words, there must be definite causes for every fact on this plane of reality. If physical, biological, and psychic realities were not subject to the law of determinism, the physical sciences, biology, or psychology could not exist. Without accepting the principle of social determinism, we cannot attempt to search for the laws of social reality, and without this sociology cannot exist. It follows that, as we study the rational facts sociologically, we must look at social phenomena in order to discover the immediate causes of these facts.

As in the realm of biological phenomena, so a fact must perform a useful function in the life of the community to which it pertains in order to be considered a part of the reality of social phenomena. It is true that social facts do not exist to serve such functions. They arise as the necessary consequence of preceding social causes. But once they exist, they must perform certain social functions in order to maintain

THE EVOLUTION OF SOCIETY 117

their continued existence. A social fact may adjust its previous function in accordance with changing social conditions. We should, therefore, determine not only the causes of social phenomena but also the social functions that they perform at different times.

Besides the causes and the functions of social facts, their value has also to be determined. The only means at our disposal for measuring the value of social facts is statistics. Statistical data, showing the rates of crimes, such as homicide or theft, or the rate of divorce in a certain country, are indices which serve to measure social sentiments concerning the inviolability of the life of the individual, security of property, the sanctity of marriage. . . .

III

Having observed the characteristics of social phenomena, let us now see what constitutes the social facts themselves. As social phenomena constitute an independent realm of reality, they should be found outside the realms of physical, biological, and psychological phenomena. And the only phenomena which we can observe outside of these are social groups and institutions.

A social group is a totality of individuals connected with each other by a special solidarity, such as a family, a village community, a tribe, a class, a caste, a corporation, a Church (*ümmet*), a state, or a nation. The social institution is a pattern of thinking or action, such as religious beliefs and ritual, norms of morality and law, the rules of language or aesthetics, economic methods, or scientific techniques, imposed by these groups upon their members, who accept it voluntarily or because of constraint.

Communities dissimilar in respect of the groups and institutions they comprise may be classified, as plants and animals are, into species and genera. If the individual cases in a realm of reality cannot be reduced to species and genera, or to general types, there can be no science to deal with this realm of reality. Science deals only with generalities. To discover general laws, it is necessary to ascertain general types.

A satisfactory general classification of communities has not yet been devised. However, until a final classification has been formulated, a tentative and preliminary classification is obviously needed to serve researches. For this purpose we propose below a tentative scheme of classification.

118 TURKISH NATIONALISM AND WESTERN CIVILIZATION

Communities may be divided into two genera: 'primitive communities' and 'nations'. Primitive communities are the early social type for which the Germans use the term *Naturvölker*. The basic social unit which characterizes these peoples is the clan. The clan is a family group comprising hundreds or even thousands of persons who are related to each other by a religious kinship. The symbol representing the clan is the name of the fictitious or real being who is accepted as the ancestor of its members. This common ancestor is also believed to be the private deity of the clan. Among the members of the clan, the law of common responsibility or group talion operates.

While there is the idea neither of public authority nor of personal rights among the primitive peoples, there is belief in a private law in which the object of the law is the clan. It is true that several clans combine to make phratries and tribes and confederations of tribes, but even these larger groups are, like the clan, still family groups. The tribes or confederations of tribes are the first grouping of the clans; the other groupings come into existence as secondary groupings through the disintegration of these confederations. Therefore, the chiefs of the phratries, or of the tribes, or of the confederations of tribes, are still family heads, like the clan chiefs, exercising only a private authority. Punishment in these societies is enforced in the form of retaliation and vengeance, and may be bought with blood money. The authority in the clan is of a religious character, and the chief of the clan has, at the same time, a religious function.

Primitive communities may be classified into four species:

(a) *Undifferentiated Communities with a Clan Basis*, such as the Australian aborigines. These peoples are composed of several totemic clans among whom there is no hierarchical differentiation. As the clans in these communities are not differentiated, they constitute the most simple organization of primitive communities.

(b) *Differentiated Communities with a Clan Basis*. In these communities, the totemic clans still exist, but they are in a state of disintegration. Upon this primary basis, certain social organs such as classes, warrior bands, religious sects, and shamans begin to appear, all developing from the clan. The North American Indians belong to this category.

(c) *Tribal Communities in which Totemic Institution is Entirely Lacking*. In these communities the totem (which was believed to be the common ancestor and the emblem of the clan, in the form of an

THE EVOLUTION OF SOCIETY

animal or plant, or in exceptional cases an inanimate object) is transformed into a real human being. With the exception of certain vestiges of clan institutions, these societies cease to be totemic in any way. Descent in the clans of these tribal communities is patrilineal, while the totemic clans were matrilineal. In these communities, the clan loses its power of solidarity, and in its stead tribal solidarity gains importance as the tribe begins to realize its own distinctive homogeneity in contrast to the above types. The Dahomey of Africa represent this category.

(d) *Degenerate Primitive Communities*, where the clan has entirely disintegrated and no national organization has developed. Some ethnographers have mistaken these peoples for the most simple type of primitive community just because they are composed of families and lack any clan organization. But this is not the case. The small families seem to stem from patriarchal families, and these in turn have originated from matriarchal clans. Therefore, the simplicity observed has been the product of the disintegration of the clans resulting from a social retrogression. The Veddas of Ceylon belong to this category.*

By the weakening or disappearance of the clan or tribe, the rise of national feelings, which is the indication of the emergence of the institution of public authority and public law, is seen in *nations*. With the rise and development of writing, literature, and history, the community feels itself a unified body. At the same time, with the development of the division of labour and specialization, different social functions are performed by special social organs.

Nations are divided into four sub-species. (a) The first is the *theocratic nation*. In this type the nation senses its own existence and unity, and expresses it in a common deity and public authority. Private law and the institutions of clan and tribe disappear and give place to a religious public law as the law of God. In theocratic nations, the law is of a ritualistic nature, and is laid down in the books of ritual which contain the commandments that govern ritual, as seen, for example, in the code of Manu of the Hindus. The religious public authority is personified in the ruler whose legitimacy is based on divine sanction. When this authority extends from the ruler to the lords, a feudal organization emerges. Clans are transformed into village communities by settling a certain territory. The village community was autonomous so long as the clan organization existed, but failed to retain its auton-

* This classification is based upon the one developed in *L'Année Sociologique*, Vols. XI and XII.

120 TURKISH NATIONALISM AND WESTERN CIVILIZATION

omy with the disintegration of the clan system, and became dependent upon external supports. The ownership of land was transferred to the hands of the feudal lords, and the villages became fiefs and the peasants serfs. As the interpretation of law lay in the hands of representatives of religion, the ruler was not vested with legislative authority; his was a purely administrative function. We may call these communities *nations with a village basis* or *administrative nations*. The ancient Eastern and Medieval European states, and the Abbasi Caliphate belong to this category.

(*b*) The second type is the *legislative nation*. In these nations, the cities freed themselves from the authority of feudal lords and began to administer their affairs through their municipal organization or joined the ruler against feudal authority. When cities assumed this form, they became communes. Urban civilization extended to the country, where the institutions of private property and individual liberty found ground. Thus the villages, too, were transformed into smaller communes. The administration of the city was based on public opinion. In the capital cities, a political public opinion arose apart from religious public opinion. The ruler of the nation acquired a legislative authority and secular law came into being. Government was no longer based on a divine law, but on the sovereignty of the people; that is, on political public opinion. In the theocratic type, the nation personified itself in a religious executive power, but now a political legislative power represents the nation. Communities of this type may be called *nations with a city basis*. France or Italy may be cited as examples.

(*c*) The third type is the *culture-nation*. Many of the institutions of a community may be shared commonly by several nations living in proximity. The whole of these communities which have common institutions may be called a *civilization-group*, and the whole of their common institutions a *civilization*. Primitive peoples and theocratic and legislative nations do not have independent national civilizations, but participate in a commonly shared international civilization. Although they have their own peculiar language and customs, these institutions do not yet colour international institutions. As soon as a nation puts the stamp of its own language and ethos on the institutions of an international civilization and adapts them to its own spirit, it becomes a nation having an independent and national civilization; that is, a *culture*. A community becomes a nation in its real sense only by having such an independent culture. With the beginnings of a national

THE EVOLUTION OF SOCIETY

culture, an intimate harmony establishes itself among the institutions of the international civilization, and this integration makes them organs of a living organism. Culture is composed of interlocking systems, each being composed of interlocking institutions. The systems composing a culture are religious, moral, legal, aesthetic, linguistic, economic, and technical. There is an intimate harmony between these systems as well as among the institutions of each system. The sources of this harmony existing among the institutions are the religious, moral, legal, etc., mores upon which the institutions are based. Harmony exists among the various areas of public opinion within a nation because all are based on the same social structure. The social life of the communities changes and evolves in accordance with the changes in their social structures. The classification of the communities, therefore, should be based on this principle.

Just as there is in legislative nations a separate political authority parallel to the religious authority, so in culture-nations there are cultural authorities independent of the religious and political authorities. Cultural authorities are great personalities recognized as leaders in the fields of morality, economy, fine arts, literature, and pure and applied sciences. As cultural interpretations originate from these authorities, they are spontaneously recognized by the members of the nation because of the universal confidence which their distinguished careers in their respective fields inspire. In culture-nations, the people are personified by the representation of their culture because culture consists of a concrete manifestation of the national consciousness expressed in various forms of institutions.

Culture may also express itself in a material organization. Various cultural corporative organizations may be connected to a centre of specialization in the metropolitan city where a great cultural league composed of the representatives of these centres may be formed. We may call this type of nation a *nation with a corporative basis*.

A community does not lose all of its previous institutions as it evolves from the lower to the higher species. The basic organizations originally found in each species maintain their existence by performing a special function. Thus, the kinship organization of the primitive peoples, the religious organization of the theocratic nations, the legal organization of the legislative nations, survive in the culture-nation in the form of 'family', 'Church', and 'state' respectively. The culture-nation emerges with the addition to the family, Church, and state,

122 TURKISH NATIONALISM AND WESTERN CIVILIZATION

surviving from the previous stages of ethnic evolution, of a cultural organization. As the establishment of the legislative organ puts an end to the tyranny of the executive power, so the emergence of the cultural authority will eliminate the corruptions of the legislative power and of the press. Therefore, it is only in the culture-nations that an independent judiciary may be instituted entirely separate from the executive and legislative powers. The most advanced nations are evolving towards this stage, although none has reached it.

(*d*) The fourth type is constituted by those nations which have lost their independence after once having been independent, such as the Polish nation.

Nations that are in a stage of transition from one species to another constitute a secondary category of species. These are also of four types: (*a*) the tribal-theocratic peoples, such as the Moroccans; (*b*) theocratic-legislative nations, such as the present-day [1915] Russians, (*c*) legislative-cultural nations, such as the Germans, the British, and the Americans, and (*d*) semi-independent nations, such as the Finns.

Once the genera and the species of peoples are established, it becomes possible to determine which elements of the social structure as well as of the institutions are of a pathological nature. It is obvious that the institutions that exist as survivals from an inferior species are pathological institutions. Thus, if in a culture-nation there are some survivals from the primitive peoples or from the theocratic or legislative species, these institutions are of a pathological character. Once the maladies of the community are diagnosed their treatment becomes possible, as scientific research is a useful guide to the practical arts.

It follows that in order to derive scientific conclusions from the researches to be undertaken on the Turks, it is necessary to establish the following points: firstly, to which civilizations have the Turks belonged at various stages of their history; secondly, to which species in the social evolution described above have they belonged; thirdly, what are the anomalies among their institutions that are irreconcilable with the institutions of the species to which they now belong; and fourthly, which institutions of international civilization have entered into Turkish life and what changes have they undergone?

The data to be used in the study of these points are provided by history, ethnology, and statistics. As the authenticity and value of those data will be scrutinized, it will also be necessary to determine to which group, which social space and time, the institutions indicated by

THE EVOLUTION OF SOCIETY 123

these data belonged. The Turkish people have lived in different societies in the same periods, and have joined various spheres of civilization at various times. Only through a scientific study of Turkish life from the beginning to our time shall we be able to know in which directions it should be oriented and by what means this will be achieved.

CLASSIFICATION OF SOCIAL SPECIES[2]

For historians each tribe or nation or civilization is unique, having its own peculiar characteristics. For them, therefore, there are no social species; there are only social individualities. Each society is itself an individual which cannot be classified into a species.

For philosophers [of history], on the other hand, states, nations, civilizations, and tribes are transitory stages or manifestations of human society in different times and places. For them, therefore, there is only one social species—that is, Humanity. All societies are individuals of this single species. As social phenomena are, for them, products of the developments of tendencies rooted in human nature, all societies are essentially the same. There is only one social evolution and that is the evolution of Humanity. Various societies represent different stages or periods of this evolution.

For the historian an historical event never repeats itself. All historical events are individual, unique, and unprecedented. If science deals with generalities instead of individual cases, therefore, history can never be a science. Science seeks to discover recurring causal relations between facts; it seeks to discover laws. Historians deny history as a science when they deny general facts. From this point of view it is not possible for a science of politics or of education to be derived from history. Institutions which may prove to be useful for one society may not be so for another. The laws of each society constitute an independent system, *sui generis*. Societies cannot be compared with each other; nor can the institutions of one society be valid for another. The institutions of each society develop spontaneously from its own particular social life. Social arts, such as politics and education, can carry on and strengthen the characteristics of the national life, but cannot modify or ameliorate that life.

For philosophers, all societies bear the same nature and character and are moved by the same needs. Therefore, laws may be formed to suit all of them. A certain institution which is useful for one is applicable to all. (Not all historians and philosophers, of course, are of these opinions. Our description applies not to all but to the majority.)

Sociologists find grains of truth in both views. They rather reconcile both views by their theory according to which society may be classified into species and genera like plants and animals. . . . For sociologists, institutions found in a certain social species will not be found in another one and are not valid there. . . . On the other hand, sociologists believe that the institutions of a society of a certain species are common to all societies which belong to the same species. Therefore, the borrowing of institutions between societies of the same species is natural, but borrowing from a society of a different species is not.

Societies are divided above all into two genera: primitive societies and nations.

A society is a group of men united by moral solidarity. Solidarity is of two kinds: one consists of likeness of sentiments and beliefs; the other is the product of the social division of labour. The first is 'mechanical solidarity', the second 'organic solidarity'. The first is the result of likeness of sentiments and beliefs, the second is the result of similarity of aptitudes and skills. The first makes individuals the cells of a social organism, the second the specialized organs of a social organism. . . . In primitive societies only mechanical solidarity operates. Division of labour in these societies is based on sex and age differentiations, but there is no social division of labour or it is in its beginnings. Primitive society is not primarily composed of individuals but of parts which are all alike, and each of these segments is composed again of like segments. Each of these segments has its own solidarity and produces a higher group by combining with corresponding segments. These societies are called segmentary because they look like fissiparous organisms.

In nations, on the other hand, these segments disappear and give place to groups which are products of the social division of labour. For this reason nations have both kinds of solidarity. Nations may also be called organic societies. In segmentary societies individuals are only cells. In organic societies, on the other hand, they are also organs having specialized functions. In segmentary societies there is a strong connection only between the individual and society. In organic society, on the other hand, the individual is tied to society both directly and indirectly (through other individuals who are dependent on, and complementary to, each other).

THE EVOLUTION OF SOCIETY

Primitive societies are divided into four species: undifferentiated clan societies . . . differentiated clan societies . . . tribal societies . . . and primitive societies in which clan organization has disappeared. . . .

Nations have not yet been subjected to a scientific classification. We propose, without claiming scientific authority, to classify nations into five species according to their social structures: (a) feudal nations . . . which may be called *societies with a village basis*; (b) communal societies . . . which may be called *societies with an urban basis*; (c) City-states. . . ; (d) societies with a compound structure, in which towns are communes but villages are feudal domains (towards the end of the Middle Ages, German towns freed themselves from seignorial subjugation and developed into communes, but villages remained seignorial domains. In France, on the other hand, urban civilization spread to the villages and brought them into a communal organization. After the sixteenth century, the sovereign authority of kings and feudal lords increased as a result of certain new ideas and trends, and thus towns became again subjected to feudal domination. This was the main factor preventing the national unification of Germany until the last century); (e) corporative societies. . . . The basic unit in primitive societies is the clan as a unit of kinship and religion; in the species of nations mentioned above, the basic units are territorial groups; that is, villages and towns. The basic units in corporative societies, on the other hand, are corporate bodies which have a national character. These latter are concentrated in metropolitan centres. Guilds exist in communal societies, but their activities are confined to the communes. In corporative societies these organizations assume a national character by having federative councils in metropolitan centres composed of their delegates. This form of civilization may be called metropolitan, and is today the highest form of civilization. The most advanced nations of Europe are developing in this direction.

In the light of this classification, it will be seen that the Turkish nation belongs to the communal type and that in the future it will develop to a corporative nation.

A NOTE ON THE TERMS 'SOCIETY' AND 'COMMUNITY'[3]

. . . All social groups are made up of concentric circles of varying sizes. From the point of view of [the degree of] social consciousness, solidarity, and organization, there is only one which is more funda-

126 TURKISH NATIONALISM AND WESTERN CIVILIZATION

mental than either the larger or the smaller circles; we call this group 'society'. The group that is larger than societies and that includes societies we call 'community', and the groups that are narrower than societies and included in these we call 'secondary groups'. Only 'society' may be likened to a social organism. Secondary groups are merely various organs within this organism, and communities are unions made up of several societies. The collective consciousness in communities is always too weak as compared to that which exists in societies.

Societies, like plants and animals, are differentiated into species and genera. Primarily, societies are classified into two big genera: tribes and nations. The nations are composed of two kinds of secondary groups: territorial groups, such as provinces, counties, districts, and villages; and occupational groups, which are the products of division of labour.

Although nations are big groups, there are still larger communities. For example, the Turks of Turkey constitute a nation. The Turkish ethnic unity, which comprises all Turks, constitutes a community. Similarly, the *ümmet* of Islam to which we belong constitutes a community, as does European internationality. Every society has a political organization, either as a state or as a tribe. Communities are weaker than societies because they are not states [they lack political organization]—they are only civilization-groups.

Tribes are also composed of several concentric groups, but these are neither territorial nor occupational groups. We call them ethnic groups. As they appear, on the one hand, as families and, on the other, as political bodies, we also call them 'politico-familial' groups. They are usually based on a real or fictitious bond of kinship, and within each one there is a solidarity based on blood feud or on warfare. . . .

THE RISE OF THE NATIONS[4]

In order to define the word 'nation', it is necessary first of all to distinguish it from other seemingly kindred concepts—race, ethnic community (*kavm*), Church (*ümmet*), people, and state. The concept of race is essentially a biological concept used in zoology, and denotes types of bodily constitution, such as the Arab or Hungarian or English breed of horses. Later on, with the birth of anthropology, this word was used to denote the bodily types of human beings. For instance, in

THE EVOLUTION OF SOCIETY 127

Europe people are classified into three main physical types, under categories of dolicho-cephalic fair, dolicho-cephalic brunette, and brachy-cephalic. However, there is no society in which all of the individuals conform to any single type. In all societies there are individuals who belong to each of these types. Even within a family these three types may be observed. Thus the nation as a social group is not necessarily identical with the concept of race.

The concept 'ethnic community' is a term which is mostly confused with the term race. For example, in French the term 'éthnique' was used to connote the idea 'racial'. Even today the British writers use the terms ethnology and anthropology interchangeably. Only recently have French authors distinguished between these two terms. For example, de Lapouge proposed the use of the terms 'éthne' or 'éthnie' instead of 'race'. And thus, today, the terms 'raciale' and 'éthnique' are used to represent '*ırk*' and '*kavm*' in Turkish. '*Kavm*' means a group of individuals who have a common language and usage, i.e. Arab, Turkish, German, and Serbian *kavm*s. Thus it seems preferable to apply the term 'ethnic family' (*famille éthnique*) instead of race when speaking of a group of *kavm*s that are related to each other. For example, Semitic, Indo-European, or Ural-Altaic *kavm*s constitute in each case a separate ethnic family or group.

The term '*ümmet*' or religious community corresponds in use to the term '*église*' (Church), and therefore we can use it in this sense because we already use such expressions as 'Muhammadan *ümmet*', 'Christian *ümmet*', 'Mosaic *ümmet*', as well as the *ümmet* of Islam, *ümmet* of *Ijabah* [the people who obey a prophet's call], of *davah* [the people invited by a prophet], etc. As ethnic groups constitute larger groups on the basis of affinity, so the *ümmet*s may constitute larger groupings. For example, the Muslim, Christian, and Jewish *ümmet*s, in Kur'anic terminology, constitute together the Abrahamic religion.

The term *halk* (people) is sometimes used [in Turkish] for *kavm* and sometimes for the citizens of a state, and at other times for the nation. For scientific purposes it is preferable to limit the use of this word so that it refers to the main bulk of a nation excluding the élite. Thus we may use the word *halkiyat* for 'folklore'.

The state is a group that has its own government, territory, and population. States may be classified into ethnic, imperial (*sultanī*), and national states. For example, the Umayyad state was an ethnic state because its organization was based on *kavm* instead of *ümmet*. The

128 TURKISH NATIONALISM AND WESTERN CIVILIZATION

population was differentiated into three castes—Arabs, *Mawālī*, and *Ahl al-dhimma*. The non-Arabs were called *Mawālī*, and though enfranchised were deprived of many rights. The *Ahl al-dhimma* were non-Muslims, and were in the lowest status from the legal point of view. The Abbasi state, on the other hand, was an imperial state. This state was founded with the assistance of the *Mawālī*, and, besides, there was a political sect called the *Shu'ūbiyah*, which proclaimed the equality of the *kavm*s. In the time of al-Ma'mūn, the *Shu'ūbi*s began to predominate over those who believed that the Arabs should constitute the basis of the state. And thus, the Arab and non-Arab Muslims acquired an equal footing and the Abbasi state became an empire on the basis of *ümmet*. The legal equality of the *Ahl al-dhimma* with the Muslims [in the Ottoman Empire] was accomplished only with the promulgation of Gülhane charter [of 1839]. It was after that that the Ottoman state became an empire on the basis of equality.

Nation-states, on the other hand, arise when these empires disintegrate. In Europe the nation-states arose only when the Roman and German empires disintegrated. However, today there is no pure nation-state except the German state. All the other states of Europe are mixtures of national and imperial forms of state. For example, the British state is a nation-state in Great Britain, but an empire-state over in Ireland and overseas. The people who constitute the nation-state in France are called citizens, whereas the people of the French empire are called subjects. During this war [World War I], the Austrian and Russian empires seem to be changing into confederations of nation-states. It seems, therefore, that the future of all states will be in the direction of nation-states. The nation is that ethnic group which, as it emerges after a long period of fusion within an empire, strives to regain and revive its identity.

A *kavm* seeks to achieve perfection by creating an ethnic religion, an ethnic state, and an ethnic civilization. But most *kavm*s have been unable to fulfil these three aims of the ethnic character. Some of them remained politically as tribes and some of them became city-states. Sometimes their religions and civilizations were confined to political units, and sometimes extended to the whole *kavm*. But *kavm*s as such rarely achieved both political and civic unity at the same time. However, it seems that there is a tendency for all *kavm*s to achieve this unity. It appears that the main obstacles in the way of this natural evolution of *kavm*s, apart from certain geographical factors, are three social

THE EVOLUTION OF SOCIETY 129

factors. These are the emergence of universal states, or universal religions, and universal civilizations. We have seen that the universal state was the imperial state. In this connection also we have seen the differences between the imperial state, on the one hand, and the ethnic and nation-states, on the other.

The universal religions which unite several ethnic groups are *ümmet* religions. Thus Christianity, Islam, and Buddhism are *ümmet*-religions. The teachings of these religions are organized into bodies or systems of jurisprudence, and apply to several societies of different ethnic origins. The ethnic religions, on the other hand, neither produce systems of jurisprudence nor apply to several ethnic communities. They apply only to a certain ethnic community or one of its segments.

The universal civilizations are those that bring several ethnic communities under their influence. The ethnic civilization, in contrast to this, is one which is peculiar only to a certain ethnic community. Its conception of the universe and humanity is confined only to the limits of itself. An ethnic community loses its own original character whenever it is subject to the effects of these three larger forces.

How can we understand the decline of the character of an ethnic community? The best guide for us in this respect is language. As soon as an ethnic community starts to lose its own language, it starts to lose its character. As the disappearance of the language is a sign of loss in ethnic character, so the revival of that language after many centuries is the best sign that that ethnic community has started to revive once again, but this time under the guise of a nation. A nation, when it shakes off the forces of a larger state, religion, or civilization starts to awaken first by reviving its language. Therefore, in studying the formation of nations we must first find out how ethnic languages disappear under the influence of the above-mentioned larger unities, and then see how they revive again. . . .

The universality of the state, religion, or civilization facilitates the assimilation of the various ethnic communities, but at the same time this universality is nòt the factor that determines which ethnic unit will assimilate the others. We can only say that, in general, the one with the strongest character assimilates those which have weaker characters. But the dominance of the stronger character is not confined only to religious, political and civil fields. Thus, the Romans were politically predominant over the Hellenes in the East; but they themselves became Hellenized, and perhaps that was due to the superiority of the Greek

130 TURKISH NATIONALISM AND WESTERN CIVILIZATION

civilization. On the other hand, the Romans were superior in civilization to the conquering Slavs in Dalmatia, but they became Slavicized under political dominance. And when the Bulgar Turks invaded the Balkans they forgot their religion, adopted the Cyrillic Christianity of the Slavs, and became Slavicized. When the Mongols of Jengiz's time adopted the civilization and religion of the Turks under Islam, they became Turkified. The Romans imposed their language upon the Gauls and Spaniards through their state, their religion, and their civilization. The Arabs Arabicized the Syrians and Egyptians, but became Persianized under the superiority of the Sassanian civilization of Iran. The Franks who conquered France adopted the Latin used there. The Varangians invaded Russia, but became Russified. The Normans became French in France and Italian in Italy. The conquering Germans imposed their language on the Baltic Slavs, and the conquering Spaniards upon the Mexicans and Peruvians. The conquering Turks were assimilated into the indigenous peoples of India, Egypt, and northern Africa.

If two ethnic communities live together and if one does not assimilate the other, it is because they have either differing religions or civilizations. We can, therefore, see in the Abbasi and Ottoman Empires that the non-Muslims were not assimilated because of the difference of religion. The Irish remained non-Anglicized because of their Catholic tradition. The Rumanian aristocracy of Transylvania became Hungarian as soon as it adopted the Catholic faith, whereas the masses who belonged to the Orthodox Church remained Rumanians in spite of all efforts on the part of Catholic Rumanians to assimilate them. The Poles maintained their identity, in spite of all attempts by the Orthodox Russians to assimilate them, because they remained Catholics. The Turkish tribes living in the province of Diyarbekir became Kurdish because both were Sunnis, while the Turkomans who were [Muslim heterodox] *Alevis* continued to be immune to Kurdification. Prior to their Islamization, the Turks had been exposed to numerous attempts at assimilation both by the Chinese in China and the Europeans in Europe, but after their adoption of Islam, their identity remained immune to assimilation in the same places. They became assimilated with the Islamic peoples. Nizam al-Mulk in his *Siyasetname* called Iranized Turks 'Turk', whereas he called 'Turkomans' those who had not accepted the Iranian civilization but maintained their older civilization. The Turkomans, thanks to their different

THE EVOLUTION OF SOCIETY

civilization, had not been Persianized in Iran. But when they came to Kurdistan, they were assimilated with the Kurds. Cities are an important factor in civilization. Since the urban population of Kurdistan is Turkish, Kurds became Turkified when they settled in the cities. Since the cities in Arabia are predominantly populated by Arabs, therefore, Turks, Kurds, etc., become Arabicized when they settled there.

We have seen how ethnic peoples lose their character together with their language. Some ethnic communities can never be reborn once they have been fused into a larger body. Since the Gauls became completely assimilated with the Latins and Franks, their language and nationality could never be resurrected. But many ethnic communities have achieved a rebirth after they had lost their character and language. In this process of rebirth, rejuvenation first appears in the language. Although the Czechs living in Austria had been assimilated to the Germans, they started a national movement with a Czech Renascence, so that the Czech language and literature, and thus the Czech nationality, were reborn. In Britain the Irish are experiencing the same rebirth. In Russia the Ukranians constitute another example. In Turkey the Karaman Greeks and many Armenians revived their languages after they had been Turkified.

Among some ethnic communities, assimilation occurs only on the level of the official and literary language, and then the rejuvenation becomes easier. The '*divan*' [court] language of the Anatolian Seljuks, for example, was Persian, but it was changed to Turkish when Mehmed Bey of Karaman took over the government. In Hungary the Magyar language was not used as a written language, as all documents referring to religious and official transactions were written in Latin until 1849. Even until recent times greetings in Latin were not uncommon. Many authors regretted the disappearance of Latin when Hungarian was revived.

We have stated already that the birth of a national language starts with the dissolution of the empire-state and the *ümmet*-religion. Thus in Germany the national language experienced a revival with Luther's Reformation. Reformation means the dissolution of the *ümmet*-religion. The revivals of national languages in Ireland, and in the land of the Czechs and the Ukrainians, started with the decline of the British, Austrian, and Russian empires. The birth of various nationalities in the Balkans similarly coincided with the breaking up of the Ottoman Empire. The beginnings of Albanian nationality started with a language revival.

132 TURKISH NATIONALISM AND WESTERN CIVILIZATION

However, the birth of a nationality may be the result of a reaction against a universal civilization. The German nationality started also as a protest against the influence of French civilization and literature. The birth of a nation means using the national language in religion, giving national expression to that religion, regaining political independence, and establishing one's own culture independently of a universal civilization.

In short, ethnic communities lose their identity in the course of history by becoming a part of a larger religious or political community and of a larger civilization, which itself is common to all ethnic units united within it. They emerge once again as nations by rescuing their character from the bonds of these three larger unities. They undergo important changes during their life in these three universal communities. It is because of this that when a nation is reborn it ceases to be the same old ethnic community. It has undergone a transformation and, hence, it cannot aim at a return to its past *in toto*.

An ethnic community during its participation in the common life of the empire-state, church-religion, and the inter-ethnic civilization experiences an evolution even when it is under subjugation. Its language undergoes a religious and civil process of selection, and it gets the chance to select the best from the various patterns with which it comes into contact. Especially the subjugated ethnic units get rid of their own aristocratic strata, thanks to the persecution dealt out by the conquerors. Because of this, they assume a more democratic character and, hence, tend to be more homogeneous nations. The Bulgarians, the Serbs, and the Greeks, for example, as soon as they had seceded from the Ottoman Empire, succeeded in achieving constitutional states better than those of the South American Spaniards. The dominant ethnic element, in spite of all the benefits it gets from assimilation, usually suffers from its own dominance because its governing class becomes cosmopolitan and remains above the masses. The Germans of Austria and the Turks of the Ottoman Empire are examples.

Ethnic society was a segmentary society composed of tribes and city-states; whereas a nation has to be a democratic society through centralization, homogeneity, and division of labour. This can only be achieved after a passage of time in common participation. Thus the *ümmet*, the empire, and common civilization are stages of evolution prior to the rise of the nation. But when nations begin to organize themselves they cannot compromise with the imperial political organ-

THE EVOLUTION OF SOCIETY 133

ization, with the *ümmet* organization, or with their common civilization. Their political organization tends to be constitutional; their laws tend to be independent of religion; and the society tends to be democratic. It also becomes necessary to achieve a modernization in religion because, if religion does not become translated into the national language, and if it is not experienced in a national life, it means that the *ümmet* life still persists. Similarly, if national culture does not disentangle itself from international civilization, it means that a national life has not been started.

One of the differences between a nation and an ethnic society is that the latter is monopolistic; it tends to monopolize religion to itself; it tends to think of humanity as co-extensive with itself; even through its cosmogony it tries to interpret the birth of the whole universe in terms of its own ethnic origin. Thus, *ümmet* is more humanistic than the ethnic societies because it does not monopolize humanity and civilization to any one ethnic community; it confines them rather to an area of religion which embraces several ethnic societies. But, in comparison with modern civilization, the *ümmet* too looks monopolistic.

Modern civilization, on the other hand, is not a monopoly of the followers of only a single religion. Modern civilization, which is based on science, may comprise nations that belong to other religions. The nations are not parts of an *ümmet*, but are units of modern civilization. Several imperial states could be the units of an *ümmet*, but the nations or modern states cannot be units of an *ümmet*. The nation is not monopolistic, like an ethnic society or an *ümmet*. For a nation considers modern civilization a whole and itself a unit of it.

The Turkish *kavm* existed before the Islamic *ümmet* and the Seljuk and Ottoman Empires. It had its own ethnic civilization before it entered into a common Iranian civilization. The Iranian civilization and the [Islamic] *ümmet* and [Ottoman] imperial organizations in which the Turks participated destroyed many of their ethnic institutions, but this participation prepared the way for the Turks to develop into a nationality. The *Tanzimat*'s failure to revive national culture and its tendency also to imitate European civilization more or less damaged the nation's feelings. But this served to sever it from the influences of the Iranian civilization and from the dominance of the spirit of the [Islamic] *ümmet* and [Ottoman] empire organizations.

Civilization is a whole that is common to various nations, and is the product of the positive sciences, their methods, and techniques. A

134 TURKISH NATIONALISM AND WESTERN CIVILIZATION

national culture, on the other hand, is the sum total of the religious, moral, and aesthetic values as well as the language peculiar to the nation. Nations tend towards homogeneity among themselves from the point of view of civilization, but towards differentiation from the point of view of culture. Thus, we can find those things which are international only in civilization, and those which are national only in culture.

WHAT IS A NATION?[5]

Turkism means furthering the ascendancy of the Turkish nation. In order to understand the nature of Turkism, therefore, we have to define the nature of the group which we call nation. Let us discuss various theories of nationality.

1. According to the racist Turkists, nation and race mean one and the same thing. The term 'race', however, is basically a term used in zoology. Animal species are classified into various types according to their anatomical characteristics. These types are called races. For example, there are different anatomic types of horses called Arab, English, or Hungarian breed. Men also used to be classified into white, black, yellow, and red races. Though it is a crude classification, it is still in use. Anthropology divides the peoples of Europe into three main races on the basis of cranial forms and of the colour of eyes and hair—as dolicho-cephalic fair, dolicho-cephalic brunette, and brachy-cephalic. No nation in Europe, however, belongs to only one of these races. In every nation there are men in varying proportions who belong to each of these. Even within the same family there may be a dolicho-cephalic fair, a dolicho-cephalic brunette, and a brachy-cephalic individual. It is true that anthropologists once believed in the existence of a relation between anatomical types and social traits. But several studies . . . have proven that anatomical traits do not have any effect whatsoever upon social characteristics, and thus this belief has been completely discarded. If racial characteristics have nothing to do with social characteristics, they have also nothing to do with nationality, which is the sum total of social characteristics. Therefore, we must look to another field to discover the meaning of nationality.

2. Ethnicist Turkists identify nationality with ethnic group (*kavm*). Ethnic group means a group of consanguines descending from the same parents and into which no foreign blood has ever been mixed. Men in ancient societies believed that they were pure, unmixed ethnic

THE EVOLUTION OF SOCIETY 135

units. But even in prehistoric times they were not ethnically pure. Events such as the taking of prisoners in wars, the capturing of women, criminals taking refuge in another society, marriages, migrations, assimilation, always led to intermixtures among peoples. French scholars, such as Camille Julien and Meillet, believe that no pure people existed even in the most ancient times. If this is so, is it not absurd to look for pure peoples in historical periods after so many ethnic intermixtures? Furthermore, from a sociological point of view men are born as asocial beings. Social consciousness is not innate. Man does not bring with him language, religion, aesthetic feeling, political, legal, or economic institutions. All these he acquires later, from society and through education. Social traits are not transmitted through biological inheritance but only through education. Therefore, ethnic purity does not play the slightest role in the formation of a nation. Although ethnic purity has never existed in any society, ancient societies did cherish ethnic ideals. This was due to religious factors, because in these societies the deity was believed to be the primordial father of the society. He was the god only of those who descended from him. He did not like foreigners to enter his shrine or to participate in the worship of his own children; and he passed judgment according to his own laws. Thus, in spite of the fact that several foreigners were absorbed in different ways, such as through adoption, the society itself was still believed to consist only of the descendants of the primordial father. We find this belief of pseudo-ethnic purity among the ancient Greek city-states, among the pre-Islamic Arabs, the ancient Turks, in short, in all societies which were in the 'city-state' (il) stage of social evolution. While it was quite normal to have such beliefs at that stage of social evolution, it is pathological to hold these same views at the stage of social evolution which we have reached to-day. In these ancient societies, social unity rested entirely on the ties of religious unity. And as religious unity was confined to the unity of kinship, social unity—in the final analysis—rested upon the sense of consanguinity. At the present-day stage of evolution, on the other hand, social solidarity rests on cultural unity. And since the means for the transmission of culture is education, culture has nothing to do with ethnic affinity.

3. The Turkists who believe in the primacy of geographical factors maintain that the nation is the totality of men who inhabit a certain geographic region. For them, there is an Iranian, a Swiss, a Belgian, a

136 TURKISH NATIONALISM AND WESTERN CIVILIZATION

British nation; whereas in Iran there are actually three nationalities—Persians, Kurds, and Turks—living together; in Switzerland again three—the Germans, the French, and the Italians. In Belgium, the Walloons, who are originally French [Celtic], and the Flemish, who are originally Germanic, live together; and in Great Britain, the Anglo-Saxon, Scottish, Welsh, and Irish nationalities live together. As these are all different from one another in language and culture, it is difficult to call these groups nations. Sometimes there are several nations within the same geographical region, and sometimes a certain nation may inhabit separate geographical regions. The Oghuz Turks, for example, are found today in Turkey, Azerbayjan, Iran, and Khwārizm. As their language and culture are the same, is it correct to call them different nations?

4. The Ottomanists believed that all peoples living within the Ottoman Empire constituted a nation. It was, however, a grave mistake on their part to believe that the peoples of an empire constituted a single nation, because within this collection of peoples there were several culturally independent nations.

5. The pan-Islamists believed that all Muslims constituted a single nation. In fact, people who belong to the same religion constitute what we call an *ümmet*. Therefore, all Muslims constitute an *ümmet*. The nation which is only a community in language and culture is something different.

6. The individualists believe that the nation of a person is merely that society to which he believes he belongs. It is true that, outwardly, people think that they are free in their choice of a particular society. In fact, men do not have this freedom and independence. . . . Every person belongs to a nation through his value judgments because he acquires all social sentiments through education, and becomes identified with his nation. . . . It is not in his hands to dissociate himself from his society. Nationality is a reality external to the individual. A man may be ignorant of his nationality, but he may discover it by inquiry and study; i.e. a nation is not a voluntary association like a political party which he may join at his own volition.

What, then, is a nation? What kind of unifying force is there that is superior to, and dominant over, racial, ethnic, geographic, political, and volitional forces? Sociology teaches us that this unifying force lies in education and culture; in other words, in the community of sentiments. Man receives his most intimate, most inner feelings through early education. As an infant he begins to be affected by the mother tongue through the lullabies to which he listens in his cradle. It is for this reason that the language we love most is our mother tongue. It is through language that we acquire our religious, moral, and aesthetic sentiments which shape our soul. We become deeply attached to the society in which we acquire these sentiments. Even when we can live in another society with better means of comfort, we prefer living in our own society with all its discomforts. . . . Our taste, our feelings, and aspirations are all inspired by the society in which we have spent our lives and in which we were educated. We hear their echoes only in that society. The obstacle that prevents us from being cut off from our own society and joined to another one is the fact that we cannot possibly erase the imprints of the education we have received in our own society.

It follows from these statements that nation is not a racial, ethnic, geographical, political, or voluntary group or association. Nation is a group composed of men and women who have gone through the same education, who have received the same acquisitions in language, religion, morality, and aesthetics. The Turkish folk express the same idea by simply saying: 'The one whose language is my language, and whose faith is my faith, is of me'. Men want to live together, not with those who carry the same blood in their veins, but with those who share the same language and the same faith. Our human personality is not our physical body but our mind and soul. If our physical excellences come from our racial traits, our moral virtues come from the society in which we are raised. . . . Thus, it is absurd to base nationality on lineage. It is only shared education and ideals which are most essential to nationality. . . .

There is one practical conclusion to be drawn from these considerations. Among us there are several citizens whose grandfathers, in the past, had come from Arab lands or from Albania. We should not, by any means, discriminate them from other citizens, as they were educated as Turks and have remained faithful to the Turkish ideals. How can we treat as aliens to our nationality those men who have shared not only the blessings but also the misfortunes of our national life? How can we deny Turkish nationality especially to those who have given great services and made great sacrifices for the cause of the Turkish nation? [There are many persons among us who, although racially not Turks, are thoroughly Turkish in culture and spirit . . .

138 TURKISH NATIONALISM AND WESTERN CIVILIZATION

who cannot identify themselves with any except Turkish nationality and do not serve any except Turkish national ideals.] Genealogy is demanded only for horses, because among animals—whose excellences are all due to hereditary characteristics and to inborn instincts—racial purity is of major importance. Among human beings, on the other hand, it is absurd to insist on lineage. If we accept the doctrine contrary to this view, we will lose many of our intellectuals and fighters. As this is not desirable, it becomes necessary to consider everyone a Turk who calls himself a Turk and to punish only those who are traitors. [To deny them Turkish nationality is an error which is due to the failure to know scientifically the nature of nation.]

VILLAGES AND THE COMMUNE

I[6]

Village and town are two important forms of community which develop naturally; they are created neither by legislation nor by administration. Administrative divisions like province, county, or district are nothing but artificial units, while families, tribes, villages, and cities are natural organisms. . . . As these natural organisms were not created by legislation, their nature also cannot be changed by it.

There are several types of village and city. The oldest type of village is the *oba*, which is a collection of tents. It is called *aul* among the Eastern and Northern Turks and *hayy* among the Arabs. The earliest village came into existence with the settlement of the *oba* in houses instead of tents. In order to determine the various types of village community, therefore, we must first see what the different types of *oba* are.

There are three such types: those based on the clan, those having a feudal structure, and those having a democratic form. By comparing these three types, we can see the difference between the various types of village community.

The first type is represented by the Arab *hayy*, which consists of a clan. The Arabic word *sammiya* (which we use for the term *clan*) derives from *sammi*, which means those named after the same name. The Arab *hayy* consists of all individuals who carry the same family name. . . . The distinguishing characteristic of the Arab *hayy* is the equality of its members. The head of the clan, who is the first among equals, is called *shaikh*. He is like the head of a family. The members

THE EVOLUTION OF SOCIETY 139

of the *sammiya* are tied to each other by the solidarity of blood revenge. The whole clan is responsible for the crime of any of its members, and to take up the revenge of any member is the sacred duty of the clan. *Diya* [blood money] is paid and received by the clan. In addition to the legal solidarity, the members are also tied by an economic solidarity. Upon the death of a member, the others are his heirs and share his properties. Thus, the Arab *hayy* is a great family.

In the feudal *oba* the conditions are different. First of all, there is a chief who is not equal to the other members. Secondly, the chief considers the *oba* the object of his exploitation. In other words, the members of the *oba* are his serfs. Thirdly, this chief is subordinated to a higher chief who, in turn, is under a still higher one. Thus, the feudal *oba* is something like a migratory feudal domain.

The democratic *oba* is unlike either the clan or the feudal *oba*. The Turkish *oba*, which belongs to this type, is a migratory community. Its families live side by side on the basis of neighbourhood. Not all of them are necessarily relatives. The head (*aksakal*, white-beard) is chosen by election. In the Arab *hayy* the *shaikh*s are the 'big in descent', while in the Turkish type the head is elected either by the people or by the chiefs of tribes or of a confederation of tribes (*beys* of *boy* or *il*). Unlike the case with the feudal chief, the *oba* is not the object of his exploitation. Legally, all members are his equals.

As we pointed out above, three types of village community—the clan-like, feudal, and democratic types—were born with the settlement of these three types of *oba*. Arab villages are based on clan organization, while Turkish villages are democratic communes. The latter were commune-like types even when they were unsettled *oba*s. But with their sedentarization, their democratic character developed more fully. The existence of that miraculous trait [of democracy] among Turkish villagers is the result of this happy situation. The commune is like a small republic. And the Turkish villages, with their mosques, schools, common pastures, woods, and harvest places, are like small, self-governing republics. Each has its own treasure-chest, getting its income from *vakf* and *avâriz* taxes. Their administration is independent of the government. It operates without any written law and through a natural folk organization. Arab villages never live without a chief and lord, whereas Turkish villages have neither. . . .

While Turkish villages in Turkey are communes, the towns, unfortunately, did not develop into communes. In Europe, on the other

140 TURKISH NATIONALISM AND WESTERN CIVILIZATION

hand, communes first developed in towns and then extended to the village communities. This failure of the Turkish towns to develop into communes is, however, not without reason. In every town there were different religious communities. Each religious community maintained itself as a religious commune through its religious endowment. Each had its own independent treasure, schools, hospitals, and charity institutions, and thus did not co-operate to produce a common urban unity. It is true that in each town there was a municipal administration instituted by law. But the maintenance of the autonomous organization of these communities prevented the towns from becoming genuine urban communes. This is the reason why in [Turkish] towns, even in Istanbul, for example, all of the public utilities of the municipality, such as water supply, fountains, hospitals, and charity institutions, were owned by *evkaf*; that is, by a religious community. Conflicts between the [Muslim] administration of *evkaf* and the [Christian] Patriarchates never ceased to exist. The same conflicts were waged in other towns between municipal administrations, on the one hand, and the *evkaf* or religious community organizations, on the other.

What can be done in order to make towns genuine cities, to create a genuine commune unity and solidarity? The only means to do this is to relegate the right to supervise . . . the administration of *vakf*, and even all religious community affairs, to municipal administrations in the towns and to county councils in the villages. . . . In democratic régimes, public affairs should be administered or controlled by the representatives of the people. . . .

II[7]

When we study the ethnic structure of our southern provinces, we find that the Turks are mostly concentrated in towns and the Kurds mostly in villages and *oba*s. . . . The villages of the southern provinces are Turkish or Kurdish, but Turkish villages are outside of the areas where feudalism exists. . . .

The basis of tribal and rural civilization is feudalism. In these provinces it has political and economic forms . . . but in both forms villages are feudal domains. Peasants are not unlike the medieval European serfs. They cannot move to another village without the permission of the lord of the village. These lords are entitled to use any of the properties of the villagers at their will. They can exact taxes and

THE EVOLUTION OF SOCIETY 141

decide on all legal matters; thus, they have even jurisdictional powers. As tribes are migrating villages, conditions there are exactly the same. Tribal chiefs have judicial functions within the tribe, and receive dues from produce, earnings, and law-suits. As the Kurds say: 'This or that chief or lord *eats* this or that district or tribe'; which means that the chiefs exploit the villages or tribes that are considered their sources of subsistence.

The area best suited to study these conditions in villages and tribes is the province of Diyarbekir. In this area there are three types of tribe: (*a*) nomadic tribes—these are not settled in villages, do not know agriculture, and live on animal herds; (*b*) semi-nomadic tribes, which are settled in villages, practise agriculture, but still engage in animal raising; (*c*) settled tribes. . . . Villages are of two types, called either 'chieftains' villages' or 'people's villages'. The latter constitute the only type which are free from feudal economic bonds; the rest are all feudal in character . . .; free persons are economically in a serf status, and are either share-croppers or field labourers. As they are indebted to the chiefs, they cannot change their villages without the permission of the chiefs. They work only on behalf of the chiefs; their lands are even claimed by them. The 'chieftains' villages' are, however, relatively freer than settled tribes. In the latter the chiefs have the right to use the properties of the villagers, to decide legal matters, and to exact taxes. The life, property, and honour of the people are in the hands of the chiefs. This is so also in nomadic and semi-nomadic tribes. To see the complete contradiction between the laws [of the state] and the actual practices, one should look at these feudal tribes of the Diyarbekir region. One will see here concretely how medieval feudal institutions are still alive in a country with a constitutional régime.

Seeing these instances of economic feudalism, we can easily explain why the Turks are concentrated in the towns. In the southern provinces freedom and equality, which the Turks have always loved, are found only in the towns where there are no chiefs, lords, or tribal leaders. Thus, following a natural instinct, the Turks have always turned to towns. Turkoman tribes which did not find the chance to settle in towns or in free villages have either been assimilated by the Kurds or have perished. . . .

142 TURKISH NATIONALISM AND WESTERN CIVILIZATION

IS TURKEY A MODERN NATION?[8]

Societies may be studied either with respect to culture or with respect to civilization, and they have been classified from the point of view of either civilization or culture. It is thus possible to ascertain to which type of civilization, and also to which cultural pattern, a certain society belongs. In order to see the position of Turkish society, therefore, we have to consider from these two points of view.

From the point of view of civilization, societies have passed through the following stages: (a) the Stone Age, in which men made their tools from stones (the foundation of civilization are tools from the use of which certain techniques develop); (b) the Bronze Age; (c) the stage of handicraft, in which tools developed from simple to complex forms; (d) the Steam Age, which was followed by the use of coal and electric energy and gave rise to the age of machine industry.

Civilization, however, represents not the real personality of a society but its acquisitions. Like learning in the life of individuals, civilization is something acquired and learned. It may be acquired even by borrowing from outside. Thus, the stage of civilization in which the society is found does not indicate to us the real objective of that society.

From the point of view of culture, societies are found in the following forms: (a) tribal societies . . .; (b) ethnic states, in which . . . the state is still based on kinship (people dependent upon the ethnic state do not yet enjoy rights of citizenship. Nobility is based on descent. The dominant ethnic group constitutes the nation in a real sense— Ancient Greek and Roman states belonged to this category); (c) imperial states, in which domination of one ethnic group disappears through fusion between several ethnic groups. The governing class is segregated from the common people and constitutes a citizen body . . . and is not based on heredity and descent, but selected through military organization or education. . . .

In the old Ottoman Empire, lords, scholars, and peasantry were differentiated even if they all belonged to the same ethnic stock. Only those who were connected with the court enjoyed prerogatives. The Ottoman system passed through two stages: in the first there were *ziamet* holders, the *sipahis*, and high government officials; in the second period arose feudal *âyans* who established their domination over certain districts, freeing themselves from the strict control of the central authority. In the later years of the Ottomans, the rulers could not rule

THE EVOLUTION OF SOCIETY 143

without the support of these feudal lords. This was feudalism. This period was followed by a régime of political equality in which the state became legislative.

There are three main points to be considered in discussing the culture of a people: social structure, religion, and language. These are the criteria indicating to which social species a society belongs.

When we look at Anatolia from the point of view of social structure, we find that neither a tribal nor a feudal organization exists there now. There are only village communities and peasantry who own their lands. Peasants are not dependent upon lords. They are under one [political] rule. That means that there is an entirely democratic social structure . . . which is also homogeneous from the point of view of ethnic composition. Each community administers its mosque and school. There exists, not a tribal solidarity, but a unity within a state. The whole nation is like a family. That means that a national solidarity exists in Turkey. . . .

As to the religious aspect of the situation, Islam is a religion which is compatible with the modern state. In Christianity there is a spiritual sovereignty, headed by popes, which is incompatible with the modern state, because this spiritual sovereignty has also a political authority. In this system, called Papalism, spiritual and temporal authorities compete with each other for independence and preponderance. . . . This led France to separate the state from the Church, to abolish the official status of religion, and thus to secularize the state. This means that Catholicism is an obstacle to the foundation of a modern state. In Eastern Christianity . . . after Peter the Great . . . political government completely overran the religious authority. This system is called Caesaro-Papism, in which religion has lost its autonomy in Russia. . .

Turkish culture, therefore, is based on a social structure which is democratic, and on a religion which is modern. This religion knows no holy synods, popes, or religious councils. In Islam, truth is that which is held by the majority. Islam is not an obstacle to the foundation of a modern state. As long as Christianity wanted people to conform to the Church on everything, religion proved to be an obstacle to the development of science and of the state in Europe.

A modern nation has to have its own language. From the point of view of culture, the Turks' own language is the language of the masses. The revival of this language will lead to the realization of a modern life. It is imperative to turn to the people.

144 TURKISH NATIONALISM AND WESTERN CIVILIZATION

Thus, we see that Turkey, from the point of view of social structure, is democratic and thus modern. From the point of view of religion, it will be modern once it is secularized. The movement towards the people will make it modern from the point of view of language. Thus, Turkey is capable of becoming a modern state.

THE TURKISH RENAISSANCE AND LITERATURE [9]

If we compare different societies with each other scientifically, we find that all societies pass through the same stages of evolution. Some thinkers do not believe in the validity of such comparisons. Yet sociology, like all other sciences which are based on the method of comparison between facts, can only be founded on such comparisons between societies and between social facts. Rejecting the method of comparison leads to the rejection of the possibility of a science of society from the beginning. It is true, however, that like all other sciences in their infancy, sociology too, in its early history, was not free from shortcomings in its application of the comparative method. Perfect classifications and definitions can be formulated only in the more developed states of a science. Thus it will be too much to expect such a perfection from a science which is still in its primitive stage.

Among human societies there have been three groups of peoples which have entered into the stage of religious civilization. These are the Christian peoples, the Muslim peoples, and the Buddhist peoples.

Since the historical evolution of the Christian peoples has been studied so far more extensively, the historical stages these peoples have passed through may be taken as a basis of comparison for the other two groups. Let us take, for example, the evolution of the Germanic peoples. We know that these peoples passed from a 'tribal' stage into an 'ethnic' stage, and then into the stage of Christian Church-religion and civilization as a third stage, which historically corresponds to what we commonly call Middle Ages. The Germans, however, following the Italians, entered a fourth stage, that of the age of Renaissance. Renaissance is that stage in which societies, finding themselves at variance with the religious morality and civilization of the Church, began to aspire to a secular art, morality, and civilization. First of all, the Italians, having experienced these aspirations, led the others in creating a new outlook in art, morality, law, and state. They turned to the pre-Christian Greek and Latin civilizations as the models of this new outlook.

THE EVOLUTION OF SOCIETY

Other European nations gradually followed the Italians and reached this stage in their historical evolution. The spirit dominating this stage was characterized by human ideals which constituted the basis of humanism, the humanities, and classical education. It was the stage of cosmopolitanism and internationalism,—in short, of humanism—through which societies pass upon the dissolution of the spirit of the Church-religion and before the coming of the era of nationality. In Europe, nationalism arose after the Reformation and Romanticism. The Renaissance, after having destroyed the literature and the arts of the Age of the Church, replaced them with the classical literature and arts which were modelled on the Greek and Latin masterpieces. This movement turned against the spirit of religiosity, then devoid of effective vitality, and unjustly extended its attacks to the still-living parts of religion. These living religious feelings, then, produced a twofold reaction both against the Renaissance and against the medieval ecclesiastical civilization. From this reaction was born the Reformation.

The Reformation, basically, was the first emergence of national consciousness in the realms of religion and morality. The societies that achieved the Reformation were the first societies to take the first steps towards national unity. Then a second reaction against Classicism followed, in which there was a revival of the ancient legends, old folk-tales, and epics which had survived from the ethnic stage and lived through oral traditions of the people. From this reaction arose the movement of thought which we call Romanticism. Romanticism was the second manifestation of national consciousness within literature and art. The economic and political unifications were later manifestations of the same thing.

We may notice that the Turks also passed through such stages. They also had their tribal and ethnic stages before they accepted Islam. We find the descriptions of these stages in the book of *Dede Korkut*.[10] When the Turks became Muslims, they entered into a new stage of civilization: they became part of the Islamic *ümmet*. Thus, they had an *ümmet* literature in place of their old ethnic literature. The Turkish literature from the time of Nevaî down to the *Tanzimat* period is the literature of the *ümmet* stage. As the literature of the European peoples before the Renaissance had a character of religiosity, so the Turkish literature of that stage had its roots either directly in religiosity (as, for example, is the case in the *Mevlid* of Süleyman Chelebi), or in *tasawwuf*, or indirectly in the reactions against this religiosity.

146 TURKISH NATIONALISM AND WESTERN CIVILIZATION

The Turkish Renaissance begins with the *Tanzimat*. I use this term to denote the movement of Westernization which had started with the Tulip Period and continued with interruptions. The Turks found the secular civilization which they wanted to introduce over against the civilization of religiosity, not in a dead past but in a living present, that is, in the West. In literature this movement, which started with Shinasi, began to show to the Turkish people a new horizon of civilization, a new *Weltanschauung*, totally different from the spirit of religiosity which had then become distorted and totally lifeless.

Yet this movement, which was continued by Namık Kemal and Abdülhak Hâmid, had not freed itself from the vestiges of the old *ümmet* world-outlook. The flavour of the *ümmet* period, through the influence of Arabic and Persian literatures, still persisted in their literature. The first radical innovator was Tevfik Fikret, who rebelled against this spirit of religiosity of the *ümmet* literature.

Tevfik Fikret was the man who completed the Turkish literary Renaissance, and who, by his unblemished, pure, and noble example, showed the Turks the new *Weltanschauung* which Western civilization represented. Turkish classical literature, which started with the *Tanzimat*, found its best expression through him.

Fuzulî, Bâkî, Nedîm were not classical poets of the Turks because they belonged to the *ümmet* period of Turkish literary history. There are not two separate classical literatures, one in the West and the other in the East. There is only one classical literature and art, which arose only in the West. European artists created Western classical literature by imitating ancient Greek and Latin writers. Turkish writers, from Shinasi to Fikret, imitated that European classical literature and created their own classical period. Namık Kemal and Abdülhak Hâmid were not romantics. They were classical writers who, however, had not been entirely freed from the *ümmet* literary traditions.

We seem thus, that the real mission of Tevfik Fikret was to bring the Turkish literary Renaissance, in language, in art, and in morality, to its completion. Fikret fulfilled his mission. If he was more humane and more of a humanist than the other representatives of the Turkish Renaissance, it was because he had genuine belief in his mission. He was the great radical who cast the final and the decisive blow to the spirit of religiosity of the *ümmet* civilization.

But, like the men of the European Renaissance, Fikret too had a mission only to put an end to the previous stage. As the men of the

THE EVOLUTION OF SOCIETY 147

European Renaissance could not start the age of Nationality, so too he could not do it here. But as it was in the West, so it was in Turkey, that if there had not been a Renaissance to give a decisive blow to the *ümmet* spirit, there could not have been a turning towards a Reformation, a Romanticism, and towards the rise of the nationalistic spirit in their genuine forms. In between two positives there should be a negative!

Fikret was the genius who fulfilled his role by secularizing and humanizing Turkish literature. As the basis of classical education in Europe is the classical literature, in Turkey too the basis of classical education will be the classic works of its writers from Shinasi to Fikret. As to Turkish Romanticism, this could only rise from Turkish nationalism because Romanticism means the expression of the national spirit in literature.

CHAPTER VI

SOCIAL VALUES AND INSTITUTIONS

VALUE JUDGMENTS[1]

OUR statements about things are of two kinds: they are statements either of facts or of values. When we say 'sugar is sweet' or 'the orange is round', we express judgments about the properties of sugar and the orange. When we say, 'a father is respectable', 'home is dear', 'the flag is sacred', we express judgments about the values attached to father, home, or flag.

Properties are intrinsic to the nature of the things. Sweetness or roundness are inherent in the nature of sugar and the orange. Therefore, the validity of a statement of fact depends upon its correspondence to an external object in space, or in other words to a material reality. Value, on the other hand, reflects the emphasis society places on certain things which do not intrinsically have the properties implied in the value judgments. The family believes in the respectability of the father, the nation in the sacredness of the soil or of the flag. Therefore, the validity of a value judgment is not determined by its correspondence to a physical object in the external world, but by its correspondence to a social reality which exists in the minds of people. In other words, what the value judgment refers to is found, not in the nature of things but in the beliefs of society.

However, we may only conclude from these statements that value judgments do not reflect a physical reality. The beliefs which are referents of these judgments are as much external facts as they are mental ones. The beliefs are mental facts in relation to society, but external facts in relation to the individual. This external reality is called social reality and has its own nature.

As individuals are reared under the training of society, they participate in the social-beliefs in most cases unconsciously. In the course of this participation, individuals feel only vaguely that their beliefs correspond to an external reality which is outside and independent of themselves. Failing to realize that this external reality is nothing but

SOCIAL VALUES AND INSTITUTIONS 149

the beliefs of society, they tend to take it as a metaphysical or a mysterious thing. When this act of participation ceases to exist, individuals clearly perceive the existence of an external reality in the form of social beliefs because when they reject and deny the values based on social beliefs, they meet with the moral reaction of society or physical punishment, and thus actually experience its existence.

Individuals derive certain judgments of fact from the physical nature of things; similarly, they derive certain value judgments from the social nature of institutions or practices of society. Just as judgments of fact reflect an external reality, so do value judgments. As individuals by themselves cannot create the properties of things, so they cannot invent the values of the things. As properties originate from the physical nature, so values are natural products of social reality. Individuals discover properties or values, but cannot create them. Men who discover the laws of nature can control natural forces; those who learn the laws of society can regulate and lead social forces. The effectiveness of men over society is similar to their control over nature. The second is possible only with knowledge about nature, the first with that about society. Institutions which make up a society are based on numerous values deriving from social beliefs. These values are classified into religious, legal, economic, aesthetic, or linguistic values. None of them derives either from the nature of physical reality or from the nature of man; all are born from the beliefs of society and are living in the social consciousness. As societies are found in different species and genera, value systems differ with the societies of the various species and genera. . . .

MORAL VALUES AND SOCIETY[2]

Morality consists of certain rules that are distinguished by two characteristics: they are obligatory and they are desirable.

The obligatory character of the moral rules is manifested by the social sanctions they carry. When we do not observe moral rules, public opinion condemns us; or when we observe them, it approves our action. The existence of this sanctioning power is an indication of the fact that moral rules are not products of our instincts. It is the society that proposes them to us. Moral rules not only are not derived from the instincts, but also they are even antithetical to them Moral rules have an external power of constraint upon us just because of their opposition to our instincts. Actions, such as eating, drinking, sleeping, fear, or anger, are instinctive and, thus, they do not need an external sanctioning power. Moral rules need such external sanctions because they tend to suppress or inhibit instincts and to further and encourage actions contrary to them. Therefore, morality is not, in origin, individual but social.

Moral rules, although they are obligatory and supported by sanctions, are observed in most cases without a conscious awareness of their character of constraint because of their desirability to ourselves. A virtuous person in most cases does not think of the approval or disapproval of public opinion; he is virtuous for the sake of virtue. However, again our inclination and attraction to moral rules do not imply that they are products of our instincts because this moral attraction may be seen only among socialized individuals. However, men have to exercise a great effort in order to conform to these rules. Being socialized implies the existence of a social consciousness as opposed to our individual instincts. Therefore, that which shows the attraction towards moral rules is not our instinctive life but our social consciousness. It is the society to which we belong which becomes interiorized in our soul and makes us attracted by moral rules. From the day we begin to experience social life, we have not only a physical organism but also acquire a personality made up of our organism plus a social consciousness. Our organic make-up is dependent upon instincts, while our social consciousness leads us towards moral behaviour. It appears, thus, that morality is social and not individual in origin.

The first of these two characteristics of moral rules is called duty, and the second goodness. The sense of duty is the manifestation of moral rules in the form of obligation, and the sense of the good their manifestation in the form of desirability. Among the moral philosophers, Kant emphasized the elements of duty in morality, while Guyeau emphasized goodness. The latter tried to establish a morality without obligation and sanction, on the basis of 'goodness for goodness' sake'. For Kant the basis of morality is 'duty for duty's sake'. In fact, moral rules create in us both the sense of duty and the sense of the good. Perfectly socialized individuals view the good as moral without obligation and sanction, because they are fascinated and enraptured by it with all their hearts; while those who are not socialized always feel the existence of the sanctioning powers behind the moral rules.

The consciousness of the society to which we belong shows us which rules are to be taken as duty and which as good. We cannot determine moral rules by our individual consciousness or reason. It is the social consciousness which distinguishes and determines moral values. If so, then there are types of morality because there are types of society. The morality of a certain social type is normal only for that type; others are pathological for it. In the realm of living organisms we find the same thing. For example, breathing through gills is normal for fish but not for mammals, just as the latter's breathing through lungs is not normal for the fish. Likewise, the institution of *vendetta* is normal in a tribal society while being pathological in nations.

The foregoing analysis shows that society is the source of the moral rules and that it is the factor which determines moral values. Let us inquire now into the aims of the moral rules.

Moral rules refer to certain actions which are opposed to our individual desires or instincts. Therefore, they imply certain sacrifices on the part of individuals. Every moral rule demands a sacrifice from one of our desires. The aim of morality is not the self, as it requires certain sacrifices from the physical side of human beings. Anything which is sacrificed cannot be the object of the sacrifice; the object of the sacrifice has to be something different from that which is sacrificed. This object can neither be the material aspect of the individual nor that of other persons, as there is no difference between the two. The thing for which the sacrifice is made must be superior to that which is being sacrificed. Only the inferior can be sacrificed for the superior and only the superior can be an aim for the inferior. If the self cannot be the aim of itself, another self also cannot be an aim for it. Therefore, if the individual cannot be the aim of morality, and as there is no being inferior to individuality, only something which is superior to it can be the object of morality. And this being which is superior to individuality is nothing but society. Society has its own consciousness from which the individual derives his superior qualities or his moral being. Prior to social life, human beings were no different from animal beings. That which gives them human qualities is the culture which society provides. Elements of culture, such as language, knowledge, religion, morality, and aesthetic standards, originate in general in society and create higher faculties in men. Therefore, the object of morality is society which is nothing but supra-individual. Moral sacrifices of the person are for the sake of society.

152 TURKISH NATIONALISM AND WESTERN CIVILIZATION

Against this view which restricts the ultimacy of morality to society, it will be said that there are certain moral duties with regard to our own selves. It is true that there are certain moral duties for our own selves as well as for others. But this self is not our physical, organic self. We do duty to our own selves when we forsake our organic desires and interests for the sake of our moral elevation, which is nothing but an effort to be more fully socialized. Therefore, the basis of the duties towards the self is sacrificing individuality for society. That which is the object of morality is not the 'individual' but the 'social'. As a matter of fact, the word 'personality' does not mean individuality, but signifies 'society' as it exists in the individual. Culture, being the sum total of the precipitations [of society] in individual souls, is not individual but social.

The personalities of others are moral objects for me because they are parts of the social culture. Individuals become moral objects because, and in so far as, they are socialized. This relativity shows that individuals are objects of morality not by themselves but in relation to society. The reason why criminals cease to be objects of morality is that they are asocial, and the perfection great men attain is due to their high degree of socialization through their personifying society in themselves.

If the object of morality is society, the nature of ideals becomes clarified. Ideals imply something for which we believe it is worth sacrificing our lives and the object of morality implies the same meaning. Thus, an ideal is nothing but society or an intensive experiencing of social life.

MORES[3]

In order to understand what *mores* (*'urf*) are, let us first see what they are not. . . . *Mores* are generally mistaken for customs [Turkish *âdet*, Arabic *'ādat*]. There is a partial general-particular relationship between these two terms. In other words, some customs are *mores* and some *mores* are customs; but not all customs are *mores* and not all *mores* are customs.

A custom is a social rule coming from predecessors. It is something different from individual habit. Customs are not individual but are social, and they are socially transmitted from generation to generation. A newly invented social rule is not a custom; it is an innovation (*bid'a*). Customs are always transmitted to the present generation from previ-

SOCIAL VALUES AND INSTITUTIONS 153

ous generations. This transmission takes place, not through biological inheritance but through social inheritance or education.

Customs are not *mores* because there are both accepted and rejected customs. Rejected customs are also socially transmitted simply because they were approved customs in previous generations. Any action which had not, at least once, won the acceptance of the public cannot become transmitted socially, and thus cannot be a custom. But a rule accepted by the public in past generations may become a rejected custom in the new generation. In other words, it is natural that there are both approved and rejected customs. There can never be rejected *mores*. *Mores* are those rules which are accepted by the whole community. Thus, generally approved customs remain within the *mores*, but rejected customs are outside of the *mores*. Therefore not all customs are *mores*.

Let us see now how all *mores* are not always customs. Innovations, like customs, are either approved or rejected by the community. An innovation is something which is not transmitted from preceding generations. It is something originated in a new generation. I do not call it social because it is not yet accepted by the whole community. An innovation rejected by the community is not social, it is only individual. In other words, it is a social rule in another community which has now been introduced into the community in question by certain individuals. Therefore, social innovations—that is, innovations that have become accepted by the community—are added into the *mores*, but individual innovations—that is, those that are not yet accepted by the whole community—are outside of the *mores*. The general acceptance of the *mores* by a community is an essential condition. Accepted customs and accepted innovations which fulfil this condition become incorporated into the *mores*; rejected customs and innovations which fail to fulfil this condition remain excluded from the *mores*.

The term *mores*, however, does not simply mean 'rules accepted by the community'. It also implies the faculty of distinguishing the values of accepted and rejected rules. Rules of conduct accepted through this faculty are *ma'rūf* (approved, 'moral'[4]) and those rejected are *munkar* (rejected). The first consists of those rules which are approved, and the second of those which are disapproved, by the community. Thus, the term *mores* means both social rules of conduct and the social conscience (*vicdan*).

How do we distinguish *mores* from individual actions? To be a

154 TURKISH NATIONALISM AND WESTERN CIVILIZATION

social norm, a rule should be above the biological nature of man as well as of his [individual] volition. Actions springing from the biological nature of man are not social actions. Actions done instinctively are transmitted through biological inheritance. These are biological but not social phenomena. Actions which we do of our own will, actions which we are free to choose, are not social but psychological actions. Social actions exist outside of biological nature because just as life is qualitatively different from the chemical elements which make it up, so the community has a special quality which cannot be reduced to biological nature. Community is not a numerical sum total of individuals, but has a reality *sui generis*, a product of the interaction of individual psyches. Social reality has its own nature distinct from biological nature. As life is something more than the elements constituting it (none of them—such as hydrogen, oxygen, nitrogen, carbon —has a trace of life), so what we call social reality is above organic nature. Therefore, the representations and judgments of this new level of mind which is above the individual minds and the rules which they imply must also be above the individual level.

Social norms are above individual wills. The will of the individual is a product of his temperament and character. As each individual has temperament and character different from that of other individuals, actions emanating from individual wills are not of a uniform nature, and thus they cannot be rules for others. Even when, under certain conditions, these actions show certain accidental similarities, still they are not norms. A rule means an action whose execution is necessary or obligatory. A mere accidental similarity between certain actions does not imply identity in obligatory character.

If social rules or *mores* are outside the plane of biological nature and are above the individual wills, they have to make themselves acceptable either through coercion or attraction. When we study accepted customs and approved innovations, we see that they really have these two qualities. They maintain their existence and win general acceptance and currency either through their coercive power of punishment, or through their attraction by their power of gaining deference. The first quality we call the sanctioning power and the second the prestige power of the *mores*.

Whenever we fail to observe a social rule, expressed as an accepted custom or as an approved innovation, we encounter ridicule or reproach or condemnation from the people. This reaction of public

SOCIAL VALUES AND INSTITUTIONS

opinion is a social punishment in fear of which we observe many of the positive or negative rules. However, observing these rules is not always due to the anticipation of a social punishment or to the fear of this social power. They are followed also because they are liked by most people; they attract them by their prestige power. We do not need to be afraid of a law of which we approve. Only those who do not like it are afraid of it.

Thus, *mores* impose themselves through the love they inspire and through the fear they cast. The first is the quality of *jamāl* (beauty), and the second the quality of *jalāl* (majesty) of *mores*, so to speak. Once these qualities of the *mores* are clarified, it will be easily understood that acts which are approved (*ma'rūf*, 'moral') are those which we like to do as well as have to do. They are both desired and obligatory, as well as possible. Their obligatory character makes them more easily distinguishable from individual actions. Some people think that their own opinions are social rules, and even claim sanctioning and prestige powers for them. The easiest way to test such claims is to invite such persons to do in front of the public what they claim as social rules. If they fail, it means that what they wanted to impose were not social rules. A social action is one which is practicable and, when practised, approvable. There is a sanctioning power favourable to social action which facilitates its execution, whereas an impracticable action faces sanctions contrary to itself, and thus it can never become a social rule. Actions actually practised are done mostly either instinctively or consciously, or by following the customs of the community or by imitating the customs of other communities. Thus, every action practised in a community is not necessarily a part of the *mores*. *Mores* contain only those which have the above-mentioned qualities.

Mores are certain ideal rules proposed by the conscience of community-ideals which individuals aspire to reach with great enthusiasms but never do reach fully. Community, through its sanctioning power and prestige, always drives individuals towards this social sublimity ['*illiyyīn*, the name of the highest of the eight paradises mentioned in the Kur'an]. But as the feet of men are in the animal nature, men cannot elevate themselves above this 'biological inferior'. Only their ideas reach social sublimity. It was because of this difference between *mores* and individual behaviour that certain thinkers like Max Nordau called the *mores* 'social lies'. Max Nordau is wrong in his opinion because the conscience of community is very sincere in its proposals of rules of conduct for its members, and individuals, too, are motivated by a sincere desire and aspiration to reach these ideals. The alleged lie is due to the gap existing between biological nature and social nature. As life fails to conquer matter and does not produce intelligence in every organism, so society, too, fails to inspire its charismatic power in every individual and to make everyone a virtuous person. There is a great distance between bestiality and virtue. A Persian poet said: 'My hand is short whereas the date is on the palm-tree'. Imam 'Ali expressed the view that this is not a shortcoming for men when he said: 'The value of a man lies in his strivings after a goal'. It was because individual actions are always separated from the *mores* by a wide gap that the Kur'an enjoins commanding the *ma'rūf* and forbidding the *munkar*. If all actions practised in general were *ma'rūf* and those not observed at all were *munkar*, believers would not be invited to fight (*mujāhada*) to confirm the *ma'rūf* and reject the *munkar*.

It follows that we have to discover the *'urf*, not in the actions expressed in a community but in the rules which are believed in with a social faith and loved with a social love. Current actions approach these rules more or less, and in this they are always under the pressure of the powers of sanctioning and prestige of the social rules, but never completely reach them. The reason why social rules have an ideal character is simply that fundamentally they spring from the social conscience.

MANIFESTATIONS OF THE NATIONAL ETHOS[5]

I

One of the problems for which sociology is trying to give an explanation is the question of the way in which great men arise in the evolution of society and the part they play in this evolution. Are the men we call 'great men' the products of the concomitance of certain social factors or are they the products of a mysterious *élan vital*?

We must first of all discuss the last question because, while the view which believes that great men are products of social evolution does not invalidate the principle of social causation, the idea that great men are born out of an impulse of the organism implies that society is determined by external mysterious forces is governed by indeterminism. We must, therefore, first discuss the way in which great men originate before we discuss their role in history.

SOCIAL VALUES AND INSTITUTIONS 157

It must be borne in mind that there is more than one type of great man. The rise of each type may be different from that of the others. In my opinion, these exceptional men may be classified into two main groups: the reformer and the inventor. The reformer (messenger of a religion, a conqueror, a great revolutionary leader, a hero) is characterized by a strong faith and intense will powerful enough to initiate new movements in history. The inventor, on the other hand, is the man who has achieved great strides in the progress of a branch of learning and civilization by an invention or discovery.

The existence of these two types corresponds to the existence of the two types of social solidarity. The two prerequisites of human society are the existence of like sentiments on the one hand, and of the division of labour on the other. The first gives rise to the first kind of solidarity which is based on the likeness of feelings. The second type of solidarity is based on differentiation of works. The intensification of the first type of solidarity gives rise to the reformer, while increasing division of labour leads to the rise of the inventor.

Among the primitives, division of labour hardly exists. Since every community is divided into several interlocking segments such as clan, age-group, phratry, there are no common sentiments shared by the whole. The community has common language, but common sentiments are found only within the special confines of clans or phratries. For the rise of common sentiments within the community as a whole, this segmentary organization must disintegrate. In other words, clans or phratries must disappear. The existence of these special units are obstacles to the rise of a common unity. Among the primitive peoples, the clans are subdivided into smaller groups as they grow because the clan is a family sharing a common life. The growth of a family may continue to a certain limit until it breaks into more than one group. As the phratry grows, it provides a better security against external attacks. Therefore, as the clan, on the one side, is divided into smaller units in accordance with the rule, the phratry, on the other side, tends to grow through propagation or through the assimilation of conquered peoples. As this social expansion continues, it finally gives rise to the confederations of the phratries. If the community lives in a mountainous or desert region, it cannot grow beyond these limits. If it is settled in the plains with rivers or with sea-shores, it settles as a village or as a town, and finally ceases to need any organization of clans and phratries. The main reason for this decisive dissolving in-

158 TURKISH NATIONALISM AND WESTERN CIVILIZATION

fluence of the city over the older organization is the division of labour.

It is with the dissolution of the segmentary organization under certain social factors that the sentiments common to the whole come into existence. It is with the rise of the collective conscience, which is the expression of these common sentiments, that the people begin to feel their existence as a unity, and recognize the authority of one or several chiefs as representatives of the collective conscience. However, even the rise of common sentiments is not sufficient to explain the rise of the reformer. For the rise of such men an extraordinary event, such as a calamity or a great victory or a crisis, should take place in the life of the community. The community does realize its own collective sentiments as the expression of its unified existence only when such critical moments arise. Among the Arabs, for example, certain institutions common to the greater part of the people—such as the market-place of *'Ukaẓ*, the month of taboos (*shehr-i harâm*), and pilgrimage (*hajj*)—had existed long before the so-called Elephant Incident. But, as Jurji Zaydan pointed out (*Medeniyet-i Islâmiye Tarihi*, Turkish trans., I, pp. 24, 25), neither great men of warfare nor orators appeared among them until this event. As the attack made by an enemy—entirely foreign to Arabs both ethnically and religiously—on the *Ka'ba*, the common symbol of the 'sacred' to all Arabs, meant the greatest of national calamities, it gave rise to a sudden burst of collective consciousness and to a clear realization of national unity. Thus, following the Elephant Incident, we see the rise of a series of great warriors, orators, the *ḥanīf*s, and the poets of the *mu'allaqāt*. When we study the history of other peoples, we find the same thing: the rise of the collective feelings following the dissolution of the segmentary organization of society, and later, when a national event ignites the collective consciousness, the rise of the reformer.

The reformer, then, is a precursor who in his own soul experiences in a most distinct and intensified manner the trends of unification and rejuvenation already begun among the people. In the field of individual psychology, an unconscious state remains ineffective till it rises to the conscious level to gain a tremendous effectiveness. The same is true in social psychology. When the urge towards unity, remaining unconscious in society, suddenly becomes expressed by a certain individual and becomes consciously felt, the movement invades all souls quickly. And once the consciousness of the people develops, it does not disappear again. It follows, then, that the reformer plays the role of cons-

SOCIAL VALUES AND INSTITUTIONS 159

ciousness in the trends towards nationhood already begun in a people.

This process of rising into the consciousness, however, takes place in most cases in a symbolic manner. The reformer comes forward as a fighter (*mujāhid*) for the cause of a religious truth or humanitarian love or political justice and freedom or as a world conqueror, while in reality he is just a symbol of a national effervescence and remains unaware of this. The recent movement of nationalism in Turkey had expressed itself under strange substitutions, such as the symbols of *Tanʒimat*, *Meşrutiyet*, Fraternity [between religions], and Pan-Islamic symbols. Our reformers and heroic leaders came along to the field of fighting with such symbols in their hands.

This discussion on the origin of the reformer shows that this type of great man is the product and the symbol of the awakening of the common national sentiments already existing in the unconscious. Let us see the case in relation to the inventor, and let us first trace the origin and the growth of the division of labour in society.

The division of labour among primitive peoples is found only within the confines of the clans. In the matriarchal clans the bridegroom, for example, is in the position of a worker. In the patriarchal family the women, children, and the slaves have to do the work ordered by the head of the family. Within these two social types, the superiority of the uterine heirs in the first case, or of the paterfamilias and agnatic heirs in the second, is the expression of the value attached by the clan religion to the maternal or to the paternal descent. The belief in the taboo forbidding certain things to be done by family heads or by certain classes is also a factor in the division of labour based on religion. This kind of division of labour based on religious beliefs makes the phratry, among some peoples, confined to certain exclusive crafts, and thus reduces them to castes, the members of which are forbidden to marry or eat with members of other castes.*

The division of labour begins only with the rise of urban centres, with its far-reaching consequences. We have already seen that, as common sentiments begin to function, 'public authority' emerges as represented by a chief or chiefs. With the rise of public authority emerges what we call a city-state. When the city-state ceases to be a

* There is a contradiction, from the point of view of marriage, between a maternal clan and the caste. As the individuals within a maternal clan are taboo to each other, they are exogamous; while in the second they are endogamous, as the members of the other castes are not their equals. This is discussed in detail by Durkheim in his essay on 'La prohibition de l'inceste et ses origines' [see *l'Année Sociologique*, I (1898), 1–70].

160 TURKISH NATIONALISM AND WESTERN CIVILIZATION

cluster of migrating families (*oba*) or scattered villages, and settles around a sacred place as the symbol of the new sentiments, a real urban centre comes into existence. The urban centre could not come into existence as long as common sentiments of clan or of phratry, and their respective religious beliefs and authorities, continue to exist. When a religion and a public authority common to the greatest portion of the community come into existence, the urban centre becomes organized around a sacred place and a citadel. Common sentiments lead people to be close to each other and to sacred symbols. The resultant situation is the settlement of a great mass of people in a relatively small area, i.e. an urban centre. The urban centre means an agglomeration of hundreds of villages clustered within the same walls. When they were in a scattered form over a large area, they could get their subsistence merely through animal breeding and agriculture. When they are placed into the smaller area of an urban centre, the same population cannot be fed by the lands surrounding the urban centre. Darwin's principle of the struggle for existence operates because, as this great naturalist has shown, the more the area narrows down and the more the food becomes scarce, the more intense becomes competition between organisms of the same species. . . . As long as the inhabitants of a city practise the same occupations, they become competitors to each other. With division of labour, the competition subsides. Thus, there is one way to get rid of the intense competition produced by social density, and that is through the invention of new occupations. Division of labour, therefore, is produced mechanically by social factors. Urban life forces people to invent and improve new trades. With increasing specialization in each trade, men acquire a better command over their work, and hence there arises professional solidarity, in addition to social solidarity. The rise of professional values leads to the completion of the disintegration of the older tribal values, and causes the collective consciousness to decrease in quantity but to become more human in quality. With the progress of the division of labour, the segmentary organization disappears altogether. As the tribal organization disappears, foreigners from outside join the society. With the domination of one urban centre over others, the ethnic state emerges. The dominating one, having become the capital centre, the seat of government, grows more quickly and leads to further differentiation of occupations. The pressures put by the needs of new trades and new inventions become more conscious. Each inventor finds at his

SOCIAL VALUES AND INSTITUTIONS

disposal previous inventions as an accumulated capital and synthesizes them into new ones.

It follows, then, that . . . the rise of the inventor is a product of the division of labour. Like the reformer, the inventor too is, at first, the product of social evolution and then a factor of it. Just as it is the innovation itself which makes the reformer and not the reformer which makes the innovation, so the force which creates the inventor is the need felt by the social conscience and pre-existing conditions. In the absence of preceding conditions and the need created by social competition, no inventor ever arises. These conditions and needs are the creations of urban centres, and especially of the capital centres. It should be borne in mind also that division of labour exists only among the members of a group having collective sentiments. The specialist is not merely a supplement to another specialist, but also a special organ and thus an integral part of a nation. The differentiation of work and the exchange taking place between different nations, therefore, are not of the same nature with social division of labour. Durkheim calls it 'mutual parasitism' [symbiosis]. It is because of this fact that in certain cities division of labour does not develop and does not give rise to the inventor. Real urban centres are those which have at their hearts a 'city' as the spirit of the urban body, so to speak. Thus urban centres, such as those found in India, where the urban population is made up of castes among whom a civil unity does not exist, or those found in Turkey consisting of communities having no national unity, can only be called conglomerations of villages. Naturally, there can be no social division of labour and no inventions under such conditions.

II

In order to distinguish social from psychological facts, we have to differentiate the meanings of 'conscience' and of 'consciousness'. In French, both meanings are expressed by *conscience*, but this is used in psychology in the first sense and in sociology in the second. As the words we use for them in Turkish [*vicdan* for conscience and *şuur* for consciousness] are different, we are in a better position to express social ideals.[6]

Consciousness means perception of sensations, through our senses, of pains or pleasures within our organism, or of qualities outside of us, such as colour, smell, sound, taste, warmth, cold, etc. This faculty, which is also shared by animals, is of an individual and organic nature.

162 TURKISH NATIONALISM AND WESTERN CIVILIZATION

Conscience, on the other hand, is the faculty which perceives, not material qualities but values which are spiritual. Acceptance of an object as sacred implies a religious value. Acceptance of an object as good implies an ethical value. Acceptance of something as glorious implies a political value. To take something as a matter of justice implies a legal value. Our judgment on the eloquence of a word implies linguistic values. If something is regarded as beautiful, an aesthetic value is implied. The price of an object implies an economic value. Exactitude of an idea implies a logical value. Conscience means the state of expressing these values within ourselves.

If we examine values more carefully, we shall see that they are not immanent qualities emanating from the nature of the things-in-themselves. Values are certain qualities attached to and superimposed on their objects. Using Kant's terminology, we may call them transcendental qualities. Kant had perceived the existence of a reality above individuals which was imperative, but he had failed to see that it was social reality and called it transcendental reality. Modern sociology confirms Kant's views by substituting 'social' for 'transcendental'.

Values, of whatever kind they may be, are basically subjective and not objective. This subjectivity, however, is with respect to society and not to the individual. The individual experiences values as external reality, independent of his feelings and desires. He is always under the impact of values. When the individual comes into this world, he does not bring with him any innate idea about values. He acquires them through education and from his social environment. Society, however, does not acquire values from any source outside itself. The only source of values is the society itself. In fact, the real essence of society is nothing but the sum total of values. Whenever an emotional crowd situation arises by the gathering of individuals, the immediate result is the creation of a feeling of value. Common sentiments arising out of interaction within the crowd are nothing but sentimental attachments to the objects regarded as sacred or glorious or good, etc. Thus, values are social institutions, external to the individual but internal to the society. Conscience is the internalization of these external values by the individual minds.*

* For further discussion see my articles 'On Good and Bad', '*Mores*', 'Value Judgments' in *Islam Mecmuası* [Nos. 8, 10 (these two translated in this volume), 17, respectively, Istanbul, 1917], and É. Durkheim, 'Jugements des valeurs et jugements des réalités' [reprinted in *Sociologie et Philosophie*, Paris, 1924. English translation, *Sociology and Philosophy*, translated by D. F. Pocock, Cohen & West Ltd., 1953, pp. 80–97].

SOCIAL VALUES AND INSTITUTIONS 163

In societies where collective sentiments exist but social division of labour have not yet developed, social values are common to all the members of the collectivity. The experience of these sentiments by individuals constitute collective conscience. In societies that have developed a division of labour, a professional conscience develops in each field of occupation, in addition to the collective conscience. In such societies collective conscience has two contents. In the beginnings both the collective and the professional consciences are experienced by individuals at an unconscious level. This unconscious sharing of collective conscience, which is concomitant with the changes in social structure, is suddenly made the focus of attention of individuals by an exceptional man. The individual who is instrumental in bringing the unconsciously felt trends into a clear state of perception is the Great Man. The one who symbolizes a cultural trend of the collective conscience is the reformer, and the one who represents a trend in civilization in the professional conscience is the inventor.

We see, therefore, that as there is an individual consciousness, there is also a kind of consciousness of the nations. So long as national conscience is experienced by individuals, but only at an unconscious level and not in a distinct form, it is far from being a 'national consciousness'. Sometimes even a reformer mistakes the national ethos for a religious or political ideal, a case in which we can only speak of the existence of an *ümmet* consciousness. Namık Kemal, for example, represented national consciousness as an *ümmet* consciousness and as a state consciousness, but not as a national consciousness. National consciousness awakens only with the birth of national ideals in a distinct form. In certain individuals it may exist, seemingly but not really, because they do not experience collective conscience or national values in their souls, and thus their experiences of national consciousness are more intellectual and imitative than emotional and sincere. Great men, although they are the consciousness of social trends, do not calculate in most cases what they are doing in a conscious fashion or do not act with a reflective will or with a critical method. . . . They are in a way the mediums of social conscience. . . . Nations are in a state of absent-mindedness under normal conditions. Under such conditions, social trends are experienced unconsciously and are not intensified. When a social trend develops into a conscious state in certain individuals, it assumes a thousand-fold intensity. The nation, evolving in a gradual manner, suddenly undergoes an instantaneous and intensive trans-

164 TURKISH NATIONALISM AND WESTERN CIVILIZATION

formation. It drives forward with an historical jump and puts an end to what Nietzsche called 'social rumination'. They are the moments of revolution of a religious, political, and moral nature.

The fact that men who are mediums of social conscience seem to be moved by an external inspiration, is another factor which enhances great men's social effectiveness. Great men constitute the creative imagination of nations and, as such, they are devoid of a reflective will and analytical method. This inspired form of creative intelligence is called 'genius'. It is this absent-minded genius who awakens the nations from their absent-mindedness and makes them achieve historic drives. It should be borne in mind, however, that just as their inspirations do come from the collective conscience, men of genius do appear only at the inspired moments of ingenious nations. The man of genius is a person who, beyond his will, makes his own soul a reflecting surface to the ingenious power concealed in the nation. The coming of a genius requires also certain organic preconditions besides social ones. Every person does not have the capacity to become a social medium. Social conditions, thus, are necessary but not sufficient causes for the rise of great men. . . . For the advancement of a nation, men of genius are not necessarily required. Because, besides the inspired imagination of a nation, there is also an analytic and critical mind which is expressed by its men of learning.

III

It is seen, therefore, that sociology does not deny the influence of the individual over society, as some erroneously claim, but as Durkheim said, it explains the nature of this influence. The influence of the individual is exercised through men either of genius or of reason. Genius is the spontaneous realization of the changes taking place in society unconsciously, which can be carried out, however, also through reason and science [of society]. . . . Genius is not acquired but is inborn, while any person may become a student of society. Not every nation produces men of genius, and this is not something to be ashamed of. But nations having no sociologists fail to plan their course of action. Furthermore, as we have shown, men of genius arise in most cases in a homogeneous social milieu. In a heterogeneous milieu the order and the progress of society is the art of [the experts of] sociology.

In order to understand the role of sociology, we must first distinguish it from ideologies. An ideologist is a utopian who fails to see that nature is an ordered system governed by uniform laws, and thinks that he can impose over nature whatever he likes. The utopian once had [cf., *supra*, 'New Life and Values'] tried to control physical nature by magic, alchemy, and astrology, or to control biological nature by charms or incantations or witchcraft. When the lights of science dispersed these myths, the only field remaining for him in which to play freely was the realm of social nature, which had so far remained unknown. The same men still believe that society is something to be shaped through legislation and instruction in any form they like. . . . But no legislation can make institutions of those practices which are rejected by social conscience; no instruction can make beliefs of those ideas which are rejected by social conscience. Institutions and beliefs constitute an independent spiritual reality, the social reality of the sociologist, which has its existence in the conscience of the nation above the desires and wishes of individuals. The laws governing this reality cannot be imposed; they may only be discovered. To influence this reality one has to discover its laws and obey them. . . . The sociologist may influence the evolution of society only by knowing its laws and obeying them. . . . His function is not to impose and institute, but to discover the elements of national conscience in the unconscious level and to bring them up to the conscious level; in other words, to bring them on to the written page. Science has to assume the same attitude towards the social nature as it has taken towards physical and biological nature. . . . The social thinker must forget ideologies. From now on he must listen to the nation which is crying 'ideals are nothing but my tendencies; values are nothing but my sentiments; language, morality, law, art, in short, everything, is in me; don't try to invent them by yourself, but try to discover them in me. Progress means going down deeper into me. I am your conscience and you be my consciousness. Seek me so that I may disclose myself to you.'

IV

How to study nations? How to discover the national ethos? This, the objective method of sociology will tell us. It is the duty, especially of the Turkish thinker, to make national researches in accordance with these methods, because it is the Turkish nation whose institutions found in its life are in greatest opposition to the institutions found in its books, due to the fact that the Turks have lived everywhere mixed

166 TURKISH NATIONALISM AND WESTERN CIVILIZATION

with other nationalities. The Turkish sociologist should discover, on the one hand, the stage in which the Turkish people stand in the social evolution, and discuss such questions as the spheres of civilization to which it belongs, the differences that exist between these civilizations and Turkish culture. On the other hand, he should study the laws governing the order and the progress of societies and, by doing this, he should try to ameliorate, in terms of these laws, the pathological factors which have arrested the growth of the national life and should give a normative orientation to the evolution of the nation. . . .

The rules of society exist in the social conscience, on the one hand, and are codified in the books, on the other. We call those which come under the first, *culture*, and those which come under the latter, *learning*. Culture is the complex of the rules of language, politics, religion, morality, aesthetics, law, and economics, which exist on an unconscious level in the life of a nation. The culture of a nation is not something to be imposed or instituted. As it is already existing, it is only to be discovered and codified. It may be brought from life to the written page, from the unconscious to the conscious. We cannot say 'to build the national culture', but we must say 'to discover or to seek national culture'. This does not mean, however, that culture is something to be found in the individual. Culture is the complex of several normative rules to which individuals always aspire but never attain. The fact that we call those very rare persons who symbolize the national ethos in any one of the social groupings men of genius is an indication of the fact that the elevation of individual life to the level of national life is extremely difficult and rare. We call the man who discovers the *génie de la langue* the genius of language and the man who symbolizes the national morality a moral genius. Thus, national life should not be sought in the habits and conduct of the individual, but in ideals which are inspired in individuals by the national experiences and institutions. Secondly, it does not mean either that national life consists either of national conduct read in history books, or in a future stage contemplated in our imagination. National life is the life which actually exists. Life in the past ceases to be alive, and the life to come is not yet born. National life is the life actually existing now.* In our search for the national

---

* This does not mean that I am against the attempt to study our past and to discover our future. I believe that we should study the past only to understand the present and not to return to it, and as the future is something to be born out of the present, it can only be surmised by an adequate knowledge of the present.

SOCIAL VALUES AND INSTITUTIONS 167

language, for example, we shall find it neither in the *Qāmūs* or *Burhān-i Qāti'* nor in the *Divân-ı Lûgat-üt Türk* or *Lûgat-ı Çağatay*. It will not be found again in the creative imagination of the 'purists'. It will be enough to study by scientific methods the actual language as spoken in Istanbul. I should not be accused of conservatism as I emphasize the present. The conservative is the man who believes in the unchangeable words of books. To believe in life one should not be the worshipper of the 'unchangeable'. Life is a creative evolution, a moving ideal which changes perpetually. The 'present' in the social realm is not the sum total of the habits and the conduct of the individual, but of ideals and aspirations felt in the national conscience which are not attained by individuals, who may never reach them. Culture is the nation's very intimate life which is lived above the individuals and is of an ideational nature.

V

As no nation ever lived in isolation without having any contact with other nations, there has always been exchange of institutions among those who were in contact with each other. These exchanges took place only among those who were in contact with each other, and did not extend to all nations. Thus, the nations are differentiated into group-ings on the basis of exchange of institutions. We call these groupings civilization-groups, and the sum total of the common institutions a *civilization*. In ancient ages there was a Mediterranean civilization consti-tuted by the common contributions of the nations who exchanged through the Mediterranean sea. Today there is a Buddhistic civilization, an Islamic civilization, a European civilization, etc. Furthermore, a certain nation may once, in one stage of its history, be a part of one civilization and of another in another stage. The Turks, for example, belonged once to the Taoist civilization. They had several institutions in common with the Chinese, the Mongolians, the Manchurians, the Tibetans, the Cambodians, and the Finns. Later, they entered into the Islamic civilization, and then they began to accept European civiliza-tion in the last century. Survivals of the Taoist civilization among the Turks may be found today only among the *tandırname* traditions of old women and, possibly, in the customs and folk poems, yet unknown to us, of the peasants and of nomads. The Islamic and European civilizations actually and formally exist side by side [within Turkish life].

168 TURKISH NATIONALISM AND WESTERN CIVILIZATION

If we take European civilization as an example, we find that among European nations there are only common words, but each one understands a different meaning by the same word they use commonly. The word 'nation', for example, has different connotations for the French and the Germans. The word 'state' means different things to the British, French, and Germans. The same is true for the word 'constitution' or 'freedom'. The word 'culture' might be a better example. The French understand 'learning' (*irfan*), while the German understands *hars* by the same word. It might be concluded from this that the French put more emphasis on learning and the Germans more on culture, but this is not the case at all. It is true, however, that the French attach greater value to learning and the Anglo-Saxons to culture. As the Germans are attaching importance to both, they have proved their superiority over both, as we see today [this article was written during World War I]. It follows, then, that European nations are living their own national lives in spite of the fact that they outwardly have a common civilization.

Institutions, like language, have an aspect of form and one of meaning. Institutions common within a civilization group are common only in appearance; that is, in form. From the point of view of meaning—that is, of intimate life—each nation has its own peculiar institutions. And the sum total of such institutions of a nation constitutes its culture. When one nation borrows certain institutions from another, it takes only certain forms whose real meanings are not defined. When these forms enter into the national life, they assume new meanings which become indigenous, and sincere sentiments evolve in the national conscience. When we borrowed words from the Arabs and Persians, we took only certain forms of words. The national meanings we have attached to these words are unintelligible to their original owners, and it is because of this fact that those who look at the *Qāmūs* or the *Burhān-i Qāti'* for the meanings of these words are doomed to remain foreigners to the national language. In short, certain concepts and institutions in words and forms, and the civilization which is the sum total of them all, may be common to several nations; but national conscience is never commonly shared.

VI

The change and the evolution of social institutions depend upon the changes in the social structure. For that reason, there is a discipline

SOCIAL VALUES AND INSTITUTIONS 169

that studies the social structure of nations which we might call national morphology. The science derived from the comparative study of several nations might be called comparative morphology. The science called comparative linguistics or comparative law may also be called sociology of language, sociology of law, etc. Comparative morphology is simply called social morphology. There is a more general and more abstract science derived from the comparative study of these sciences which is called general sociology. The subject-matter of general sociology is the comparative study of the cultures of all nations. We might call the discipline derived from the study of the culture of a certain nation national sociology.

The sociology of a nation is a synthesis of social disciplines relating to that nation, national linguistics, national ethics, national law, etc. If certain nations belong to the same social species, their cultures are similar; if they belong to the same civilization group, their civilizations are similar to each other. Therefore, for the establishment of sociology on the basis of comparison it is first necessary to establish national sociology, but national sociology presupposes the findings of sociology in order to know to which social species and civilization the nation in question belongs. Thus, all social sciences and social disciplines have to utilize each other's data. . . . Social disciplines are always national, because their subject-matter is the institutions of a nation. They are, however, objective disciplines at the same time because they are interested in observing and discovering the institutions existing in the nation. They will show not 'what it should be' but 'how it is'. They are, however, normative disciplines also, because once the rules of national institutions are discovered and become known, they assume an obligatory character for the members of the nation. We do not learn the grammatical rules of our language with only a theoretical interest, but we make the rules we have learned norms in our speech and writing. Thus, social disciplines are both objective knowledge and practical arts based on objective information. This is true also in national history. National history is, on the one hand, an objective discipline based on facts substantiated by evidences, and also an art of an educational and normative character. We see, therefore, that social disciplines are national on the one hand, and normative and educational on the other. The social sciences, on the other hand, are both objective and international like the other exact sciences such as mathematics, physical science, and biology. Their bearing upon the arts is in much the same

170 TURKISH NATIONALISM AND WESTERN CIVILIZATION

way. In mathematics, physics, and biology there is nothing practical; but the arts such as engineering, chemistry, or medicine apply only on the basis of the knowledge discovered in these sciences. In much the same way, there is nothing of a practical nature in the social sciences, but arts such as education and politics can only exist on the basis of these sciences. The only difference between these two categories of science [the physical and the social sciences] is the fact that the subject-matter of the social sciences is national phenomena, in general and in abstract if not of a particular concrete nation.

We may conclude that if the books of a particular nation contain knowledge concerning the social disciplines relevant to that nation, as well as knowledge concerning the general and abstract social sciences, these books are a source of exceedingly fruitful and useful learning (*irfan*), because this learning teaches the particular and concrete rules constituting national culture, and the general and abstract laws to which this culture is subject. Otherwise, if it consists of the arbitrary wishful thinking and dreams of the ideologists as to 'how should it be?', or of the traditional and unscientific doctrines borrowed from other nations, learning to be acquired from them is merely morbid and harmful. A person corrupted by the acquisition of such learning cannot think in terms of how he lives or cannot live in terms of what he thinks. His whole life is wasted in indecision and pessimism due to the failure to solve the contradictions between Life and Book. All of us have experienced this in our lives. In spite of the fact that Turkish culture is living like a hidden treasure of genius in our unconscious conscience, there has risen a thick curtain between it and ourselves by learning acquired from instruction. The language, the morality, the law, the fine arts, etc., with which we actually live are different in nature from that learning relating to them which we acquire from books. As our life is not reflected in our books, our learning does not affect our life. As our culture does not penetrate into our learning, our learning does not extend to our culture. As there is no connection or mutual understanding between our consciousness and our conscience, we live as double-minded sick men. The only way to put an end to this malady is to study Turkish culture, to develop our national sociology from it, and to entrust our education only to works written on this principle.

SOCIAL VALUES AND INSTITUTIONS

THE METHODS OF CULTURAL SOCIOLOGY[7]

I

Human phenomena are of two kinds: those which are associated with consciousness and those which are not. Those which always remain unassociated with consciousness are biological phenomena and are studied by biology. Those which are always or sometimes associated with the states of consciousness are treated by psychology. Psychological phenomena are sensations, perceptions, or behaviour, and may be generally classified into two groups: (*a*) the individual psychological ones, such as the sensations or actions originating from the biological organism of the individual—the science which deals with them is psychology; (*b*) the social psychological ones, such as those patterns of thought and action which originate from the social group in which the individual lives—the science dealing with them is sociology.

The patterns of thought and action imposed by the social group to which the individual belongs are called *traditions* (*an'ane* [in Arabic '*an'ana*]). Traditions are classified into religious, moral, legal, linguistic, aesthetic, and economic groups. Religious traditions, for example, consist of the religious beliefs and rituals. Linguistic, aesthetic, and economic norms are the traditions of their respective spheres of life.

The sum total of these traditions, which are related to each other in their origins, is called a *civilization*. Such traditions are shared by different societies, are found in common forms in different societies, and, hence, are of an international character. The sum total of the peoples belonging to a common civilization is called a *civilization-group*. A nation may sometimes have the traditions of more than one civilization and, thus, may belong to more than one civilization-group. The Ottoman Turks, for example, have retained several traditions stemming from the old civilization of the Turks as well as those coming from the Islamic and European civilizations.

A tradition is a pattern of thought or of action which implies a judgment of goodness or badness, or, in recent terminology, *value judgment*. But in every nation there is a social conscience which is made up of *mores* (*common opinion*, '*urf*) determining the judgments of goodness or badness, or value judgments, which are entirely peculiar to that nation. The traditions are international but the *mores* are only nationally accepted. The forces which make a nation consist of association

172 TURKISH NATIONALISM AND WESTERN CIVILIZATION

(*ta'āruf*) among its own members, and of dissociation (*tanākur*)[8] between them, on the one side, and the members of other nations, on the other. Association (*ta'āruf*) is a participation in common *mores* (*'urf*), and dissociation (*tanākur*) means divergence in *mores*. The hadith: 'The souls are arrayed armies: those which recognize one another become akin; those who are strangers to one another become mutually opposed' [*al-arwāḥu ajnūdun mujannadatun famā ta'ārafa minhu 'talafa wamā tanākara 'ḫtalafa*] is an expression of this truth. As each nation has been living in particular social conditions it is natural that each should have its own particular value judgments or *mores* (*'urf*). The real ethos of a nation is reflected, not in its traditions but in its *mores*. There may be conflicts between the traditions and the *mores* of a nation. A certain tradition may be congruent or incongruent with the *mores*. Congruence between the two gives rise to an *institution*; otherwise, if the tradition remains but plays no part in the life of the nation, it is the *fossil* of an extinct civilization. If it still lingers on as a continuation of the past in the present without fitting itself to present *mores*, it is then called a *survival*.

It follows that the social conscience, the ethos, of a nation is reflected only in its institutions. Institutions are not international but national. The sum total of the institutions of a nation constitutes its *culture*. Like *mores* and institutions, culture is thus of an entirely national character. An institution is not necessarily a by-product of the adaptation of a tradition to the *mores*. There are institutions which come into existence merely by assimilation into the *mores* even when they have no place in traditions. Thus, for example, the *Mevlid* [recital of the Prophet's Birthday Poem] is even today a living ritual [in Turkey] in spite of the fact that it never had any place in the traditions of *fiḳh* [Islamic jurisprudence]. A tradition may be just a fossil in one country and a living institution in another. The criminal injunctions of the *fiḳh*, for example, became fossils in Turkey because they did not fit into the Turkish *mores*, but they are still living institutions in Hejaz or Yemen. Polygamy could maintain its existence among the Turks only as a survival. Just as there are institutions directly emerging within a culture, there are also certain traditions which are taken from international civilization and fitted into its *mores*. In some cases, a culture may borrow traditions from more than one civilization, as we see in the Turkish culture [of the Ottoman Turks] which has taken traditions from old Turkish, Islamic, and European civilizations.

SOCIAL VALUES AND INSTITUTIONS 173

The branch of science which studies the laws upon which societies and institutions are dependent, by comparing civilizations and cultures, is called *comparative sociology*. The one which studies how the culture of a nation is distinguished from the civilization to which it belongs and how it develops its own specific characteristics and how it develops within its own uniqueness is called *cultural sociology*. Comparative sociology is a positive science because it is entirely objective. Cultural sociology, on the other hand, has to remain as an art [a normative science], in spite of the fact that it rests heavily upon the first, because it cannot free itself from subjectivity. Comparative sociology, which deals with the comparison of these and of all the civilizations and cultures, is the most general and the most abstract field of the social sciences. But the branches of cultural sociology which deal with religion, law, economics, language, and art from a national point of view are normative disciplines.

II

In the beginning every tradition is of the nature of an institution based on national *mores*. But when it assumes an international character, following borrowings by other nations, it transforms itself into a tradition because there are no international *mores*. An international tradition is like a container without a content. Since each nation makes the content of this tradition its own *mores*, the fact that the traditions are empty containers is not usually noticed. The international container ceases to be a tradition by being united with the national content and thus by turning into an institution. Since the process of assimilation takes place unconsciously, no one notices the change. Even when a tradition, in its transformation into an institution, becomes subject to a partial alteration, again no one notices it. People think that the tradition is still living in its original form. If the art of writing, the book, and the school had not existed at all, the process would continue quite naturally. But the fact that the traditions became written down and preserved in their original form in places of instruction such as the *medrese* [religious school] and the *mektep* [secular school] produces obstacles to this natural process. The traditional containers preserved by such means may remain devoid of any national content. The traditions of Turkish culture, for example, are not written down in any book and, therefore, did not have the support of any *mektep* or *medrese*;

thus, they were either forgotten entirely or evolved along with the national *mores* by fitting themselves into the latter. But Islamic traditions and the traditions coming from Europe have remained immune from this assimilation thanks to the conservatism of the old *medrese* and [to the formalism] of the old *mektep*. Turkish culture has thus assimilated the old Turkish traditions but has failed to do so in relation to the Islamic and European traditions and, hence, it did not realize its formation completely. Two factors are needed to do this, one being a new type of *medrese* and the other a new type of *mektep*.

Traditions may clash with two kinds of conscience,[9] one being individual and the other social. The individual *conscience* is the consciousness of the person, and its function is to observe sensations. The observation of sensation is an individual experience and consists mainly of the act of distinguishing qualities. Whenever a conflict arises between the tradition and individual experience, it gives rise to scientific criticism from which originate positive knowledge and the faculty which we call pure reason.

The social *conscience*, on the other hand, with which the traditions may come to grips is the *mores*. Just as consciousness is the perception which distinguishes the qualities of things, so the *mores* give rise to another kind of perception whose function it is to distinguish the values of things. The perception of qualities is an individual process, the determination of values is a social process. Just as the observations of consciousness are an individual experience, so the expression of the *mores* constitutes the social experience. Clashes between tradition and social experience give rise to cultural criticism as a result of which the faculty which we call common sense arises together with the national learning (*irfan*). Kant named abstract reason 'pure reason' and common sense 'practical reason'. Having demolished metaphysics, which is the support of the social values—e.g. religion and ethics—by his critique of pure reason, he constructed it over again in his critique of practical reason. This indicates that abstract reason is the child of the clash between tradition and individual experience, and common sense the child of the clash between traditions and *mores*. Hence, in the determination of good and bad, or of the social values, abstract reason cannot be used as a criterion. Abstract reason plays its part only with respect to judgments of reality. As traditions were derived basically from the *mores*, they could be used as criteria in this matter, but in most cases they fall short in their performance of this function because, since they

SOCIAL VALUES AND INSTITUTIONS 175

do not contain the *mores* in themselves, they are either empty containers [forms] or misleading survivals. The real criteria for value judgments are, therefore, only *mores* or common sense, which are the product of the instinctive criticism of the traditions through the *mores*. But the most inspiring expression of common sense is the man of genius. The genius is the person who excels in common sense or the person who feels and experiences the *mores* in their clearest form. The *mores* are like rays of light diffused into the conscience of the people. They do not turn into burning flame, however, until they are intensified by the focus of a lens. The soul of the genius is that lens. He is like a lens held to the sun of society. As the burning force of the lens comes from the sun, so the effectiveness of the genius lies in his being a reflection of the *mores*. Those who put the dictates of common sense into practice are heroes. A genius is the hero of theory and the hero the genius of practice. Another type of man who is the carrier of common sense to a lesser degree is he whom we call the sage (*'ārif*). The real representatives of a nation are the men of genius, the hero, and the sage. It is a mistake to look at the average man as a national type. We ought to see the national type in the men of genius. The average man represents only the sum total of the individual consciences, but he never represents the social conscience or the national personality. The élite of a nation are the men of genius, the heroes, and the sages. The scholar and the scientist acquire only certain skills through training. Even a simple person may become a scholar or a scientist, but never a genius, a hero, or a sage. Hence, the scholar or the scientist cannot be regarded as the élite of a nation unless they are endowed also with common sense. They may achieve greatness in scientific and technical fields through their acquisition of abstract reason, but as abstract reason cannot be used as a criterion in matters of value, so neither their ideas nor their actions can be taken as a gauge in national sociology. Among the specialists of science, the only persons who can say anything with regard to matters of value are those who are specialized in national sociology because, although they also conduct their studies through abstract reason, their subject-matter consists of common sense or its source, the *mores*, and thus they have authority.

The national type manifests itself also during great social upheavals or in times of crisis which immerse the souls of individuals within the social soul. Thus, for example, the national type of the Turk emerged in its most striking form during the critical defence of the Dardanelles.

176 TURKISH NATIONALISM AND WESTERN CIVILIZATION

National life is not that life which we live in ordinary times of tranquillity. In these times we live only our individual lives. It is because of this that the genius and the hero do not appear in times of peace. Great men appear only in critical times. Extraordinary events obliterate individualities. Individuals in the days of crisis and excitement live only the national life. The individual seems indifferent to values in the times of tranquillity, while the crowds arising at times of crisis sanctify or condemn an object towards which they project their whole attention. Then thoughts become faith, ideas become ideals, wishes become wills, and feelings become ecstasies (*vecd*). A state of crisis may be likened to a microscope, it has a magnifying power which brings social feelings into distinct shapes. The *mores* of the nation, which under ordinary conditions remain concealed, unfold themselves clearly in this manner. In order to discover the sources of the new Turkish revival, which is in itself the full expression of the Turkish *mores*, we have to trace back to the Graeco-Turkish War [of 1897], leading ultimately to the emergence of certain forces which had remained hidden until then. The Reval Meeting was the event which suddenly worked the forces which until then had been fighting only against the Macedonian bandits and the people of Rumeli who until then had remained only as spectators of the fighting into a frenzy. The events of July 24th [the so-called Young Turk Revolution of 1908] and the counter-revolution of 'March 31' [April 13, 1909], the Turko-Italian and the Balkan wars, and finally the present World War [I], all contributed to the rise of various national movements [among the Turks]. In short, if one of the mirrors of the national values is the élite, the other is the national enthusiasm created by extraordinary events.

The common sense of a nation expresses itself best in exceptional persons and at exceptional times. Although it is reflected instinctively in the genius, in the hero, or in the sage, this is not, however, enough. It must also be possible to grasp the common sense of a nation by methodical means. If this were not possible, one could not speak of a national sociology based on method. To grasp the common sense of a nation simply means to be able to identify its *mores*. In other words, it means to distinguish them from the fossilized practices and from the survivals. Thus, the problem amounts basically to the question of how the *mores* and the institutions of a nation are distinguished.

III

To do this, the first method to be employed by cultural sociology is the method of 'convergence' (*ta'āruf*). This procedure aims at seeking common ground among the conflicting trends which take place in national life. Within the national life there are certain social trends which may clash with each other. They may be contradictory on several points. However, they may also converge on certain points. These common points are, therefore, the ones which signify the *mores*.

In Turkey, for example, there have been three major social movements; namely, the movements of Turkism, Islamism, and Modernism. The existence of these divergent movements is a lively evidence of the fact that the elements which we took from three civilizations are still not assimilated and still conflict with each other. All of these three movements represent the same traditionalism. In spite of these divergences, however, there is also a convergence (*ta'āruf*) among them since all of them refer equally to the same problems of the same nation. The existence of this convergence between them and the existence of divergence (*tanākur*) between them, on the one hand, and those of the other nations, on the other, are indications of the fact that all three movements agree on the same *mores*.

Groups existing in a society are like connected containers. Just as the water in these containers always maintains an equal level, the groups within a nation also maintain a relation of convergence (*ta'āruf*) among themselves. But as the *mores* normally remain concealed in the conscience of the people and those which have been made manifest are traditions, the outsider, observing the behaviour of individuals, sees, at first sight, only the divergence of ideas and does not notice the basic similarity in the souls [of the people]. There may be certain traditions represented by one of the groups which are, in many cases, accepted by others too. That means that these traditions, whatever may be their sources, have become commonly accepted beliefs and practices, or the institutions of all. As examples from language are more convenient than others, let us mention a few to illustrate this. We have borrowed, for example, foreign words like *telefon* (telephone), *telegraf* (telegraph), or *salon*, which are used by both an Islamist and a Turkist. That means that these words have become established institutions of the language. There are several Arabic and Persian words which were likewise accepted by the Turkists as parts of the Turkish language, such as

178 TURKISH NATIONALISM AND WESTERN CIVILIZATION

kitap [*kitāb*=book], *millet* [*milla*= nation], and *devlet* [*dawla*= state], all referring to institutions. No Turkist would entertain any desire to replace them by equivalents derived from pure Turkish. The Islamists and the Modernists, on the other hand, have never thought of expelling the pure Turkish words still in use among the Ottoman Turks.

These facts show that there are common points or institutions agreed on by the three groups with respect to language. The simple reason is that there are linguistic *mores*. Not all of the originally Turkish words have become assimilated to the Ottoman Turkish. Several Turkish words which the linguistic *mores* did not assimilate have been rejected from the Ottoman Turkish; that is to say, words such as *sayru, savcu, göʒgü* have become mere fossils. Some, on the other hand, could have entered Ottoman Turkish only by undergoing modification either in spelling or in meaning, as *ölü* from *ölük, sarı* from *sarıg, ulu* from *uluğ, yordam* from *erdem*, and *deniʒ* from *tengiʒ*. In the same manner, all Arabic and Persian words borrowed could not be used in the Turkish language in their original forms. In most cases they underwent considerable changes when they were incorporated into Turkish; thus *nerdubān* became *merdiven, çarçūbe* became *çerçeve, ghirbāl* became *kalbur, ʒukāk* became *sokak*. The first forms in these examples are perfect examples of the fossils, and the second of the institutions. Words derived from the European languages have undergone the same process of modification.

As the existence of common points among the divergent three groups derives from the accepted *mores*, the conflicts are the consequences of their traditionalisms. The traditionalist Turkist, for example, attempts to introduce such fossil words as *uluğ* or *göʒgü*, which had been rejected by the *mores* of the people. Such attempts cause resentment among the Islamists and the Westernists. Or, when the traditionalist Islamist insists that the correct Arabic form for the word 'attention' is *taḥdīk* or *iltifāt* and not the current *dikkat* [which is also derived from Arabic], and that the correct form should be used in Turkish, or when he attempts to revive *nerdubān, çarçūbe, ʒukāk*, and *ghirbāl* to take the place of the Turkified forms, others just laugh. Those who prefer to pronounce *Europe, Paris*, and *cigarette* the French way instead of saying *Avrupa, Paris*, and *cigara*, simply make themselves ridiculous, as we read in Recaizade Ekrem's novel *Araba Sevdası (Love in the Carriage)*.

Those examples indicate that Turkish culture is not identical with the civilization of the Turks. The latter is the sum total of Turkish traditions. The culture of the Turks, on the other hand, is the sum total of the institutions which are actually alive in the *mores* of the Ottoman Turks and which have come down from various origins. It is only the traditionalists of the Turkists that over-emphasize and want to revive the old civilization. The culture-ist Turkists, on the other hand, put the emphasis on the living culture of the people.

If we extend these observations on the language to other fields of social life, we shall always notice great differences between the traditionalist Turkist and the culture-ist Turkist, and it will become evident that the latter can reconcile himself with the Islamist and the Modernist without difficulty. Since the factors that bring a nation into existence are the principles of convergence (*ta'āruf*) and divergence (*tanākur*), the traditions taken from among international traditions are assimilated into the forms of institutions, and these institutions are always more or less different from the international forms of the tradition. It follows, then, that the national culture, even if it has not yet become a conscious one, always exists. It is necessary only to bring it into consciousness by distinguishing it from international civilization. In order to do this, it is necessary to distinguish the living institutions of the *mores* from the survivals which no longer live in the *mores*. Since the traditions mutually agreed upon by the opposing groups in a nation are national institutions living in the *mores*, we can discover the national *mores* and culture by discovering the common ground of all contending groups.

The second method to be employed in cultural sociology is that of discovering the latent or explicit divergence (*tanākur*) between the institutions of various nations belonging to the same sphere of civilization. This procedure will lead us to the point where we can see how a tradition undergoes alterations in the process of its assimilation within different nations and how it creates institutions within these nations which differ from one another. Nations belonging to the same civilization often look alike from outside, but are different in reality. In order to realize this point, the observer should not be deceived by superficial similarities existing between certain traditions. He must look at the variations between the institutions existing in different nations respectively.

European civilization, for example, is commonly shared by various European nations. But the German nation, for example, tends to distinguish its own religious, cultural, ethical, and legal values, and

180 TURKISH NATIONALISM AND WESTERN CIVILIZATION

differentiates its own aesthetic and literary taste, and even its scientific and economic practices, from the corresponding ones in the other nations. It is through such acts of differentiation that the culture of the German nation marks its own existence. Likewise, the Ottoman Turk would distinguish his peculiar *mores*, and thus make his culture a conscious reality only by discovering how its own institutions differ from those of the other Turkish peoples, from those of the other Muslim peoples, and from those of the Europeans.

The third procedure to be followed will be the method of conciliation (*te'lif*). Although a nation is a group of people sharing the same *mores*, divergent groups within it might be conciliated. In order to do this it is, first of all, necessary to differentiate the civilizational and the cultural forms found among these groups. Thus, for example, the civilizational form of Islamism is *fiķh*-ism. To be a Muslim, it is not absolutely necessary to be a *fiķh*-ist however. *Fiķh* is a scholastic (*medresevî*) tradition which had its origins only in the second century of the *Hijra*. The most glorious period of Islam was the period preceding the rise of *fiķh*. And today we see that an Islamic life is being lived without being perfectly fitted into *fiķh*. In the history of Islam, the *ahl al-Hadith* had rejected *fiķh*, the *Mutakaddimūn* had rejected *kalām*, and, later, the *Mutasawwif*s lived a lively Islamic culture by replacing the 'reason' (*ķāl*) of *fiķh* and of *kalām* by 'experience' (*ħāl*). The supporters of *'urf* today also want a living Islamic culture.

The civilizational form of Turkism, on the other hand, is the doctrine which claims to revive the old [Turkish] *töre* [customary law]. But those who accept it do not realize that before the traditional customary law came into existence there was a civilization of the Turks and, furthermore, the customary law took different forms in the Gültekin [Orkhon] inscriptions, in *Kutadgu Bilik*, in the *Yasa* of Jengiz, in the *Tüzükât* of Timur, and in the *Kanunname*'s of Fatih [Mehmet the Conqueror] and of Süleyman [the Magnificent]. Furthermore, the contemporary cultural life of the Ottoman Turks is creating a new Turkish civilization through its dissemination among all the Turks. Thus, just as Islamism does not mean *fiķh*-ism, in much the same way Turkism is not *töre*-ism. And again, it is a mistake to take Modernism as necessarily meaning Europeanism. Modernization and Europeanization are quite different things. There is similarity but not identity between the two.

It follows, then, that *fiķh*-ism, *töre*-ism, and Europeanism are not

SOCIAL VALUES AND INSTITUTIONS 181

reconcilable with each other at all. Each is equally traditionalist and imitationist. On the other hand, the genuine Islamism, the true Turkism, and the real Modernism are reconcilable with each other, not only in the unconscious conscience of the nation, where they are already coexisting and co-operating, but also on the conscious level.

The fourth procedure to be followed in cultural sociology is the method of exemplification (*istişhād*). Newspapers and journals like to discover social trends by using the questionnaire technique. As the national conscience is not exemplified in the average type of person, this method is useless in discovering sociological truths. The national conscience is exemplified only in the genius, in the hero, or in the sage. The questionnaires should, therefore, be applied only in their cases. However, even then it is far from being always useful because these men would tend to express, at the time of the inquiry, not their feelings but only their intellectualized opinions. Furthermore, those who are not living now cannot be questioned. On the other hand, these men have in their most sincere, least artificial moments made utterances and performed deeds, without any formalism, which are the most valuable documents for national sociology. It is therefore the task of the method of exemplification to utilize such exemplary ideas or acts as documents. Thus, for example, we can obtain many data from the activities and writings of Namık Kemal because his refusal to accept *Tanzimat in toto*, his belief in the sovereignty of the rights [of the Muslim-Turkish people] as expressed in the letter he wrote to Abdul Hamid during the preparation of the Constitution of 1876, are exemplifications of the national conscience. Apart from great men, great events also are important sources of data for understanding the trends of the national conscience. The events of 'March 31' [April 13, 1909], for example, were a reaction against the tendencies which were curtailing the position of the sovereign, the position of the Turks and of the Muslims, and exaggerating the importance of the policy of reconciliation between the religious communities [within the Ottoman Empire].

The fifth procedure to be utilized in discovering the national ethos is aimed at the determination of social types. Comparative sociology constructs social types by classifying the forms of society into genera and species. Thus, every nation occupies a position as a species in a genus. As the *mores* and the institutions found in each genus and species and the law governing them are knowable, it will be possible to understand the *mores* and the institutions of a nation once its genus and

182 TURKISH NATIONALISM AND WESTERN CIVILIZATION

species are determined. In this manner the institutions will be distinguished easily from the fossils and survivals.

Societies are divided into two great genera: tribes and states. There are three species of state: city-states, sultanistic states, and modern states. The Turks in their pre-Islamic period in Asia belonged to the first species. During their Ottoman period, they constituted a Sultanate by substituting *sancakbeys* for *boybeys*. From the time of *Tanzimat* and the Constitutional Revolution, the Ottoman state began its transformation towards a modern state. A modern state is one which is based on a legislative organ, an independent culture, and a national economy.

Once the genera and species of societies are determined, it becomes easier to identify which traditions are the survivals [of a previous species] and which ones have become institutions. *Mores* and institutions are normal social facts [for each species]. The fossilized ones and the survivals, on the other hand, are pathological phenomena. The task of national sociology is to devise measures to be taken against the revival of fossils, to eliminate the survivals, and to strengthen the institutions. However, in some cases both *mores* and institutions may become pathological, as in the case of an institution which becomes retarded in its evolution by certain arresting factors, and thus fails to reach the stage of development it should reach with reference to the species in which it is normally found. Because of arrested growth, certain *mores* and institutions lag behind. Thus, for example, since the division of labour is not developed among us in the field of religion, and since the men of piety and the men of [religious] law have not assumed specialized functions, everybody considers himself charged with these functions. This has been the main factor in the co-existence among us of religious laxity, fanaticism, and hypocrisy. The discovery of the species to which a nation belongs will remedy such anomalous conditions.

To measure the authority and effectiveness of value judgments or social values, we have one more method, and that is statistical procedure. It is possible to ascertain statistically to what extent people observe a certain tradition which exists among different nations. Through a comparative analysis of these statistical data, it will be possible to show that a certain tradition is practised among various nations in varying degrees. Through this procedure the *mores* of the nations will be ascertained in a comparatively objective way also.

SOCIAL VALUES AND INSTITUTIONS

Cultural sociology may develop methods in addition to those which we have enumerated so far. For the present we deem these sufficient. However, there is an important point with regard to the problem of the determination of national *mores* which should be taken into account above everything else: the investigator engaged in research work on the national *mores* should not have any monopolistic bias in favour of any of the civilizations to which the nation belongs. For example, those who seek to identify the *mores* of the Ottoman Turks should not have any excluding preference for any of the old Turkish or Islamic or European civilizations. The traditionalists cannot perceive the living *mores*. It should never be forgotten either that the *mores* never rest on official sanctions and that, on the contrary, the official rules derive their moral sanction from the *mores*. The faiths and laws lose their moral sanction as soon as they contradict the *mores*, and thus they cannot for long have a material power to enforce them since through non-use such institutions become obsolete by themselves.

The greatest danger in cultural sociology is to confuse *mores* with customs and usages. There are accepted or rejected customs and usages. As long as they conform to the *mores*, they are regarded as accepted customs and usages; as long as they remain discordant with the *mores*, they are regarded as rejected customs and usages. Therefore, customs and usages are not of the same category as the *mores*. The word '*urf* used in the Kur'an corresponds to the term *opinion* [in French]. The *mores* of a nation are the social conscience of the time in which they exist. And this social conscience can only be an accepted one; it can never be a rejected one.

CHAPTER VII

RELIGION, EDUCATION, AND FAMILY

SOCIAL FUNCTIONS OF RELIGION[1]

I

THE social functions of religion differ according to various types of society. In one of our previous essays we specified two such types, viz. primitive societies and organic societies.

In primitive societies there is only one kind of authority—that is, religious authority—because no political or cultural authority developed in them independently. The authority in primitive societies is still based on *mores* (or in the Kur'anic term, on *'urf*), and the *mores* among primitive societies are of a religious nature. There are no political or cultural *mores* among them.

In organic societies, at first political *mores* and later cultural *mores* take shape in addition to religious *mores*. In the same manner, a political and a cultural authority exist in organic societies in addition to the religious authority.

A collectivity (*hey'et*) united by religious *mores* and subject to a religious authority is called an *ümmet*. A collectivity united by political *mores* and subject to a political authority is called a *state*. The collectivity which is the product and the union of cultural *mores* under a cultural authority is called a *nation*.

It follows, therefore, that primitive societies are of the character of an *ümmet*. No political or national institutions have developed among them. In organic societies, on the other hand, all three exist simultaneously but separately, *ümmet* giving rise to the state which prepares the way for the nation. The organization of the independent but auxiliary religious, political, and cultural institutions in these societies, as a result of the differentiation of functions, gives rise to the three kinds of *mores* and the authorities based on them. Keeping in view this differentiation between the two types, let us now discuss the social functions of religion within them.

RELIGION, EDUCATION, AND FAMILY 185

In primitive societies, the religious institutions perform the functions of the other two institutions because these societies do not have political and cultural organs. In other words, *ümmet* functions also as state and nation. All social institutions, in general, derive their power and value from some authority or, more correctly, *mores*. In primitive societies there is only the religious authority and *mores*. All institutions of primitive societies, therefore, necessarily spring from religion and acquire their power and value from this source of sacredness.

The fact that in organic society only a part of the institutional life rests on religious *mores* while in primitive society all institutions rest on religious *mores*, should not lead us to think that religion is serving a more useful task in primitive societies. Religious *mores* invest the institutions to which they are related with a supernatural or, in clearer terms, a charismatic power and value. This power may be useful in its relation to institutions which are relatively spiritual and represent the collective conscience of society, but it becomes harmful when it is extended to worldly or secular, and especially to material, institutions because it prevents these institutions from adapting themselves to the expediences of life. Therefore, the predominance of religious *mores* over all institutions is not something to be desired for organic societies.

In organic societies religious *mores* still exist, but they cover only those ideals and sentiments which have to remain spiritual and sacred. They do not extend over those institutions which are of a worldly and secular character. The latter institutions derive their power and role either from political or from cultural *mores* and evolve in accordance with the expediencies of life. Political *mores* transform themselves into laws when they win the support of legal sanctions. Cultural *mores*, which have several forms such as moral, aesthetic, linguistic, economic, and technical, do not invest the institutions to which they are related with charismatic sanctions, as in the case of religious institutions, but they determine the right in human conduct, beauty in works of art, correctness in language, economy in commodities, rationality in economy, and utility in techniques.

In the organic society these come into existence through division of labour, and develop independently of standards of social values or of *mores*. Each of them performs its function in its own field independently. Therefore, we should seek the functions of religion in organic society because only there can we see religion in its own sphere.

II

One of the great tasks of religion in organic society is to leave other institutions free within their own spheres. As religion consists of a body of beliefs and rituals, it is necessary to seek social functions of religion (in terms of their worldly functions) with respect to these two groups of phenomena*

There have always been certain convictions on the worldly functions of rituals and beliefs. For example, some confuse religious purification (*şer'î taharet*) with the 'purification in accordance with medicine' (*tıbbî taharet*) and try to interpret the religious obligations of washing (*gusül* and *abdest*) as if they were wisely meant to eliminate germs. Since the religious purification means essentially avoidance of moral filth, there is no justification for attributing it to some other motives. Washing with ordinary water is no substitute for antiseptics, and secondly, religious purification may even be carried out, if necessary, by simply using earth, which would be essentially a symbolic act. Again, some people attempt to evaluate prayers in terms of utility, that is physical exercise, or fasting in terms of dietary exercises. It is, I believe, a mistake to reduce religion to such materialistic terms.

We have to seek the social functions of religion, not in any utilitarian sense but in the moral functions they perform because all social facts are basically moral or ethical or ideational phenomena. The study of social facts should be undertaken only in accordance with the methods of sociology. Let us, then, attempt to see the social role of religion in terms of sociological methods.

Religion divides everything into two categories—the sacred and the profane.[2] The thing worshipped and everything connected with it are sacred, everything outside of the sacred is profane. The fundamental principle of religion consists of prohibiting the profane thing from approaching or from being in contact with that which is sacred. There is an absolute and irreconcilable contrast between the two. It is the greatest sacrilege to bring the profane into contact with the sacred and to profane the sacred. Besides the other-worldly sanctions behind this prohibition, there are also worldly charismatic sanctions for it. This worldly power charged with a mysterious charisma is believed to

---

* Showing the other-worldly function of religion is beyond the subject of this essay. This is the task not of the sociologist but of the theologian and the scholar of *fıkh*.

strike like lightning those believers who commit sacrilegious acts and destroy them.

On the other hand, the nature of ritual consists of an act of approach by the man who is profane to his deity. Thus, ritual can take place only when the worshipper cleanses himself from the state of profanity; the worshipper himself becomes sacred in order to approach deity. For this reason, worship consists of two phases: in the first place the worshipper tries to extricate himself from the profane things. This is negative ritual. In the second place, the pious who is now outside of the profane begins to present his spirit to his deity. This is the positive ritual. The negative ritual consists of the following acts [in Islam]: (a) ablution of the whole body and parts of the body, purification from bodily excrements, cleanliness from menstrual discharges, covering private parts of the body, and fasting; (b) turning towards the *Ka'ba* (*Kibla*), performing prayers at certain places and times, starting to do things from the right side; (c) prohibiting the utterance of profane words and looking around during prayer, wearing the clothes of *ihrām* at *mikat* and prohibiting clothes of luxury, prohibiting adornment by cutting hair and nails when in *ihrām*; (d) sacrifice of animals as a symbol of self-sacrifice, paying alms (*ʒakāt* and . . . *fitra*), *jihād*, and pilgrimage.

We can see in these prohibitions and obligations, first, certain personal organic functions and the acts of eating and drinking, secondly, the times and places men enjoy (such as houses, places of business and of enjoyment which are not places of worship)* thirdly, things that men are inclined to do, such as talking, dressing, adorning themselves, and, fourthly, things that men are ambitious to do. These are all profane, in general. In other words, anything individual is profane. Therefore, the aim of negative ritual is to isolate the individual from his individuality, to elevate him to the status which is 'the negation of individuality', that is 'forsaking the world'. Moral uncleanness is nothing but the desires of the individual, or individuality, from which rituals like ablution purify him symbolically. Other negative rituals are also designed to isolate the individual from all desires and ambitions and moral blemishes. Man, looked at from a physiological point of view, is only an egoistic animal. To have society, it is, above everything, necessary to weaken this love for the ego. So long as man

---

* There are sacred places, and times in which prayers take place—*Ka'ba* [Mecca], *Kibla* [the direction to which the worshipper turns], mosque, holidays, fasting-month, Friday [the Sabbath], hours of prayer. The social nature of these will be noted later.

188 TURKISH NATIONALISM AND WESTERN CIVILIZATION

remains unable to control his individual desires and egoistic ambitions and so long as he is trained not to be ready to make great sacrifices of his individuality, he cannot be 'civilized by nature'.

Social life imposes several obligations such as observing the rights of property, life, and honour of others, working and refraining from sloth, learning reading and writing, justice and honesty, paying taxes, making sacrifices in times of war, and helping the families of the dead and of invalids by certain financial sacrifices. These are all irreconcilable with egoistic inclinations. To fulfil these duties, one has to develop a will powerful enough to overcome individual ambitions. In short, the individual has to 'negate' himself in community before he may 'survive' in it. Regarding everything which has an individual character as profane, regarding it as transitory, bad and taboo, negative rituals arm man against temptation. He elevates himself to the status of a genuine human being by acquiring a will-power to overcome his desires in this training school of self-control. In this way, a self-seeking being becomes a sacrificing citizen. It might be argued that if this religious policing did not exist, a moral and a legal policing of men would not be possible. Negative ritual transforms the individual into a social being by a continuous and effective training. Thus, even the negative rituals of religion are by themselves important social factors. They are, in a sense, nothing but means to attaining positive rituals.

But certain men of piety seriously take them as ends in themselves. These great heroes of faith spend their days in fasting and nights in prayer, live in solitude for years, kill their desires by renunciation and self-torture, make poverty an object of pride, renounce property, wealth and even, as Ibrahim Edhem did, crown and throne, family and children, and train themselves to respond to humiliation and insult with kindness and compassion. It is neither possible nor without harm to make everybody a man of piety, but among every people it becomes indispensable to have a limited number of them symbolizing the power of character and self-discipline. They serve as models for those who are weak in will, who strengthen their own morale by seeing what miracles an intensified will is capable of performing.

Against this characterization of piety, one might say that the pious man is retiring to a purely individual life by his withdrawal from society. Does this not mean that he escapes society and retires to individuality? The answer will be as follows: the solitary escapes from the world of business and of enjoyment only as centres of desire and

RELIGION, EDUCATION, AND FAMILY 189

ambition. He deprives himself of the comforts and delights of life, such as talking, sleeping, eating, drinking, and of avoidance of pain and displeasure. By doing these things, he fights against the desires of individuality and elevates himself above these desires. It is true that this is not sufficient for becoming socialized, but it is an indispensable prerequisite. Furthermore, as long as the individual desires remain extinguished in his soul, social counterparts may take their place. The solitary seeks escape from the earthly plenum in order to reach the heavenly one.

III

The positive rituals are based on three conditions—they should be performed after negative rituals; they should be performed in a collectivity; and they should be carried on periodically.

The reason for the priority of negative to positive ritual is given already. To explain the second condition—that is, performance in a collectivity—let us first discuss the effects of the collectivity upon the soul.

When we see that other people do not share a sentiment or an idea, we too do not attach value to it. True, we feel or think it, but we do not will or believe it as a belief. The individual mind is unable to elevate feelings into will, ideas into ideals, or intellectual attitudes into dogmas; it is both quantitatively and qualitatively incapable of it. It is quantitatively incapable because the mind cannot reach the boiling-point, the state of ecstasy, without the inspiration of the collectivity. Without reaching this point, intense psychological experiences such as determination, conviction, and faith cannot be attained. It is qualitatively incapable because our senses can perceive only the material qualities of bodies such as colour, smell, taste etc., and are unable to perceive good and bad in objects because they lack the 'sense of value'. Animals do not have a normative faculty which might enable them to form judgments of goodness, sacredness, or reverence. Values and the faculty of perceiving them exist only where there is social life.

When a number of individuals constitutes a collectivity, a new psychological element which we call the collective soul comes into existence as a product of interaction between individual souls. The collective soul is different from the individual soul both quantitatively and qualitatively. When individuals form a collectivity, a wave of excitement and ecstasy begins to invade their souls. You can never see

190 TURKISH NATIONALISM AND WESTERN CIVILIZATION

individual psychological states such as insensitivity, indifference, and quietism among the individuals in a crowd. Their souls are under the captivity of an intense emotion, a deep rapture. Such states, furthermore, are different from individual experiences such as appetite, anger, and fear, which we also find among animals, and are even opposite to the collective emotions. Individual emotions work upwards, from the oragnism towards the soul; collective emotions, on the other hand, originate in the soul and are new factors commanding organic emotions in the soul. These emotions are not amoral like bestial emotions. They are charged with judgments of approval or disapproval, reverence or contempt, sanctification or condemnation towards the particular things to which they refer. As long as the individual is not surrounded by the collectivity, he remains in a state of moral indifference. In this state his only concern is the avoidance of pain and the search for pleasure. He has neither an ideal to venerate nor anything to hate. He neither sanctifies anything nor condemns anyone. He knows neither kindness nor enmity. The collectivity, on the other hand, has faith and firmness, it is never indifferent. It believes in what it thinks, sanctifies what it believes, and condemns those who are against it. The collective soul knows no scepticism, hopelessness, or pessimism. The faith, hope, and optimism which we see in individuals are products of social life. As all individuals live in a social environment, no one can escape the impacts of the collective soul. Society creates the personality of the individual through its language, literature, traditions, science, law, and morals; in short, through its culture. The more the individual participates in various aspects of social life and the more he specializes in his particular occupation, the stronger the personality he will acquire. In individuals who are deprived of the common and special blessings of social life, personality is almost non-existent.

Once these points are understood, it becomes quite easy to explain why positive rituals should be performed in collectivity. We have pointed out above that the ritual means the approach of the profane worshipper to the sacred object of worship and that the profane is prohibited from approaching the sacred. The worshipper first frees himself from individuality; that is, from the profane state through negative ritual. But for the approach to the sacred this is not enough. It is also necessary that he make himself sacred or fill his soul with a sanctifying power. We say that this faculty does not exist in the individual state. Therefore the reason for the necessity of performing the

RELIGION, EDUCATION, AND FAMILY 191

ritual in collectivity is the fact that to become sacred it is necessary to become social. The worshipper seeks to reach an audience with his deity, a sacred communion with it. To do this, it is necessary, above all, to silence the 'bestial ego' which is awake in the soul, and then to arouse 'the sacred self' which lies in a dormant state. To do the first it is necessary to be freed from individuality; to do the second it is necessary to come into a state of collectivity. It is only when a person frees himself from profanity and acquires a sacred nature that he can enter into that audience for which he longs so much.

Positive rituals consist [in Islam] of prayers five times a day, *teravih* [Arabic, *tarāwīh*] prayer [during the fasting month], Friday prayer, holy-day (*bayram*, [Arabic, *'id*]) prayers, and the pilgrimage. Of these, daily prayers and the *teravih* prayer may be performed individually although, in principle, they are expected to be performed collectively. Individual performance of them is permissible because the personality, as the product of culture, carries a permanent sacredness in the soul. The power of sanctity needed for approach to the sacred does exist in a person when he is alone, but if isolation from collectivity continues for a longer period, this power may weaken. Thus, performance of Friday and holy-day prayers individually is not permitted.

Prayers should, furthermore, be performed in places which are consecrated, that is separated from ordinary places. Quite naturally, such places are regarded as more sacred than the profane places. Places of prayer in Islam are *masjid*s, mosques (*cami* [Arabic, *jāmi'*]), great mosques (*cami-i kebir*), *Ka'ba*, and *Arafāt*. In every neighbourhood and village there exists a *masjid* in which daily prayers and *teravih* prayers are performed. In every district and county there is a mosque, in which Friday and holy-day prayers are performed in addition to the above. The necessities of life led to the existence of a great mosque in every big city besides the ordinary mosques and, thus, a larger meeting-place is provided for Friday prayers. However, there is no definite general rule on this; both Friday and holy-day prayers may be performed in the ordinary mosques as well as in the great mosques.

Thus, the *masjid* is the social space where the people of a neighbourhood or a village get together; the mosque is the one where the people of a district or county form the congregation; and the great mosque is the one where people of a big city or province form a religious collectivity.

192 TURKISH NATIONALISM AND WESTERN CIVILIZATION

As the local groups coming together in these places of worship are members conscious of belonging to a nation, these gatherings assume a national character. The *Ka'ba* and the *Arafāt*, on the other hand, bring a huge collectivity every year from among the able-bodied members of the *ümmet* of Islam. All nationalities within Islam attend these gatherings through their representatives. Fasting during the month of *Ramaẓan* is nothing but a negative ritual, preparing for this positive phase of ritual. The time extending from the end of *Ramaẓan* to the beginning of the Feast Month of Sacrifice ['*īd aḍhā*] [about two months] is the interval in which pilgrims from distant lands may travel to the holy place.

The periodicity of positive rituals is a fact also necessitated by social life. Besides the religious aspect, social life also has economic, aesthetic, etc., aspects. Individual members of society find enjoyment in eating, sleeping, working, leisure, entering legal relations, etc. There must be certain periods of time for prayer so that the people may come together at the places of worship. Thus, like all social affairs, religious activities, too, become periodic and punctual. Every religion has its own calendar.

We do not need to go into further details to show the social functions of the positive rituals. They simply bring together at certain places and at certain times individuals who, because of the necessities of life, have to live scattered and make them convene with each other for a holy aim. As all kinds of meetings produce a sense of holiness in souls, so the meetings with a holy purpose certainly generate the same feeling in a much more intensified manner. The feeling of holiness is such an elixir that we may aptly call it 'sacred power'. Any idea touched by it turns into a belief, any sentiment into a conviction. It turns the sad person into a cheerful one, the pessimist into an optimist, the sceptic into a believer. The 'sacred power' makes the coward courageous, the slothful industrious, the sick healthy, the immoral virtuous, the indifferent an idealist, the weak determined, the egoist altruistic. Men who in ordinary times and places seek different gods are brought together at national times and places by these gatherings to experience a national life.

In short, the social function of rituals expresses itself as the renunciation of individuality, and the social function of positive ritual as the fulfilment of nationality. Religion is the most important factor in the creation of national consciousness as it unites men through common sentiments and beliefs. It is because of this that genuinely religious men

RELIGION, EDUCATION, AND FAMILY 193

are those who have national fervour, and that genuine nationalists are
those who believe in the eternity of faith.

ISLAMIC JURISPRUDENCE AND SOCIOLOGY[3]

Human actions may be studied from two points of view; namely,
from the point of view of utility and from that of goodness or badness.
The disciplines which study human actions from the point of view of
utility and non-utility, such as hygiene, economics, and the science of
administration, may be called the sciences of management (*tadbīr*
[T. *tedbir*]). These disciplines may take different names such as *tedbir-i
nefs*, *tedbir-i menẓil*, *tedbiri-i devlet*, depending on the relevance of
utility and non-utility to the individual, or the family, or the city, or the
state.

The science that studies human actions according to the criteria of
goodness or badness is called *fiḳh* in Islam. Actions which are classified
on the basis of goodness or badness may be divided into religious rites
(*menâsik-i Islâmiye*) and legal relations (*hukuk-u Islâmiye*).* Thus, *fiḳh*
contains two sections, Islamic ritual and Islamic jurisprudence. (Since
the last century the term *fiḳh* has been applied to the second section and
has become almost synonymous with Islamic jurisprudence.)

The utility or non-utility of actions is defined by reason based on
experience. The goodness or badness of the actions is also defined,
according to the Mutazilites, by reason. But the goodness or badness
of an action when judged by reason is nothing but its utility or non-
utility. To distinguish the utility or non-utility of an action is something different from distinguishing its goodness or badness. Good is
not good because it is useful, it is good because it is believed to be
good. It is true that good is also useful from the point of view of
society. But the usefulness of the good is not the cause of the belief in
its goodness, it is the result of it. Good, when circumscribed by utility,
ceases to be good. It is because of this fact that good has to be absolute
and categorical. This observation is not limited solely to religious
values; it is true also in the realm of political and national ideals. When
a people tries to revive its language from oblivion, it does not do it
because of any consideration of utility. It does it because it cherishes
its language. A patriot, dying for the sake of his fatherland, does not

---

* Since the morality of actions is nothing but an aspect of these two categories of action
fiḳh did not codify ethics separately as a special branch.

194 TURKISH NATIONALISM AND WESTERN CIVILIZATION

believe that the fatherland is merely the place where he gets his daily bread. Sometimes thousands of soldiers risk their lives just to keep the enemy from getting hold of their flag although there may be no actual harm in its being captured by the enemy since it is just a piece of cloth. The sun is obviously more useful to men than the moon, but in spite of this truth, we continue to believe in the crescent as a cherished symbol. When the people prefer the fez or fur cap to the hat, they do it not because they think one is more hygienic or cheaper than the other, but because these objects symbolize a meaning, a value cherished in the national consciousness. These examples indicate that when we measure sacredness with utility and analyse the cherished objects in terms of reason, what we call 'social conscience' becomes nothing other than 'practical reason' (*mudebbire*). Hygiene or economics takes the place of morals when we consider moral values in terms of practical interests.

The rationalist or utilitarian approach to morals, which is rejected in contemporary philosophy and sociology, had also been rejected in the past by the scholars of *Ahl al-sunna*. According to them, good or bad is determined by religion (the *shar'*), though it may be comprehensible in terms of reason. The *shar'* determines the goodness or the badness of actions using two criteria. The first is the *nass* and the second is '*urf*. The *nass* is expressed in the Book and in the *Sunna*, while the '*urf* is the conscience of the society expressed in the actual conduct and living of the community. Actions with respect to goodness or badness are judged obligatory (incumbent, *vājib*) or forbidden (*harām*) in terms of the *nass*, and as customary (equitable, *ma'rūf*) or rejected (*munkar*) in terms of the '*urf*. The actions that are neither obligatory nor forbidden, and neither customary nor rejected, are accepted as permissible (*mubāh*).*

Yet, the function of '*urf* does not consist only in distinguishing between actions that are socially accepted and those that are socially rejected. The hadith '*mā ra'aha'l-mu'minūna hasanan fa-huwa'inda 'llāhi 'l-hasanu*' (what the faithful regard as good is good with God), and the maxim of the *fikh* 'action according to '*urf* is like acting on the *nass*' imply that under necessity '*urf* may take the place of *nass*.

Muslims have to obey the commands and prohibitions expressed in the *nass* as they have to command that which is customary (*ma'rūf*)

---

*The actions classified as commendable (*mandub*) and objectionable (*makruh*) are only graduations between those that are obligatory and rejected.

and forbid that which is rejected (*munkar*). But the latter is nothing more than those actions which are cherished or rejected by the social consciousness.

Therefore, on the one hand, *fiķh* is based on revelation, and on the other, on society. In other words, Islamic *sharī'a* is both divine and social. The transmitted principles of *fiķh* are absolute and unchangeable. The Holy Kur'an is preserved and the *Sunna* is recorded as far as possible. The divine part of the *sharī'a*, being a divine act, is in a state of absolute perfection; hence, it is exempt from any evolution or progress. The fundamentals of the faith cannot be subject to the law of evolution like social institutions. Religion is religion when it is believed in as free from any defect. A religion ceases to be religion when its ultimate principles are believed not to be absolute and unchangeable.

The social principles of *fiķh*, on the other hand, are subject to the transformations taking place in the forms and structures of society, and hence are subject to changes along with society. Every '*urf* is invariably the '*urf* of a certain social type. A norm which is customary in a certain social type may be a norm rejected in another social type. Even a glance at history and ethnology will show us that the customs, the usages, and folkways do change from time to time and differ from society to society.

It is true that good or bad is not an individual and rational product as the intellectualistic philosophers held but is supra-rational and social as the idealistic philosophers hold. But this social and absolute character does not prevent these norms from being subject to change from society to society. Social absoluteness cannot be reconciled with being conditional, but may be reconciled with relativity. The social absoluteness of a norm implies its being unconditional and categorical in a certain social type. For example, the laws of a state have an absolute character of enforcement within their own territory though the laws of different states may not be the same. This is so also in the case of morality. The goodness or badness of actions is relative to the type of society in which they are current. For that reason, the norms have to change not only with the changes in time but also with the transformations of the types of the societies to which they are relative. For example, in a tribe the gens is responsible for the actions of the individuals; whereas in the civil society this rule cannot be applied. Again, in a tribal society private authority—that is, the authority of the chief of the clan—is more powerful than the public authority, that is, the

196 TURKISH NATIONALISM AND WESTERN CIVILIZATION

sovereignty of the tribal chief. In civil society the gens narrows down to the family and the tribe grows up to be a state. Through this transformation the application of this rule would lead to the infringement on, and decline in, the public authority which is the basis of public law. Sociology shows us that the family has passed from the stages of the maternal clan to the patriarchal and the dual type of family (moiety). The families observable today among various peoples belong to either one of these types, or to transitory forms. In each type, the legal relations between husband, wife, and children differ. Therefore, is it possible to subject all of them to the same laws? As a matter of fact, is it not because of this that changes of the rules are allowed to be made considering the fact that social types undergo transformation?

It is true that, in the matters of *nass*, *ijtihād* [the exercise of one's own judgment as to what the law is in a given matter] is not permissible, but in cases where *nass* does not exist, acting according to *'urf* is like acting according to *nass*. According to certain scholars of *fiḳh*, if *nass* is the product of *'urf*, *ijtihād* is permissible in matters of *nass* too. Then the scope of *'urf* in *fiḳh* becomes more expanded.

From the above discussion we arrive at the following conclusion: The sources of *fiḳh* are two: traditional (*naḳlī*) *sharī'a*, and social *sharī'a*. But the social *sharī'a* is in a continuous process of 'becoming', like all social phenomena. It follows, then, that that part of *fiḳh* is not only liable to evolution in accordance with social evolution, but also *has* to change. The fundamentals of *fiḳh* related to *nass* are eternally constant and unchangeable, whereas the social applications of these fundamentals which are based on the *'urf* of the public and on the *ijmā* (consensus) of the scholars of *fiḳh* have to adapt themselves in accordance with the necessities of life.

THE SOCIAL SOURCES OF ISLAMIC JURISPRUDENCE[4]

One of the sources of *fiḳh* is *nass*, the other is *'urf*. The first source of *fiḳh* is conceived with utmost care, and thus there has originated, besides the several sciences based on the Kur'an and Hadith, a special science called the *Fundamentals of Fiḳh*, which shows the ways in which the provisions of *fiḳh* are derived and differentiated from the body of *nass*. Would it not have been possible to make similar careful studies on *'urf*? Would it not have been possible to elaborate a sociological method to show how *'urf* has varied within different social groups and changed

RELIGION, EDUCATION, AND FAMILY 197

with the stages of the evolution of these groups, and also to show how the variations and evolution in 'urf have influenced fikh itself? It would be unjust to expect the past centuries to create a science based on such studies, since sociology was developed only very recently as a positive science.

In every community there is the 'urf, the by-product of its real legal life, which constitutes the living law of the community. It is the norms living in the consciousness of the people which interpret, and apply to the actual, the formulae written in the law books. It is because of this fact that the 'urf, which was not at first regarded as an original source of fikh, forced itself into being accepted by the fakihs through other means.

The Islamic community first resorted to the Kur'an in its search for legal satisfaction. But this community was in a process of continuous growth and expansion, and it was inevitable that its social life, and hence its 'urfs and customs, should be subject to grave transformation. Then, the community, being unable to find an applicable answer in this source [Kur'an] for some of the 'urfs which were of almost unlimited varieties, had to resort to the sunna and hadīth. Even Imām Mālik accepted the social traditions of the people of Medina, by assuming that these were the forms of the sunna diffused among the people (sünnet-i şâyi'a). But when the endless necessities of life which had been covered by 'urf in the past raised questions that proved to be unanswered even in these sources, ijmā and qiyās were resorted to. At the same time the Great Imām [Abū Hanīfa] realized that the 'urf should be taken as an independent source, and he established the rule of approbation (istihsān), which consisted of preferring the practices most expedient to the public, to qiyās. And Imām Abū Yūsuf formulated the following rule: 'When a nass and an 'urf differ from each other in a particular situation, the 'urf is to be preferred if the nass was derived from 'urf.'

There has been only one scholar of fikh who did not accept the 'urf and the ijtihād, and who accepted no principle other than that of the acceptance of the ostensible (ʒāhir) meaning of the nass. He was Dāvūd bin 'Ali, the imām of the Ẓāhirī sect. This sect, which denied the necessities of life, received a punishment deserving of its attitude —that is, it was not accepted by life. Thus, in spite of all the efforts of some persons who were seeking fame by attempting to revive the Ẓāhirī sect, it could not survive anywhere and left almost no trace of its influence.

198 TURKISH NATIONALISM AND WESTERN CIVILIZATION

It is seen, therefore, that as *ijtihād* was born from the need for adaptation to the *'urf*, so the growth and differentiation of *fikh* went hand in hand with the development and differentiation of the *'urf*. In order to write the history of *fikh*, it is necessary to know the *'urf* of the Muslim peoples. Yes, the Islamic *sharī'a* is the tree of *Tuba* which has its roots in the heavens, but the *raison d'être* of this tree is to live in an earthly environment and atmosphere, and to get its air, heat, and light from the social *'urf* to satisfy the civil needs. It cannot be said that this tree, after giving fruits during some centuries, does not need to get its food any more. Those who believe that the Islamic *sharī'a* will remain the *sharī'a* of every age to the last have to accept the fact that the tree should always be living and fruitful. A law which does not live and give life cannot be the regulator of life. It is evident, therefore, that there must be social fundamentals as well as dogmatic fundamentals of *fikh*. It remains for the scholars of *fikh* and the sociologists of our time to elaborate this branch of knowledge which has so far been neglected. I say scholars of *fikh* and sociologists because the job cannot be done by either group alone. This science cannot be established without the co-operation of the two.

The various forms of expression of the *'urf* are public opinion, *mores*, customs, usages, and tradition. The consensus of the scholars of *fikh* and the negative decisions of the *shūra* are a kind of expression of the *'urf* too. We may question even sociologically whether unbroken tradition (*tavātur*) is also free from the negating influence of the *'urf*.

We have, therefore, first, to classify and define scientifically the various forms of *'urf*. Secondly, we have to define the moral, legal, and political aspects of the *'urf* and discover the differences between them. Thirdly, as in studying other natural phenomena, we must study *'urf* to see if there are certain and necessary laws according to which its changes and evolution operate.

European sociologists show by the comparative methods of ethnology, history, and statistics that under 'similar social conditions' certain moral and legal institutions and certain religious beliefs assume certain social patterns and that where identical forms of social life exist, there is a development towards identical institutions. It has even been demonstrated that in societies of the same type, even the secondary customs and usages show complete similarity in spite of the fact that these societies have been so remote from each other both temporally and spatially as to preclude any possibility of contact. The uniformity

RELIGION, EDUCATION, AND FAMILY 199

of this similarity observed between the institutions which belonged to the same social type is the best proof of the existence of the law of determinism in social life. Certain of our *'ulamā* have regarded the natural laws which are observable in natural phenomena as the *sunna* of God. Is it not compatible with religious feelings to extend this understanding to the natural determinism observable in the natural laws of society?

If social consciousness, moral beliefs, legal usages, and political opinions of peoples and nations are dependent on natural laws which are independent of individual will yet governing them, what can be the power which establishes these *sunna* and the laws other than the eternal purpose? Therefore, does not *'urf* too have a divine nature in an implicit and figurative sense, if not in an actual and open way? Imām Abū Yūsuf says, 'If *nass* is derived from *'urf*, then *'urf* is preferable'. Therefore, is it not possible to say that the *nass* relative to temporal affairs and social life is a derivative of the *'urf*? When we accept social determinism and the uniformity of social phenomena as the expression of the way of God, it becomes natural to regard this divine *sunna* as the basis of the *nass* relating to the social life.

Yet, the sociology of the sources of *fiķh*, although studying the social origins of *fiķh*, can in no way claim to replace the science of *fiķh*. In the same way, *nass* also never claimed to hold such a monopoly over *fiķh*. The functions of *iftā* and *qaḍā* are not the business of the scholars of the sources of *fiķh*, but of the scholars of *fiķh* whose duty it is to apply the rules of the *fiķh*. As to the scholars of the sources of *fiķh*, they have two functions: to lead the scholars of *fiķh* in the field of the *nass* on the one hand, and in the field of sociology on the other. The scholars of *fiķh* cannot dispense with either of these methods.

RELIGION AND LAW[5]

In a primitive society every person is required to satisfy all his needs by himself. In advanced societies, on the other hand, each person performs the work in which he is trained. The factor that relieves people from doing several jobs is what we call social division of labour.

Now, why should this principle, which is accepted in every sphere of life, not be applied in religious life? Are branches of [religious] learning so simple as to be mastered by every person without having specialized training? Why should there not be trained specialists in religion who would master religious knowledge, with all its sublimity and pro-

200 TURKISH NATIONALISM AND WESTERN CIVILIZATION

fundity? Are matters of the propagation of faith, religious education, and piety so insignificant as to be left to the private initiative of ordinary persons?

It is observed that soldiers drafted from Anatolian villages are pitifully ignorant of their religion. This is due to the fact that the job of teaching religion is believed to be within any person's competence. As a consequence, a special religious organization has not developed to handle religious teaching properly.

It is true that there were religious institutions in Islam. But, as we [Muslims] always tended to combine things rather than divide them, these institutions assumed several functions at the same time, in spite of the fact that Islam, from the beginning, had differentiated matters of piety (*diyanet* [Arabic *diyānah*]) from the affairs of jurisprudence (*kaʐa* [Arabic *qaḍā*]). From the earliest centuries the office of the *muftī* and of the *qāḍī* were separately established to issue judgments relating to matters of piety and of law respectively. The Great Imām [Abū Hanīfa], who was in his time the *muftī* of the *umma*, persistently refused to accept any appointment as the supreme judge, and he even risked his life for this cause. He believed that the two offices could not be united in one person.

Piety and the matter of jurisprudence are so different from each other that in several cases the same thing may be impermissible from the point of view of piety yet possible from a judicial point of view. For example, taking interest is not permissible from the point of view of piety, whereas it is permissible through *dawr-i sharʾī* [the method of paying interest by a fictitious transfer]. The right to sue may become null and void by the lapse of time but never from the point of view of piety. To bequeath to an heir is not permitted by piety, but it is judicially practised through [the principle of] disposal of possession (*nafy-i mulk*) or the principle that an heir may be appointed as trustee for the property bequeathed to notable righteous persons. Likewise, *hulla* is not permissible by piety, but it is practised through judicial ways. Polygamy is impermissible by piety because there is no possibility of righteousness, and its impossibility for the common people is confirmed by the Kurʾan; yet polygamy was permitted by the judiciary. Divorce is the most hated of what is permissible (*ʾabghaḍ al-halāl*) for piety, but was not restricted [in law] by any negative condition.

These examples show that piety and judicial judgment are different things. When a judgment is demanded from a *muftī*, to which should his judgment refer? Undoubtedly it would refer to the provisions of piety. The decree of the *qāḍī*, on the other hand, is a judicial judgment. Obviously these two things are not the same. When the Great Imām [Abū Hanīfa] avoided uniting the two functions in his person, he was acting so righteously that it was for him worthwhile to risk his life. The following verse shows the necessity of the existence of a class of men charged with the duty of dissemination of faith. 'The believers should not march forth altogether; and the believers should not all go out to fight. Of every troop of them, a party only should go forth, that they (who are left behind) may gain sound knowledge in religion, and that they may warn their people when they return to them that they may beware' [Kur'an, IX, 122, Pickthall's trans.]. From the beginning there were persons charged with the duty of the dissemination of religion; such were *muftī*s, teachers, shaikhs, *imām*s, *khatīb*s, preachers, and pilgrimage guides.

If these ever become organized as an orderly religious organization under a Ministry of Pious Affairs, we may be sure that the function of religious teaching will be fulfilled everywhere in the World of Islam. Why should the principle of division of labour not be applied in this sphere of life too? A person may be a specialist in jurisprudence, but may not be in religion; and vice versa. Why should the same persons combine the two competences in themselves? Even if we accept that they do, still it is absolutely impermissible to charge them with the two functions which are irreconcilable in one person at the same time.

Piety has to do with that aspect of life that is sacred, and it is not permissible to mix earthly considerations with it, such as expediency, concession, and casuistry. The legal aspect of life, on the other hand, has to be subjected to economic, hygienic, technical, and many other secular considerations.

The reason for our lagging behind other nations in religious heedfulness lies in the backwardness of our judicial methods and practices in spite of the utmost perfection of the principles of our religion. It is because of the confusion of the two things that those who are dissatisfied with judicial conditions become unfaithful to religion in the long run. Whenever these two things are mixed, each becomes harmful to the other, because their respective foundations serve different purposes. When *muftī*s issue their religious judgments and *qāḍī*s perform their judicial functions separately, both will succeed in maintaining the purity and integrity of their own fields.

202 TURKISH NATIONALISM AND WESTERN CIVILIZATION

A wise man once said that the expression 'differences in community' of the *nass* saying, 'the differences in my community are a blessing to it' (*ikhtilāf ummati rahmatuhu*) implied division of labour and specialization, and it seems to be a justifiable interpretation. If it is so, let us pray to God to bestow that blessing upon us.

STATE AND RELIGION[6]

The discussions that took place in the annual convention of the [Party of] Union and Progress have given expression to a sincere contention that Islam can be reconciled with modern civilization.

There have been men in Turkey who have held this view. Especially Namık Kemal and Cevdet Paşa should be mentioned among them. There is, however, another group which believed the contrary. According to the latter group, Islam would neither be reconciled with, nor would it ever adapt itself to, contemporary civilization.

It is interesting to note that each group contained within itself two factions which represented certain diametrically opposite views. Theoretically, both started with similar premises but arrived, in practice, at entirely contradictory conclusions. One of these factions we may call 'the zealots of Europeanism', and the other 'the zealots of scholasticism'.

The first believed that, as the principles of Islam cannot be reconciled with contemporary civilization, we have to drop them altogether and adapt ourselves, in a material as well as in a spiritual sense, to European civilization. The second believed that as the bases of Islam are irreconcilable with contemporary civilization, the latter civilization ought to be rejected *in toto* in order to maintain the existing traditions.

It is obvious that both views are entirely blind to the facts. People can neither entirely drop the religion they hold sacred, nor can they dispense with the necessities of contemporary civilization. Reason demands, not that one be sacrificed at the expense of the other, but that an attempt be made to reconcile the two.

Unfortunately, the leaders of *Tanzimat* did not follow this latter course when they initiated the drive towards modernization. In their reforms they wanted to modernize the Ottoman state, but because of their mistaken interpretations, they reduced the state to an inorganic condition and divested it of its Islamic form altogether.

The first mistake they made was their belief that the Caliphate of

RELIGION, EDUCATION, AND FAMILY   203

Islam and the Islamic state were different things which disregarded the fact that the Caliph was actually the temporal head of the state and that the organization of the Caliphate corresponded to the organization of the state.

As can be seen in Mawardi's *Aḥkām al- Sulṭāniyya*, the Sultanate is a function of the sovereignty of the Caliph and cannot be separated from it. Thus, contrary to the conception of the leaders of the *Tanẓimat*, Caliphate and Sultanate are not two separate functions united in one person. The Grand Vizir was not an unconditional deputy of the Sultan, who was believed to be independent of the office of Caliphacy, but was actually the unconditional deputy of the Caliph, and the imperial seal that he carried was the seal of the Caliph, as was the case among the Abbasi Caliphs. To assume that the *Shaikh-ul-Islām* was the unconditional deputy of the Caliph, and to attribute to him a spiritual leadership comparable to that of the Pope, is a grave mistake from the point of view of the *sharī'a*.

The second mistake of the leaders of *Tanẓimat* was their acceptance of two kinds of judiciary. To them, Sultanate and Caliphate, though united in one person, were two independent authorities each having separate judicial functions—one delegated to the office of the *Shaikh-ul-Islām* as the deputy of the Caliph, and the other to the Grand Vizir as the Sultan's deputy. Following this assumption in 1836, they placed the *qāḍī-askers* and the *qāḍī* of Istanbul under the office of *Shaikh-ul-Islām* and, as the *shar'ī qāḍīs* were under the *qāḍī-askers*, the office of *Shaikh-ul-Islām* became the highest [judicial] office. In the past, however, these judges had always been under the office of Grand Vizir, because in Islam there were not two kinds of judiciary and the functions of *iftā* and *qaḍā* could not be united in the same person. Judicial power was the exclusive right of the Caliph and the absolute deputy of the latter was the Grand Vizir. *Qāḍīs* were the Caliph's delegates, and exercised judicial functions on his behalf. Therefore, they were selected and appointed by the Caliph's deputy. *Muftīs* [who exercised the function of *iftā*], on the other hand, were not officers of the Caliph. They were simply announcers (*muballigh*) of the commandments of God. Consequently, their office was too lofty to be subjected to a higher earthly authority. The functions of *iftā* and *qaḍā* could not be joined in one person, and it was for this reason that the Great Imām Abū Ḥanīfa and Zenbilli Ali, the *Shaikh-ul-Islām* of Selim I, did not accept the appointment to the office of the highest judiciary. These examples

204 TURKISH NATIONALISM AND WESTERN CIVILIZATION

show sufficiently how lofty and sacred was the office of *iftā* in Islam.

As both *muftī* and *qāḍī* were guided by the law of *fiḳh*, why should this difference in status between the two exist? The reason is that the *fiḳh* contained provisions with regard to both piety and justice, and that *qāḍī*s were charged with the execution of the judicial provisions while the *muftī*s were conveyers of religious injunctions on behalf of God. Religious injunctions impose religious obligations whose sanctions are exclusively other-worldly, whereas judicial injunctions are backed only by earthly sanctions. Therefore, judicial injunctions, although still religious, constitute an independent category outside of the injunctions concerning matters of piety. They are what we today call law. Thus, in Islam law refers to the provisions of religion (*dīn*), but not to those of piety (*diyanet*). All injunctions of religion are one in nature, but owing to the separation between earthly and other-worldly sanctions, they are necessarily divided into these two categories. As the *qāḍī* is charged with the task of maintaining an earthly order and with the fulfilment of social needs in general, he has to take the various expediencies of life into consideration.

Thus, the *qāḍī* had to judge or accept judgments on various matters whose execution was not permissible from the point of view of piety. For example, charging interest is not permissible from the point of view of piety at all, because all Muslims are brothers and exacting interest from brothers is something to be morally condemned in every nation. The *qāḍī*, on the other hand, was forced by the necessities of social life to permit this absolutely impious act when, under the name of *ribḥ-i mulzam* (unavoidable interest), he had to lend at interest the funds deposited for orphans. Likewise, while it was not permissible to bequeath to an heir (*lā wasiyya bi al-wārith*), the *qāḍī* gave implicit permission under the principle of 'the disposal of property'. Contemporary judicial expediencies forced them to regard intoxicating drinks as *mal-i mutaqawwim* [a commodity capable of legal ownership and transfer], but this compulsory acceptance did not imply acceptance of intoxicating drinks as lawful objects from the point of view of piety.

Uniting *iftā* and *qaḍā* under the same office and having the judicial decrees of the *sharī'a* courts ratified by the *iftā* has given rise to the impression that things permitted judicially are also permissible from the point of view of piety. This is harmful from the point of view of morality and piety. Islam has manifested its moral sublimity in its injunctions of piety. Judicial injunctions are nothing but acts of

RELIGION, EDUCATION, AND FAMILY 205

tolerance on behalf of religion in accordance with the necessities of time. When the Prophet said: '*Bu'ithtu bilḥanīfiyyati-s-semḥā*' ('I was sent with a straightforward and the most generous faith'), he meant that the provisions of piety were *hanīf* (straightforward) and the judicial toleration was *samīh* (generous). The *hanīf*s are those who act in accordance with the religious commands given by the *muftī*, and the *samīh*s are those who benefit from the implicit permission of the *qāḍī*. The *tasawwuf* calls the first *ahl-i aẕīmet* [men resolved to act according to law without concession] and the second *ahl-i rukhṣat* [men of concession]. The right of the claimant may become null and void by forfeit, but the right itself is not nullified. 'The man of concession' may refrain from paying his debts on the basis of such a judicial permission, whereas 'the man of resolution' does not hesitate to pay such a debt in compliance with the *fatwā* which demands that which is due from the pious.

To identify morality with law is a sign of moral decline in a nation, and again, in the same manner, to identify piety with legality indicates ethical decadence. Putting the *sharī'a* courts under the office of *Shaikh-ul-Islam* has given rise to this lamentable consequence. Seeing that this office became an authority based on the earthly sanctions of coercion like those of the judiciary, the people began to disregard other-worldly sanctions. As the office of *iftā* began to handle matters of judiciary and undertook the task of ratifying judicial decrees, the idea that the *sharī'a* was nothing but the judicial judgments became a firm belief among the people. The multiplicity of the judicial authorities undermined the safety of the provisions of piety and gave rise to the belief that Caliphate and Sultanate were separate authorities. This led some people to believe that there were two kinds of Islamic government in this country. Under the impression of such a belief, there are not a few persons who think that Islam is a religion with two governments, as is Catholicism. The erroneous interpretations of the men of *Tanẕimat* have been responsible for these unsound beliefs so that gradually the state has ceased to be an Islamic state.

Was this policy necessitated by their efforts to modernize the state? It will be shown below that, on the contrary, they made the state even less modern.

The aim of a modern state is to unite all its organs within its own organization by legal ties in order to make them organs of public service or of private associations. In modern states public services are incorporated into official departments of the government. Private associations are constituted in accordance with the laws of the state and with the authorizing permission of the state. Thus, their existence does not infringe on the political authority of the state. In a state where this policy is not followed, associations and organizations tend to establish their own authority over their members, and actually tend to become states within the state. The sociological criterion indicating the existence or non-existence of a political authority in any organization is the existence or non-existence of a judicial authority. When a social group is in a position to exercise the judicial function, it is vested with political authority and thus possesses something which is peculiar only to the state.

It is known that before the period of *Tanzimat*, foreign embassies and Christian Orthodox patriarchates had judicial rights and they exercised a kind of political authority thus. We cannot blame the statesmen of the *Tanzimat* for these ancient deviations. However, they accepted them as reasonable and legitimate and, furthermore, they themselves attempted to create a similar situation even for the Muslims. Thus, instead of abolishing or diminishing these deviations, they furthered and strengthened them.

To understand the *Tanzimat*ists' view of government, it suffices to discuss the meanings of two terms which they introduced into the vocabulary of government, namely 'community' [*Cemaat* in Turkish usage; *millet* in Western publications] and 'affairs of cult'. To understand the first, let us look at the groups which correspond to these 'communities' in Europe. We find, for example, Protestant and Jewish congregations living in France, or Russian and American nationals living in Paris. However, neither these non-Catholic Churches nor these foreign nationals are of the same nature as these so-called 'communities'. The 'communities', native or foreign, which existed in Turkey enjoyed political powers, legal immunities, and even a political authority, none of which was possessed by those communities in France. Protestants, Jews, Russians, or Americans in France are under the exclusive jurisdiction of the state of France in all their legal dealings. And this is not peculiar only to France or even to Europe. It is the same everywhere wherever a modern state exists, including Japan.

It follows, then, that in modern states there cannot exist any organization of the nature of these 'communities'. It is one of the truisms of public law to see them either as organs of public service or as private

RELIGION, EDUCATION, AND FAMILY 207

associations. The statesmen of *Tanẓimat* were not followers of this principle. For them, the Ottoman state was not a political community made up of citizens, but a confederation made up of 'communities'. Since they assumed that under the headship of the Caliph there existed a 'community' of Muslims like those of the native or foreign 'communities', therefore this confederation of 'communities' did not seem to them anything unreasonable. The Sultan, from their point of view, would be the suzerain of the confederation and the Caliph, the Greek Patriarch or foreign ambassadors would be his vassals. But as the Sultan was at the same time the Caliph, they believed that the right of precedence of the Muslim 'community' had been guaranteed by this policy.

This conception of 'communities', each vested with a partial autonomy, which was held by the statesmen of the *Tanẓimat* was, according to them, a result of their respect for the principle of religious freedom. They called these groups 'religious communities', and the legal provisions by which these 'communities' were vested with autonomy, they called provisions of 'the affairs of cult'. Thus, judicial matters with respect to the family, for example, became matters of cult and not of law! All scholars agree that rules having judicial sanctions are legal rules. Of the matters relating to family, those which are not brought before the judge, or those which do not necessitate any judicial sanction, are not matters of law. Among them, those which are based on the sanctioning power of public opinion are matters of morality and those which are backed by other-worldly sanctions are matters of piety. The statesmen of the *Tanẓimat* called these matters *umur-u meẓhebiye* (affairs of cult), exploiting the ambiguity of the word *meẓheb* [Arabic *madbhab*]. This word, however, means exactly what the word *'doctrine'* means in French. The *meẓheb* of an *imām* refers to a doctrine of *fiḳh*. For *umur-u meẓhebiye* the French use the term *affaires cultuelles*, as they also use the name *ministères des cultes* for the ministry of *meẓheb*s. As the word for cult in Islam is *'ibāda*, the correct translations would be *umur-u ta 'abbudiye* and *ibâdat naẓareti* respectively. The first means nothing but *umur-u diyaniye* (affairs of piety). Freedom of religion should mean freedom in the affairs of worship or piety. In order to realize this freedom, it is not necessary to create political communities out of communities of cult or to invest them with legal privileges. Âli Paşa, one of the leading statesmen of the period of *Tanẓimat*, found nothing objectionable in granting the Armenians the right to have a kind of 'national assembly' and 'national constitution', in

208 TURKISH NATIONALISM AND WESTERN CIVILIZATION

addition to the already existing privileges of the Armenian 'community'.

One of the logical consequences of the *Tanẓimat*ist view was the idea of establishing a Muslim 'community' alongside the others. As a first step towards this end, *sharī'a* courts were connected with the office of *Shaikh-ul-Islam*. The projects to establish Muslim 'communities' were to constitute the second step. Happily the only one, constituted in Edirne, was never extended to other provinces. As we have seen above, these communities had, in fact, a political character. In other words, they were, so to speak, pseudo-states. As our state was an Islamic state under the Caliphate, there would be another Islamic state under the name of the Muslim 'community'—a situation full of grave inconveniences. Besides the inevitable clashes that were likely to arise between these two Islamic organizations, there was a still greater danger because, by our own example, we should have formally recognized and confirmed the legitimacy of the external and internal Capitulations.

Although this project of organizing a Muslim 'community' was never materialized, something else was done which was equally harmful: in addition to the judicial function of the state, another judicial function was created for the office of *fatwā*. It was believed that accepting the duality of the judicial office and identifying the affairs of piety with those of the judiciary were in accordance with the principles of Islam. Thus, the Islamic state could never have become a modern state, confirming a claim put forward by certain European scholars, and consequently could never be independent internally or externally. We should have had no right to abolish the Capitulations. However, there were further consequences. As is known, the Ministry of Justice is entitled to submit laws to the Legislative Assembly whenever it deems any law unsatisfactory or contrary to the demands of contemporary life. By accepting these proposed Bills as a whole or with modifications, a continuous improvement of the laws is guaranteed. The same need was also recognized in the office of *iftā*. The procedure accepted by this office under such a condition was as follows: in case a judgment, believed to be in accord with the needs of the time, was not found existing in the Hanafite *fiḳh*, it was compared with either other disputed opinions of the Hanafites or other doctrines of the four schools of jurisprudence. It was finally decided on the basis of the principle that 'it is necessary to follow whatever the head of the believers commands

RELIGION, EDUCATION, AND FAMILY 209

in questions subject to *ijtihād'*, and was submitted for the ratification of the Caliph. This procedure, which was the result of connecting the *sharī'a* courts to the office of *iftā*, is in accordance neither with the Constitution nor with *sharī'a*. It was not in accordance with the first because, since the decrees of the Caliph are of the nature of law, the procedure necessarily leads to the promulgation of laws not passed by the Legislative Assembly. And it was not in harmony with *sharī'a* because the *iftā* authority is not vested in the Caliph but lies in the *nass* whose interpreters and conveyors are the *muftīs*. As an *ijtihād* cannot abrogate other *ijtihād*s, the decree of the Caliph cannot force a *muftī* to comply with it.

As the decree of the Chief Administrator is of the nature of law, and as the *qāḍī*s are the delegates of the Caliph, his decrees are incumbent only upon the *qāḍī*s. Therefore, preferring one judgment to another on questions that are subject to *ijtihād* is a procedure already followed by the legislative authority in its enactment of laws and has nothing to do with matters of *iftā*. In short, the acceptance of such a procedure has given rise, on the one hand, to the practice of submitting the ratification of the *fatwā* to the Head of the Believers, which is contrary to the *sharī'a*, and, on the other hand, to the anti-constitutional practice of allowing the office of *fatwā* to legislate laws directly and without the knowledge of the government or of the Legislative Assembly.

Another consequence of this system of a multiple judiciary that aggravated the situation further was the non-existence of a codified *sharī'a* law, because whenever a case came before the court, the judicial ruling for the case was sought by the court from the office of *fatwā*. This *fatwā* is a kind of law applicable only retrospectively, whereas the provisions of modern codes of law are applicable only to future cases and the right to prepare such laws is reserved exclusively by the legislative body. By issuing such laws, the office of *iftā* performs a legislative act according to one opinion, and acts as a legal counsel according to another. But the latter is absolutely prohibited; as the conversation—recorded in the *Yearbook of Mashikhat*—which took place between Selim I, one of our greatest Caliphs, and Zenbilli Ali, one of our greatest *Shaikh-ul-Islam*s, shows the way in which matters of piety should be differentiated from those of the judiciary.[7] As to the legislative function of the office of the *iftā*, we have already shown that it is contrary to the constitutional régime. An additional drawback to the system of a multiple judiciary follows from the fact that civil and

210 TURKISH NATIONALISM AND WESTERN CIVILIZATION

sharī'a courts issue different and even contradictory decrees on the same issues, and thus throw the government into uncertainty.

All of these effects which we have enumerated so far are compatible neither with the modern state nor with the Islamic state. The affairs of piety and those of the judiciary constitute different areas of public service in a state. They should be taken care of by independent ministries. As the Ministry of Justice deals with judicial affairs, all the judicial organs should necessarily be connected with this Ministry; and as the office of the *Shaikh-ul-Islam* is the Ministry of Affairs of Piety, the complete administration of religious affairs should be given to this sublime office. The *sharī'a* courts together with the *Board of Sharī'a Affairs* and the organizations of the *Qāḍī-asker* should be attached to the Ministry of Justice, but neither their activities nor their organization should be changed. Already Clause 118 of the Constitution makes it clear that the provisions of *fiḳh* should be the basis of the preparation of laws in general, and the scholars of law admit that legal provisions concerning the family, in comparison with other fields of legal provision, are, comparatively, more deeply bound by tradition.

The good results of the institutional separation of affairs of piety from those of the judiciary will not be simply a better distribution of justice. Its greatest advantage will be rather with regard to matters of piety. The office of the *Shaikh-ul-Islam*, which so far has had no time to be interested in matters of piety because of its preoccupation with material affairs, such as the interest transactions on the property of orphans and the administration of the *ahliyya* courts, will then be freed from such non-essential activities and will be able to look after 'the care of our other-worldly affairs', as Ali Zenbilli has put it, and to care for the necessary religious education of the people of Islam.

The affairs of piety, which will be the supreme religious task of the office of the *Mashikhat* of Islam, consist mainly of two things—matters of belief and matters of worship (*'ibāda*). Worship in Islam may be performed at any place; that which should be carried out in a congregation takes place only in the mosques. The inculcation of the beliefs and the education about the rites of prayer are based on knowledge (*'ilm*) and carried through experience (*ḥāl*). The centres of the first are *medreses*, and of the latter, convents. It seems, therefore, that the mosque, the *medrese*, and the convent are three basic Islamic institutions which will be administered by the *Mashikhat*. These institutions so far have been administered by the Ministry of Evkaf (*awkāf*). But

RELIGION, EDUCATION, AND FAMILY

this ministry, being a kind of Ministry of Finance, can administer only their material and financial affairs. Matters of learning and of education have been entirely neglected by it. With the administration of these religious affairs by the *Mashikhat*, there will certainly be a new development in the affairs of piety, because this office has two supreme councils composed of men who have authority on matters of Islamic learning and education which did not exist in the Ministry of Evkaf. One of these councils is the *Board of Fatwā (fetva emaneti)* which is an academy of *Fikh*, and the other is the *Board of Mashayikh (Meclis-i-Meşayih)* which is a kind of academy of *tasawwuf*. If, in addition to these, a *Board of Mutakallimīn (Meclis-i Mütekellimin)* is instituted as an academy of *kalām*, a complete *Learned Council of Religious Studies* will be obtained by amalgamating these three boards.

Since Islam is a religion based on learning and enlightenment, its guides in matters of piety should be men of learning and wisdom (*'ulamā* and *'urafa*). Whenever we look for the organization of piety in Islam, which is free from such (*bid'a*) institutions as priesthood and spiritual government, it is found exclusively in the organizations of learning. In Islam religion is nothing but a form of intellectual enlightenment. For Muslims, the *muftī* is nothing but an erudite scholar in *fikh*; the *mutakallim* a doctor, a scrutinizing student of Islamic beliefs, and the *shaikh* a sage (*'ārif*) who has insight into matters of conscience. Thanks to this superior feature of Islam, we may regard these boards as academies of piety.

Three other departments are needed in the *Mashikhat* in addition to these boards for the administration of the mosques, of the *medreses*, and of the convents. The department now called the *Department of Instructions* corresponds to the second of these three, but for each of the others none exists because, until now, appointments to positions such as those held by the professors of religious seminaries (*mudarris*), the prayer leaders (*imāms*), the sermon readers (*khatībs*), and the chief shaikh of convents (*postnishīn*) were made by the Ministry of Evkaf. As the *Mashikhat* did not appropriate these tasks to itself, it was not equipped by the department to handle them.

Let us now survey the unfortunate consequences of the failure to include these functions under the *Mashikhat*. As the Ministry of Evkaf was a purely financial administration, it could not deal adequately either with the training of the ministers and preachers in their proper institutions of learning or with appointments to proper positions. One

212 TURKISH NATIONALISM AND WESTERN CIVILIZATION

can calculate the unfortunate consequences of this failure from the experiences of the army officers in charge of training new conscripts. According to their reports, most of the soldiers coming from the villages do not know their *mezheb* or even the name of the Prophet. But this religious ignorance is not peculiar to the peasants. You will find the same state of ignorance amongst the poorer classes of the towns and cities. How can such a grave state of religious ignorance be allowed to reign in a religion whose basis is learning?

One of the groups for whose training no special care was taken is the teachers of religion in the [secular] schools. The position of these teachers before the young students who have learned something about mathematical and positive sciences is really tragic. These persons, utterly unable to give reasonable and logical answers to the questions asked by students, do nothing but say, 'Shut up, you infidels!' and thereby degrade their religion before the eyes of the younger generation. The youngsters cannot understand that what has failed before their questions is not the religion of Islam itself but the teacher of religion. Thus, the teacher's ignorance gives rise to a shaking of the faith in the students. The decline of religious beliefs in the schools is due not to an insoluble conflict between the Islamic faith and positive science, but to the utter incompetence of the teachers of religion. A religion like Islam, which is based on reason in metaphysics and on *'urf* in sociology, cannot be in conflict with positive sciences. In addition to the incompetence of the teachers of religion, a condition which has favoured disorganization in religious teaching in schools is the inadequacy of the religious text-books. These books should be written only by genuine scholars. The training of ministers and preachers and of qualified teachers of religion in the secular schools as well as the preparation of scholarly books on faith and worship—all these could be handled adequately by the *Mashikhat*.

The damage created by the dissociation of the *Mashikhat* from the matters of piety was not confined only to the growth of ignorance in religion and to the decline of faith. Another consequence has been a decreasing participation in the performance of religious worship and a diminishing attendance at the mosques. Is nothing going to be done to counteract this trend? Would an honest and sympathetic minister, an eloquent reader of *Khutba*, a wise preacher, a *mu'azzin*, and a *hāfiz* with good voices to make the call to prayer and to recite the Kur'an not increase the number of attendants? Is it not possible in this age of hygienic appliances to build running-water facilities so that ablution might be taken comfortably and to have clean prayer-grounds untouched by wet socks? Today there are several measures demanded to be taken by modern hygienic, aesthetic, and rational standards. Not only are there no religious prohibitions against these, but also they imply several material and spiritual benefits. With the use of electric bulbs in Istanbul the mosques look more hygienic and more aesthetically pleasing. It is obvious that the application of such measures, decided by adequate and competent authorities, will help to increase the attendance at the mosques. These could be planned and applied only by a supreme authority which would have matters of piety as its sole concern, and this supreme authority can be no other than the *Mashikhat*. This authority must educate functionaries such as ministers, preachers, and readers of *Khutba* as well as the *muftīs*, the piofessors of the *medreses*, and experts in religious knowledge in order to give a proper orientation to matters of piety. Professional and specialized *medreses*, therefore, should be established to educate them. In addition to the existing *medreses*, specialized schools to educate preachers, sermoners, muezzins, and Kur'an reciters, and the leaders of the religious orders, should be established. And finally, a school which would be on a higher level than the others for educating *medrese* professors should be opened. The latter *medrese* should contain departments of Arabic Studies, *tafsīr*, *hadīth*, *Kalām*, and *fiḳh*.

One more function of the *Mashikhat* of Islam should be to make the *tarikat*s a social institution in accordance with their original aims and to transform the convents into genuine educational institutions.

Besides these tasks, it should educate the trusted men (*umana*) of religion to be sent all over the World of Islam for the purpose of the furtherance of piety.

The *Board of Fatwā* should prepare an *Encyclopedia of the Fatwā*, the *Board of Mutakallimīn* should prepare books on the Science of *Kalām*, the *Council of Mashayikh* on *tasawwuf*, and a *Committee of Authors and Translators* should be instituted to prepare or translate from Arabic such works as are needed by the public, e.g. on the history of *kalām*, the history of *tasawwuf*, the *siyar* of the Prophets, *tafsir*, and the compendia of the *hadīth*s.

In short, the organization of all the institutions and organizations needed to meet the requirements of the affairs of piety, the building of mosques in villages which do not have any, the opening of *medreses*

214 TURKISH NATIONALISM AND WESTERN CIVILIZATION

wherever they do not exist, the support of needed personnel by providing them with adequate salaries so that the functionaries and scholars of religion can live decently—all these tasks should be carried out by the office of the *Shaikh-ul-Islam*.

ISLAM AND MODERN CIVILIZATION[8]

I

In one of our previous essays we have put forth the thesis that Islam and modern civilization are compatible. There are two possible procedures to verify this thesis: the first is to compare the foundations of Islam with those of modern civilization directly; the second is to enquire whether the points of incompatibility or agreement between Christianity and modern civilization present favourable or unfavourable implications for Islam. Here we shall first follow the second course because it will show us that to the extent to which Christianity remained remote from the principles of Islam, it failed to reconcile itself with modern civilization, and that it was able to reconcile itself with modern civilization only to the extent to which it approached [the principles of] Islam.

There is strong evidence for the argument that Islam is the most modern religion and in no way conflicting with modern science.

The first reason for the existence of a fundamental opposition between Christianity and Islam should be sought in the social conditions existing at the time of their rise. Christianity originated within a community that was under the domination of a powerful state and that had no hopes for political independence. Islam, on the other hand, flourished among a people free from external domination who had the capacity to establish an independent state although they lacked such an organization at the time. 'State' means a public authority which has the power to enforce its judicial rules over the individuals whose safety it undertakes. At the time of the rise of Christianity, the Roman state and its laws were in force. Christianity found a political organization already in existence, and thus it took the matters of organizing a government and maintaining laws as matters outside the concern of religion. It accepted the separation of state and religion as a principle, and formulated it in the slogan 'render unto Caesar that which is Caesar's and unto God that which is God's'. Thus, Christianity seems at first sight

RELIGION, EDUCATION, AND FAMILY 215

like a religion that has left judicial powers entirely to the government, and has concerned itself exclusively with pronouncements on matters of righteousness and ethical teachings.

The real nature of things, however, was not that way at all. Christianity, by accepting the state outside of religion, was relegating the state to a non-sacred realm. It did not appropriate the state to itself because it looked down on it. This attitude, originally due to the fact that the Romans were foreign to the early Christians both from the point of view of nationality and of religion, did not disappear altogether even when the conditions changed. Although Christianity took on political government outside of the realm of religion, it nevertheless brought to the world a new government under the name of Heavenly Kingdom. Thus, two kinds of government came into existence in Christendom, one as the non-sacred, temporal government, and the other as the sacred, spiritual government. If Christianity had not found an already existing order of state at the time of its birth, it would have attempted undoubtedly to create one, and then it would have regarded it as a sacred being of its own creation. As this government would have been within the religion, and as such a sacred institution, no need would have been felt to establish a spiritual government. If this had happened, there would be no duality of temporal and spiritual governments, but something similar to the case existing in Islam.

Europeans who have compared Christianity and Islam usually believe that Islam's acceptance of judicial matters as part of religion, and of the state organization as part of religious organization, is a defect in Islam. Even some Muslims who have received their ideas from the same sources think the same way. However, when the problem is investigated more carefully, it appears that this is not a defect but, on the contrary, a merit.

In Islam, religious provisions are divided into three categories—those relating to piety, to morality, and to judicial affairs. All of them are religious because they are sacred. Religion is the sum total of all beliefs that are taken as sacred by an *umma*. Aesthetic and rational rules are non-sacred, and therefore they are outside of religion. Islam takes ethical and legal rules as religious rules and thus makes them sacred. This conception is contrary to the interpretations of ethics and law from the point of view of utilitarianism, historical materialism, and the doctrine of social contract. Over against these points of view, it attributes to them a supra-individual, sacred, and transcendental

216 TURKISH NATIONALISM AND WESTERN CIVILIZATION

character. Modern sociology entirely justifies and confirms this point of view of Islam.

Although Islam brings everything sacred under religion, at the same time it divides them into three categories, ascribing to each a different sanction. The sanctions of the rules of piety are other-worldly sanctions; those of the judicial rules, legal sanctions; and of the ethical rules, the sanctions of *'urf*. In Islam, which commands in accordance with *ma'ruf* and prohibits in accordance with *munkar*, criteria of ethical rules are *mores* (*'urf*, or opinion of the whole). All the investigations of modern sociology have but confirmed the same thing.

When Christianity accepted the need for a spiritual government, it did not take it as a mere metaphysical expression. This government, although spiritual, would not content itself with a mere spiritual sanction; it would also demand a material sanction. Islam believed in the existence of a supreme court in the Hereafter and that the accounts of piety of our actions be settled there. Christianity, in its attempts to support its spiritual government by a material sanction, went much farther by bringing that court into this world and institutionalizing it, in the Middle Ages, in the so-called courts of inquisition. In Islam, the maxim *'shari'a* decides for *ẓāhir'* [outward appearance] is well known. The spiritual courts of Christianity extended their penetrating inquisitiveness to the realm of the inner private conscience of man and attempted to measure the faith of persons. But the spiritual government was composed not only of these courts. It also had its councils, which were a sort of parliament legislating laws on matters of piety and making ecclesiastical laws.

As politics is based on national sentiments perceived by men of action through experience, the rule of the majority in political matters may be an adequate basis. On these matters the opinions of the experienced ignorant may, in many cases, be better than those given by inexperienced learned persons. Thus, in politics, the fact that the learned are few and the ignorant many may not be an obstacle to the rule of the majority. Matters of piety, on the other hand, are entirely matters of learning and specialization. Thus, it is not permissible to decide matters of piety on the basis of the rule of the majority in such Councils, and to make such decisions obligatory. The opinion of the majority cannot be binding on matters of piety, just as it cannot be on questions of science. The majority commits few mistakes on political matters, and no great harm proceeds from them. On matters of piety, on the other hand, the error is greater and its consequences for other-worldly salvation are more dangerous. For this reason, Islam never constituted any Council and never made enactments on any matter of faith or worship on the basis of majority opinion as if this were issued as law. The Councils did not content themselves with promulgating beliefs and prayers in the form of laws, but they issued laws providing earthly punishments for matters of conscience, forgetting that only the sublime court of the Hereafter can do this. As spiritual public authority was vested in the Councils and in the Papacy, the decrees of the latter were regarded as binding when the Councils were not in session. The interpretations of the Popes were infallible, like those of the decrees of the Councils. The meaning of the Islamic saying '*ijtihād* does not abrogate *ijtihād*' will be understood better when we compare it with the idea of infallibility of the Popes and Councils, which may abrogate all opinions of the learned. In Islam, the *fatwā* issued by a certain office does not prevent the *muftīs* from issuing *fatwās* in accordance with their own opinions. The *ḥadīth* saying: 'Consult yourself, etc.' (*Istaftaka nafsaka wa in aftāka*, etc.) shows how wide are the limits of the freedom of *ijtihād* in Islam. The acceptance of the maxim '*ijtihād* does not abrogate *ijtihād*' does not mean that a judicial decision (*qaḍā*) does not abrogate others. A judicial decision (*qaḍā*) abrogates another act of a court, but one *iftā* does not abrogate another *iftā*. *The Board of Examination of Shar'* (*Meclis-i Tedkikat-ı Şer'iye*) abrogates the decisions of the *shar'* courts by cassation, and the *qāḍīs*, as delegates of the Caliph, are under the obligation of following what the Caliph has decreed on those matters which are subject to *ijtihād*. The *muftīs*, on the other hand, do not have to make their *iftās* within such limitations. In Christianity the '*muftīs*' have to follow the '*fatwās*' of the Pope or of the Councils. In the Greek Orthodox Church, too, the decrees of the Holy Synod have the authority of a kind of *iftā* in a similar manner. In Islam any person who has the qualifications to *iftā* has the right to exercise it, but no one may ever have the same authority on the basis of position. Only Revelation is the authority behind the *iftā*.

Islam's inclusion of judicial provisions into the provisions of religion, and its acceptance of the sacredness of the state is not a shortcoming but a merit, for if it had seen government and law as profane and secular institutions it would have invented a spiritual government such as we find in Christianity. It was because Islam did otherwise that organizations having a spiritual authority or the authority to issue

218 TURKISH NATIONALISM AND WESTERN CIVILIZATION

decrees on matters of faith, such as Councils, Holy Synods, Inquisition courts, and ecclesiastical courts, were not established in it. Islam did not establish institutions contrary to the laws of nature and life such as a priesthood. It was because Islam had brought state, law, and court into the realm of the sacred that those traits such as loyalty to the secular ruler, a genuine fraternity and solidarity among the believers, sacrifice of interests and life for the sake of *jihād*, tolerance and respect towards the opinions of others, which are the very basis of a permanent order in society, were cultivated among all Muslims as common virtues.

Let us now look at the modes of relation between spiritual and temporal governments, and the differences existing between these and the régime accepted in Islam.

II

These modes of relations may be reduced to four basic régimes: The first form is what we may call Papalism, which is based on the universal authority of the Popes. In this form, all authority on matters of both piety and politics are combined in the office of Papacy. According to this system, Christian ecclesiastical sovereigns in general, such as bishops, are subject to the authority of the Pope. Gregory VII had said: 'Why should not the Papacy, having acquired the right of leadership in spiritual matters, also acquire the right to conduct temporal affairs? Temporal powers may see the glories of sovereignty higher than those of the bishops. The differences between the two will be understood by looking at their origins. Rulership is the product of the vanity of man while the bishopric is the institution of God.' Long before these words were uttered, Saint Ambrose had declared that the superiority of the bishop over the ruler is like the superiority of gold over silver. These declarations from the authorities suffice to expound the Catholic view on the matter.

The second form is the papacy of the Caesars (Caesaro-Papism). This existed in Russia and means that the ruler has the functions of papacy. Since the end of the sixteenth century the Muscovy patriarchs, supported by the Russian episcopates, severed themselves from the Patriarchate of Constantinople, and since then they began to get supreme power into their hands, which caused the Tsars some concern. Consequently, at a Council which convened at Moscow in 1667, Nikon was dismissed from his office. However, this defeat did not stop the

RELIGION, EDUCATION, AND FAMILY 219

successors of Nikon from following the older policy. Finally, in 1719, Peter the Great declared himself the head of the Russian Church and put an end to the ambitious aims of the Patriarchs. The next year Peter assembled a Holy Synod composed of archbishops, bishops, and archimandrites. The Holy Synod was headed by the Tsar, the members were appointed and decisions were ratified by him to be enforced. Thus, the Tsar became an absolute ruler in religion over matters of faith, worship, and discipline.

This régime disrupted the safe conduct of both political and religious affairs. In accordance with political considerations, Tsars could intervene in the foundations of religion by forcing the Holy Synod to issue decrees contrary to the provisions of religion. They thus arrested social progress and prevented political and social innovations, by utilizing men of religion, who became their most loyal instruments, in their attempts to keep people under their absolute rule. However, that was the result of the efforts to find a remedy against the principles of Christianity which were unfavourable to the establishment of an independent government. The Russians could establish an independent state only by accepting the papacy of the Tsars.

The third system is the concordate system. The relation between temporal and spiritual governments found a solution in the Orthodox Church in the form of a harmful but durable system, while in Catholicism it remained in constant anarchy. Popes used to claim authority over political matters, and the rulers declined to accept such claims because just as religion cannot recognize a power above itself neither can the state. In the Orthodox Church religion was sacrificed for the sake of the state. In Roman Catholicism, on the other hand, Popes wanted to sacrifice the state for the sake of religion, and sought as vicars of God to become the rulers of the rulers over the earth following the ancient Roman Caesars. When the temporal rulers were powerful, they rejected such a condition of dependence, which is contrary to the nature of state, and issued decrees about the limits of this authority of the bishops within their territories. When the Popes realized that they were unable to curb the powers of the kings, they began to negotiate with them, trying to conclude concordats that would be in their own favour as far as possible. But these concordats were never made sincerely. The Popes accepted them only temporarily in order to regain once again complete jurisdiction under a favourable situation. They even did not conceal their belief that these concordats were

220 TURKISH NATIONALISM AND WESTERN CIVILIZATION

unilateral only and that they were not binding on the Church. The history of Europe is full of such concordats, continuously changing and always dragging both sides into conflicts.

The fourth system is the separation of the state from the Church. The impossibility of maintaining the relationship between the state and the Church under the concordat régime was realized at last in France and the French Parliament decided to separate these two powers from each other completely. From that time on, France did not have an official religion, and the churches ceased to have any official character. They would be just private associations under the Statute of Associations. Thus, the state became completely laicized and religion unofficial. Although this has been a grave source of sickness for the French nation, it was nevertheless a necessary consequence of Catholicism.

The only natural consequence of the conflict of Christianity with the political government could be either Caesaro-Papism or laicism. The ideal [of the universal authority] of the 'Popes' has been realized only in Tibet. But this was due to a tricky measure of the Chinese government. In the first century of the Hijra, the kingdom of Tibet had conquered a great portion of China and Turkestan and had established a great empire. The Chinese succeeded in expelling the Tibetan king by encouraging the Dalai Lamas and supporting them with military forces. From that time on, Dalai Lamas remained in Tibet as absolute sovereigns; but the Tibetan people came to their present state of backwardness under such a government.

The above explanations show that Christianity is irreconcilable with a modern state. Let us now look at Islam from that point of view. In Islam, both state and law are within religion. The provisions of religion comprise judicial rules and prescriptions of piety. The execution of judicial functions are given to the Caliph. The *fakih*s, proven to be qualified as *mufti*s, are charged with the task of purveying the provisions of piety. They are under the judicial authority of the Caliphs, but are not bound in their *iftā*s by the latter's opinions. *Qāḍī*s are delegates of the Caliph and exercise their judicial functions as his deputies and, thus, on the matters which are subject to *ijtihād*, they are bound to follow the judgment preferred by the Caliphs even if this judgment is not in accord with the *iftā*, or even if it is beyond the opinions of any of the four schools of *fikh*, because the Caliph's opinion and decree is 'to be carried out judicially' and, as such, it is of the nature of law, whereas any opinion which is to be carried out as *iftā* is not of a legal nature.

There are, for example, several judgments given as *iftā*s in the *fikh*s of the Shāfi'ī, Mālikī, and Hanbalī schools which the *muftī*s of these schools follow in their *iftā*s. In the Ottoman lands, on the other hand, the *qāḍī*s judged only according to the Hanafī *fikh*. Thus, only the pronouncements of the Hanafī *fikh* were judicially followed and had assumed the nature of law; those of the other three schools remained subject to *iftā*. Furthermore, the Ottoman Caliphate had accepted only five of the books of *fatwā* of the Hanafī school as subject to judicial application and the *qāḍī*s judged only on the basis of these. But even the Hanafī *muftī*s were not under any obligation to restrict themselves to these five books of *fatwā*. The codification of the *Mejelle-i Ahkâm-ı Adliye* (*Compendium of Judicial Rules*) was meant only to show the provisions to be judicially followed by the *qāḍī*s and not to be provisions followed in *iftā*s of *muftī*s.

It follows from these considerations that *muftī*s are absolutely free and independent in declaring the provisions of piety, although they are dependent upon the ruler or the Caliph, because the Caliph, although having judicial authority, lacks any authority over matters of piety such as the Catholic Pope or the Russian Tsar enjoyed. However, the *muftī* does not have any authority over matters of piety either. The *muftī* only has the authority of *iftā*, simply because of his competence in learning. There is a great difference between 'authority' and 'competence'. Thus, the judicial right belongs exclusively to the Caliph since he has judicial authority. But the *iftā* authority of the *muftī* does not give the right of *iftā* to him exclusively. There is no question of a right of *iftā*; there is only the question of competence in *iftā*. The fact that the *muftī* has no authority over matters of piety shows that there is no *iftā* government of the *muftī*s in addition to the judicial government of the Caliphs. There is only one government in Islam, which is the Caliph's government. Thus, the Caliph is entirely independent in his judicial government; and the *muftī* is equally independent in teaching and declaring the provisions of piety. Neither do judicial provisions obstruct the safe application of the provisions of piety, nor do the latter intrude into the safe course of the judiciary.

In one of our previous essays [see *supra*, '*Religion and Law*'] we have shown that *qaḍā* and *iftā* cannot be united in one office. But there are exceptions to this rule. There was no harm in their unification in the Prophet Muhammad's person. He was in a position which would not confuse the two because, in addition to these two functions, he had the

222 TURKISH NATIONALISM AND WESTERN CIVILIZATION

function of *risalah* also. Whenever he failed in either of the first two, Revelation corrected him.

In a secondary form, *iftā* and *qaḍā* may unite in the Caliph because the *qāḍīs* who are the Caliph's delegates have to follow his opinion. If the *qāḍī* is dependent in his judicial action and independent in his capacity as *muftī*, he will be in a difficult position. What will happen if his opinion does not agree with the Caliph's opinion? Therefore, it would be strange for him to exercise his *iftā* according to his own opinion after judging the contrary opinion of the Caliph. Furthermore, judicial provisions have been compromised with certain exigencies under legal casuistry. When the *qāḍī* follows them and when he acts as a sort of judiciary, how can he issue a *fatwā* in contradiction to it? How can he have two consciences at the same time to pronounce the same thing both permissible and non-permissible? The *qāḍī* may exercise *iftā* only if he can face these difficulties in his position.

Let us now turn to our main topic. It has been seen above that Islam is not contrary to a modern state, but, on the contrary, the Islamic state means a modern state. But how did it happen that the modern states came into existence only in Christendom?

When we study the history of Christianity, we see that, following the Crusades, a new movement started in Europe which was then acquainted with Islamic culture. This movement aimed at imitating Islamic civilization and religion. It penetrated Europe with time, and finally culminated in Protestantism as a new religion entirely in contradistinction to the traditional principles of Christianity. This new religion rejected the priesthood, and the existence of two kinds of government, spiritual and temporal. It also rejected the Papacy, the Councils, the Inquisition; in short, all institutions which had existed in Christianity as contrary to the principles of Islam. Are we not justified if we look at this religion as a more or less Islamicized form of Christianity? The modern state came into existence in Europe first in the Protestant countries. The constitutional régime appeared in England, the first nation-state was established in the United States, and the first culture-state came into existence in Germany. The racialist sociologists would believe that the superiority in civilization of these nations and of the Scandinavian nations was due to the fact that these nations belonged to the Germanic and Anglo-Saxon races. The sociologists of religion, on the other hand, believe that the decline of the Latin nations was due to their Catholicism, the backwardness of the Russians was a

RELIGION, EDUCATION, AND FAMILY 223

consequence of their Orthodoxy, and the progress of the Anglo-Saxon nations was the result of the fact that they had freed themselves from the Catholic traditions and approached the principles of Islam. If these principles taken by Protestantism from Islam were factors in this progress, do they not also constitute an experimental proof that Islam is the most modern and most reasonable religion? This being so, how is the attempt of the statesmen of *Tanzimat* to organize the Islamic community in imitation of the [minority] 'communities' existing in our country justifiable? Christian organizations appeared in a dependent people and they might suit only dependent 'communities'. Free nations and free states can reconcile themselves only with the institutions of Islam because Islam originated in a free people who wanted to create an independent state.

THE CALIPHATE

I[9]

Foremost among a man's social duties is that of knowing his nationality and his religious community (*ümmet*). One has also to know and understand the differences between the social grouping called 'nation' and that of '*ümmet*'. As Europe is in a much more advanced stage of social evolution, every person there knows this difference, and is consciously aware of his connection with a certain nationality and religion. In the East, on the other hand, the connotatioror of these two terms are not yet clearly known and, hence, many people cannot give an adequate answer when they are asked: 'To what nation do you belong? And to which *ümmet* do you belong?' It is necessary, therefore, that we clarify the meanings of these two terms in order to identify our social position.

Ümmet is the grouping constituted by men of the same religion. Christians, for example, constitute an *ümmet*. Likewise the Jews constitute another, and so do the Muslims. Thus, each religion existing in the world constitutes an *ümmet*. The common connecting element in each *ümmet* is religion. In the grouping called 'nation', on the other hand, language, morals, law, and political institutions, fine arts, economic organization, science, philosophy, and technology, are also common unifying elements, in addition to religion. Within a certain *ümmet*, there may be different languages, moral standards, legal and political institutions, aesthetic tastes, economic and educational institutions. Within a certain nation, on the other hand, these spheres of social life have to have a uniformity and unity. And the totality of these we call 'culture'. Culture is an all-inclusive term, comprising all social institutions. Therefore, we may define the nation simply as the 'sum total of men who belong to the same culture'.

It follows from these definitions that the group which we call society as the one comprising all spheres of life is not *ümmet* but nation. *Ümmet* is, in most cases, a collection of several societies or nations. And thus *ümmet* is, in many cases, international. As a matter of fact, internationality first emerged with the emergence of *ümmet*. Early international institutions were nothing but religious institutions. In the Middle Ages, European internationality was nothing but Christendom. Its international institutions were institutions of the Church. National institutions were not fully differentiated from the institutions of religion. Among us, too, these two areas of organization were fused with each other until recently.

Social evolution leads to increasing division of labour, and this, in turn, necessitates a differentiation between groupings referring to different social categories. As this took place in Europe, among us, too, national organization began to be differentiated from the *ümmet* organization. After the armistice [following World War I] particularly, two important factors accelerated this differentiation. The first is the dissolution of great empires which had contained several nationalities and, as a consequence, the emergence of each nation as a state. Formerly, the religious head of an *ümmet* could, to some extent, be the political head of an empire comprising several nations. When these nations emerged as separate states, the religious head of the *ümmet* could not be the political head of only one of these nations. The function of the head of an *ümmet* is to serve the religious life of the Muslims. The function of the state, on the other hand, is to serve national life. When the two are united in one person, there may be occasions on which either the general interests of the *ümmet* will be sacrificed for the sake of the particular interests of one nation or the political aims of a nation for the sake of the *ümmet* ideals.

The second factor causing differentiation between groupings is the rise of the principle of popular sovereignty, which gained force in recent times as a result of the development of political consciousness and which obviated the claims of single persons to be the sole possessors of sovereignty. Historical experiences have shown that the interest of nations and those of dynasties are different things. Especially after the armistice, the treason of the ruler and of the prime minister who was his son-in-law, their alliance with the enemies of the nation, the crimes against the nation which they committed as tools of these enemies, were all due to the usurpation of the rights of the people for the interests of the court. These bitter experiences have shown to the Turkish people that from now on it is impossible for them to trust their political fate to the hands of court governments which think of nothing but their own selfish interests. Consequently, the Turkish nation resumed the right of sovereignty which was its own, and relegated its legislative and executive powers to the Grand National Assembly. In this way national organization assumed a particular form.

When national organization took this particular form, the organization of *ümmet* had the chance to manifest itself in a more striking and brilliant form. The person who is at the head of the *ümmet* organization and who is regarded as the religious guide is the Caliph. The Prophet had delegated Abū Bakr to lead the prayers during the illness which ended with his death. The office of Caliphacy was born out of this delegation of religious leadership. It is very well known that in Islam prayers are performed in congregation five times a day. In order to perform this worship, the congregation is led by an *imām*. Friday and holiday prayers should be performed not only in congregation but also as an *ümmet*. It is for this reason that the two latter prayers cannot be performed in village and neighbourhood *masjīd*s. They can be performed only in the great mosques of the cities. The *imām*s and the *khatīb*s who read prayers and deliver sermons in these mosques have to be specially commissioned by the Caliph. This obligation shows that as the congregations are led by a particular *imām*, so these latter are also led by a higher and universal *imām*. Thus, on Fridays and holidays the whole Islamic *ümmet* performs prayers as a unified community under the universal leadership of the Caliph. For this reason, the office of Caliphacy is defined as the 'supreme imamate'. The fact that the Friday and holiday sermons are delivered in the name of the Caliph, and the existence of various alternatives as to the performance of Friday and holiday prayers in the absence of the Caliph, indicate that the essential function of the Caliph is the fulfilment of the supreme imamate.

During the Prophet's life-time there was only one *imām*, who was none other than his blessed self. The one-ness of imamate was regarded

226 TURKISH NATIONALISM AND WESTERN CIVILIZATION

as the clearest symbol of the unity of the *ümmet*. Later on, the number of *masjīd*s and mosques as well as *imāms* increased. This multiplicity could lead to the curtailment of the idea of the one-ness of the Islamic *ümmet*. With the establishment of the office of Caliphacy this danger was overcome. The Caliph meant the highest *imām*, the *imām* of *imāms*. The several *imāms* had to be guided by a highest *imām* in such a way as to single out the unity of the *ümmet*.

From that time on, the Islamic *ümmet* has taken the one-ness of this highest *imām* or Caliph as the expression of its existence, unity, and solidarity. How could it be permissible to defame such an office, the symbol of the unity of the Islamic *ümmet*, through the politics of a particular nation, and inevitably to disfigure it through the unavoidable and human faults of politics? In the time of the Seljuks in Baghdad and of *Kölemen*s [Mamluks] in Egypt, the headships of the *ümmet* and of the nation were naturally separated from each other. In these periods the Caliph was performing only a religious function with regard to the *ümmet*. All affairs with regard to political authority were carried on by the sultans of the Seljuks in Baghdad and of the *Kölemen*s in Egypt. These were the greatest periods in the history of Islam, both politically and religiously. It was only when Selim I had again unified these two offices that the decline of the Ottoman Empire ensued; its religious as well as its political life began to deteriorate. A study of the history of Islam from this point of view will bring several important truths to light.

The ceremony of the election of the new Caliph in all mosques of Islam last Friday[10] was a day of great rejoicing which spiritually united all Muslims of the world. That day all Muslims, who had gained a supreme *imām* as the head of the *ümmet* exclusively, realized their solidarity in a sense more intense than in the past. Until now the religious authority of the Ottoman Caliphs was confined to those Muslims who were their political subjects. Their religious authority over Muslims in other states was rejected by the other governments because they could not be sure that this religious authority was free from political designs. Now that the Caliph will no longer be subject to the politics of any nation, he will enjoy free communication with the Muslim *muftī*s of all lands; he will issue decrees to all *imām*s and *khatīb*s; in short, he will exercise his right of religious authority over all religious institutions. No Muslim of non-Muslim state will prevent the fufilment of this religious function.

We see, therefore, that the present-day Caliphacy is a thousand times more powerful than it was in the past. Although Turkey and the Turkish nation is its main support, all Muslim states and nations will support it materially and spiritually. But its real and most powerful source will be the greatness of Islam which has today forced the European world to respect it.

As to the question of confining the right of election to the Caliphacy only to the house of Osman, we believe it is correct. This respectable family is a blessed dynasty which has served and elevated the Turkish nation for a thousand years and both Islam and the Turkish nation for six centuries. With the acceptance of this rule, a right acquired historically through competence has been recognized by its inheritors, and at the same time the conflicts and ambitions of the election will be reduced to a minimum. We are deeply thankful to the Grand National Assembly and its famous President for their success in giving to the office of the Caliphacy a character that is compatible with the principle of popular and national sovereignty, which is the foundation of modern states and through which genuine Islamic unity in religious life might be realized.

II[11]

Our Prophet sent letters to each of the rulers of his time—to the rulers of Byzantium, of Egypt, and of Abysinnia. These letters invited neighbouring nations to embrace Islam and delivered to them a proposal which read approximately as follows: 'Your political organizations and governments will remain as they are and you will rule in your countries as in the past. The only thing which I want from you is the acceptance of the faith and prayers of Islam.'

Let us suppose that these rulers and their subject peoples had accepted Islam. How, then, would Islam be organized? We can only imagine. Each nation in the Islamic world would have its political independence. Each nation would possess a governmental organization suitable to its race and culture. However, this political independence could not impede religious unity. All the Muslim nations would be united into a great religious community under the name of the Muhammadan *ümmet*. At the head of this religious community would be the Prophet himself as long as he lived and the Caliphs after his death; and their mission would consist of inviting non-believers to the right path and believers

228 TURKISH NATIONALISM AND WESTERN CIVILIZATION

to devotion. Thus, beside the political organization of nations there would be an entirely independent Islamic organization.

But, unfortunately, history did not follow the course here envisaged. Neighbouring rulers did not accept the Islamic religion through preaching and teaching. Under these conditions, the declaration of *jihād* became necessary. Neighbouring countries became incorporated into the realm of Islam by means of war.

At that time, the Arabs had not yet established political institutions and a government. For this reason, the organizations of state and community developed side by side among the Muslims. The two organizations ceased to be independent by being fused with each other. But, the Kur'an confirms the necessity and the importance of nations by the verse: 'We have created you male and female, and have made you nations and tribes that you may know one another' [XILIX, 13, Pickthall's trans.]. 'Knowing each other' means undertsanding and communication. Communication between men is carried on by means of language. Individuals speaking different languages cannot know what one another thinks; there is mutual opposition (*tanākur*) among them. But among those who speak the same language there is mutual understanding (*ta'āruf*). The Prophet said in one of his *hadīth*s: 'Spirits are like arrayed armies. Those who know one another become akin; those who are strangers to one another become mutually opposed.' Therefore, in order to have agreement it is always necessary to know one another. Mutual opposition (*tanākur*), on the other hand, gives rise to disagreement. Thus, real and complete agreement which is a prerequisite for the state can be realized only within a nation, which is a group with *ta'āruf*. These revealed pronouncements imply that Islam does not condone imperialism.

An independent Islamic organization, which would undoubtedly have been realized if the conversion had taken place of those rulers and their peoples who at the beginning of Islam received the letter of our Prophet, was not fully established until now. Today, we are in a position to expect the realization of such an organization in its proper form.

The outlines of this organization should be somewhat as follows: in *ümmet* organization, the basic unit is the *masjīd* of the neighbourhood. *Masjīd*s should be tied to mosques and mosques to the great mosques of the cities. Each great mosque should be headed by a *muftī*. The *muftī*s of each state must be connected to the *muftī* of the capital, the *Shaikh-ul-Islām*. And the *Shaikh-ul-Islām*s of all nations must be under the office of the Caliph. The *medrese*s and the establishments of religious orders should also take their places in this organization according to their rank.

The Caliphacy, until now, has not been able to create such an organization, because it was not independent. When the Caliphacy and the Sultanate were united in one person, either one of the two dominated the other. At the time of the early four Caliphs, when piety preceded everything, the Caliphacy was essential and the rulership was a secondary function. In the reign of the Umayyads, Abbasids, and Ottomans, the Caliphacy was subordinate to the Sultanate, as it was captured by the swords of the *amīr*s who had material power. As a consequence, in these epochs the Caliphacy was not independent, whereas in reality both the powers of the Caliphacy and of political sovereignty should be independent.

The Turkish revolution of today has assured the complete independence and freedom of these two powers. As the right of sovereignty of the Turks has passed entirely to the people, the Caliphacy too has won its independence by being separated from the Sultanate. Now the office of Caliphate, having won its independence, will be able to establish the religious organization mentioned above, and will be able to call, at such times as it shall deem necessary, international religious councils such as council of *muftī*s, of '*ulamā*, and council of religious education. It goes without saying that these religious meetings will be as creative as the *ümmet* organization. Thanks to these creative meetings, our religious life which has been for many centuries in a state of lethargic slumber will re-awaken, and, in accordance with the promise of our Prophet, the splendour of Islam will shine in much the same way as it shone in its Golden Age.

III[12]

The Caliphacy has taken four forms in the history of Islam. As these four types are each of a different nature, we shall call them by different names.

The primary function of the *Rāshidūn* Caliphs was Caliphacy. Since there was no state organization at that time, these Caliphs were invested with political authority or sovereignty in addition to their original function. We call this type the 'Caliph-Ruler' type. The primary function of the Umayyad, Abbasi, and Ottoman Caliphs, on the other

230 TURKISH NATIONALISM AND WESTERN CIVILIZATION

hand, was political rulership. They were invested with Caliphal authority in addition to their original political authority. We shall call this type the 'Ruler-Caliph' type. In Baghdad at the time of the Seljuks and in Egypt during the reign of the Mamluk Sultans, the Caliphs were not only divested of any political authority, but also were without any religious organization, which they needed to carry out their religious functions. As they themselves were not *mujtahid*s and *muftī*s, they needed an organization composed of competent scholars and, as they were unable to go everywhere, they needed a vast religious organization. Because of the non-existence of a religious organization, these Caliphs failed to perform their religious functions in a real sense. They had under their control neither a *Shaikh-ul-Islam* nor a *Board of Religious Scholars*. As the office of Supreme Judge was only a state office, it could not be regarded as part of a religious organization. We shall call this type 'Caliphacy without organization'. Finally, the last type which is to be born now will be separate from political sovereignty and will be able to produce a vast *ümmet* organization, and thus will be in a position to fulfil its religious functions in a true sense. We may call this type the 'independent and organized Caliphacy'.

Let us now discuss the four different forms the functions of the Caliphacy have taken, now that we have established these four types.

1. Under the 'Caliph-Rulers', leadership in prayers, in preaching on Friday and holiday gatherings, and in the guidance of pilgrims and execution of the rites of pilgrimage was actually carried on by the Caliphs themselves. As they were personally qualified to have the authority of *ijtihād*, they developed their interpretations on questions of beliefs and worship like any other *mujtahid*. As at that time there were no schools of law and theology or mystic sects, there were naturally neither separate *imām*s on matters of belief and worship nor spiritual guides to direct the inner life of the believers. On these matters, too, leadership was actually the task of the Caliphs. The same Caliphs also collected the *Sura*'s of the Kur'an and edited it as a codified book. To protect sacred places, e.g. Mecca and Medina, to preserve holy trusts, to propagate the Book of God and the *Sunna* of the Prophet over the whole world, were also their primary tasks. These Caliphs, in short, were performing the tasks of *imām*s, preachers, masters of pilgrimage and heads of pilgrims, *muftī*s, spiritual guides, collectors of the Kur'an, guardians of sacred objects and propagators and preachers of the faith all at the same time. As they personally had reached a supreme status

RELIGION, EDUCATION, AND FAMILY 231

and were to be looked upon as genuine examples in matters of piety and righteousness, they were really the *imām*s of the *ümmet* of Islam. Unfortunately, however, even these Caliphs assumed political authority and rulership, and thus they could not remain aloof from the inevitable conflicts of political life. As a consequence of involvement in politics, religious schisms arose which divided Islam into *Sunnī*s, *Shīʿī*s, and *Khārijī*s. It seems that, if they had not assumed political in addition to their religious authority, they would have been able to fulfil the latter function more fully.

2. In the 'Ruler-Caliph' type, the Caliphs did not have any superiority with regard to matters of piety and righteousness and lacked any competence and authority in religious scholarship. As a consequence, there originated *imām*s of religious scholarship, such as the Four *Imām*s, among persons who had these qualities. The Caliphs ceased to perform personally functions of leadership and preaching, in prayers and in pilgrimages, and delegated others for these functions. Works such as preaching, teaching, interpreting, and propagating were carried on disinterestedly by pious members of the community on their own initiative. The religion of Islam was elevated through these individual efforts, various branches of religious scholarship were established, and the *ümmet* of Islam developed a rich culture. In all these activities the Ruler-Caliphs not only failed to play a positive role but even played a negative one. Their political activities had reduced their religious functions to a secondary position.

3. The reasons why under the 'Caliphs without organization', the Caliphs failed to perform their functions properly, have been explained above. As Ruler-Caliphs emphasized their political functions, they did not need to build a religious organization. Thus, the Islamic *ümmet* of four hundred million believers remained devoid of even a simple religious organization. The third type of Caliphs had inherited, from their predecessors, an office which was not based on any organization. Places of worship were *vakf*s and were independent of each other [without any supporting organizational structure], and there was not a connection between them and any central authority connecting each with the rest. When the whole system of sensory and motor nerves becomes paralysed, no relation may exist between the brain and the organs of the body. The Islamic *ümmet*, having innumerable mosques, religious colleges, and mystic orders, was in such a condition although it was supposed to be tied to a central authority under the name of the

232 TURKISH NATIONALISM AND WESTERN CIVILIZATION

Caliphacy. As there were none of the international means of communication such as newspapers and telegraph during that period, the centre and outlying areas had no knowledge of each other. Furthermore, the Caliphacy, even in the centre, did not have any consultative organ composed of religious scholars comparable to the present-day *Board of Religious Scholars*. These Caliphs, who were not necessarily experts themselves, could not perform their religious functions without the aid of religious councils composed of scholars of religious affairs. Even if they had had these bodies for the propagation of religion, they could not have mobilized the great body composed of *muftī*s, scholars, *imām*s, *shaikh*s, preachers, teachers, and missionaries to elevate God's word.

4. The future Caliphs will be able to perform their religious duties in a much better way than their predecessors, as they are independent of political authority and have a religious organization. *Dār-ul-Hikmat al-Islāmiyya* is a kind of religious academy designed to be a consultative staff to the Caliph. The most distinguished scholars all over the Islamic world should be appointed to this board. The Islamic *ümmet* will entrust matters of scholarship to the scholarly authority of this board rather than to the personal scholarship and virtues of the Caliph.

Some people have for a long time proposed an *ümmet* organization comparable to the religious community organizations which existed in the past among the non-Muslims in the Ottoman Empire. These organizations of non-Muslims were, in fact, not simply spiritual organizations. They also had legislative, executive, and judicial powers as if they were temporal organizations. These powers were internal extra-territorial rights or Cult Privileges (*Imtiyazat-ı Mezhebiye*). Each of the religious communities having these political privileges was, in fact, a state on a small scale. The modern conception of national sovereignty cannot sacrifice to any group other than the whole nation even a small portion of the three political functions of the state. Therefore, the new religious organization has to be different from that of the non-Muslim communities. This organization may be appropriately termed mosque-organizations, having the office of *muftī* at every district centre and *mashikhat* at every state capital. As politics has so far not entered into mosques no harm may come from the mosque organizations. As religious communities (*cemaats*) so far have been centres of political separatism the use of this word may lead to an unconscious imitation of previous events.

RELIGION, EDUCATION, AND FAMILY 233

In a previous essay I have shown what an *ümmet* organization should be like. As this organization would simply connect the already existing institutions to the office of the Caliphacy, it will materialize easily. If the whole *ümmet* establishes the necessary contact with the central religious office, the Caliphacy will be able to fulfil its religious functions in their true sense. Since telegraphs, postal services, railways, and steamers are bringing distant places into proximity, very soon the Islamic *ümmet* will become a great family. It is up to the men of religion and to the members of the *Board of Religious Scholars (Dār-ul-Hikmat al-Islāmiyya)* to decide what will be the nature of religious duties appropriate to the needs of our time. We only wish that God might make our beloved Caliph successful in carrying out these sacred tasks.

THE NATURE OF ISLAMIC EDUCATION[13]

The term 'Islamic education' implies two things: the educational views of Islam and the education of children in accordance with Islamic beliefs.

To study the educational views of Islam is the job of the history of education. Here I shall not discuss the history of education in Islam, but rather present-day problems. In other words, I shall try to show that the religion of Islam is one of our ideals in education.

If we study the curriculum of a [Turkish] school, we notice that [Turkish] children are taught according to three categories of learning: (1) They are taught language, literature, and history, which are Turkish language, literature, and history; (2) they are educated in the Kur'an, *tecvit* [reading the Kur'an with the proper rhythm and pronunciation], catechism, and the history of Islam and Islamic languages [Arabic and Persian]; (3) they are also trained in mathematics, natural sciences, and foreign [European] languages, which will aid them in their further studies in these sciences, as well as such skills as handicrafts and gymnastics.

This shows that the aims we pursue in our education are three: Turkism, Islamism, and Modernism. No Turkish father can fail to have his child educated in the Turkish language or allow him to remain ignorant of Turkish history. Also he cannot let him be ignorant of Islamic beliefs and rituals, or unacquainted with the history of Islam. But he also wants his child to be trained as a modern man, in addition

234 TURKISH NATIONALISM AND WESTERN CIVILIZATION

to his education as a Turk and a Muslim. It seems, therefore, that complete education for us would comprise three fields: Turkish education, Islamic education, and modern education.

Before the *Tanzimat*, Turkish children were educated solely in Islamic studies. Reforms of the *Tanzimat* period tried to introduce secular education. At first, there were grave conflicts between religious and secular education. Instruction in drawing and the French language met with strong opposition when introduced into secular schools. It was claimed that teaching the roundness of the earth or the heliocentric system was contrary to dogma, and it became necessary to seek evidence in dogma to support the truths which have been proven by observation and reason. However, with the passage of time, secular education gradually became established and rooted. But, unfortunately, the more secular education gained prestige, the more Islamic education lost its importance. It is true that religious instruction in the [secular] school curricula continued to occupy an important place. But the decline seen in Islamic education was in quality rather than in quantity: Religious instruction lost its vitality. Teachers of religion continued to look down on the sciences as objectionable upstarts (*bid'at*), and thus lost their prestige in the eyes of the students. Moreover, the application of scientific educational methods to this religious education had not even been started.

The confusions and the consequent calamities under which the Turkish-Islamic world was suffering at that time led to the birth of two appealing ideals—Turkish nationalism and Islamic internationalism. Young intellectuals awakened under the blows of these calamities to realize that our difficulties were due to our lack of ideals in education. We did not wish, they said, to give our children either a national or a religious education; whereas it is evident that the real forces which lead individuals to the highest sacrifices for cherished aims are religious and national feelings. But not only did we fail to give our children a Turkish and Islamic education, we also did not succeed in giving them a modern education. However, it is modern education which might have enabled our children to make and use the technical instruments which are produced and used by advanced nations. By our failures, we proved that we were incapable of using modern techniques in military as well as in economic spheres. The test of science is action. By our failures in action we demonstrated our ignorance in sciences. Thus, both our institutions of higher learning, which should have trained

RELIGION, EDUCATION, AND FAMILY 235

specialized scientists, and our colleges, which should have educated citizens, did not achieve their aims.

At the present time, three groups of intellectuals are trying to lay the foundations of a new education. On the one hand, Turkist pedagogues are pointing out the important role that national traditions should play; the modernist pedagogues, on the other hand, are showing new methods to be applied in education based on the idea of the practical and economic applications of modern science. In the third place, however, it is also necessary to discover the foundations upon which a new Islamic education may be based.

These three aspects of education must aid and complement each other. But if we fail to define the function and delimit the sphere of each in a reasonable way without overstressing any one of them, they may be contradictory and even hostile to each other. When secular education transgresses its own material realm and reaches into the spiritual realm, it clashes with the education of Turkish and Islamic ideals. To distinguish the boundaries between national and religious education, on the other hand, is more difficult. It requires extensive studies to show which of the Islamic traditions definitely belong to the Islamic religion, and which of them, in fact, were but Arabic, Persian, or Turkish traditions.

Thus, Islamic education must recognize the function of national and modern education, but must not leave them to take over its own function. In the meantime, Islamic education has to distinguish the genuine beliefs and traditions of Islam from the traditions and additions (innovations, *bid'at*) borrowed, first from the Arabs and later from other peoples.

NATIONAL EDUCATION[14]

I

We call the sum total of the value judgments that constitute the ethos of a people its culture. Education simply means inculcating this culture in the habitual attitudes of the individual members of that people. We call the sum total of all reality judgments current among a people its techniques. Training as opposed to education, therefore, consists of instructing individuals in these particular techniques. Since value judgments differ from society to society, culture is always national; hence, education, which means the inculcation of the culture,

236 TURKISH NATIONALISM AND WESTERN CIVILIZATION

should be national. Reality judgments or techniques, on the other hand, are anational* and, therefore, training children in rational [scientific] knowledge should be anational.

We may classify societies into three types or stages of social evolution, according to whether their education is national or not. (*a*) In pre-literate societies education is national but also incomplete. The child acquires the national culture within the life of the tribe without having books, school, or teachers. However, the culture he acquires is not the total culture of the ethnic whole, but rather the partial culture of only one tribe. (*b*) The peoples whose religions are based on divine scriptures, or those who have adapted a secular innovation, become a part of a certain civilization-group. That civilization is taught to children through books and teachers. National culture becomes overshadowed by the traditions of international civilization. Civilization is the product of all reality judgments of the peoples who belong to the same *ümmet* or to the same level of material development. Within a civilization-group, education tends to be of an international rather than a national character. It tends to inculcate the international civilization rather than the national culture. (*c*) The modern nations who regain their political independence and cultural freedom from international civilization-groups immediately set out to re-discover their national cultures. When they do this, they begin to emphasize education in national culture at the expense of training in the techniques of a particular civilization. It is then that national education reigns over everything.

We [Turks] also have passed through the same phases. Among the Oghuz, the forefathers of the Ottoman Turks, national education was regional and partial. When these Turks adopted Islam and founded Seljuk and Ottoman states, they adopted also a civilization with its books, schools, and teachers. This civilization, which was a collective product of the Arabs, Persians, and even Turks, imprinted itself upon the minds which it trained. Thus, [among the Turks] *divan* literature replaced the *şölen* literature and the *töre* gave place to *fikh*. In the meantime, however, the *şölen* literature continued in the anonymous literature of the folk, and was carried on by minstrels and mystic poets.

---

* There is a difference between 'anational' and 'non-national'. All value judgments which are foreign to the national ethos of a people are non-national. As reality judgments are neutral from the point of view of national ethos, they are neither national nor non-national but simply anational.

RELIGION, EDUCATION, AND FAMILY 237

Turkish mythology and language maintained their existence silently in the hearts of the people. The *töre* of the Oghuz found its way into the Ottoman secular laws, and was taught in the Schools of the Pages, of the Janissaries, and of the Palace. When the *medrese* was transforming the Turks into non-Turks, these institutions were transforming non-Turks into Turks. Thanks to these national institutions, international civilization failed to annihilate the national culture altogether. But with the continuation of culture alongside civilization, a series of dichotomies in language, law, morality, and fine arts was created. Two systems lived side by side, one on the upper, the other on the lower level, without ever becoming assimilated. With the coming of the *Tanzimat* era a new civilization shining with its modern advancement began to be imposed upon us. The schools, the books, and the teachers of this new civilization began to dominate our education. We now belonged officially to two civilizations. As the old institutions of the folk culture were disintegrated, national culture disappeared altogether. [Instead of the dichotomy and conflict between Ottoman civilization and Turkish culture] there now began a new conflict between the two civilizations whose sources and foundations were different. Over against the *divan* literature appeared the *salon* literature, and modern [secular] law arose before the *fikh*. The *medrese* and the *mektep* [the secular school] became the centres of two opposite forms of education. Both were non-national, both trained the youth without any cultural education. And finally came the trend of Turkism. It originally appeared as a result of the need felt to discover the national *culture*, but was understood by some as an attempt to revive and re-institute the ancient Turkish *civilization*. Thus, the number of the civilizations inhibiting our national culture has risen from two to three. We are even faced with strange proposals, such as reviving fossilized ancient Turkish words, or forging artificial words by using dead particles of Turkish, or introducing words from the *Chağatay*, from the *Kazak*, and from the *Tatar* dialects. There were those who advised dropping the living culture of the Turks and going back to the ancient Turkish civilization which had in reality been dead for a long time. The genuine Turkists who turned their attention to culture rather than civilization went against such dangerous aberrations by clarifying the true meaning of this new movement. Consequently, it is now clearly understood that Turkism is nothing but a search for national culture.

In order to discover the national culture one must, first of all, be

238 TURKISH NATIONALISM AND WESTERN CIVILIZATION

completely free from prejudice in favour of any particular civilization and tradition. Anyone who is a particular admirer of European or Arab-Persian civilization cannot understand the national culture just as one who admires the old civilization of the Turks cannot. Secondly, one has to discover and distinguish the obvious or latent differences between the institutions of the nations who share the same civilization. It is only in this way that one can see what kinds of transformation a commonly shared tradition has undergone in different nations, and how it has given rise to dissimilar institutions. Different nations which belong to the same civilization may look alike on the surface, but may, in reality, be quite different from each other. In order to see this, one should not be deceived by the similarities between traditions, but should look at the differences between the institutions. And, thirdly, one should try to discover the latent points of convergence between the trends of social conciliation which seem irreconcilable.

From the outside the life of a nation may appear like a heterogeneous mixture of traditions derived from diverse civilizations, but in reality it is a homogeneous culture composed of institutions in harmony with each other. A nation that lives and grows necessarily has a homogeneous culture. The crises seen among the intellectuals of a nation are not necessarily expressions of certain maladjustments within the culture. A healthy society may have unhealthy intellectuals because the store of knowledge (*irfan*)* of such individuals has been picked up from diverse international civilizations, and is, in most cases, something quite different from the national culture. Such a knowledge is healthy and creative only when it reflects national culture. Among the nations in which national culture is not cultivated, individual education, in most cases, is entirely cut loose from the national culture. National culture manifests itself in the thoughts of the men of genius and in the deeds of great men. These two types of individuals represent national culture and constitute the élite. Intellectuals, because they acquire their education only through their studies, are neither representatives of the culture nor are they the élite of the nation. The confusions seen in the minds of the intellectuals should not necessarily be taken as symptoms of maladjustments in the culture of a nation.

In spite of the fact that our intellectual life is dominated by morbid minds, the people's culture is healthy and creative. It is only when we

---

* I use the term *irfan* to meet the French *la culture*, while I use 'culture' (*hars* [Arabic *karth*]) in its German meaning.

RELIGION, EDUCATION, AND FAMILY   239

discover it, by the scientific methods of sociology, that we shall be in a position to enter into a period of national education.

II

Until now our chief guide in education has been psychology. Psychology, however, is a mixed discipline because it studies organic-psychic phenomena, on the one hand, and socio-psychic ones on the other, failing to make a clear distinction between the two. In fact, the first is the legitimate subject-matter of biology; the second that of sociology. Psychology can treat only phenomena which pertain exclusively to the individual. Recent developments in sociology have shown that socio-psychic phenomena are entirely different from the organic-psychic ones. The social mind is of a transcendental character in relation to organic-psychic phenomena. Because of the fundamental difference between these two groups of phenomena, we have to distinguish between their manifestation in the particular individuals by using the terms soul and mind. Soul is an [organic-psychic] function, whereas mind is made up of religious, moral, aesthetic, intellectual, linguistic, and economic [socio-psychic] functions. Therefore, the manifestations of the culture in individual minds can be studied only by sociology.

This distinction is bound to give rise to a new approach to the problems of education . . . because the mind is something transmitted to each new generation through education. The mind acquired by the members of society is nothing but the culture of that society. However, this is peculiar not only to intellectual education; it is true also for physical education. Physical education does not consist simply in developing the kinetic activities, like those of baby animals which are produced by the natural growth of the organism, but is also a matter of the physical formation of the bodies of the members of a society in accordance with the ideals of that society.

Since I view education from that angle, I do not approve the aims of education formulated by Mr Ismail Hakkı [Baltacioğlu] in the last issue of this journal. I do not believe that the educational aims of the twentieth century are represented only by those nations which are the strongest and most advanced in this century. The peculiar culture of any one nation may be the aim of education only for that nation. If the Turkish child is to live in Turkish society, he must be educated accord-

240 TURKISH NATIONALISM AND WESTERN CIVILIZATION

ing to Turkish culture. The survival of the Turkish nation in the twentieth century illustrates the fact that Turkish culture has a survival value for this century. This means that the Turkish child will get a contemporary education only when he is educated according to that culture. The reason why our educational institutions are yielding bad results is not that our education is based on national culture but rather that it is torn between diverse international civilizations. To reform our education correctly, we will have to emphasize, not civilization over against culture but, on the contrary, culture over against civilization.

The most advanced nations of the twentieth century are the carriers of civilization. Our national culture has to reconcile itself with the fundamentals of that civilization. But the traditions of European civilization, like those of the Turkish and Islamic civilizations, should be permitted to be part of the life of the nation only when they have been thoroughly absorbed by the national culture. Just as every nation erects customs houses and political frontiers to inspect imported goods and foreigners, so they ought to erect cultural frontiers and customs houses. European civilization cannot be adopted by our national culture simply by importations through certain individuals. On the contrary, it will be the real property of the individual members of the nation only when it is absorbed by the national culture. I shall elaborate this point later.

Another point proposed by Mr Ismail Hakkı as an aim of education is the desirability of training productive citizens. Utilitarian considerations may be a legitimate aim in teaching. But education can never be based on utilitarian principles. In recent years education in Turkey has been oriented in an extremely wrong direction: economic utilitarianism. 'To gain money' has been shown to fathers, teachers, and the youth as the main principle of education. I wonder if the civilized nations of the twentieth century really hold the same view. For me, education is something different from training in skills. The main intention of training is to give basic knowledge, and then later to give instruction in professional and specialized skills. Certainly, the aim of teaching is utilitarian. But, in addition to instruction in knowledge and skill, there is also an educative process whose aim is the cultivation, in the minds of an élite, of non-utilitarian and altruistic sentiments which do not seek ulterior interests. Primary schools, trade and professional schools, are institutions of training. But the lycées whose function it is to educate the élite are purely educational institutions. Their graduates are the future lawyers, doctors, writers, government officials, and teachers who make up the élite of the nation. If they are not educated as unselfish, patriotic, self-sacrificing men, the nation cannot benefit from their leadership in her difficulties. During their undergraduate years the youth, who are later expected to specialize as doctors, engineers, chemists, etc., badly need teaching in literature, philosophy, and social sciences; in other words, in cultural sciences. Later they are going to study in great detail the sciences in their respective fields of specialization. As they will not get a cultural education as graduates, they need a thorough cultural education as undergraduates. Therefore, these schools should be entirely devoted to education in the humanities.

III

What is the object of education? Is it the individual or the nation? For psychologists it is the individual, for sociologists the nation. The psychologist claims the personality is found within the individual, whereas the sociologist maintains that it exists within the nation as a whole. In making this claim, the sociologist does not intend to deny the role of the individual. A nation is composed of active and living elements, and also of elements which are passive and lifeless. The active and living elements are human beings and the lifeless ones are the traditions. These latter become institutions only when they come to life within the minds of the men who constitute the nation. Thus, institutions are living expressions in the minds of men of inanimate traditions. The sociologist emphasizes culture because he sees the traditions as the lifeless, and the human beings as the living, realities. He seeks living society not in the civilization-group but rather in the nation, because the first is a medley of lifeless traditions while the second is an organic whole composed of human beings. Furthermore, individual members of a society may be classified as anational, nonnational, or national types. The child is an anational member of the society when he is born into it because he does not automatically inherit anything relating to the culture or values of the nation. Children may become entirely devoid of any national culture if, in their schooling, they acquire only the lifeless traditions of an old or new civilization. Traditions cannot become living institutions in the passive mind of children. Their minds can register the traditions like a phonograph, but they are unable to give life to them. This is not, however, peculiar to children. Aged persons too, as individuals, can fail to give life and meaning to the lifeless traditions. The transformation of the traditions into living institutions takes place only in a collectivity of individuals or, in better terms, in crowd situations. Sociologically, the living members of a society are those who take part in collective national experiences. Trends of public opinion, changes in value attachments, movements of ideologies, come into existence as a result of the collective behaviour of the members of the society. As I have explained the rise of new ideals during the times of great national crises, disasters or victories several times, I will not repeat the explanation here. Since the basis of the value structure of a society is the national ideals, naturally the whole value system changes following a transformation of the ideals of a nation. Therefore, the rise of the living institutions from the lifeless forms of traditions can be expected, not from the private experiences of individual beings but from their collective experiences.

Therefore, when the formal tradition of the formal civilization is replaced in the education of the children by the religious moral, legal, aesthetic, etc., values which live in the heart of the nation, only then will the educational institutions produce thoroughly national members of the nation. It will be only then that the school will exercise an educational role in the midst of our national crises. Certainly, the most important source of education lies in national crises. Just as a national disaster once educated Prussia, so now our national crises are educating us. The idealism of our children and youth is the product not of the teachers but rather of our national crises. Today they experience an intensive education which is given not by the school but by the national life.

We can, however, not expect this educative role to be played always by national crises. Crises cannot and should not go on continuously. When a crisis in the life of the nation passes on, the ideals which it creates are symbolized in a national day or in slogans and symbols. These continue to influence the educational life of the nation. The education resulting from the national crises should also be continued by the schools, particularly the lycées. Undergraduates constitute the portion of the youth that is most vulnerable to crises. Young minds stimulated by positive sciences are prone to analyse values in terms of the logic of natural sciences, and may fall into grave doubts which may cause acute crises in their minds. Disbelief in things once cherished is one of the most painful tensions that youth can suffer. In Europe, in order to help students in this period of crises, the humanities are introduced into the lycée education to counteract the influence of the natural sciences. As the humanities serve to protect national culture against the natural sciences, they should be the main pillars of education and teaching.

Three types may be differentiated among the youth during the crisis period: (a) the type in which national culture has lost its entire meaning under the onslaught of the analytical effects of the natural sciences. This is the Epicurean type which is found everywhere. The Epicureans not only disbelieve in ideals, they hate them. (b) Culture may lose its rational basis in the mind of the individual, but may continue to have a sentimental support. The type which represents this state does not merely believe, like the Epicureans, in the philosophy of life whose maxim is: 'the maximum pleasure and the minimum pain' or 'the maximum gain and the minimum loss'. He, on the contrary, seeks pain. This is the Stoic type which is less frequently found. It is the type who is unable to believe in what he loves. (c) The third type is the one in whose mind culture has both rational and sentimental foundations. He is attached to the values and believes in them. These are idealists. The Epicurean is a complete non-national type. The Stoic is national by emotion but non-national by intellect. The idealist is entirely a national type.

The aim of education is to develop this national type. The creation of such types means the creation of a nation. And it also means the creation of individual personalities because the individual acquires genuine personality only as he becomes a genuine representative of his culture. Only infants and animals are anational, and therefore these human beings who disbelieve in their national culture are degenerate, devoid of personality. The individual has a genuine personality in direct relation to the degree to which he has incorporated the culture in himself. If individuality means personality, it is absolutely incorrect to claim that national education does not further the development of individuals. The aim of national education is to build representative personalities, and thus, to build men as well as the nation.

Those who reject his understanding of national education have been misled by a wrong view once put forward by exponents of *Völkerpsychologie*, according to which the national type is simply the average type. Modern sociology, which has enabled us to dispense with this

244 TURKISH NATIONALISM AND WESTERN CIVILIZATION

pseudo-science called *Völkerpsychologie*, has conclusively proven the inadequacy of that view on the national type. As Durkheim has conclusively shown, the average is only an abstract of the individual type, whereas the national type is represented not by the average but by the type which incorporates the minds of the nation. The real representatives of a nation are men of genius and heroes of action. The genius is the hero of the intellect, and the hero is the genius of the will. Only these chosen ones represent the intellect and the will of a nation. The national type is to be looked for, not among the library erudites who carry in their heads the anational learning, but in the heroic type of the nation. . . .

After clarification of these points we should warn the reader not to get the impression that we claim that education is moulding children on the pattern of the national type, which might lead him to believe that we want our children to look like the peasants of Anatolia. . . . We do not believe that social values are represented in the average type. . . .

It is believed erroneously by certain people that my views on education are like those peculiar to the Germans. These men believe that the Anglo-Saxon education is a non-national education. As a matter of fact, English education is the most national education. No people are more attached to their national institutions than the British. They are distinguished from the Germans by their emphasis on the 'community' as opposed to the Germans' emphasis on the state. As we also rely on the state, we are perhaps nearer to the Germans. . . . In short, it is not true that the German education is collectivistic whereas the Anglo-Saxon is individualistic. Both are national and cultural. Only among the French is education civilizationistic rather than culturistic. The French regard themselves not as the continuation of the Gauls but rather as the inheritors of the classical Greek and Roman civilizations. French culture is nothing but a modernized version of this classical civilization. The Germans and the Anglo-Saxons have ceded from the Latin civilization by religious and aesthetic reactions, such as the Reformation and Romanticism. Luther and Shakespeare represent the national reactions, as opposed to Catholicism and the classical dramas. France remained both classical and Catholic without following the same reaction. . . .

When I defined education as 'the adaptation of the individuals to the national culture', and when I added the adjective 'national' as natural and indispensible, I believed that I was reacting against the

French rather than against the Anglo-Saxon education. We have good reason to instigate such a reaction against French education, because the system prevalent in our country ever since the *Tanzimat* era has been precisely this French civilization-education. The system in force before that era was similarly a civilization-education. At the present time we are proposing to instigate national education as culture-education and to dispense with civilization-education.

IV

Above I had distinguished education from training, the former as the individual's adaptation to culture, the latter as the individual's adaptation to technology; showing that culture is national and technology anational, I concluded that education is national whereas training is anational. As I had discussed the relevance of education and training to *nationality* from the point of view of culture and technology, I will discuss here the same thing with respect to *modernity*, again from the same point of view.

As education is a manifestation of culture, the existence of a modern education in a society will be possible only with the existence of a modern culture in that society. . . .

The nation is the social type in which the state is based on popular sovereignty. . . . Among diverse types of society it is only the nation that can be called a modern state. The word 'modern' does not necessarily refer to the present time, but mainly to the societal advancement attained today. The nation is a modern society just as its culture is a modern culture. Like modern culture, modern education can be found only in the social species which we call nation. The Turks in the pre-Islamic period lived first as confederates of tribes . . .; then in the Islamic era as an *ümmet*. The old Ottoman state, for example, was an *ümmet*, retaining, however, certain aspects of the older Turkish confederates. As the Ottoman Turks founded a state on the basis of an *ümmet*, they destroyed tribal and hereditary aristocratic institutions and replaced the [feudal] lords by the appointed lords of the emperor. [In Persia] the Safavids [another dynasty stemming from the Oghuz Turks, from whom the Ottoman dynasty also stemmed], on the other hand, returned to the older [tribal] confederacy as they promised the Turkomans to restore the old tribal and aristocratic institutions. In their organization, in which each tribe had a hereditary *khan*, the shah was the *khan* of the *khans*. Two parts of the ancient Oghuz, thus, established two contradictory systems, one in Persia and the other in Turkey. Since the Ottoman Turks eliminated tribal chiefs and feudal seigneurs, Turkey became a national state, while in Persia both still exist. The Ottoman Turks are today in a stage of transition from an *ümmet* form to a modern nation. They have a modern culture which is yet on an unconscious level. As it will not be difficult to awaken it, the foundation of a modern education already exists among us. As I indicated above, modern education can exist only in a modern state, and it can be realized only by awakening national culture, not by importing it from somewhere else.

Modern training, on the other hand, presents an entirely different situation. Modern training means instructing the members of a nation in all of modern technology, which does not necessarily exist in the nation originally but may exist outside of it and may be taken from there. The modern technology of our time is the basis of contemporary civilization; that is, of European civilization. Our joining European civilization is occasioned by its technology, just as our union with Islamic civilization was by religion. It is erroneous to think that the Turks having a modern culture is a result of their joining European civilization. Our culture is national because our social structure is national. We can even say that at the time when European societies had a feudal structure, we had a democratic one. In order to understand that modern culture and technology owe their existence to different origins, it is enough to note that although the Turks had a national culture, at least unconsciously, they still lack any part of modern technology. Or, Persia, for example, may introduce all modern techniques from Europe, but may not develop a modern culture as long as she lacks a modern social structure and as long as she continues her present-day tribal and feudal institutions.

Modern education, like modern culture, is a manifestation of the very life of the nation. Modern training, on the other hand, can be adopted from a civilization which, like modern technology, is international. Therefore, we have to make our education thoroughly national. If we achieve this, if our society, in structure and type, becomes a modern society, our education in the long run will acquire a modern character. Otherwise, that is, if our society is still far from being modern, we must not expect to be able to give our children a modern education. . . .

In short, in modern society children get their modern education only when they are given a national education. In a society which is not modern, the children will get neither a modern nor a national education merely through the attempt at giving them a modern education. On the contrary, the product of such an attempt will be nothing but a youth devoid of character, stability, and culture. As we believe that we are a modern society, it is enough for us to see to it that our education becomes national. When it does, we will inevitably have a modern education. For us, the aim of a national education would imply at the same time the realization of the aims of modern education. We do not have to adopt either cultural values or education from Europe. If our cultural values and our education are similar to those of European societies, this is due not to any copying but to the fact that, perhaps, we belong to the same social type. . . .

As the educator is a representative of the nation, the trainer is the leader of modernity. As the aim of education is national cultivation, the aim of training is modernity. The professor and the teacher are both educators and instructors at the same time. Training has both educational and instructive functions. This double character serves the national integration as well as modern progress.

Let me, therefore, conclude my discussion in the following way: while we are not in need of Europe from the point of view of culture and education, we badly need it from the point of view of techniques and learning. Let us try to acquire everything in techniques from Europe, but let us find our culture only in our own national soul.

To nationalize education and to modernize teaching—these are the two goals we should aim at in the field of education!

MODERN FAMILY AND NATIONAL CULTURE[15]

I

Psychologists divide psychological phenomena under three faculties, called sensibility, intelligence, and will. Like the individual, every nation has its own soul, and if we wish to draw parallels between sociology and psychology, we may divide the soul of a nation into three sets of mechanisms, namely culture, civilization, and state. Corresponding to the faculty of sensibility in individual psychology, we may call the sentient experiences of a nation its culture. Corresponding to the faculty of intelligence in individual psychology, the rational concepts of a nation constitute a civilization. And finally, corresponding to the will in individual psychology, nations manifest their will in the state.

The culture of a nation is unique to itself. Its sources are the religious, moral, and aesthetic experiences of the nation. These experiences constitute the most intimate, the innermost feelings, of the nation. These inner feelings are intimate expressions of the nation's personality, as its language is a mirror of its historical and social life.

The civilization of a nation, on the other hand, is not peculiar to itself alone. Civilization is composed of sciences, techniques, and methods which are transmitted from nation to nation. . . . The fact that civilization is commonly shared by many nations indicates that nations do not live in isolation, that they are parts of larger groups: the larger circle comprising the nations of the same civilization we call a civilization-group.

The differentiation of nations with regard to culture and their similarities with regard to civilization resemble the disagreement about sentiments and the agreement on rational matters between individuals. The old saying 'There is only one road for reason' signifies clearly its unifying role. The proverbs: 'Do not argue about taste', 'You can argue about doctrine, but you cannot argue about manners' show that in most cases men disagree on matters of feeling. Nations unite in a civilization because there is only one way to attain that which is rational for them; they differ in culture because their tastes and manners are peculiar to themselves.

The state, which is the sum total of the institutions of law, should in its ideal form be national, like culture. But this ideal form has scarcely materialized up to our time. In most cases, we find a nation either politically organized in several forms of state or a state comprising several nations. . . .

Over against the contention that specific religious, moral, and aesthetic feelings constitute the culture of a nation, one may say that several nations are found which share the same feelings. It is true that several nations share the same religion, morality, and aesthetics in their doctrinal, technical, and methodological aspects. These rational or intellectual elements belong to the structure of civilization irrespective of the institution to which they may refer. Contrariwise, sentimental and emotional elements—such as taste, manners, and intuition, no matter to what institution they may refer—always constitute the elements of culture.

II

We belonged to Iranian civilization before the *Tanẓimat* era. Our rational sciences, techniques, and methods at that time (whether they had been taken over originally from Greece or India) were derived from the *shu'ubīyah* civilization, a product of the Abbasī period which was in general under Iranian influence. Another name which we may use for this *shu'ubīyah* civilization is Iranian civilization. When we were in the period of transition from this civilization to European civilization, we should have changed only our reason and way of thinking, techniques, and methods. We should have taken over from Europe only the lessons of the new civilization. But, as the leaders of the *Tanẓimat* did not recognize the existence of culture as distinct from that of civilization, they wanted to extend the process of Europeanization even to the most intimate sources of our national personality. That was their greatest mistake.

Doubtless, we would not have been able to survive at that age without accepting and assimilating European civilization unconditionally. Since the leaders of the *Tanẓimat* realized this and put it into practice, we are deeply indebted to them. Under the circumstances of their age, their understanding of a renascence could not be otherwise. But to think in this way today would be unpardonable.

Yes, we shall accept European civilization unconditionally. But because of our national culture, we shall still remain distinct from the other European nations in that civilization, just as the French, the English, the Germans, and the Russians are fundamentally separated from each other by their respective cultures, in spite of the fact that all of them belong to the same civilization. The differences between the cultures of these nations are deepening every day rather than disappearing. National personalities are becoming more and more strong, vital, and pronounced. In view of the fact that the European nations, although they share the same origins as far as religion and race are concerned, differ so profoundly from each other, is it not natural that the Turks, who do not share the same religious and racial origins, should have a culture more at variance with them?

However, we do not claim that our old culture will remain intact once we enter European civilization. Just as the faculties of sensibility, intelligence, and will, in individual psychology, interact, so in the make-up of national personality, culture, civilization, and state affect

250 TURKISH NATIONALISM AND WESTERN CIVILIZATION

each other. Therefore, the innovations to take place in our civilization and state will certainly pave the way for several changes and developments in our cultural life. It is true that changes in culture depend upon changes in the social structure. However, cultural changes are not due solely to structural changes; civic and political changes affect the social structure as well and, therefore, lead indirectly to cultural changes. Just as there is an interdependence between individual psychological faculties, so the social mechanisms, culture, civilization, and state too are dependent upon each other. Therefore, we must admit that our national culture will undergo changes in the process of Westernization.

It is, however, wrong to think that this change will take place only by using Europe as a model and simply imitating it, as we did in our civic and political reforms. Civic and political changes may take place in a purely mechanical way, somewhat like the growth of inanimate objects, by mere additions from the outside. Change in culture, on the other hand, is comparable to the creative evolution which takes place in living organisms under the impulse of an internal *élan*. A new civilization and system of law can change national feelings only when they penetrate into the soul of the nation and become assimilated within it. Neither through instruction nor through legislation, neither through imitation nor through suggestion, can one directly change deep-seated feelings. Reformers can inculcate new feelings in a nation only when they have established a spiritual influence over the people, and this influence exists only in those men who have been influenced and educated by the nation itself. The suggestive power of reformers and educators is derived, not from a common civilization but from the national culture.

III

It follows from these observations that we have to be the disciples of Europe in civilization, but entirely independent of it in culture. With respect to law, which is the basis of the state, the situation is twofold: to the extent that law is based on moral feelings it has one foot in culture, but as it is based on modern sciences, methods, and techniques, it has its other foot in civilization. This double feature, which is found in the state and other institutions, is also characteristic of the institution of the family, which is the main subject of this essay. When we were patterning our civilization after that of Europe, the acceptance of certain European conceptions of family and womanhood, in place of the older ones, was inevitable. The rise of the movements for modern family and modern womanhood in our country were consequences of this necessity. But when we study the question more closely, we find that each European nation holds a different and characteristic conception of family and womanhood although there is a certain underlying attitude which is common to all. Undoubtedly, this common attitude is the product of their common civilization as much as different and unique feelings are expressions of independent national cultures. Thus, within the same common European family-pattern we find the varieties of the typical English family, French family, German family, etc. As an example, we may take the problem of the fair treatment of women and feminism, which I have discussed in a previous paper. These two problems, which characterize modern European civilization with regard to family, refer to attitudes that are commonly shared in that civilization. These two attitudes, however, manifest themselves in each of the European nations in entirely different psychological forms. Each nation, being too jealous in preserving its own uniqueness, does not deign to imitate the others. The guardian of national culture is national pride. Jealousy and pride, which are usually bad traits with respect to other matters, are regarded as very praiseworthy with regard to the preservation of culture. A nation maintains its existence by protecting its own national character. A nation which regards other nations as its superior is degenerate.

If so, we Turks can recognize the Europeans as superior in civilization. In civilization we can be their disciples and their imitators. But, beware, we should never view the culture of other nations as superior to our own! We should by no means be the disciples or imitators of other nations in matters of culture. We can take over unconditionally civic modes of thinking from Europe. Our progress in civilization will follow the lines of the European civilization. There is no danger, no harm, in this. But the growth of our culture can never follow the same route. Our culture can grow only from inside and by an inner evolution, although it will evolve in accordance with the changes taking place in our social structure and in our civic and political organizations, exactly as a seed grows and flourishes in its own inner development by utilizing earth, water, and air.

In Turkey, the institutions of the family as well as other institutions are now undergoing severe crises because of our failure to see these

252 TURKISH NATIONALISM AND WESTERN CIVILIZATION

fundamental differences between the progress of civilizations and the growth of cultures. The Westernists, on the one side, are emphasizing the importance of progress in civilization because of their unawareness of the existence of national culture; thus, they urge, as they do for everything, blind imitation of Europe in matters of the family ultimately leading towards the destruction of the national family as they strive to attain the modern family. On the other side, the extremist Easternists wholeheartedly reject the modern family and the modern conception of womanhood because of their fear of the disintegration of the traditional family. From our point of view, both of these extremist views are wrong. There is no doubt that the Turkish family will be modernized by the introduction of new conceptions from European civilization. But the Turkish family will be a copy neither of the French or English nor of the German family. Turkish womanhood certainly will better itself by benefiting from the progress of modern civilization. But the Turkish woman will not be a copy-cat of French or of English or of German womanhood.

The growth of culture follows the path of the inner evolution which all living beings undergo. The cultural evolution of family and womanhood, therefore, can follow the same process. It is for this reason that we can more or less predict the shape of the future Turkish family in its civic aspects, but we do not have at our disposal any objective criteria by which to decide the future cultural course that the Turkish family and womanhood will follow. We can identify the product to be born out of the living organism only when it is born.

Although we are unable to determine the future of our national family in a positive way, we can, however, help it to evolve normally in a negative way. Can we not apply the method of negative education —which Jean Jacques Rousseau recommended to protect nature against civilization—in order to protect, in our case, our culture against civilization? In order to do this, we must reject everything that looks as if it were only sheer imitation of the types of family and womanhood in other nations. As we succeed in this rejection, social evolution will follow its normal course and will one day give rise to our national family and our own womanhood.

THE FOUNDATIONS OF THE TURKISH FAMILY[16]

In the previous essay we saw that we can guess the civic elements which the Turkish family is likely to assume in the future. A similar

RELIGION, EDUCATION, AND FAMILY

prediction, however, is rather impossible for the cultural elements of the family.

This view is in accord with the philosophy of Bergson, the most original thinker of our time. For him the changes to take place in the realm of physical reality are predictable, whereas those to occur in the biological reality are not. . . . In my view, social reality too has a mechanical and an organic aspect. Progress and retrogression in civilization, for example, belong to the mechanical aspect of social life and, as such, they are predictable on the basis of our knowledge of the preceding causes. Cultural evolution and decline, on the other hand, belong to the organic aspect of social reality, and are elusive of any determination before their actual happening.

Although Bergson believed that we are unable to predict the events of biological reality, he, at the same time, believed that they could be grasped by intuition. Life, according to him, is an *élan vital*. In order to grasp where this *élan* is driving us, we have to go back to its beginnings and experience continuously the current of evolution it has undergone. Only then can we feel which phases this drive will pass through in the future. Bergson tried to grasp the orientations of the *élan vital* by using this method in his *Creative Evolution*. I believe that this method is more applicable in the field of cultural sociology. Thus, in order to anticipate the future course of the family among the Turks, we have to go back to its origins.

In a previous essay[17] I have shown that among the ancient Turks women had a legal status equal with, or even sometimes superior to, that of men. . . . Why?

Among primitive societies religious life manifested itself in two different systems: in religion and in magic. At this stage of society magic constituted a system partially separate from the religious system but not yet entirely divorced from it. Therefore, in societies at this stage the religious and magical systems were equal in importance. René Maunier shows that in Melanesia harvest work, which consisted of a series of magical activities, was done by women because they were believed to possess magical powers. He says: 'The idea of the magical powers of women explains how women were left outside of the religion in the relatively advanced society of the Melanesians where women previously had had religious functions. The powers ascribed to them were originally magical powers. This conception belonged to a period in which religion and magic were mixed. When religion and magic

254 TURKISH NATIONALISM AND WESTERN CIVILIZATION

became differentiated from and antagonistic to each other, women were relegated to the sphere of magic because they were considered as carriers of evil powers and were kept apart from sacred objects' ('Vie religieuse et vie économique', *La division du travail*, p. 36, note). . . . Among the ancient Turks, the magical system was represented by shamanism and the religious system by *töre*. . . . As these two systems had an equal value among them . . . there was equality between men and women. . . . The non-equality between men and women in some other societies was connected with the unequal status of magic and religion. The more the antagonism between religion and magic deepened, the more the inequality of men and women widened. In ancient Persian magianism . . . there was no difference between religion and magic . . . and women were not looked down upon. When Zoroaster founded his new religion which was based on asceticism, he divorced religion from magic; then women began to be looked upon as impure. Thus, in all ascetic religions . . . magic is prohibited and women occupy a lower status. Women were equal to men among the ancient Turks because their religion was not an ascetic one. The religion of Islam was, in the Prophet's time, a religion of enthusiasm, and women were not regarded as inferior, though it [Islam] prohibited but did not reject magic as false. But when the ascetic conceptions of the Iranian and Greek Orthodox religions penetrated through to the Muslims in the Abbasi period, the ideas about the inferiority of women spread among the Muslims too. When the Turks came into contact with them they also were influenced by the same ideas throughout the centuries. It was only when the importance of magic reappeared under another name [that is to say, as civilization] during the *Tanẓimat* period that women began to gain higher status. Culture is a product of religion, whereas civilization is an evolution from ancient magic. . . . Contemporary civilization is the successor of ancient magic. Both are not national but international. Both aim at utilitarian purposes and, thus, are antagonistic to ascetic religion and morality; both have given higher status to women. If the intensity of the intrinsically altruistic and sacrifice-demanding religious and moral feelings are not tempered by the secularizing influences of magic and civilization, these feelings become intensely ascetic. The basis of an ecstatic religion is love; that of an ascetic religion, fear. The believer in ecstatic religion loves his God, whereas the ascetic is afraid of his deity. The one avoids only inferior pleasures, whereas the other extends this avoidance even to aesthetic pleasures. Thus, the disappearance of magic intensified the ascetic character of the religions and led to the loss of the value of women as well as of fine arts. Now, with the rise of [secular] civilization, religion is changing from an ascetic to an ecstatic character, and with this transformation women as well as fine arts are regaining their equal status. . . .

We see, in short, that the equality of men and women among the ancient Turks was connected with the equal status of the systems of religion and magic. The existence of a higher sexual morality among them . . . [18] was due to the fact that the goddess of fertility, who was regarded as the enemy of chastity among the Chaldeans and Greeks, was held in esteem by the Turks as the guardian of innocence and virtue.

PART IV

T.N.W.C.— 17

CHAPTER VIII

NEW ORIENTATIONS

TOWARDS THE PEOPLE[1]

ONE of the fundamental principles of Turkism is the drive towards 'going to the people'. . . . What is meant by going to the people? Who are to go to these people?

The intellectuals and the thinkers of a nation constitute its élite. The members of the élite are separated from the masses by their higher education and learning. It is they who ought to go to the people. But why? Some would answer: in order to carry culture to the masses. But, as we have shown elsewhere, culture is something which is alive only among the people themselves. The élite are those who lack it. Then, how can the élite, lacking culture, carry culture to the common people who are a living embodiment of culture?

To answer the question, let us first answer the following questions: what do the élite and the people have? The élite are the carriers of civilization and the people the holders of culture. Therefore, the élite's approach to the people should only have the following two purposes: to receive a training in culture from the people and to carry civilization to them. Yes, it is only with these two purposes that the élite should go to the people. The élite will find culture only there and no-where else. . . .

The élite do not acquire national culture through education from childhood. The schools in which they study are not the people's schools or national schools. Our élite get their education without acquiring national culture. Their education merely serves to de-nationalize them. They need to compensate the shortcoming by mixing with the people, by living with them, by learning their language, by observing the way they use their vernacular, by listening to their proverbs, their traditional wit and wisdom, by noting their mode of thinking and their style of feeling, by listening to their poetry and music, by seeing their plays and dances, by penetrating into their religiosity and morality, by tasting beauty in the simplicity of their

260 TURKISH NATIONALISM AND WESTERN CIVILIZATION

clothes, their architecture, and their furniture. They should learn the folk-tales, anecdotes, epics, and beliefs, which are survivals from the ancient *töre*. . . . They should read their books, the books of the minstrels from Korkut Ata onwards, the hymns of mystics from Yunus Emre onwards, the people's humour from Nasreddin Hoca onwards, and discover the *karagöz* [shadow plays] and the *ortaoyunu* [open-air plays]. They have to find the old coffee-houses of the people where epics are being read, experience the nights of the holy month, the Friday communal feast gatherings, the religious holidays to which children look forward with so much enthusiasm. They have to build national museums in which works of art of the people will be exhibited.

It is only this way, only through such a contact with the national folk culture, and only by saturating their souls with the Turkish culture that the élite of the Turkish nation will nationalize themselves. It was through such a national education that Pushkin became the national poet of the Russians. Men like Dante, Petrarch, Rousseau, Goethe, Schiller, D'Annunzio became great creators of art and literature only because they had received their inspirations from the people.

As sociology has shown, genius is hidden in the people. An artist becomes a genius only because he becomes a manifestation of the aesthetic taste of the people. The reason why we lack great artists is that our men of art do not receive their aesthetic inspirations from the living museum of the people. No one, so far, has valued the art of the people. The old Ottoman élite scorned the peasant as 'stupid Turk'; the people of Anatolia were ridiculed as 'outsiders'; the title given to the people was 'vulgar'. The 'refined' were the Ottoman élite, who were the slaves of the court. As they had despised the people, nothing in language, poetry, literature, music, philosophy, ethics, politics, and economics has survived from the heritage of this ancient élite. The Turkish people have to start again from ABC. They did not even have a name as a nation until recently. The *Tanzimat*ists said to them: 'You are Ottomans. Don't claim a national existence distinct from other nations. If you do, you will cause the destruction of the Ottoman Empire.' The poor Turk, scared to lose his fatherland, had to say: 'By God, I am not a Turk, I am nothing but an Ottoman.'

But the Ottomanists could not see that in spite of whatever they did, foreign [non-Turkish] nations would do their best to secede from the Ottoman Commonweath because such artificial commonwealths composed of several nations could no longer survive. Each nation would be

NEW ORIENTATIONS

independent and would have its own homogeneous, genuine, natural social life. This trend of social evolution, which had started in Western Europe five centuries earlier, certainly would start in Eastern Europe too. The downfall of the Austro-Hungarian, Russian, and Ottoman Empires after the [first] World War has shown that this is very near. What would be the fate of the Turks once they faced this catastrophe without a realization that they themselves were a nation, that they too had their own home and their rights in the Ottoman Empire? Were they to say: 'As the Ottoman Empire fell, we do not have national hope, or political aspiration any more?' When the Wilsonian points were known, certain conscientious Ottomanists, who until then had remained indifferent to Turkism, began to say: 'What would be our state today if Turkism had not taught many of us that we had a national home ethnographically drawn, a national existence independent of the Ottoman Empire, a national right to rule in this home in complete independence?' It was only one word, that sacred word Turk, which showed us the right path to be followed amidst anarchy.

Turkists not only taught the élite the name of the nation, but also the beautiful language of the nation. As the name they gave to the nation was taken from the people, this language also was taken from the people, because both had existed only among the people. The élite had been living the life of somnambulists until then. They, like somnambulists, had a dual personality. Their real personality was the Turk, but they thought themselves Ottomans under the delusions of their somnambulism. While their real language was Turkish, they talked an artificial language in their delirium. In poetry, they put aside their own metre and sang in artificial metres copied from the Persians.

Turkists, like a psychiatrist, tried to cure this split personality by making them believe that they were not Ottomans but Turks, that their language was Turkish, and that their poetry was the people's; they even demonstrated these scientifically. It was only then that the élite were cured from this abnormal state of somnambulism and began to think as normal men.

We must confess, however, that so far these men have taken only one step forward towards the people. To reach the people in a real sense, they must live amongst the people and get the national culture from the people. The only way to do this is for the nationalist youth to go to villages as schoolteachers. Those who are not young should at

262 TURKISH NATIONALISM AND WESTERN CIVILIZATION

least go to the towns in inner Anatolia. The Ottoman élite will become a national élite only by completely assimilating the folk culture.

The second aim of going towards the people is to carry civilization to the people. The people lack civilization and the élite have its keys. But the civilization that they should carry to the people as a precious contribution will not be Oriental civilization or its offshoot, Ottoman civilization, but Western civilization, as we shall show below.

TOWARDS GENIUS[2]

. . . Science[3] tells us what is normal and what is pathological; but this knowledge does not satisfy all our spiritual needs. Man wants to know what is 'normal' through his intellect, but he also wants to discover what is 'original' through his sensibility. 'Original' is that which is not a product of imitation but is genuine. . . . Anything 'original' is natural, sincere, beautiful, and unique. Thus, originality is the basic concept of art and aesthetics.

When we look at our life with the eye of a real artist, what do we find as 'original'? Our old literature was an imitation of Persian literature and, therefore, was not original at all. Our modern literature is an imitation of French literature and, therefore, it too is not original. The same goes for our music, old and new! Is there nothing original in this land?

If we search for it only among the élite, no, we shall not find anything original. The two types of élite which we had in our history were artificially created specimens. The old-fashioned élite of the *Enderun* and the Europeanized élite of the *Tanzimat* were like flowers raised in hot-houses. The fertile soil of the country never saw these artificial flowers; and the people who grew naturally did not know any of the works of this élite. The artists of this élite drew their ideas from outside, copied their images from foreigners, borrowed their feelings from others, and tried to create only by their intellect. They were feudal artists of a feudal society because they looked down on the people as cattle and produced only for the courts and mansions. Hence, their works were neither original nor sincere.

Fortunately, our people did not consist only of these. Outside of them there is a great mass who were looked upon as cattle before the *Tanzimat* and as 'commoner' after that era, but the democratic consciousness of today calls them 'the people'. In Turkey the people are just the opposite of the élite. Just as there is nothing original in the élite, so there is nothing which is not original in the people. Everything among the people, their way of clothing, their spirit of surrender and quietness, their unpretentious heroism, in short, their whole life, is original. We find the same originality in the people's works of art. The West knows only two original figures among us—Nasreddin Hoca and Karagöz. But, in addition to these, are the tales of *Âsık Kerem, Şah Ismail, Köroğlu* not equally original? Are not the book of Dede Korkut, the hymns of Yunus Emre, the chants of the Bektashis, the *Divan* of Dertli original? If we go farther back, the fairy-tales, ballads, epics, proverbs, and sayings have the same original quality. In music, can we not say that the folk music of Aydın, Urfa, Diyarbekir, Harput, and Egin are capable of being the bases of an original music? Our architecture, calligraphy, tile works, book-binding and illuminating, dyeing, textiles, arms, were all original pieces of folk art.

It seems, therefore, that our people are the source of original beauty; and as the power which creates original works is called 'genius', the only source of genius for us is the people because there were no men of genius in [Ottoman] art. The first school of training in art, then, will be the life of the people, the natural and sincere experience of the people.

However, these original works of the people are technically primitive; they cannot satisfy refined tastes. Originality of a work does not necessarily imply perfection. A real piece of art should be also the product of refinement. Therefore, our artists will not only be educated in the art of the people, but at the same time they should train themselves in the works of the great artists of the West. . . . It is only when these two kinds of aesthetic education are thoroughly combined that a genuine national art will be created.

Let us go back, for example, to the Renaissance period of Italy. The Italian artists of this period, especially the painters and sculptors, were admiring the great works of the ancient Greeks and Romans because these had attained the highest perfection in art. The artists of the Renaissance acquired the techniques of this ancient art with great enthusiasm and effort, but did not imitate them because ancient mythology did not appeal to the people. For the people of the Renaissance, the most beautiful woman was the Virgin Mary and the most beautiful man Jesus Christ. The duty of the artists of the people was to give an artistic expression to these symbols which were venerated

264 TURKISH NATIONALISM AND WESTERN CIVILIZATION

and beautified in the soul of the people. Michelangelo and other artists discovered the right path. They gave the technical beauty of Venus to the Virgin Mary and transferred the corporeal perfection of Apollo to Christ. The saints were given all the beauty of the mythological figures. The art of the Renaissance was born as a national art, from the synthesis of the two elements. The Catholic Church appropriated this art and made itself a museum of it. The Orthodox Church continued to represent its sacred symbols not by following Græco-Roman models but on the basis of crude patterns taken from the Semites; thus, the Orthodox Churches did not become places of any aesthetic manifestation. Following the Renaissance, other nations did the same in the rise of their national art. Great men of genius, like Shakespeare, Rousseau, and Goethe, had acquired an education in the people as well as in the classics of the ancients. . . .

The reason why genuine artists have not arisen among us is our failure to use these two great sources of creative inspiration. We have neither tasted the aesthetic experiences of the people nor been acquainted with the great works of art of the West. Even the objects of beauty of our people were shown to us by outsiders, by men like Pièrre Loti. We ourselves did not even see them. Who knows what other treasures of aesthetic value our people may have of which we are unaware? We are interested neither in them nor in the art of men of international attainment. We are restricting ourselves to that old and new literature of ours which are both devoid of any originality and genius. And this not only arrests the advancement of our artistic life but even degenerates it.

We see, therefore, that the source of genius is the people. Men of genius are conscious reflections of the people's consciousness. But they have to attain the standards of international perfection in techniques in order to be the great artists of all nations. . . . If one source of art is the creations of the people, the other source is the creations of men of international attainment. Only those who drink the magic waters of both these springs will attain great achievements in art. . . .

The religious and moral experiences of the people are equally original. Taken as a whole, we call them national culture. The intellectuals and the artists of a nation are the real élite of the nation only when they represent the culture of the people and only when their works bear originality. We can see now why the élite of the Western nations have this national character whereas ours do not, and why education raises

NEW ORIENTATIONS

moral character there and why, when it is not national, it lowers it here.

To discover genius, therefore, let us turn towards the people and to the great works of the world! This is the second objective of the youth.

REVOLUTIONISM AND CONSERVATISM[4]

In one of my articles on political parties published in *Hakimiyet-i Milliye*,[5] I had pointed out the useful role of the conservative parties in the political life of a nation. When revolutionists attempt to destroy past traditions and put new ideals in their places, conservatives raise their voices: 'If you are going to destroy only the dead traditions', they say, 'we are with you. But if you attempt to destroy living traditions, we shall oppose you!'

What are living traditions? What are the criteria by which one can distinguish dead traditions from living ones?

It is much easier to draw this distinction in Turkey than in any other country because there is among us, on the one hand, a whole tradition, called Ottoman civilization, that is entirely composed of such lifeless traditions and, on the other hand, another system which we call Turkish culture, whose traditions are all alive.

Are the grammatical rules of Arabic and Persian in the Ottoman language anything but examples of these lifeless traditions? Is *arūẓ* anything but a dead tradition? Are not *gaẓels* and *kasides*, *allafranga* poems, 'oriental' music, night-club songs, literature of superstitions and phantasies, rococo architecture, decadent poetry, pessimistic and sceptic morality, etc., etc., all lifeless traditions? Over against these, are not the language of the people, rhythms of folk poetry, the people's aesthetic taste, folk literature, folk morality, the wisdom of the people all living traditions in general?

The problem is quite clear: we are revolutionists against Ottomanism, but conservatives towards Turkish culture. The revolutionary Turkey of today is changing only the Ottoman traditions. Ottoman civilization is an Oriental civilization. Oriental civilization is not Islamic civilization. It is a continuation of Eastern Roman civilization.

Turkish revolutionism cannot by any means accept conservatism with respect to questions of civilization. Turkism is conservative only on questions of culture. This conservatism is not irreconcilable with revolutionism. Liberal revolutionists have always served national cultures. The only group which is not conservative on questions of culture is the radical group. Turkists cannot be radicals. Turkism, on the other hand, cannot be conservative on matters of civilization. Civilization is the clothes of nations. Just as individuals change their clothes so nations may do. Turks, for example, have in the past turned from the civilization of the Far East to Oriental [Near Eastern] civilization. And now there is no reason why they should not accept Western civilization provided they preserve their Turkishness and Islamic faith. The latter two constitute what we call Turkish culture.

In our acceptance of Western civilization, the most important point on which to be alert is the problem of the preservation of our national unity and integrity. Turkish revolutionists should be conservatives only in this sense. On this point we are in agreement with the conservatives. To be conservative on matters of culture is not at all an obstacle to progress. National culture is something living; it is something which evolves by itself. As culture is the product of the unconscious ego of society, no one can interfere with it on the basis of his individual consciousness. National culture always marches towards the right path and meets with success through divine guidance; it never errs.

The only part of our life that we can improve by conscious control is civilization. Civilization, in itself, is the product of individual consciousness. We have to accept the civilization of the West, because, if we do not we shall be enslaved by the powers of the West. To master the civilization of the West, or to be mastered by the powers of the West: between these alternatives we must choose! Today this truth is well understood: in order to defend our freedom and independence against Europe, we have to conquer the civilization of the Europeans. European civilization consists of positive sciences, industrial technology, and social organization [division of labour]. If we had not introduced modern military techniques and methods of training from Europe, how could we defend ourselves today against the aggressors? The whole strength of Europe, the only superiority of it, lies in its civilization. It was only by means of its civilization that Europe has been able to defeat Muslim nations and has become the master of the world.

Why, then, should we ever hesitate in taking over this civilization which has proved so successful? Did not our faith make it a duty for us to take over all kinds of science and learning, as it is said: 'Seek knowledge even if it be in China', and 'Learning is the lost property of the believer; he should take it wherever he finds it'? And the science and learning of today are nothing other than what we call Western civilization.

Western civilization is a continuation of ancient Mediterranean civilization. The earliest founders of the Mediterranean civilization were Turanian peoples, such as Sumerians, Elamites, Phoenicians, Hittites, Scythians, the Hyksos, and the Cumans. There was a Turanian Age in history before the ancient ages. The early inhabitants of Western Asia were Turks. These ancient Turks, who were attacked by Semites from the south and by Aryans from the north, were forced to turn temporarily towards the Far East. But this temporary Eastern affinity does not prove anything against our affinity towards Western civilization. The earliest founders of the early Mediterranean civilization were our forefathers. Much later, Muslim Arabs, Persians, and Turks again improved this civilization and became the teachers of the uncivilized Europeans. By destroying the Western and Eastern Roman Empires, they brought about revolutions which twice changed the ages of history in Europe. Even today we have prepared the ground for the opening of a new era in history by causing the fall of the Tsarist régime in Russia.[6] We are connected with Western civilization through several contributions, and thus have a share in it.

What shall we take from European civilization? Not a national language, of course, because we have a national language spoken by the masses. But we want methods of linguistics. Thus, what we shall take is not the language but the science of language. We shall also develop our own modern neologisms corresponding to European scientific and industrial terms. We shall certainly not take our standards of beauty from Europe because, fortunately, there is the national treasure of art of our own people. But, again, we need the methods of aesthetics, and these we shall take from the West. And, again, we shall certainly not take national morality from the West because our people have their own. But we do not know the methods of scientific inquiry in this field. Thus, what we need is not a European moral code but the science of ethics. It is no more necessary, after these examples, to say that we shall not take religion from Europe. It is religion that separates us from Europe more than anything else. Europe will always remain Christian as we shall remain Muslim. But, this, of course, will not prevent us from introducing the science of comparative religion from the West, because it is a science that studies all religions from the same

268 TURKISH NATIONALISM AND WESTERN CIVILIZATION

point of view and has elaborated methods whereby religions are studied objectively.

These observations lead us to the conclusion that we shall take from Europe not merely the results of these sciences in Europe. Rather we shall take and use the methods of the sciences to reach the truth by ourselves. We shall take not the products but the techniques of the applied sciences and technology. We shall, therefore, not copy the composition of European composers, but learn the methods and the techniques of modern music by which we shall harmonize the melodies sung by our people. The aim, therefore, is to arrange our national melodies on the basis of the techniques of modern music and produce our own modern national works of music. In the field of literature, our aesthetic sense should be cultivated by translating Western classics into our own language. The classical literature of Europe is a healthy literature. The kind of literature brought by decadents and phantasists is morbid. The Ottomans copied only this morbid literature because Ottoman society was senile. The Turkish nation is a young nation which has emerged out of the ashes with full vigour. It is even yet in its infancy. How can one give the works of worn-out and sick nations into the hands of the people of a youthful nation? The emergence of such a healthy, young, and alert nation out of an old, sick, and senile Ottoman nation is one of the miracles of our time. How can we explain it? Was there a hidden world in Turkey which so far escaped the notice of everybody? Yes, indeed. It was the Turkish people—living a life of *Ergenekon*[7] with their own language, literature, morality, philosophy, in short, with their own national culture. The Ottoman civilization had fallen upon them and concealed them from sight. They are now emerging from this *Ergenekon* under the leadership of the Grey Wolf as a healthy and gifted nation.

TOWARDS WESTERN CIVILIZATION[8]

I

As an old Turkish saying runs: 'Know your work, your food, and your mate', so modern sociology would tell us 'know your nation, your religion, and your civilization'.

The publications of the Turkists and national disasters taught us more or less where our nationality and our religious community lie.

On these two points there seems hardly any disagreement. But on the question of the civilization to which we belong, there are still differences and, perhaps, serious conflicts of view. It is necessary, therefore, to begin with this question in our discussion of the problems of the nation.

One of the reasons for the ambiguity in the question of civilization is the confusion existing with regard to the concepts 'civilization' and 'being civilized'. Formerly, human societies were believed to belong to one of three states: savagery, barbarism, or civilization. Today, the word 'savagery' has been discarded altogether from the vocabulary of science. It is recognized today that even primitive peoples, once believed to be savage, have their own form of civilization. It is even accepted that these primitive societies pass through certain stages of evolution and, thus, there are those who hesitate to use the term 'primitive' for these peoples.

If civilization is something which exists in all human societies, we might ask whether this is true also of animal societies. Civilization is the sum total of certain institutions; that is, of certain ways of thinking and acting. Animal societies are governed by instincts that are transmitted through biological inheritance. Among them, even division of labour and specialization are hereditary. Classes, the king, the labourers, and the soldiers are born with certain organs necessary for the performance of their functions. In animal societies there is nothing similar to the institutions that are transmitted through tradition and education. Thus, we cannot speak of the existence of civilization in animal societies. We can, therefore, derive two principles with respect to civilization: (a) civilization is found in all human societies; (b) civilization is found only in human societies. As stated above, civilization is the sum total of certain institutions. The sum total of the institutions peculiar to a particular nation, however, is called *culture*. As we also call all institutions within a particular *ümmet*, religion, what would be the position of the term *civilization* with respect to culture and religion? From a sociological point of view, we shall call the sum total of the institutions found commonly among different societies which belong to different cultures and religions, a civilization. Societies foreign to each other from the point of view of culture or of religion may belong to the same civilization. Just as differences in culture do not necessarily bar sharing in the same religion, so differences in culture and in religion do not prevent association within the same civilization. Thus, for example,

270 TURKISH NATIONALISM AND WESTERN CIVILIZATION

the Jews and the Japanese share the same civilization with European nations although they differ from them both in culture and religion.

A second reason for the existence of vagueness about the problem of civilization is the supposition that there is only one kind of civilization. In fact, there are several kinds of civilization. Australian aborigines, North American Indians, African tribes, Oceanic tribes belong to different areas of civilization. In ancient times, there was a Mediterranean civilization shared by the nations of the Mediterranean basin. The Ancient Greek and through it the Roman civilizations were offshoots of this Mediterranean civilization. Later, Roman civilization gave way to the Eastern and Western civilizations. In East Asia there was the civilization of the Far East to which Chinese, Mongols, Tunguz, Tibetans, and Indo-Chinese have belonged, even until now. Archaeologists, studying human remains under the earth, can tell us the civilization areas of prehistoric peoples. Students of folklore also find that tales, myths, epics, and proverbs are distributed to different areas of civilization. These examples show that civilization areas had geographical bases and were delimited by distinct boundaries. A folktale or a tool, for example, was diffused to certain limits but not farther because every civilization had its own system. Each civilization had its own logic, its own aesthetic standards, its own *Weltanschauung*. For this reason, different civilizations could not mix freely with each other. Again, for the same reason, when a society does not take a certain civilization in its entirety as a system, it fails to take its parts also. Even if it takes some parts, it fails to digest and assimilate them. As in religion, so also in civilization it has to be taken from its inside and not from its outside. Civilization, too, requires sincere believing and loyalty. Our *Tanzimat* reformers, who failed to understand this point, attempted to introduce European civilization by imitating appearances only. Their attempt was destined to fail.

Just as geographic areas of civilizations are distinct from each other, their separate historical evolutions are also independent of each other. In each, evolution has a beginning and an end. But, as civilization-groups are wider than culture-groups, the life span of a civilization-group is longer than that of a culture-group.

Furthermore, when a nation advances to the higher stages of its evolution, it finds it necessary to change its civilization too. The Japanese, for example, dropped the civilization of the Far East and took over Western civilization. A striking example in this connection is given by the Turks. The Turks have adopted three distinct and dissimilar civilizations during the course of their social evolution. When they were in the stage of ethnic-state organization, they belonged to the civilization of the Far East. When they passed to the stage of the sultanistic state, they entered into the area of Eastern civilization. And today, in their transition to the stage of nation-state, we see the rise among them of a strong movement which is determined to accept Western civilization. Traces of Far Eastern civilization are still found among the illiterate masses who carry oral traditions. The traditions of *tandırname* beliefs still living among them are nothing but the survivals of beliefs and rites which were basically derived from the Far Eastern civilization. Folk-tales are survivals of old myths and epics. Comparative studies to be made between the old [pre-Islamic] religion of the Turks and religions of other peoples of the Far Eastern civilization, and between these religions and the folk-tales and beliefs of present-day illiterate people will reveal the truth of this statement. These studies may also show the nature of the relation of the Turks to the groups called 'Altai' or 'Mongolian race'. To classify Turks who are fairer and more handsome than Aryans with the 'yellow race' has no scientific foundation, as the supposition of a linguistic unity among the ethnic groups, usually called the 'Altai race', is far from being proven. It is very probable that all of these groups, which are vaguely called a 'race', are nothing but different groups all belonging to the Far Eastern civilization. If this is so, our only affinity with Finno-Ugrians, Tunguz, and the Mongols consists of a common sharing of the same civilization and of our domination over them for a long period. It is quite possible that through such an association certain similarities in language have taken place.

The conversion of the Turks to Islam and their entrance into the area of Eastern civilization took place simultaneously. For this reason, many would call the Eastern civilization Islamic civilization. As pointed out above, peoples belonging to different religions may belong to the same civilization. In other words, civilization and religion are two different things. Otherwise there could not be any institution common to the groups who belonged to different religions. Since religion consists only of sacred institutions, beliefs, and rituals, non-sacred institutions such as scientific ideas, technological tools, aesthetic standards constitute a separate system outside of religion. Positive sciences such as mathematics, physics, biology, psychology and sociol-

272 TURKISH NATIONALISM AND WESTERN CIVILIZATION

ogy, industrial methods, and fine arts, are not connected with religions. Thus, no civilization can ever be called after a religion. There is neither a Christian nor an Islamic civilization. Just as it is incorrect to call Western civilization a Christian civilization, so it is equally incorrect to call Eastern civilization an Islamic civilization.

II

We should seek the sources of the Eastern as well as of the Western civilization, not in the religions of Islam or of Christianity but in other realms. Mediterranean civilization was created in ancient times with the contributions of Egyptians, Sumerians, Hittites, Assyrians, Phoenicians, etc. This civilization had reached its perfection among the Greeks whom the Romans succeeded. The Roman Empire carried this civilization to several nations who were living under their domination, but finally broke up into Eastern and Western states. This breach, however, was not only a matter of political partitioning. It paved the way for the partitioning of the Mediterranean civilization into two parts. Since Europeans were the inheritors of West Rome, they appropriated Western Roman civilization and improved it, and, thus, the new Western civilization came into existence. Muslim Arabs, on the other hand, became the inheritors of the Eastern Roman civilization. In order to prove that this was the case, let us look at certain elements of Eastern civilization. The earliest models of Arab architecture were of Byzantine origin. Turkish architecture was a product of the combination of the two. It is true that neither Arabs nor Turks simply copied their models. They created their own original architecture by adding creative perfections through the inspiration of their religious beliefs and moral ideals. This process of making them original products was due to the religious temperament and national culture of Arabs and of Turks. In spite of this, historians of art assume that their architecture was modelled after Byzantine architecture. In the East there was the Oriental music of the upper strata. Fārābī had taken this music from the Byzantines and adapted it to Arabic. This music spread among the upper classes of Arabs, Persians, and Turks, but failed to penetrate into the depths of the lower strata. It remained only within the circles of the upper strata. Thus, Muslim peoples failed to show as much originality in Eastern music as they did in architecture. Turkish masses continued to play their older music which they had when they

NEW ORIENTATIONS 273

belonged to the civilization of the Far East, and produced a folk music out of it. The Arab and Persian peoples did the same thing. Thus, Eastern music never became a national music among the Eastern peoples. Another reason why we cannot call this music Islamic is the fact that it is owned equally by non-Muslim peoples of the East, belonging to the Greek Orthodox, Armenian, and Jewish faiths.

Through translations, the Arabs received logic, philosophy, natural sciences, and mathematics from the Byzantines, and developed their aesthetic and philological sciences, such as rhetoric, prosody, grammar, and syntax, on Byzantine models. Medicine was taken from Hippocrates, Galen, and their disciples. In short, the Arabs took over from the Byzantines whatever they found among them in rational and experimental sciences, in pure and applied science and philosophy; later the Persians and the Turks took these from the Arabs. Independent Arab philosophers were divided into peripatetic and illuminationist schools. The first were Aristotle's and the second Plato's followers. Muslim religious thinkers were divided into *mutakallimūn* (theologians) and mystics. The first were followers of the atomistic philosophies of Democritus and Epicurus, the latter of the Neo-Platonism of the Alexandrian Plotinus. There were also disciples of Pythagoras and Zeno; the followers of the latter were called *Riwakiyyūn* (Stoics). Muhiyyud-din Arabī's *a'yān-i thābita* (eternal essences) were nothing other than Plato's ideal patterns. Besides metaphysics, ethics, politics, and economics were taken from Aristotle. Books on ethics, such as *Akhlāq-i Nāsirī, Akhlāq-i Jalālī* and *Akhlāq-i 'Alā'ī*, contained sections on ethics, politics, and *tedbir-i menẓil*, and all were basically copied from Aristotle.

Throughout the course of the Middle Ages, Eastern and Western civilizations were not much differentiated from each other. As Muslims could not effect any appreciable transformations within Eastern civilization, so the Christians failed in bringing perfection within Western civilization.

During the Middle Ages, however, we see the rise of two institutions in Europe. Opera originated in feudal castles; in the south of Western Europe, chivalrous love and a new aesthetics of *salon* and womanhood developed. The first contributed to the perfection of music and gave rise to modern European music. As quarter tones which had existed in Greek music were not suitable for opera, they fell into disuse, but through the influence of the opera, [polyphonic]

274 TURKISH NATIONALISM AND WESTERN CIVILIZATION

harmony was introduced into music and monophonic melodies were dropped. The second novelty contributed to the introduction of women into social life without their losing their chastity and sanctity. When the Muslims were introducing, from the Christian Byzantium and Magian Iran, the practices of feminine seclusion such as harem and veil, Western Europe was bringing women into social life.

With the exception of such differences, there was much in common between the Eastern and Western civilizations during the whole medieval period. Corresponding to medieval Muslim architecture, there was a religious architecture in Europe, the Gothic. Corresponding to the *hikmat* of Muslims, we find scholastic philosophy taught in European schools. . . . In both [the Muslim and the Christian scholasticism] all truths were known, because they were given truths transmitted through traditions. The task of the scholars of *hikmat* was to prove and confirm these truths through reason. Hence, they did not wish to be called philosophers because they regarded those as non-believers. Scholastic thinkers of the Christian Church shared the same view. Both Muslim thinkers and Christian scholastics took Aristotle as their teacher. For both, the aim of knowledge was to reconcile religion and Aristotelian philosophy.

III

Ethical, religious, scientific, and aesthetic revolutions in Europe—such as the Renaissance, the Reformation, the new philosophy, and Romanticism—put an end to medieval life. The same revolutions did not, however, take place in the Muslim world; for that reason we are still living in a medieval age. Europe put an end to scholasticism; we, on the other hand, are still under its domination.

What is the cause of this difference, in spite of the parallelisms of several centuries? Historians have suggested several explanations, but we shall accept a sociological explanation. In the great urban centres of Europe, the increase in moral density gave rise to the development of division of labour which, in turn, brought forth occupational specialization and the specialist. With this process of specialization, the individual won in Europe a personality with a new spiritual structure. With this fundamental revolution there was born a new Man with a new spirit, a new mentality, and a new set of ideals.

The new life springing from the spirit of the new Man did not fit

NEW ORIENTATIONS 275

into the old framework. Thus this was broken and destroyed. The liberated new life turned its creative forces in every direction and achieved great developments and improvements in every field of life; especially through the industrial revolution it gave modern civilization its characteristic mark.

In the East, on the other hand, great urban centres with advanced social density did not develop. The existing great centres of the East were not homogeneous in population and lacked the means of social contacts, hence of moral density. Because of the absence of a social division of labour, specialization and individualist personality, large-scale industry did not appear in the East. As the nations of the East did not develop a new spirit and a new life, they were unable inevitably to move their civilization farther from its medieval form. Things remain as they are according to the law of inertia if there is no cause to move them.

While Western and Central Europe freed themselves from medieval civilization, the Christians of the Orthodox Church in the East still were not freed from it. Russians, for example, remained within Eastern civilization up to the time of Peter the Great. Peter had many difficulties in his struggle to free the Russians from Eastern civilization and to introduce them to Western civilization. In order to learn what sort of methods should be followed in transforming a nation from Eastern to Western civilization, it suffices to study the history of Peter's reforms. While Russians, until then, were generally believed to be incapable of any progress, they began after these forced reforms to progress very quickly. This historical fact alone is enough to prove that Eastern civilization is averse to progress and Western civilization is the avenue to advancement.

IV

It was mentioned above that the basis of European civilization is the division of labour which produced, not only differentiation of specialized trades and professions, but also specialization in learning. We find the same differentiation in art. Social life underwent the same process of differentiation. Political authority was divided into legislative, judicial, and executive functions. The whole political organization was separated from the religious organization. Due to the progress of division of labour, administration of justice assumed a new strength;

276 TURKISH NATIONALISM AND WESTERN CIVILIZATION

economic, scientific, and artistic activities were developed to their utmost.

Muslim states, once equal or, from military and political points of view, sometimes even superior to those of Europe, began to sink lower as a result of the advancement made in Europe through the progress of the division of labour. A society can compete with other societies in both military and political fields only if it is equipped with equal weapons. Thanks to their extraordinary advances in industry, Europeans are able to manufacture horrible weapons of warfare. We, on the other hand, have to face these weapons with ordinary guns and rifles. How can the Islamic world ultimately survive under such conditions? How can we maintain our religious and national independence?

V

There is only one road to salvation: To advance in order to reach—that is, in order to be equal to—Europeans in the sciences and industry as well as in military and judicial institutions. And there is only one means to achieve this: to adapt ourselves to Western civilization completely!

In the past, the makers of *Tanʒimat* recognized this and set about to introduce European civilization. However, whatever they wanted to take from Europe, they always took not fully but by half. They created, for example, neither a real university nor a uniform judicial organization. Before they took measures to modernize national production, they wanted to change the habits of consuming, clothing, eating, building, and furniture. On the other hand, not even a nucleus of industry on European standards was built because the policy makers of *Tanʒimat* attempted their reforms without studying conditions and without putting forth definite aims and plans. They were always taking only half-measures in whatever they attempted to do.

Another great mistake committed by the leaders of *Tanʒimat* was their attempt to create a mental amalgam made up of a mixture of East and West. They failed to see that the two, with their diametrically opposed principles, could not be reconciled. The still existing dichotomy in our political structure, the dual court system, the two types of schools, the two systems of taxation, two budgets, the two sets of laws, are all products of this mistake. The dichotomies are almost endless. Religious and secular schools were not only two different institutions of education, but within each there was again the same dichotomy. Only in military and medical schools was education carried out exclusively along European lines. We owe to these institutions the generals and doctors who today save the life of the nation and the lives of the citizens. The training of specialists within these fields, in a way equal to their European colleagues, was made possible only because of the immunity of these two institutions from dichotomy. If the methods of warfare of the Janissaries or the medical practices of the old-fashioned surgeons were mixed into these modern institutions, we would not have our celebrated generals and doctors today. These two institutions of learning must be models for the educational revolution that has to materialize. Any attempt to reconcile East and West means carrying medieval conditions to the modern age and trying to keep them alive. Just as it was impossible to reconcile Janissary methods with a modern military system, just as it was futile to synchronize old-fashioned medicine with scientific medicine, so it is hopeless to carry the old and the new conceptions of law, the modern and the traditional conceptions of science, the old and the new standards of ethics, side by side. Unfortunately, only in the military arts and medicine was Janissary-ism abolished. It is still surviving in other professions as a ghost of medievalism. A few months ago a new society was founded in Istanbul in order to bring Turkey into the League of Nations. What will be the use of it as long as Turkey does not enter definitely into European civilization? A nation condemned to every political interference by Capitulations is meant to be a nation outside of European civilization. Japan is accepted as a European power, but we are still regarded as an Asiatic nation. This is due to nothing but our non-acceptance of European civilization in a true sense. The Japanese have been able to take the Western civilization without losing their religion and national identity; they have been able to reach the level of Europeans in every respect. Did they lose their religion and national culture? Not at all! Why, then, should we still hesitate? Can't we accept Western civilization definitely and still be Turks and Muslims?

Let us review what we have changed since we introduced Western civilization and see whether there was anything to do with our religion and nationality. We abolished, for example, the *Rumî* calendar, something sacred for us. It was the calendar of the Rum; that is, of the Byzantines. If anyone should ever regard it as something sacred, the Byzantines should do it. The same is true for dropping the use of the

Rumî hour and introducing the Western hour. What damage to our religion and culture can one expect from replacing Aristotelian deductive logic by the inductive logic of Bacon and Descartes and the scientific methods arising out of it? What did we lose when we put ancient astrology and alchemy aside and took modern astronomy and chemistry? How much truth can one find in the old books of zoology, botany, and geology? Are we not obliged to get from the West the sciences which did not at all exist in the East, such as biology, psychology, and sociology? We had already taken our old sciences from the Byzantium. By merely replacing them with those taken from Europe, what can we lose in religion or culture? By enumerating these examples endlessly, it will be seen that whatever we drop in the name of Eastern civilization was all taken originally from the Byzantines. Once this is realized, no one will ever seriously object to the dropping of the Eastern civilization and introducing Western civilization.

The solution to our problem of civilization is of a pressing nature from another aspect also. For a long time we have been concerned in our country with the question of education. In spite of many efforts, the question is still unsolved. If we scrutinize the real nature of the question, we find that basically it is nothing but an auxiliary aspect of the problem of civilization. If we solve the basic problem, the question of education will also be solved. In this country there are three layers of people differing from each other by civilization and education: the common people, the men educated in *medrese*s, the men educated in [modern] secular schools. The first still are not freed from the effects of Far Eastern civilization; the second are still living in Eastern civilization; it is only the third group which has had some benefits from Western civilization. That means that one portion of our nation is living in an ancient, another in a medieval, and a third in a modern age. How can the life of a nation be normal with such a threefold life? How can we be a real nation without unifying this threefold education? The sources of our knowledge are: first, folk-lore (the books of the minstrels, folk-tales, folk literature, proverbs, superstitious beliefs); secondly, the books translated from Arabic and Persian and taught in the *medrese*s; thirdly, modern schools and their books translated from European languages. We shall succeed in unifying our learning and education only when we have one civilization; only then shall we be a nation homogeneous intellectually and spiritually. We cannot afford to hesitate any longer.

NEW ORIENTATIONS

In short, on the basis of our above analyses the foregoing principle of our social policy will be this: to be of the Turkish nation, of the Islamic religion, and of European civilization.

TOWARDS MODERN SCIENCE [9]

In order to join the ranks of the contemporary nations, certain conditions should absolutely be fulfilled. At the top of these comes the drive towards science. As individual persons think, feel, and will, so do the nations—from this develop science and philosophy, religion and art, morality, politics, and economy. A modern nation is a creature which thinks in terms of the positive sciences. Although philosophy is more or less a matter of intuition rather than of scientific thinking, it has to be compatible with the positive sciences, and thus it is in very close relation to them. Therefore, if a nation does not want to say farewell to thinking, it has to acquire the positive sciences.

The sciences show us the causes of phenomena. If we know the cause of a certain fact, we can produce or remove it, depending upon its desirability or undesirability. At the same time, science shows us the effects and functions of facts. Therefore, it is a practical guide showing the means to be used to reach ends. When some people say: 'We must have, not men of science, but men of practice', they talk nonsense. Look at the nations of Europe and America! The most practical ones are those who think scientifically.

Another function of the sciences is to unify the members of a society through certain common ideas. As each person thinks in his own way, those who do so exclusively tend to believe that what they think is the correct way of thinking while what others think is not true. This prevents co-operation and even a common universe of discourse among people. It is for that reason that we need an impersonal frame of thinking that would unite persons on certain common ideas, and by its practical results would also prove its applicability to the nature of facts. This impersonal frame of thinking is provided by the modern sciences, which are based on objective experiments, manipulated through instruments, and subjected to positive methods.

Another function of the sciences is to tell us the good and the bad. Determining the good and bad gives rise to several conflicts in social life. For the conservative, everything old is good and everything new is bad. The radicals believe just the contrary. Both are groundless.

280 TURKISH NATIONALISM AND WESTERN CIVILIZATION

There is no relation between the badness or goodness of something and its being old or new. We expect the solution to this important problem from science. For science this problem is a question of normal versus pathological. Biology can tell us whether a fact in the organic world is normal or pathological. Why should the same not be done in psychology and sociology? ... Sociology has made great progress in recent years, so that it is in an equal position with biology in determining the normal and the pathological. ... As societies are classified into species and genera, it becomes possible to determine for which social species a certain institution is normal and for which it is pathological. Furthermore, as the course of social evolution reveals the various stages of evolution, it becomes not impossible to predict what institutions will rise in a certain society in the future. As other nations have already passed through the stages through which we are going to pass, it becomes possible to determine which institutions will be normal in any one stage and which ones will not be.

The modern state is a government of science as much as it is the sovereignty of the people. A modern nation cannot survive without large-scale industry, without public hygiene, railways, electricity, and all comforts. And a modern state also cannot survive without developing an organization based on modern law, without building a national economy and realizing real freedom and equality on the basis of democracy.

It is the positive sciences that can bring these material as well as spiritual attainments. Therefore, our first objective, as individuals and as a nation, is science.

CULTURE AND REFINEMENT [10]

In French the term 'culture' has two different meanings. We may express one of these by the word 'culture' (*hars*) [Arabic *ḥarth*], and the other by 'refinement' (*tehẕib*) [Arabic *tahdhīb*]. Many of the misconceptions regarding culture come from this dual meaning of the word *la culture*. ...

One of the differences between culture and refinement is that the first is democratic while the second is aristocratic. Culture consists of the folk traditions, the usages, *mores*, oral or unwritten literature, the language, music, and religious beliefs, the moral, aesthetic and economic institutions of the illiterate. Since the people are the source and

NEW ORIENTATIONS 281

carrier of these products, culture is democratic. Refinement, on the other hand, is something peculiar to the intelligent élite, to the educated and sophisticated intellectuals. . . . The basis of refinement is the acquisition of a good education and a sincere and unpretentious love for thinking, fine arts, literature, philosophy, science, and religion (provided it is free from any fanaticism). Thus, it is a special way of feeling, living, and thinking fostered by a special education.

Another difference between the two is that the first is national while the second is international. A man, probably under the influence of his own culture, may overestimate the culture of his own nation, but if he is sophisticated enough he will like the culture of other nations and try to enjoy it. Thus, refinement makes men more humanistically minded, more tolerant and benevolent towards everybody and every nation, and more eclectic.

This point of difference leads us to discuss the problem of nationalism and internationalism. A nation is the sum total of those men who participate in a common culture. Internationality is a group of nations who participate in a certain civilization which we may equally call a civilization-group. Some people would believe that there are not several civilizations created by different groups of nations. For them there is only one civilization, common to all men, whose members are not nations but persons. This is the view of him whom we call the 'cosmopolitan'. A cosmopolitan is a man who believes [as Tevfik Fikret, the Turkish poet, expressed it]: 'My people is mankind and my home the earth'. This view of civilization is irreconcilable with that of the nationalists. To the latter, mankind is the human species studied together with other zoological species by zoology, whereas human beings—that is, socialized individuals—live only as nations. As Turkism does not agree with those doctrines which deny the principle of nationality, it naturally rejects cosmopolitanism. Internationalism, on the other hand, is something wholly opposite to cosmopolitanism. For the internationalist, civilization does not extend to the totality of mankind. There are several civilizations. Each has its own sphere or area and each is made up not of individual human beings but of individual nations. . . . A civilization may be called a Society of Nations. . . .

It follows that each civilization-group is a circle of internationality. The existence of the national culture of a nation does not preclude its participation in an international civilization. Civilization is the sum total of the institutions commonly shared by the nations which belong to the same internationality. Within each internationality, therefore, there is the one civilization common to all nations within it and the several cultures of the individual nations. Thus, when we adopt Western civilization, we not only will share an international civilization but at the same time will get the opportunity to enjoy the cultures of the nations who belong to that civilization. As national societies are differentiated into occupational groups because of the division of labour and specialization, so also an international community is differentiated into national and unique cultures as if there were a kind of division of labour and an international specialization among these nations.

When we judge by our own national standards, we appreciate only those works which fit into our national culture. But, just as we become bored with eating the same dish every day, we also tend to be satiated with the literary works, music, or architecture of our culture. As the connoisseur changes his menu frequently, so the sophisticated person also wants to taste the works of other cultures. . . . International relations within a civilization-circle are something like a symposium. Each nation contributes its own culture, and to the degree of its contribution it is entitled to enjoy the cultures of others. One should not confuse, however, the national taste, which appreciates only the national culture, with exotic taste, which appreciates only foreign cultures. The normal pattern which we find among the European nations is that of the prevalence of the national taste as basic and permanent with the exotic taste remaining in second plane. That was not the case among the Ottomans. Among the *havas* [the élite], exotic taste had become the basic and permanent norm while national culture did not have even a secondary value. For that reason, its old literature was a product of Persian and its modern literature of French taste and no national literature ever flourished.

Therefore, when refinement takes such an abnormal dimension, it becomes harmful. Refinement is normal so long as it recognizes the value of the national culture. When it denies it, it assumes a morbid and unhealthy nature. Turkists, therefore, reject cosmopolitanism as cosmopolitans reject Turkism. But there is no point of contradiction and opposition between Turkism and internationalism. A Turkist is at the same time an internationalist. Everyone of us lives a national as well as an international life. Our national life means living our own national culture. Our international life consists of our participation in international civilization, on the one hand, and in several unique and original cultures, on the other. The civilization in which we have participated since the *Tanẓimat* era is definitely that of the West. . . .

We can see, therefore, that the 'culture' of the Turkists is neither *la culture* of the French nor *die Kultur* of the Germans.[11] For the French, French culture has acquired a world-wide form of refinement, thanks to its literary power. The Germans believe that their *Kultur* would have conquered the whole world, through their military and economic forces, if their armies had not been defeated. Our understanding of culture is not as aggressive as these. We shall build our own culture for our own taste and enjoyment. . . . Our enjoyment of other cultures will never go beyond the limits of an exotic interest. For us, anything French or English or German or Russian or Italian may only have an exotic beauty. Although we admire it, we cannot be captured by it. Our hearts are given to our own culture. For us the most beautiful is nothing but the beauty of our own culture. We do not deny that we are far behind European peoples in civilization, in learning, in economic life, and in refinement, or that we have to work hard to catch up with them. But we cannot regard any nation as culturally superior to us. For us, our own culture is the best of all cultures imaginable. Therefore, we can imitate and follow neither French *culture* nor German *Kultur*. We consider them, like the cultures of all other nations, original cultures peculiar to their own nations and get only an exotic enjoyment from any of them.

We see, therefore, that Turkism being the love of our own original culture is, nevertheless, not chauvinistic or fanatic at all. It is determined to adopt Western civilization unreservedly and as a whole, and does not entertain any disdain or contempt for the cultures of other nations. To the contrary, it appreciates and respects all cultures. However little we may sympathize with the political methods of the nations from whom we have seen enmities, we shall admire their civilization and culture and venerate their great thinkers and artists.

CHAPTER IX

THE PROGRAMME OF TURKISM

⚜

WHAT IS TURKISM?—A RECAPITULATION[1]

IN a previous article I quoted the 'New Life and New Values' which appeared originally some seven or eight years ago.[2] The ideas expressed in that article have taken clearer form with the passage of time. In it, for example, the search for genuine values, on the one hand, and the creation of a civilization for the Turks, on the other, were presented as representing the same goals. A statement such as 'the genuine civilization is the Turkish civilization which will begin with the growth of the New Life' shows this confusion clearly. Such a statement is undoubtedly chauvinistic. But every new movement inevitably goes to extremes in the beginnings. As time passed, we began to see that international civilization and national culture are different from one another. We realized that the genuine values which the proponents of the New Life were to create were not universal values to be valid for all men, but the national ideals peculiar only to the Turkish people. Furthermore, as these existed already in the soul of the nation as unconscious gropings, they had only to be uncovered and, therefore, it is incorrect to say that they should be created. As these points were now clarified, it automatically appeared that the New Life meant nothing other than the National Life.

However, one would say that if National Life is one which is already being experienced, why take pains to discover it? Something existing evidently exists even if it is not discovered. Ideals that exist in the unconscious are still motivating forces even though they are not conscious. It is true that we believed in the existence of the National Life which we are after, as existing unconsciously in the soul of the people and that we gave the name 'Turkism' to the work of making this unconscious conscious. If our people were not consciously presented with 'cultures'[3] other than their own, it would not be so urgent to make national Culture conscious because only the unconscious Culture of the nation would affect our life. But, since our national

THE PROGRAMME OF TURKISM 285

Culture has been in a state of unconscious stupor, and since non-national 'cultures'—either as survivals of the past or as imported new elements—have reigned over our life as our national consciousness, we had to proceed urgently.

Let me put it more clearly: before the rise of Turkism there were two 'cultures' in our country—the religious (*ümmet*) 'culture' and the Westernist (*Tanzimat*) 'culture'—which were inimical to each other. The souls of the educated Turks were torn in the struggle between the two. In reality, neither reflected the true inner life of the Turks of the time because long before the *ümmet* education and the [modern] secular education existed, and long before the existence of the Ottoman Turks, the Turks existed as an organized nation. The Ottoman Turks could create a Culture with a national character only out of their own life. If the [Ottoman] *Enderun* 'culture' had penetrated into the masses by following a course of independent growth and by becoming rooted in the soul of the people, it might have produced a vehicle of national education. The first step taken in the *Tanzimat* reforms was to eliminate this *Enderun* 'culture' which was already mixed with religious (*ümmet*) 'culture'.

It seems, therefore, that when the Turks entered into a phase of modern and national life, they were sentenced to remain under the un-natural tutelage of an *ümmet* 'culture', which was not modern at all, and of the *Tanzimat*ist education, which was not at all national. Both 'cultures' were kept side by side artificially without any attempt being made to reconcile and co-ordinate them. The contradictions between the two were reflected in the souls of young men who had the psycho-logical aptitude of synthesis and produced crises in their lives. Both 'cultures' were called civilizations. The Turks were destined to carry these two civilizations, which were diametrically opposed to each other, without ever being able to reconcile them, and to ignore the existence of the conflicts and contradictions between the two.

In reality, however, the two mentalities represented by these two civilizations appeared diametrically opposed to each other only under the influence of certain traditional catchwords and convictions and were not at all irreconcilable. First of all, what had existed then was a national Culture, on the one hand, and two 'culture' patterns in the form of international civilization, on the other. The *ümmet* 'culture' constituted one element of the national Culture in the form of religion. As the Turks were Muslims, Islam would naturally remain in their

286 TURKISH NATIONALISM AND WESTERN CIVILIZATION

Culture as an important element. Thus, there would not be a conflict between the *ümmet* 'culture' and the national Culture. Since religion constituted one of the sources of the national Culture, there should be a close solidarity between the two. And, equally, there would be no contradiction between the national Culture and the European 'culture' introduced with the *Tanzimat*. Only those forces which are of the same nature may be contradictory. For example, the Eastern and Western civilizations are absolutely irreconcilable. As these contradict each other, the people cannot combine both within themselves at the same time. Just as there can be no man with two religions, there can be no nation belonging to two civilizations at the same time. It is for this reason that the Turks had either to remain within Eastern civilization or to adopt Western civilization unreservedly. In doing the latter, however, they would not lose anything from their national Culture because national life, i.e. the sum total of national values, will maintain its independent existence as a national lore, which we have called Culture, so that when Western civilization and Turkish Culture confront each other within our souls, there will be no conflict at all and no crisis suffered by the youth.

Before the Turkist arrived at these conclusions, the false representatives of our culture were the representatives of the *ümmet* and those of the civilization the *Tanzimat*ists. Yes, the first were the false representatives of the old 'culture' because in so far as Islam was confined to those highbrows who were educated in Arabic and Persian, it failed to penetrate into the masses. Therefore, with the exception of the religious life, the rest of the *ümmet* 'culture' cannot be called Culture. It is only the religious life within the *ümmet* 'culture' which is a part of the national Culture. Thus, whereas the *ümmet* 'culture' is not reconcilable with Western civilization, the religion of Islam is. Since the *ümmet* 'culture' refused to view religion as a sphere of life which changes and evolves alongside the *mores* [of the people], since it insisted on identifying it with the *fikh*, which is nothing but a crystallization of the *mores* of a particular period, and since it viewed itself as a civilization inclusive of all elements of Culture aside from religion, it was unable to reconcile itself either with Western civilization or with modern science.

The *Tanzimat*ists, on the other hand, were false representatives of contemporary civilization. While European civilization did not aim at destroying the particular Culture of any nation, the *Tanzimat*ists entirely neglected the national Culture, equating Culture with civiliza-

THE PROGRAMME OF TURKISM

tion which is common to all nations. Their understanding of European civilization did not go beyond that of the Levantines of Pera.[4] They could see Europe only through the eyes of these Levantine *Frenks*. They simply imitated the superficial lustre, the luxury, and ornateness, and such other rubbish of Europe, and never seriously tried to assimilate the science, philosophy, art, and moral standards of its civilization.

We can now argue definitely that a serious interest in Culture is absolutely requisite for the rise of a genuine interest in civilization. For a civilization-group is a society above societies, made up of culture-groups or nations. As civilization consists of the sum total of the common features of several national Cultures, each national Culture would naturally distinguish itself from others, and then seek the international features it has in common with other Cultures. The nations will cling first to their own ideals; it is only after they have realized the value of national Culture that a Society of Nations is conceivable. The cosmopolitanism that existed before the era of national idealism is diametrically opposed to present-day internationalism, which is based on international law. In the Europe of today, this old cosmopolitanism no longer exists. Every person is first of all a member of a nation and then of an international community. Among us, as the meaning of nationalism is not understood in its real sense, the fiction of cosmopolitanism is in vogue over against internationalism. In Europe a person is first a man of Culture and then of civilization. One can understand the significance of civilization to the extent to which he grasps Culture. Among us, those who have grasped the significance of Culture are few, and an interest in international civilization is yet to be born. The 'civilization' of the *Tanzimat*ists was nothing but a mixture of an understanding devoid of any method and a practice stripped of any system.

Since truth results from the conflict of ideas, as Namık Kemal said, the conflict between the *ümmet* 'culture' and the *Tanzimat* 'culture' would inevitably give rise to a new sparkle of truth in the souls of the youth who were capable of yearning for a synthesis. That long-awaited sparkle was Turkism with its substitution of the national Culture for *ümmet* 'culture' and of modern civilization for the *Tanzimat*ist 'culture'. Turkism is nothing but the method of right feeling and right thinking for the Turks. Right feeling means the avoidance of error in our value judgments; right thinking means the exactness in our judgments on reality. Religious, moral, and aesthetic judgments require right feeling; science, industry, and techniques are based on

288 TURKISH NATIONALISM AND WESTERN CIVILIZATION

exact thinking. Since subjective feelings are national and objective ideas international, right feeling means sharing the feelings of the nation and correct thinking means reasoning as all civilized human beings do, on the basis of scientific thought. As the artist, the moralist, and the philosopher constitute the élite of feeling, they will fulfil their functions to the extent to which they think objectively and in a way detached from national values.

In 'New Life and New Values' we had stated that the political revolution would be based on *idées-forces*, whereas the social revolution would be based on *sentiments-forces*. Political revolutions everywhere have been the products of the dissemination of new international legal ideas. In other words, political revolutions are products of civilization and progress. Social revolutions, on the other hand, symbolize the victory of the living values of a nation over against the dead ones. And this is realized only with the awakening of the national Culture to replace imitative and conventional 'cultures'. Since the values constituting a national Culture inspire enthusiasm and excitement in the soul, they are aptly called *sentiments-forces*. And since scientific and technical concepts, on the other hand, are only cold truths free from any attachment to the emotions, they are by themselves only 'shadow ideas'. They become *idées-forces* only if they combine with the *sentiments-forces* of a particular Culture. Therefore, unless the elements of a civilization are absorbed by the Culture of a nation, they never penetrate into the life of the people. Unless the science and techniques of the West are appropriated by our national *mores*, they will not take a place in our schools or in our life. That is why a nation does not become civilized if it has not attained Cultural consciousness. Civilization produces fruits only when it is grafted on the tree of the national Culture. The *Tanzimat* failed because it tried to adapt the civilization of Europe without building the national Culture. The Turkists have learned a lesson from their experiment, hence they are convinced that an understanding of civilization is a prerequisite to an adequate understanding of Culture. It is only then that the ideas emanating from the civilization of the West will not remain mere 'shadow ideas' among us but will become genuine *idées-forces*. . . .

We see, therefore, that Turkism first started as a philosophical movement under the name of New Life, and then evolved into a practical movement inevitably arriving at conclusions that are corroborated by present-day sociology. This common conclusion teaches us

THE PROGRAMME OF TURKISM 289

that human Culture is nothing but a synthesis of national Culture and international civilization and that humanity is heading towards an international society by the federation of free nations.

THE AIM OF THE TURKISTS[5]

... Once we understand these relations between culture and civilization, we can determine the meaning of Turkism and what it is expected to do. The Ottoman civilization was destined to fall for two reasons: first of all, like all other empires, it was a non-permanent community of peoples. Not communities but societies are groups which have everlasting life; only nations are societies. Subjugated nations may forget their national identity only temporarily under the cosmopolitan rule of the empires. They are destined to awaken from their slumber of serfdom and demand their cultural independence and political sovereignty. This process started in Europe five centuries ago. It was inevitable for those empires—the Austrian, Russian, and Ottoman empires which, so far, had remained safe from this process—to undergo dissolution like their predecessors.

The second reason is the fact that the more Western civilization advanced, the more it increased its power to wipe out the civilization of the East. In Russia and among the Balkan nations the civilization of the West took the place of that of the East [which is not an Islamic civilization but a continuation of the Byzantine], and sooner or later the same transformation would take place within the Ottoman territories. ... As the civilization of the West is taking the place of that of the East everywhere, quite naturally the Ottoman civilization which was a part of Eastern civilization would fall and leave its place to Turkish culture with the religion of Islam, on the one hand, and to Western civilization, on the other. Now, the mission of the Turkists is nothing but to uncover the Turkish culture which has remained in the people, on the one hand, and to graft Western civilization in its entirety and with all its living forms on to the national culture, on the other.

What the reformists of the *Tanzimat* era did was a mere attempt to reconcile the civilizations of East and West. But two opposite civilizations cannot live side by side. As their principles are opposed to each other, each tends to corrupt the other. The principles of Western and Eastern music are irreconcilable. The experimental mind of the West cannot get along with the scholastic mind of the East. A nation is

T.N.W.C.—19

290 TURKISH NATIONALISM AND WESTERN CIVILIZATION

either Eastern or Western. Just as there can be no person with two faiths, so there can be no nation with two civilizations. As the reformists of the *Tanẓimat* era failed to see this, they failed in their reforms. The Turkists will succeed, because they have determined to adopt Western civilization as a whole and to drop the originally Byzantine civilization of the East. The Turkists are those who aim at Western civilization while remaining Turks and Muslims. Before they realize this, they have to discover and revive our national culture.

THE TURKIST PROGRAMME—LANGUAGE[6]

I

Turkey's national language is undoubtedly the Turkish of Istanbul. However, we must distinguish the Turkish dialect spoken there from the 'Ottoman Turkish' which is written but not spoken. Which one of these is our national language? . . .

The duality of written and spoken language is entirely peculiar to Istanbul. Any condition which is not found anywhere universally but only partially in one particular place is not a normal fact. Therefore, the duality which we speak of as existing in Istanbul is a pathological case. . . . In order to remove this duality, one of two courses can be taken: either the written language will be made the spoken language or the spoken one will be made the written language.

The first alternative is impracticable because the written language of Istanbul is not a natural language, but artificial like Esperanto. This 'Ottoman Esperanto'—the vocabularies, grammars, and syntaxes of Arabic, Persian, and Turkish put together—how can it be a spoken language? This mixture of artificial superfluities—three different words for the same thing, at least three grammatical rules for relative cases, for example, and at least three forms of a certain particle—how can it be a natural spoken language? . . . The impossibility of the policy of making a spoken language out of this written language is already proved by the complete failure of all the efforts that have been made for centuries. Even if it were possible to enforce this strange language by dictatorial methods, it would still not be the language of the people because it would be necessary to disseminate it among all Turks. Obviously it is impossible to impose a language upon a vast nation.

Thus, the second alternative remains: to follow the spoken language and make it the written language! This is not a new idea because the writers of the common folk have been doing it already. Alongside the Ottoman literature another, the Turkish literature, written in the language of the people, has existed for six or seven centuries.

Therefore, there is nothing to be done anew in removing this duality. The only thing to be done is just to ignore the Ottoman language as if it had never existed and to take the Turkish language, which is the basis of the folk literature, as the national language of Turkey. Thus, Turkists have simply adopted the following principle: write as the people, especially as the women of Istanbul, speak! . . .

II

Some of the critics say: 'The language of the folk also contains several originally Arabic and Persian words for which you blame the Ottomans'. It is indeed true that in the spoken language of the people there are several words taken over from Arabic. However, these words . . . differ in two ways from those taken by the *ulema* and the men of letters of the Ottoman upper classes: in the language of the common people there are nowhere several different expressions for one word. Whenever the people definitely accepted a certain word from Arabic or Persian, they have altogether dropped the Turkish one corresponding to it. For example, when the words *hasta* (sick), *ayna* (mirror), and *merdiven* (ladder) became established as accepted words, the original Turkish words *sayru, göʒgü,* and *baskiç* corresponding to the above, became entirely forgotten. It is true, however, that in some cases old Turkish expressions were retained even when equivalent Persian or Arabic ones were introduced. In these cases, however, either the meanings of the introduced words, or of the old Turkish ones, underwent changes and, thus, they were distinguished from each other by nuances in meaning. . . . The Ottoman *ulema* and writers used several Turkish, Arabic, and Persian words for the same meanings. Thus, in their language there existed for a certain meaning at least three words, one from Turkish, the other from Arabic, and the third from Persian (e.g. *su, āb, mā'* for 'water'; *gece, shab, layl* for 'night'; *ekmek, nān, khubʒ* for 'bread'; *et, gūsht, laḥm* for 'meat'). In Ottoman there was always a trinity of words for each meaning. . . .

In the second place, people corrupted the words taken from Arabic, Persian, or other foreign languages, either in meaning or in pro-

292 TURKISH NATIONALISM AND WESTERN CIVILIZATION

nunciation; in other words, they assimilated them into Turkish. . . .
The people assimilated borrowings, and made their language a living
whole in which every word had a definite function. This was done not
consciously and rationally but unconsciously and instinctively. In the
language of the people every word has a definite meaning distinct from
the meanings of other words, and there is a definite word for any
intellectual or sentimental meaning which the people experience. The
Ottoman scholars and writers believed that the modifications made by
the people in order to assimilate foreign words were corruptions, and
called the products of this assimilation *galaṭât* (corrupted words). . . .
To them, *fasaḥat* (correct pronunciation) meant only to use the words
that had entered into Turkish from Arabic and Persian, not in their
Turkified but in their original forms because, to them, the Ottoman
language was not an independent language and had no capacity of
assimilation. . . . We see, therefore, that for the people 'a corrupted
word (*galaṭ*) which has become established is better than an unfamiliar
word in its correct form (*fasîh*)', while for the *ulema* the contrary was
true. For the people, the Turkish language is the sovereign; Arabic and
Persian words must accept its phonetic and lexicological laws. . . . For
the other group, sovereignty and the right of independence belonged
only to Arabic and Persian words; Turkish had to obey their nobility
and purity. Turkish could not claim any independent existence, as it
was believed to be ninety-nine per cent Arabic and Persian.

It seemed, therefore, that the job facing the Turkists was to reject
the view of the 'correct-pronunciationists' and accept that which the
people had unconsciously maintained. The Turkists regard the pure
(*fasîh*) words of the Ottomanists as incorrect (*galaṭ*) words. They
accept it as a principle to follow the corruptions of the people not only
in pronunciation but even in spelling. . . .

III

The principles of the Turkists in language are not, however,
favourable to the views of the (Turkist) purists. In the purists' view,
for a word to be really Turkish it had to be derived from an originally
Turkish word. Therefore, for them the words . . . that were intoduced
into the language of the people from Arabic or Persian origins should
be liquidated and replaced by forgotten old Turkish words, by words
found in Chagatay, Uzbek, Tatar, Kirghiz, and other dialects, or by

new words to be coined according to newly invented grammatical rules. Turkists reject this view. First of all, no Turkish root can be claimed to be originally Turkish when we trace it to the ultimate origins. It is a scientifically established fact that many words which we think are originally Turkish were derived from Chinese, Mongolian, Tunguz, and even Indian and Persian origins. In the second place, words are symbols of the meanings they refer to and not definitions. It is not necessary to know the origins and derivations of the words. This is useful only for philologists and linguists. It is even harmful to the system and idiom of the language because, as we have seen in connection with the words that were derived from Arabic and Persian, also in the originally Turkish words, the actual meaning is sometimes different from the etymological one. . . .

For Turkists, every word that is known to, and used by, the Turkish people is Turkish. For a word to be Turkish, it is not enough to be derived originally from Turkish. Several words . . . derived from Turkish roots have become obsolete and cease to live. . . . Just as the fossils in plant and animal nature cannot be revived, so it is with linguistic fossils. . . . The language of a people is a living organism made up of its own living organs and not of dead roots. Therefore, the purification of Turkish . . . should not be based on the extremist claims of the purists.

The purists' insistence on borrowing words from various Turkish dialects should also be rejected. For various Turkish dialects, once differentiated from the ancient Turkish mother tongue, followed separate lines of development and became alienated from each other in phonetic, morphological, and lexicological aspects. If we introduce words from these dialects, we shall destroy the beauty of the Turkish of Istanbul. As a matter of fact, we do not need these words because we already have others corresponding to them. Only the ancient words that were the names of old Turkish institutions will enter into our language and then as scientific terms, as studies on ancient Turkish history discover them. But this would not imply a revival of fossils. . . .

The purists' proposal to coin new words by inventing new rules should also be rejected. Just as it is impossible to incorporate a new organism into the living body of an animal or plant, so it is impossible to introduce an invented rule into a language. . . .

Leaving aside the extremist radicalism of the purists, we still find that there are many words in Ottoman Turkish to be discarded since

294 TURKISH NATIONALISM AND WESTERN CIVILIZATION

there are several superfluous terms introduced unnecessarily into scientific neologisms. . . . In a medical dictionary, for example, there are very many Arabic and Persian words which are not needed at all. . . . Words for which there exist Turkish expressions that are in no way different in meaning should be dropped altogether.

IV

Turkists believe that a language may borrow words from other languages provided there are no exact equivalents of these words in that language. They believe, however, that a language cannot borrow rules from other languages. . . . All Arabic and Persian borrowings in the Ottoman language are used either as mere words or as forms [denoting person, gender, number, etc.]. We believe that the first group, provided they do not clash with already existing Turkish equivalents, should be retained while the other group ought to be dropped entirely. For example, the Arabic word *kātib* should not be used in Turkish in the meaning 'one who writes' But as *kâtip*, the same word has been used by the people as an independent word meaning 'clerk' or 'secretary' [thus, the word should be retained in this sense]. . . .

It follows that when a word is borrowed from Arabic or Persian as a term, other words etymologically related to it should not be taken along with it. . . . The plurals of Arabic or Persian words should likewise be rejected. . . . Languages cannot exchange particles . . ., in other words, a language cannot borrow morphemes from another one. . . . Only in some cases certain foreign words used in Turkish have assumed this character of morphemes and become mere words, such as nouns. . . .

As an exception, three particles from the Persian have entered into the popular use of Turkish. One is the particle of reference or relation (-*î*), the other two are *khâne* and *nâme* which in Persian are, in fact, nouns and not particles. . . . The first has almost become a Turkish particle, because it is added to Turkish words. But in all other cases it is certainly not a Turkish particle. . . . Although we can reduce the number of borrowed words that are constructed with this particle, unfortunately, and contrary to one of our basic principles, we have to adopt this particle in forming many of the scientific terms. Turkism, which has succeeded in overcoming all obstacles in creating a new Turkish, is forced to make a concession before this tiny particle. . . .

The words *khâne* and *nâme* may be accepted as particles since they serve to enrich the language.

Just as a language cannot borrow forms and particles from other languages, neither can it borrow rules to make [possessive and adjectival] constructions. The old Ottomans accepted all kinds of such rules from Arabic and Persian. These constructions, too, are like forms and particles, like morphemes. In every language the words in possessive and adjectival constructions are all morphemes. . . . As all kinds of construction exist in Turkish, there is no need for any Arabic or Persian constructions. These were taken over by Ottoman writers, not because of any vital necessity but simply because they believed that Arabic and Persian were more beautiful than Turkish. To them, that was true with respect to words, forms, particles, and construction. In fact, no one can claim objectively that a certain language is more beautiful than another. Every language has its own beauty. Every nation subjectively finds its own language beautiful. Certainly Arabic is beautiful, and so is Persian. But they are more beautiful for Arabs and Persians. And to us, Turkish sounds most beautiful. The beauty of words, forms, particles, and constructions is also a relative matter. They are beautiful within their respective languages. An Arabic word is beautiful in the Arabic language; a Persian construction sounds beautiful in a Persian sentence. If you could transfer the very beautiful eyes or nose of a woman to the face of another, they would not seem equally beautiful. In the same way, the beautiful aspects of a language are only ugly when put into the sentences of another language. . . .

V

Some think that the Turkist view on language questions has only certain negative principles. . . . But the new Turkish cannot be created by merely clearing away the superfluous elements borrowed from other languages. To do this is only the negative aim of Turkism. Turkism has also certain positive aims. The abnormality of the old Ottoman language did not consist only in having superfluous foreign words, verb forms, idioms, and particles. If it were so, it would be quite easy to ameliorate the language simply by dropping all these superfluous elements. The old Ottoman language suffered also from another malady: It lacked many necessary words. It is significant that a philosophical essay could not have been written [in Turkish] until the rise

296 TURKISH NATIONALISM AND WESTERN CIVILIZATION

of the Turkist movement; neither could the masterpeices of world literature have been translated [into Turkish] clearly and adequately. Therefore, a real amelioration of our language would also require the filling of these gaps by putting missing words into their proper places in the organism of the language. This is the positive aim of the New Turkists.

The words in which our language is deficient are of two kinds. The first consists of certain idioms used by the people. There are several words, expressions, and gallicisms used by the people which have not yet been incorporated into the written language. In fact, these constitute a mine of richness and beauty for the language. . . . The second deficiency consists of words of an international nature. A nation has to appropriate the words that express scientific concepts, philosophical ideas, literary images, poetic experiences of the civilization-group or internationality to which it belongs. Now that the Turks are determined to adopt Western civilization, they need new words that will express all Western concepts and meanings.

What shall we do to create these words in our language? The most fruitful course of action is to have first-rate stylists carefully translate into Turkish all the literary masterpieces and scientific and philosophical treaties written in European languages. Through these translations, several new words and modes of expression will enter into the New Turkish in addition to several means of linguistic refinement, grammatical tools and organs, syntactical mechanisms and constructions, and new possibilities to express sentimental and symbolic meanings. Then, the New Turkish will become a vehicle to express the most complex ways of thinking as well as the most sincere and original experiences.

In this process of translation, we shall come across several concepts and meanings which are entirely new to us, and it will become necessary to find equivalent words to express them in Turkish. How should this be done? For many of them there will be equivalents in our spoken Turkish, which is rich in zoological, botanical, physical, and technological terms as well as in geographic ones. The words expressing emotions and sentiments also are numerous. Thus, in the attempt to create new terms and meanings, we shall above all go to the language of the people. Then we shall create new words by using the rules of Turkish for particles, forms and relative and possessive cases. And then, if there are still words missing, we may resort to Arabic and Persian to borrow words, provided they are accepted as simple and single words.

THE PROGRAMME OF TURKISM

... Some of the foreign [Western] words should be adopted as they are. Some of these words are those that express certain conditions with respect to a nation, a period of history, or an occupation, and have become adopted in all languages, e.g. 'feudalism', 'chivalry', 'Renaissance', 'Reform', 'Jacobinism', 'socialism', 'Bolshevism', 'aristocracy', 'democracy', 'diplomacy', 'theatre', 'classicism', 'romanticism', etc. Another category of these words is those that are used as the names of tools, machines, and objects of industrial techniques. Most of them have been taken over directly by the people and, in most cases, are not translated by other nations, such as steam, railway (*chemin de fer*), telegraph, telephone, tramway, gramophone, etc.

In short, the New Turkish will come into being, first, by clearing our language of the superfluous words taken unnecessarily from Arabic and Persian, second, by enriching it with nationally used but literally ignored words and expressions, and, third, by creating international words that we do not yet have. The first process is one of clearance, the second one of culturation (*tahris* [Arabic *tahrīth*]), and the third is the process of refinement (*tehẓib* [Arabic *tahdhīb*]).

Let us summarize the principles of Turkism on language:

1. In order to build our national language, we must ignore altogether the Ottoman and, taking the Turkish which is the basis of the folk literature, accept the pronunciation of the people—especially of the women of Istanbul.

2. Those Arabic and Persian words for which Turkish equivalents exist must be dropped completely, but those for which there are no exact equivalents must be retained.

3. Those Arabic and Persian words that have become incorporated into the vernacular of the common people will be retained in their corrupted forms and meanings as Turkish, and will be spelled in accordance with the Turkish pronunciation.

4. Old, fossilized Turkish words shall not be revived when there are equivalent new words.

5. New terms will be made, first of all, from words in the vernacular. If this source fails to supply the need, new words may be coined, provided they are made in accordance with regular rules of Turkish grammar with respect to particles, conjugations, and word compounds. If such words are not found, then new words may be derived from Arabic and Persian, provided they are not compound words [made according to Arabic or Persian grammatical rules]. Foreign words

298 TURKISH NATIONALISM AND WESTERN CIVILIZATION

referring to certain ages, certain conditions of professions, and tools used in industry will be accepted directly.

6. All linguistic 'extra-territorial rights' of Arabic and Persian shall be abolished altogether; no rules of tenses, particles, or compounds shall be taken at all.

7. Every word known and used by the Turkish people will be regarded as Turkish. Every word that is familiar and not artificial to the people is national. The language of a nation is a living organism built up, not by its lifeless roots, but by its vital usages.

8. As the phonetics, morphology, and vocabulary of Istanbul Turkish are the bases of new Turkish, words, tenses, particles, or rules of word compounds shall not be taken from other Turkish dialects. These dialects, however, shall be studied carefully from a comparative point of view in order to understand Turkish syntax and idioms.

9. As investigations on the history of the ancient Turkish civilization increase in the future, several ancient Turkish words, such as the names of ancient institutions, will enter modern Turkish. These old words should be used only as terms for the institutions to which they refer; they must not be revived as parts of general vocabulary.

10. Words are not definitions of the meanings to which they refer. The meanings of the words cannot be discovered by simply knowing their etymologies.

11. A dictionary and a grammar of modern Turkish should be worked out on the basis of the above-mentioned principles. In these works, Arabic and Persian words and terms that have become incorporated into Turkish should be given, together with information on their structure and composition, not in the sections concerning the dynamics of the language, but in the sections concerning etymology which deal with the dead past and the genealogy of the language.

LITERATURE AND MUSIC

I[7]

In the Turkist programme, our literature will go through an education in two schools of art for its development: One is folk literature and the other is Western literature. Turkish poets and writers should take as their models the products of the folk art, on the one hand, and the masterpieces of the West, on the other. Without passing a period of apprenticeship in these two schools, Turkish literature can be neither

THE PROGRAMME OF TURKISM

a national nor a developed literature. Therefore, our literature will partly approach that of the people and partly that of the West.

What are the products of folk literature? They are (a) tales, anecdotes, legends, myths, narrations of the miraculous deeds of the saints, (b) proverbs, riddles, (c) songs, ballads, epics, hymns, (d) tales of *Dede Korkut, Âşık Kerem, Şah Ismail, Köroğlu,* and other popular romances, (e) the works of mystic poets and minstrels such as Yunus Emre, Kaygusuz, Karacaoğlan, Dertli, and (f) the humorous literature of Nasreddin Hoca and Karagöz. The more our literature benefits from these models, the more cultured it will be.

The second set of models for our literature are world classics extending as far back as Homer or Virgil. The best models for a newborn national literature are masterpieces of classical literature. Turkish literature should avoid the romanticists and later schools before it drinks the good old wines of the classical masters' works. Young nations need a literature that glorifies ideals and heroes. Classical literature is, in general, of this kind. The establishment of the school of neo-classics in France in an attempt to give the youth a new impulse towards idealism is an example showing the educational importance of classical literature. We cannot, however, dispense with the romanticists altogether and concentrate solely on the classicists because romanticism is ultimately based on folk literature. The romanticist movements in Europe began as movements towards the people and by taking folktales and epics as models. It follows, then, that we have to pass through both classicism and romanticism in our strivings for culture and for the cultivation of our literature. In our effort to imbibe the spirit of Western literature, we shall at the same time try to understand how Western romanticists utilized folk literature. By this apprenticeship in the school of the immortal works of the West, we may revive the process of cultivation of our own literature.

It is only after these two periods of schooling, the one in Turkish culture and the other in Western traditions, that our literature will become national as well as Western.

II[8]

Before the introduction of European music, there were two kinds of music in Turkey: one was Eastern music, which Fārābī took from the Byzantines, the other was folk music, which was a continuation of ancient Turkish music.

Eastern music, like Western music, was derived from that of the ancient Greeks. The ancient Greeks, finding insufficient the full and half tones that existed in folk music, added quarter, eighth, and six-teenth tones and called them quarter tones. Quarter tones were not natural but artificial. For this reason, they do not exist in the folk music of any nation. Therefore, Greek music was an artificial music based on unnatural tones. Furthermore, there was in this music a boring montony due to the repetition of the same tones, which again is something unnatural.

Opera, which originated in Europe in the Middle Ages, eliminated these two shortcomings of Greek music. Quarter tones were not suit-able for opera. Composers and singers of opera were from the people; thus, they were unable to understand quarter tones. Under these con-ditions, Western opera eliminated quarter tones from Western music. Furthermore, as opera was a representation of a succession of human feelings, emotions, and passions, it adopted [polyphonic] harmony and saved Western music from monophony. These two innovations prepared the way for the rise of a more fully developed Western music.

Eastern music, on the other hand, remained in its previous state. It preserved quarter tones on the one hand, and remained foreign to [polyphonic] harmony, on the other. This morbid music, after being transmitted by Fārābī to the Arabs, passed to the Persians and Otto-mans chiefly because of the esteem in which it was held at the courts. The Greek Orthodox, Armenian, Chaldean, and Syrian churches and Jewish synagogues also accepted the same music from Byzantium. In the Ottoman lands this music was the only institution common to all Ottoman ethnic and religious communities, and for this reason we may properly call it the music of the Ottoman peoples.

Today we are faced with three kinds of music: Eastern music, Western music, folk music. Which one of them is ours? Eastern music is a morbid music and non-national. Folk music represents our culture. Western music is the music of our new civilization. Thus, neither should be foreign to us.

Our national music, therefore, is to be born from a synthesis of our folk music and Western music. Our folk music provides us with a rich treasure of melodies. By collecting and arranging them on the basis of the Western musical techniques, we shall have both a national and a modern music.

THE PROGRAMME OF TURKISM 301

This will be the programme of Turkism in music. It is the task of our composers to bring this aim to fruition.

RELIGION[9]

Turkism in religion simply means having religious scriptures, sermons, and preaching all in Turkish. A nation that is unable to read and understand the scriptures of its religion quite naturally fails to understand the real nature of its religion or the teachings of its preachers, and also fails to enjoy worship. The Great Imām Abū Hanīfa even believed that reciting the verses during the daily prayers in national languages was permissible. The joy to be derived from prayers depends entirely upon a thorough understanding of the verses read during worship.

If we examine the religious life of our people, we shall notice that among the rituals that inspire ecstasy to the highest degree are those sincere and silent supplications which are offered in the native tongue after the usual prayers. Another source of the highest religious joy, which the Turks enjoy in prayers, are the hymns that are also recited or sung in the mother tongue. Again, it is essentially the singing of hymns in Turkish which gives a special colour to the *Ramaẓan* night prayers, as they combine poetry and music. During *Ramaẓan*, or in ordinary times, sermons given in Turkish are another source of religious feelings and experiences among the people. But the recital of the Birthday Poem [*Mevlid*] composed in Turkish is the ritual that gives the greatest rapture and joy to the Turks. This ritual, which combines in itself poetry and music and dramatic events, became one of the most vital forms of ritual among the Turks in spite of the fact that it was a latter-day religious innovation. The Turkish hymns and mystic poems sung in mystic convents during the rite of *ẕikr* have also been a great source of ecstasy.

These examples show that the real force which from time to time inspired religious experiences among the Turkish people, was the existence, among the religious rites, of certain rituals long permitted to be performed in the national language. Thus, in order to ensure to our religious life a greater enjoyment and stimulation, it is necessary to have the Kur'an—except during the recitals, the litanies, the supplications that are read after prayers, and the sermons—read in Turkish.

MORALITY[10]

Patriotic Morality

Among the ancient Turks, patriotism reached its highest levels. No Turk ever hesitated to sacrifice his life or his most beloved possessions for his people. . . .

In the future, too, patriotism should be the most important area of morality for the Turks because the nation and its soil are ultimately the only independent and self-existent unit. The family and occupational groups constitute only the cells and organs of this whole, while religious and international federations, although wider in scope than national unions, constitute no real social organisms but only collections of societies. These groups cover only particular aspects of the life of their members, whereas the nation is the group that is all-inclusive with respect to the life of its members.

Therefore, the ideal of the nation is above the ideals sought by other social groups, such as the family, professional group, church, and international union. Patriotic morality should rank above other moralities. . . . Turkism should give the highest value to the Nation and Fatherland.

Professional Morality

Professional morality follows patriotic morality.

The ancient Turks considered professional solidarity to be more important than kinship solidarity. . . . The ruling institution among them was divided into four professional groups . . . which later on, among the Ottomans, corresponded to the civil, military, bureaucratic, and scholarly estates. In addition to these, there were occupational organizations. The *Akhı* organization of the Anatolian Seljuks was a professional order based on the *futuwwa* principle. . . . The artisan syndicates of the Ottoman period were nothing but a continuation of these older organizations. These unions were organized on a regional basis and, therefore, lost their usefulness when national economy replaced regional economy. . . . For this reason, it is foolish to attempt to revive these old institutions. Instead, it is necessary to organize nation-wide syndicates that will have their central organization in the capital of the state. . . . In every city there must be a central committee composed of the syndicate representatives; . . . their function will consist of running the common affairs of the syndicates of the city and of organizing the economic life of the city. . . . Federations of different syndicates should establish central committees in the state capital which, in turn, will constitute, through their representatives, a general confederation of syndicates. . . . Scholarly professions should join the federation also . . . and, thus, all professions will be organized as an army and constitute the basis of the new professional morality. . . . These organizational bases . . . should control professional behaviour . . . and provide a professional ethic . . . and establish institutions of professional and mutual help.

Family Morality

The ancient family and sex morality of the Turks . . . which had reached high standards, is completely lost today. Under the influence of the Iranian and Greek civilizations, women have become enslaved and have sunk to a low legal status.

When the ideal of a national culture arose among the Turks, the revival of, and return to, these traditions were inevitable. It was for this reason that feminism in Turkey developed alongside the rise of nationalism. Turkish nationalists are both populist and feminist, not only because these two principles are valued in our age, but also because democracy and feminism were two bases of ancient Turkish life. Other nations, in their efforts to adapt themselves to modern civilization, have to keep far away from their past, whereas for the Turks it is enough to turn and look at their ancient past for inspiration. The ancient Turkish religion, being free from ascetic rites and negative rituals, from fanaticism and bigotry, had made the ancient Turks very tolerant with respect to women and to foreign peoples. . . . An impartial historian of the future will admit that democracy and feminism originated with the Turks.

Thus, the Turkish morality of the future will be based on the principles of democracy and equal rights for women as well as on national, patriotic, professional, and familial values.

Civic and Personal Morality

. . . Civilization-groups originated with the clans. In primitive societies only those who belonged to the same clan were regarded by others as having rights and respectability. In these societies, there could be no feud between the relatives within the clan; peace prevailed among its members. With the evolution of human society, the phratry

304 TURKISH NATIONALISM AND WESTERN CIVILIZATION

took the place of the clan, and was followed by the tribe and tribal confederations, city-states, ethnic states, and empires as units in which peace prevailed. With the widening of these units, the circle of persons recognized as having rights and being objects of moral obligation was increased. Thus, personal morality or civic morality gradually grew in scope.

Civic morality has two aims, one positive and the other negative. The negative aim of civic morality is justice, which implies prohibiting the violation of the security of other persons. The positive goal of civic morality is kindness, which means doing good to others. A second positive aim of civic morality is fidelity in contracts. . . .

Civic morality in the individual necessitates belief in the sacredness of personality. . . . One of the important aims of Turkism is to elevate civic morality, which is next to those moral codes of the nation, profession and family.

LAW[11]

The aim of Turkism in law is to establish modern law in Turkey. The most fundamental condition for our success in joining the ranks of modern nations is the complete cleansing of all branches of our legal structure of all traces of theocracy and clericalism.

Theocracy is the system in which laws are made by Caliphs and Sultans who are regarded as the Shadows of God on earth. Clericalism refers to the acceptance of traditions, claimed to be originally instituted by God, as unchangeable laws and to the belief that these laws can be interpreted only by spiritual authorities, believed to be the interpreters of God.

The state that is completely freed from these two characteristics of the medieval state is called the Modern State. In the first place, in a modern state the right to legislate and to administer directly belongs to the people. No office, no tradition, and no other right can restrict and limit this right. In the second place, in a modern state all members of a nation are regarded as equal to each other in every respect. No special privilege is recognized for any individual, or family, or class. States that fulfil these conditions are democratic; that is, they are governed by the people.

If the first aim of Turkism in law is to create a modern state, its second aim is to free professional organizations from the interference of public political authority and to establish professional autonomy based on the authority of the professional specialists. On the basis of this principle, civil law, commercial law, laws on industry and agriculture, and laws giving professional autonomy to professional organizations such as universities, the bar, medical associations, teachers' associations, engineers' associations, etc., should be codified.

The third aim of Turkism in law is to create the institution of the modern family. The principle of equality in the modern state necessitates the equality of men and women in marriage, divorce, inheritance, and in professional and political rights. It is, therefore, necessary to fashion the new family code and the law of elections on this basis.

In short, all provisions existing in our laws that are contrary to liberty, equality, and justice, and all traces of theocracy and clericalism should be completely eliminated.

POLITICS[12]

Turkism is not a political party movement. It is a scientific, philosophical, and literary movement. In other words, it is a movement of cultural drive and regeneration. For this reason, Turkists so far have not entered into any political struggle as a political party and certainly will not do so in the future.

Since this is so, however, Turkism cannot remain altogether indifferent to political ideals because Turkish culture, in addition to other values, implies certain political ones. For example, Turkism can never reconcile itself with clericalism and theocracy. Turkism is a secular movement and can reconcile itself only with movements of a secular nature.

The Turkism of today is supporting the People's Party because that party has materialized the sovereignty of the people; it has called our state the Turkish state and our people the Turkish nation. Until the revolution in Anatolia, the name of our state, our nation, and even our language was 'Ottoman'. No one could dare use the word 'Turkish' for them. Nobody could claim to be a Turk. When Turkists dared to do so, they became hated enemies to the court and to the conservatives. Under the leadership and direction of our great Mustafa Kemal, the Society for the Protection of Rights, from which the People's Party was later born, delivered the country from invasion and, at the same time, called our state, nation, and language by their real names and

306 TURKISH NATIONALISM AND WESTERN CIVILIZATION

delivered our political life from the last traces of absolutism and cosmopolitanism. We may even say that this society put the political programme of Turkism into practice without being aware of it. Truth is one and cannot be two. Those who seek it will finally arrive at the same ends, even if they proceed along different ways.

Turkism and Populism met on the same [political] programme because both were products of necessities and realities. As both reached the real truth, they are in complete agreement. One of the evidences of this agreement is the fact that all Turkists, without exception, have joined the struggle in Anatolia and have become its most ardent defenders. God's sword was in the hands of the Populists just as God's pen was in the hands of the Turkists. When Turkish soil was threatened, the sword and the pen joined forces. From this union was born a new Turkish nation.

In the future Populism and Turkism will always march hand in hand towards the realization of our ideals. Every Turkist will remain a Populist in politics and every Populist will be a Turkist in the field of culture. Our religious catechism tells us that our doctrine in theology is that of Māturīdī, and in jurisprudence that of Hanafī. In a similar expression we can put forth this maxim: 'Our doctrine in politics is Populism; in culture it is Turkism.'

ECONOMY

I[13]

Patriotism assumes various forms with respect to religion, morality, law, and fine arts. A real patriot should be loyal in all these spheres of life. In the Middle Ages, religious patriotism meant loyalty to the Catholic Church, but when the modern states arose, the religious state assumed a different significance.

If there are religious, moral, legal, and literary manifestations of patriotism, can we not speak of an economic patriotism? Economic life has been taken customarily as the most cosmopolitan sphere of life. The Manchester [school of political] economy which is still taught in our schools teaches that the economic mind [*vicdan* (conscience)] is something totally cosmopolitan! When there is such an official school based on the theorem of *laissez-faire*, *laissez-passer*, how can we dare to speak of a patriotic economic mind?

THE PROGRAMME OF TURKISM   307

We do not need to be frightened, however. Everybody knows now that Manchester economics is not at all a cosmopolitan doctrine, that it is nothing but the national economics of England which stands for big industry and, thus, derives only benefit from the freedom of exchange abroad and suffers no loss from it. It was the American economist John Ray and the German Friedrich List who discovered this truth; each developed a theory of national economy for his own country. The economists of other nations later followed them. It was only we poor [Turks] who remained captives of British economic theory, just as we still blindly imitate other nations and fail to free ourselves from cosmopolitanism in morality, in law, and in literature. In spite of certain sporadic attempts, [the Turkish] state was dominated by that Manchester tradition.

The abolition of the Capitulations has been not merely a step towards freeing ourselves but also a decisive move. In order to protect national industries, it was necessary to have control over the customs tariffs; this became possible only through this great effort. The [Turkish] state, following this decisive step, is showing signs of pursuing a national economic policy by establishing the National Credit Bank and by its decision to construct the Ankara railways. The decision to make an Internal Loan (as of last week) may be taken as a clear sign of our government's determination to pursue a national economic policy.

II[14]

This nation which has performed a miracle during the war can do the same in the economic field during the time of peace. What would be the path to follow to perform this miracle?

We can find the right way if we leave the wrong road that we have been following since the *Tanzimat* era. English political economy, which did not suit our national spirit, has misled us since that period. People believed that the state is incapable of building industries, that it cannot encourage and protect national industries, that the municipal administration is unfit for economic enterprises, and that economic enterprises are expected to be carried only by individuals and companies. Theories of this nature, which have no universal validity, have been responsible for the decline of our old economy and have prevented us from developing a new one. Before the *Tanzimat* era, we had a rich industry. We had developed aesthetic crafts, such as tile

308 TURKISH NATIONALISM AND WESTERN CIVILIZATION

works, rug weaving, dye techniques, book-binding, gilding, iron work, carpentry, etc. Each of these constituted a field of aesthetic creation that could be an object of honour for a great nation. After the *Tanẓimat*, these techniques disappeared and were not replaced by new ones. In the same way, our old commercial and guild organizations were totally destroyed.

Why did the theories of English political economy not fit our national life? England herself was not an agricultural country. She did not have enough land for agriculture. She had, on the other hand, abundant coal and iron reserves. Large-scale industry was developed spontaneously by the people. Overseas trade, too, made great strides in the same way. Economic growth was not dependent upon the encouragement of the government. Non-intervention of the government in business and the non-existence of import and export restrictions were enough for the growth of economic life. Therefore, the economic [interests] of the people could be expressed thus: 'Just don't disturb us; we'll do the rest.'

In our country the situation was just the opposite. Private initiative did not exist. We did not have the capacity to form companies. We did not know even the ABC's of large-scale industry. We were entirely ignorant of the skills necessary for it. Therefore, the mere existence of needs was not enough to produce a [new] economic life. Without the guidance of the state, we Turks could not take even a step in this direction. The governments, however, avoided such a policy because of the teachings of the political economists. Furthermore, it already had an important excuse: Economic Capitulations. There were various possible forms of economic aid to which the Capitulations would not be a hindrance, but the government did not want to use them. They seemed to be afraid that the spirits of the Manchester political economists would be displeased.

Fortunately, we realize today that this theory of political economy is the one suited only to the conditions of England and that each nation must develop her own system of national economy.

There is a great need for the growth of big industry in Turkey. This cannot be realized by private enterprise; it needs central and local government 'entrepreneurship'. Industries built for military needs constitute a good example. When peace comes, these will be needed no longer. Thus, will it not be possible to replace them with civil industries that will cover the needs of the country? There are several

THE PROGRAMME OF TURKISM 309

officers of the army who know industrial management. It will be a great advantage even if they can only run the already existing plants. After the peace, on the other hand, it will be easy to get machinery, technicians, and engines from Europe. Great sums now being spent for the trade schools are just wasted. Technical knowledge cannot be transplanted through instruction; it can be acquired only by apprenticeship. The best trade schools are industrial plants. Plants to be established by central and local governments will bring big profits. When private citizens, as individuals or as companies, want to buy them, they may be sold to them and new ones can be opened by the government. If the Grand National Assembly pursues such a policy by drawing up a national economic plan, it will be possible to see an economic miracle after the establishment of peace. The Turkish nation is capable of performing miracles in every field if it makes each aim a matter of a National Pact and realizes each goal with the aid of faith and idealism and by mobilizing its National Assembly, its army, and its government agencies.

We want one more miracle, following the peace, from our glorious fighters who have won independence and freedom for our country. This miracle will be nothing but the economic miracle which will lay the foundations of the civilization of our nation.

III[15]

The needs of a nation do not consist only of those spiritual needs that give rise to religion, morality, art, and language. There are also material needs that give rise to what we call economic activities . . . which are the bases of other social activities. In a society where there are no persons of means who do not have to worry about their daily bread, no science and no art or philosophy can exist. . . . As a wealthy class did not arise in Turkey through economic progress, the number of men of leisure who might occupy themselves with work done only for enjoyment has been very limited. . . . The non-existence of great scientists, artists, and philosophers in Turkey is due to the backwardness of our economic life. . . . Those who had been more or less interested in intellectual activities in Turkey were government functionaries. . . . The only incentive in their intellectual preoccupation was the desire for 'personal glorification'. In Europe such persons are called 'dilettanti'. In Europe the dilettante is not an admired type,

310 TURKISH NATIONALISM AND WESTERN CIVILIZATION

whereas among us these 'omniscients' are the most preferred of the élite. In Europe the work of the specialist is valued, whereas among us dilettantes are regarded as authorities. This is due also to economic conditions. The degree of economic advancement of a nation is proportional to its degree of division of labour. Specialization in higher activities is possible only where division of labour has reached a highly advanced stage. Professional specialization in science, art, and philosophy is dependent upon the development of an economic division of labour. . . .

The advancement of economic life is necessary, not only for increasing the number of specialists. The development of other fields of social activity depends upon the degree of economic prosperity in each of them. In a country where economic life remains backward, science, art, philosophy, or even morality and religion, can never achieve higher manifestations. . . .

IV[16]

The modern state is based on large-scale industry. New Turkey, to be a modern state, must, above all, develop a national industry. What should we do to realize this?

The new Turkey, which has to introduce the latest and most developed techniques of Europe, cannot afford to wait for the spontaneous rise of the spirit of enterprise among individuals in order to industrialize. As we have done in the field of military techniques, we have to reach European levels in industry through a national effort. We have to start by utilizing the latest developments in European techniques, without necessarily following the stages of gradual evolution. The starting-point, for example, should be electrification. We must utilize the hydraulic power of the country and put it into an electric network. The people of Turkey, who have been able to adopt European military techniques in all their details, can learn and master the most modern industrial inventions and discoveries. Military techniques, however, were not introduced by the private initiative of individuals. This was accomplished through the state. Our medicine, which is equally advanced, was also initiated through state action. Therefore, only the state can achieve the task of introducing large-scale industry in every field. The Turkish state has the power to be an independent [national] state. Turks are temperamentally *étatists*. They

THE PROGRAMME OF TURKISM 311

expect the state to take the initiative in everything new and progressive. Even social changes are introduced through the state in Turkey, and it has been the state which has safeguarded social changes against the forces of reaction.

In order that the state itself may become competent in economic enterprises, it must become an economic state. The statesmen and government employees should have economic experience and knowledge. The modern state, selecting its personnel with this point in view, is like a big business concern. . . . By following the same line, our state will, at the same time, perform a moral service because the rise of a new class of speculators will be prevented. The ambitions manifested in the Peace Conference clearly showed what a criminal people these capitalists, as they are called in Europe, are! Present-day European imperialism is based on private capitalism. If we accept the system of state capitalism, we will be able to prevent the rise of those insatiable and predatory capitalists in our country.

The state and provincial or local councils may follow one of the four possible lines with regard to economic policy: (*a*) the simplest, direct state enterprise to be carried out by its own employees; (*b*) the authorization of certain private entrepreneurs to undertake economic enterprises; (*c*) mixed enterprise, to be carried out through the combination of state and private capital; (*d*) another mixed system . . . which is the same as the method of tax farming already used in our country. . . .

By following these major economic policies, an economic revolution can be achieved in our country. . . . For example, a big programme of electrification can be applied under this system. . . . We do not need to wait for these covetous European capitalists to come and do it for us!

V[17]

In ancient times the Turks lived a nomadic life. The Turkish economy was a pastoral economy. . . . Industry among these nomad Turks used animal products. . . . The ancient Turks were not strangers to commerce. During the imperial periods, the greatest source of state revenue was Turkish trader caravans carrying silk from China to Europe and velvet from Europe to China. The main trade routes between China, India, Iran, Russia, and Byzantium were dominated by Turks. . . . We see, then, that the old Turkish emperors were interested not only in maintaining political security in the vast area of Turan stretching from Manchuria to Hungary, but also in creating an organization of international trade and exchange between the nations of Asia and Europe. . . .

In the future, Turks must again attain this economic prosperity which they enjoyed in the past. And the wealth which they shall accumulate must belong to the public. . . . As Turks love freedom and independence, they cannot be communists. But as they love equality, they cannot be individualists. The system most suited to Turkish culture is solidarism. Individual ownership is legitimate only in so far as it serves social solidarity. The attempts of the socialists and communists to abolish private ownership are not justified. However, private wealth which does not serve social solidarity cannot be regarded as legitimate. Furthermore, ownership is not necessarily individual. Together with private ownership there must be social ownership. Surplus profits that are not produced by the labour of individuals but that are the product of the sacrifices or hardships undertaken by society should belong to society. Appropriation of these surplus values by individuals is not legal.

The capital accumulated through the appropriation of the surplus values on behalf of society will be invested in industrial plants and large farms to be established for the benefit of society. The profits of these institutions of public enterprise will be spent to build houses and schools for the poor, orphans, widows, the sick, invalids, the blind and deaf, to found public gardens, museums, theatres, libraries, hygienic housing for peasants and workers, for the electrification of the whole country, in short for everything that will ensure the prosperity of the people and put an end to all kinds of misery. When this public wealth reaches a certain quantity, it may even become unnecessary to collect taxes from the people any longer, or it may at least lead to a reduction of the varieties and percentage of taxation.

The social idealism of the Turks, therefore, means preventing the usurpation of the social wealth by private individuals without abolishing private ownership, and preserving and increasing it in order to invest it for the benefit of the whole. The economic ideal of the Turks would mean, in addition, industrialization. Some believe that Turkey should always remain an agricultural nation and never indulge in industry. This is wrong. It is true that we shall never dispense with agriculture, but if we want to be a modern nation, we have to be

THE PROGRAMME OF TURKISM

industrialized. The most important revolution in Europe was the Industrial Revolution. This revolution meant the rise of a national economy in place of a regional economy and the rise of big industry in place of handicraft industry.

A national economy and large-scale industry can be achieved only through a protectionist policy. In this respect we shall follow the theories of the school of national economists. John Ray in America and Friedrich List in Germany have proved that the political economy of the Manchester school in England was not a universal and international science, but a system for a national economy peculiar to Great Britain. These two economists put forward systems of national economy for their own countries which ensured their industrialization so that today the United States and Germany have reached a stage in which both can boast of being equal to Great Britain. Now they follow the same open-door policy as Great Britain. This was made possible only through the application for many years of the protectionist policies proposed by the exponents of national economy.

Now, the first job of the Turkish economists is to study the economic conditions of Turkey and to develop a scientific and comprehensive economic plan on the basis of these scientific researches. Once this economic plan is prepared, everybody should work in accordance with it in order to industrialize our country; the Ministry of Economy should co-ordinate all of these individual activities.

TRANSLATOR'S NOTES

Chapter I (p. 35)

1. 'Babamın Vasiyeti', published in *Küçük Mecmua* (no. 17, Diyarbekir, 1923).

2. Namık Kemal (1840–88), Turkish poet and thinker who fought for a constitutional régime and infused the ideas of liberty, progress, and patriotism among the Turkish intelligentsia.

3. *Medrese*, traditional Muslim schools.

4. 'Hocamin Vasiyeti', published in *Küçük Mecmua* (no. 18, Diyarbekir, 1923).

5. A revolutionary organization formed originally by Abdullah Cevdet, İshak Sükûti and İbrahim Temo in 1889, which later developed into the Party of Union and Progress. Gökalp came to Istanbul in 1893.

6. 'Pîrimin Vasiyeti', published in *Küçük Mecmua* (no. 19, Diyarbekir, 1923).

7. Gökalp refers to Mustafa Kemal whose nationalist movement in Ankara he had joined upon his return from Malta where he had been sent by the Allies as a political prisoner.

8. From 'Millet Nedir?' published in *Küçük Mecmua* (no. 28, Diyarbekir, 1923) and in *Yeni Mecmua* (IV, nos. 70–4, Istanbul, 1923). See note 5, Chapter V below. The section taken here was dropped from the essay when it was reprinted in *Türkçülüğün Esasları*. I have put it under this section as it has relevance for the biography of the author.

9. As Gökalp's birthplace, Diyarbekir, was considered to be a Kurdish-speaking area, his adversaries—mostly from among the Islamists and Ottomanists, whose views and policies he criticized—claimed that he himself was not a Turk but a Kurd. It seems that he was annoyed by such claims and wrote the above article. However, as in his sociological understanding of nation he rejected racialism and even a common ethnic origin, he would not have ceased to preach modern Turkish nationalism even if he had been racially or ethnically a Kurd. He expressed this in a poem as a reply to Ali Kemal. The latter had for long been a controversial and shady character among the Young Turks in exile in Europe and, finally, following the end of the First World War, he became a member of the puppet anti-nationalist government of Istanbul. Because of his wild attacks on the leaders of national independence, he was regarded as an arch traitor and was finally kidnapped and lynched by a mob. Gökalp, in this poem entitled 'To The Man Who Calls Me Not A Turk', said:

> Even if I were a Turk or not,
> I am the friend of the Turk;
> Even if you were a Turk or not,
> You are an enemy of the Turk.

10. The following paragraph appeared originally in 'What Is A Nation?' (see note 5, Chapter V below), following the part I have translated under the above heading. I have transferred it to the end of the remaining part which is translated here, as it has relevance to the biography of the author.

Chapter II (p. 46)

1. 'Bugünkü Felsefe', published in *Genç Kalemler* ('Young Pens') (no. 2, Salonika, 1911), under the pseudonym Tevfik Sedat.

2. The author intentionally used the word *vicdan* (conscience) instead of *şuur* (consciousness). The distinction will be encountered in other writings to be found in this volume.

TRANSLATOR'S NOTES   315

For the sake of English style, I have rendered it in many cases by the word 'consciousness', and sometimes by *conscience* in the French sense. Cf. p. 174; see also Gökalp's footnote to the essay 'Community and Society', Chapter IV in this volume, and the first paragraph of the second section of the essay 'Manifestations of the National Ethos'; see below, Chapter VI.

3. 'Muhiddin-i Arabî', published in *Genç Kalemler* (no. 8, Salonika, 1911), under the pseudonym Tevfik Sedat.

4. Abū Bakr Muhammad, *b.* 'Ali Muhyi'l-din (1165–1240).

5. 'Yeni Hayat ve Yeni Kıymetler', published in *Genç Kalemler* (no. 8, Salonika, 1911), under the pseudonym Demirtaş.

6. Gökalp here refers to the Young Turk Revolution of 1908.

7. This word, the Turkish form of the Arabic *umma*, means the politically organized community of all Muslims, and plays an important role in Gökalp's writings. The reader will come across it frequently in the following essays. In the absence of an exact equivalent, I have retained the word in most cases in its Turkish spelling. I have, however, sometimes used 'religion' or 'church' for it whenever these expressed the meaning intended. Gökalp defines this term clearly in his essay entitled 'What Is A Nation?', which will be found in this volume; see below, Chapter V.

8. Gökalp wrote on 'New Life' in *Felsefe Mecmuası* ('Review of Philosophy') (no. 13, Salonika, 1911), in which he said:

'New life . . . is an ideal which is in the process of emerging from the social consciousness. Today this ideal has to remain somewhat ambiguous. This ambiguity will be cleared away by time and by the guidance of the social consciousness. . . . The New Life is today in a state of unconsciousness. . . . It is an ideal emerging ["not from the minds of the individuals who criticize the old values and grope for a new ideal", but] from the social consciousness. . . . The ideals have to correspond to reality; any idea without this property is not an ideal and has no basis.'

And again, in the same review (no. 16, 1911):

'. . . Ideals owe their sanctity and sublimity to the social consciousness. Patriotism, nationalism, piety, anti-militarism, anarchism, socialism, humanism . . . are all diverse expressions of the social consciousness. . . . The ideals governing men change with changing social consciousness. Religious ideals played the major role for a long period, but now the ideals directing all nations are *national ideals*. Present-day social and economic life necessitates this. . . . This is the ideal which we hope the youth will follow. Is our social consciousness likely to give birth to such an ideal? Yes. Everyone has realized today that the only ideal for the Turks is Turkism. . . . There is a growing tendency towards nationalism among the Turkish youth today. What we want is to transform this tendency into a great and sacred *faith*. There is a movement and sentiment of Turkism today, but it is not yet present as an *ideal* and as a *faith*.'

And (*ibid.*, no. 17, 1911):

'We all want, let us say, to achieve a revolution in the ethical foundations of our social life. . . . We have first of all to know how contemporary ethical values have come into existence. What factors have kept them alive until now? Do the same factors still exist today? After we have answered these questions, we shall have to answer the following: What are the conditions governing our social life today? Are these conditions compatible with the ethical norms? What kinds of change are present social conditions likely to produce tomorrow in these ethical beliefs? The extent to which we answer these questions will determine the revolution which we want to produce in our ethical life. . . . That is the New Life which we expect from the social consciousness. We accept the social

316 TURKISH NATIONALISM AND WESTERN CIVILIZATION

consciousness as our guide. We shall determine our path according to the truths which we derive from it. Thus, we do not want the changes which the socialists seek to produce because we believe that they are mere utopias and will remain utopias.'

9. 'Tarihî Maddecilik ve İçtimaî Mefkûrecilik', *Yeni Gün* (Ankara, March 8, 1923); reprinted in *Türkçülüğün Esasları* (Ankara, 1923), pp. 60–9. Although this essay does not belong to the period of the previous essays, it is taken here to show the perseverance of Gökalp's idealistic stand in his later years.

10. Despite the several striking similarities in the conceptualizations of Gökalp and his contemporary Max Weber, there is no reason to believe that either knew of, let alone was influenced by, the other. The term 'charisma' (adj., charismatic), coined by Weber, is used here throughout as it is an exact equivalent of Gökalp's meaning.

11. Gökalp here refers to the publication of the *İktisadiyat Mecmuası* (Review of Economics) which he founded in 1916 with the financial help of the Party of Union and Progress. The review continued publication for about two years, and seems to have ended with no. 67 in 1918. Gökalp's own articles in this review were on national economy. See Osman Tolga, *Ziya Gökalp ve İktisadî Fikirleri* (Istanbul, 1949), and Cavit Orhan Tütengil, *Ziya Gökalp Hakkında Bir Bibliyografya Denemesi* (Istanbul, 1949), p. 16.

12. 'Mefkûre', published in *Türk Yurdu* (V, no. 32, Istanbul, 1913), reprinted in *Türkleşmek, İslâmlaşmak, Muasırlaşmak* (Istanbul, 1918).

13. The quotation actually refers to the verses taken from a poem by Tevfik Fikret, the Turkish poet and contemporary of Ziya Gökalp.

14. Gökalp here uses the words *irfan* and *medeniyet* to denote something for which he later introduced the term *hars* (Arabic *harth*) which is translated throughout this book as *culture*.

Chapter III (p. 71)

1. 'Üç Cereyan', published in *Türk Yurdu* (III, no. 35, Istanbul, 1913), reprinted in *Türkleşmek, İslâmlaşmak, Muasırlaşmak* (Istanbul, 1918).

2. The policy of reforms initiated by the promulgation of the Reform Charter of 1839.

3. 'Millet ve Vatan', published in *Türk Yurdu* (VI, no. 66, Istanbul, 1914), reprinted in *Türkleşmek, İslâmlaşmak, Muasırlaşmak* (Istanbul, 1918).

4. *Turan* or Transoxania, the name of the territories beyond the River Oxus, the ancient home of the Turks.

5. Gökalp had used the word *beynelmileliyet* (internationality) when this essay was published in *Türk Yurdu*, but changed this term to *ümmet* when it was reprinted in the book *Türkleşmek, İslâmlaşmak, Muasırlaşmak*.

6. 'Milliyet Mefkûresi', *Türkleşmek, İslâmlaşmak, Muasırlaşmak* (Istanbul, 1918).

7. 'Lisan', published in *Türk Yurdu* (III, no. 36, Istanbul, 1913), reprinted in *Türkleşmek, İslâmlaşmak, Muasırlaşmak* (Istanbul, 1918).

Chapter IV (p. 89)

1. 'Halk Medeniyeti', published in *Halka Doğru* (I, nos. 14–15, Istanbul, 1913).

2. The Turkish word used is *ocak*, which means 'hearth'. In this essay it is translated as 'informal group' or as 'confraternity'.

3. 'An'ane ve Kaide', published in *Türk Yurdu* (IV, no. 39, Istanbul, 1913).

4. Published in *Türk Yurdu* (IV, no. 41, Istanbul, 1919), under the title of 'Cemaat ve Cemiyet' ('Community and Society'); reprinted in *Türkleşmek, İslâmlaşmak Muasırlaşmak*

TRANSLATOR'S NOTES

317

(Istanbul, 1918), under the title of 'Hars Zûmresi, Medeniyet Zûmresi' ('Culture-group and Civilization-group'). Note here that Gökalp first used the terms 'community' and 'society', but then dropped them, preferring to use 'culture' and 'civilization'. I have put his earlier terms in parentheses.

5. See Chapter II, note 2.

6. From 'Cemaat Medeniyeti, Cemiyet Medeniyeti' ('The Civilization of Community and the Civilization of Society'), published in *Türk Yurdu* (IV, no. 47, Istanbul, 1913). When the preceding article appeared in *Türk Yurdu*, a certain Armenian intellectual using the initials H. Ş. sent a comment to the review which was published in no. 46, in which, after praising the Turkist understanding of nationalism, he criticized Gökalp's idea that the basis of 'community' was religion. I have taken here passages from Gökalp's rejoinder, as a further illustration of the argument in his discussion in the previous essay.

7. Cf. 'Social Sources of Islamic Jurisprudence', Chapter VII in this volume.

8. 'Hars ve Medeniyet', *Türkçülüğün Esasları* (Istanbul, 1923), pp. 27–38. The remaining portion of this essay (from pp. 38 to 40) will be found in this volume under Chapter IX, below. See note 5 of the same chapter.

9. İbrahim Şinasi (1824–71), the Turkish editor and poet, initiated the movement of democratization of the Turkish language.

10. Mehmed Fuzuli (1495–1555), a Shi'i Turkish poet who lived in Iraq and wrote *divans* in Turkish, Persian, and Arabic. Ahmed Nedim (1681–1730), an Ottoman poet who lived in Istanbul and brought Ottoman *divan* literature to perfection. See E. J. W. Gibb, *A History of Ottoman Poetry*, III (London, 1904), pp. 70–108, and IV (London, 1905), pp. 29 ff.

11. Mahmud of Kashgar (a town in Chinese Turkestan) wrote a dictionary of Turkish in the second part of the eleventh century.

12. Jāḥiẓ (767–868) wrote a treatise entitled *Risāla fī Faḍā'il al-Turk* in which he described the characteristics and merits of the Turks.

13. *Servet-i Fünûn*, a literary school which received its name from the literary and scientific magazine of the same name. The school flourished from the last decade of the nineteenth to the early decades of the twentieth centuries.

14. The so-called Kızılbaş, who were regarded as the most heretical group of the heterodox Alevis.

15. Yunus Emre (*circa* 1249–1321), Turkish mystic poet and a younger contemporary of Rūmī. Recent researches have shown that he was a spiritual descendant of Hacı Bektaş, the thirteenth-century Turkish heterodox mystic. In contradistinction to Rūmī, Yunus wrote his mystic poems in simple pure Turkish.

Chapter V (p. 113)

1. 'Bir Kavmin Tetkikinde Tâkibolunacak Usûl', *Milli Tetebbular Mecmuası* ('The Review of National Studies') (I, no. 2, Istanbul, 1915). In this essay the word *kavm* (Arabic *ḳawm*) is used in the sense of a community united by a common ethnic origin. In translation I have rendered it as 'community' or 'ethnic community' and, in a few cases, as 'people'. This and the following essays are included here together as they show some variations.

2. 'İçtimaî Neviler', *İslâm Mecmuası* (II, no. 20, Istanbul, 1914).

3. From 'Aşiretler Hakkında Sosyoljik Tetkikler', *Doğu* (nos. 9–11, Zonguldak, 1943); first published in the newspaper *Sinop* in 1926.

4. 'Millet Nedir?' *İçtimaiyat Mecmuası* (I, no. 3, Istanbul, 1917).

318 TURKISH NATIONALISM AND WESTERN CIVILIZATION

5. 'Millet Nedir?' originally published in *Küçük Mecmua* (no. 28, Diyarbekir, 1923), and in *Yeni Mecmua* (IV, nos. 70–4, Istanbul, 1923), re-written and printed in *Türkçülüğün Esasları* (pp. 15–21) under the heading 'Türkçülük Nedir?' ('What is Turkism?'). (See the essay on 'My Nationality', Chapter I, note 8, above). The essay printed here originally included the portion which I have put under the last-mentioned essay; but this portion was dropped when it was re-written and published in the above-mentioned book. Between the two versions there is little significant difference; several sentences are exactly the same. The re-written form is longer than the original version while omitting a few sentences which appeared in the latter. Only two sentences from the earlier text are given here, in brackets.

6. 'Şehir Medeniyeti, Köy Medeniyeti', *Küçük Mecmua* (no. 30, Diyarbekir, 1923).

7. 'Köy ve Şehir', *Küçük Mecmua* (no. 33, Diyarbekir, 1923).

8. 'Türkiye Asrî Bir Cemiyet mi?', given as a lecture in 1918, published in *Doğu* (nos. 5–6, Zonguldak, 1943), from the notes taken by E. B. Şapolyo.

9. 'Tevfik Fikret ve Türk Renesansı', *Muallim* (Istanbul, 1917), a special issue in commemoration of Tevfik Fikret, the Turkish poet who died in 1915. This article is the more interesting and significant as Gökalp was far from an unconditional admirer of Fikret and his ideas; cf. Chapter II, note 13; also p. 281.

10. The Book of *Dede Korkut* is a collection of twelve tales which represented pre-Islamic Turkish epic literature surviving after the Islamization of the Turks.

Chapter VI (p. 148)

1. 'Kıymet Hükümleri', *İslâm Mecmuası* (I, no. 18, Istanbul, 1914). *İslâm Mecmuası* was one of the reviews that Gökalp founded, with the financial help of the Party of Union and Progress, to promote the publication of his ideas as well as those of his associates or disciples. This bi-monthly review continued publication from 1914 to 1917 and appeared in fifty-four issues. Gökalp published several articles in this review, a few poems, and some articles which did not bear his name (see Kâzım Nami Duru, *Ziya Gökalp*, Istanbul, 1949, p. 95). Duru reprinted the article entitled 'Din ve Şeriat', which appeared in *İslâm Mecmuası* without author's name, as Gökalp's, and claimed that there were others written by Gökalp, but printed similarly without his name. See below, note 6, Chapter VII, in this volume. It seems to me that these unsigned articles were written in co-operation with Halim Sâbit, who was the editor of the review and who had written there several articles to expound Gökalp's writings on *fıkh* and religion, which, incidentally, are clearer and more interesting than Gökalp's.

2. 'Ahlâk İçtimaî Midir?', *İçtimaiyat Mecmuası* (I, no. 3, Istanbul, 1914).

3. 'Örf Nedir?', *İslâm Mecmuası* (I, no. 14, Istanbul, 1914).

4. The Arabic word *ma'rûf* is from the root of *'urf*, which is translated here as *mores*. The English word *moral* stands in the same relation to the Latin word *mores*.

5. 'İçtimaiyat ve Fikriyat: Cemiyette Büyük Adamların Tesiri' ('Sociology and Ideology: The Influence of Great Men on Society'), *İçtimaiyat Mecmuası* (I, no. 2, Istanbul, 1917).

6. See Chapter II, note 2.

7. 'Millî İçtimaiyat' ('National Sociology'), *İçtimaiyat Mecmuası* (I, no. 1, Istanbul, 1917).

8. The author used the French words 'sympathie' and 'antipathie' respectively for these two terms in a series of articles, included in this volume, entitled 'National Education'; see Chapter VII, below. However, I have preferred to use 'association' and 'dissociation' in this translation.

9. See Chapter II, note 2.

TRANSLATOR'S NOTES

Chapter VII (p. 184)

1. 'Dinin İçtimaî Vazifeleri', *İslâm Mecmuası* (III, nos. 34 and 36, Istanbul, 1915).

2. Gökalp introduces the Arabic word *zanīm* for 'profane', and in a footnote he points to the non-existence in Islamic terminology of a word for this concept as an antonym for 'sacred' and proposes the word mentioned above as a term.

3. 'Fıkh ve İçtimaiyat', *İslâm Mecmuası* (I, no. 2, Istanbul, 1914).

4. 'İçtimaî Usul-u Fıkh', *İslâm Mecmuası* (I, no. 2, Istanbul, 1914).

5. 'Diyanet ve Kaza', *İslâm Mecmuası* (II, no. 35, Istanbul, 1915).

6. 'İttihat ve Terakki Kongresi Münasebetiyle', *İslâm Mecmuası* (IV, no. 48, 1916; V, nos. 49–50, Istanbul, 1916–17). This and the following essay cannot be claimed for Gökalp without some reservation. Neither appeared under his name in *İslâm Mecmuası*. Both betray a style which is not exactly his. However, the ideas expressed are his, as found in his other writings incorporated in this volume. It is known that he wrote these essays originally as reports to the 1916 convention of the Party of Union and Progress and that they were distributed to the party organization. I have included them here expressing also my guess that they were either written with the help of someone else, or later re-touched by another person. See Uriel Heyd, *Foundations of Turkish Nationalism* (London, 1950), pp. 35 and 90; Erich Pritsch, 'Die islamische Staatsidee. Ein geschichtlicher Überblick', *Zeitschrift für vergleichende Rechtswissenschaft* (III, no. 1, Stuttgart, 1939), pp. 58 ff. See Osman Nuri, *Mecelle-i Umur-u Belediye* (I, Istanbul, 1922), pp. 274 ff; and Kâzim Nami Duru, *Ziya Gökalp* (Istanbul, 1949), pp. 60–9, for another version of the first essay which was distributed to the party organization as a memorandum. Gökalp was assigned by the Central Committee of the Party of Union and Progress to prepare a memorandum to be submitted to the government. The ideas contained in this article were suggested in that memorandum. In the general convention of the party the transfer of the *Shar'* courts from the office of the *Shaikh-ul-Islam* to the administration of the Ministry of Justice was accepted in accordance with Gökalp's proposals. The schools under the *Evkaf* administration were also transferred to the Ministry of Education. (see Emin Erişirgil, *Bir Fikir Adamının Romanı* (Istanbul, 1951), pp. 200–2. These were early steps towards the secularization of religious courts and schools. With the fall of the government of the Party of Union and Progress following the end of the First World War, the older régime of the courts was restored by the reactionary Mehmet VI and his government. However, much more radical reforms started by Atatürk brought this process of secularization to its completion. In the meantime, the office of *Shaikh-ul-Islam*, the *Shar'* courts, and the ministry of *Evkaf* were all abolished, together with the institution of the Caliphacy. Thereupon, Gökalp's speculations about the Caliphacy and its future organization naturally remained mere utopias. However, for the sake of historical record, I have included his separate essays on the Caliphate in the following sections of this chapter, stressing in the meantime the point that this inclusion should neither be taken as an indication of approval of his ideas nor as an occasion to reopen the discussion of a matter which today is nothing but a dead issue in Turkey.

7. The reference seems to be to the two incidents, as mentioned in *İlmiye Salnamesi* (Istanbul, 1915), pp. 310–13, and quoted from *Şakayık-i Nümâniye*. According to a story, *Shaikh-ul-Islam* Mevlâna Alaeddin Ali Cemâlî, popularly known as Zenbilli, twice objected to Selim's orders for the execution of forty men in one case and of 150 men in another case on account of their violation of the ruler's laws. When Selim indignantly retorted to Ali's objection saying that the matters in question were affairs of Sultanate and that the Muftī had no right to interfere in them, Ali said that he was interfering in them not as an earthly concern but as matters of the other world because it was his duty to guard the ruler only on matters of the other world.

320 TURKISH NATIONALISM AND WESTERN CIVILIZATION

8. 'İslamiyet ve Asrî Medeniyet', *İslâm Mecmuası* (II, nos. 51–2, Istanbul, 1917); French translation 'L'État islamique peut-il être un état moderne?' in *La Pensée Turque* (nos. 5–9, Istanbul, February 16–April 16, 1917).

9. 'Hilâfetin Hakikî Mahiyeti', *Küçük Mecmua* (no. 24, Diyarbekir, 1922); also printed in *Hilâfet ve Millî Hâkimiyet* (Ankara, 1922), pp. 5–10. The differences and inconsistencies between the two previous essays and the present one are striking. This and the following two essays were written following the proclamation, on November 1, 1922, of the decision of the nationalist Turkish Grand National Assembly to abolish the Sultanate; whereupon the last Ottoman ruler, Mehmet VI, fled from Istanbul on a British ship and Abdül Mecid, the cousin of the latter, was designated by the Assembly as Caliph on November 18. However, the Caliphate also was abolished on March 3, 1924, about sixteen months after the abolition of the Sultanate and about eight months before Gökalp's death.

10. This sentence needs clarification as the reader may get from it the erroneous impression that the new Caliph was elected through a ceremony taking place in the mosques on the first Friday (November 24, 1922) following the designation of Abdül Mecid as Caliph. In fact, the new Caliph, as explained in the previous note, was designated and appointed by the Turkish Grand National Assembly, and the ceremony taking place in the mosques on Friday, November 10, 1338 (according to Ottoman fiscal date), consisted of nothing more than mentioning the name of the new Caliph in the Friday sermon.

11. 'Hilâfetin İstiklâli', *Küçük Mecmua* (no. 25, Diyarbekir, 1922); also printed in *Hilâfet ve Millî Hâkimiyet* (Ankara, 1922), pp. 55–7; French translation in *Die Welt des Islams* (N.S., I, no. 4, Leiden, Brill, 1951), pp. 300–3.

12. 'Hilâfetin Vazifeleri', *Küçük Mecmua* (no. 26, Diyarbekir, 1922); also printed in *Hilâfet ve Millî Hâkimiyet* (Ankara, 1922), pp. 58–62.

13. 'İslâm Terbiyesinin Mâhiyeti', *İslâm Mecmuası* (I, no. 1, Istanbul, 1914).

14. 'Millî Terbiye', *Muallim* (nos. 1–4, Istanbul, 1916). These essays were criticized by Sâti [al-Ḥuşarî], at that time a prominent pedagogue in Turkey, who upheld an individualistic philosophy of education as against Gökalp's collectivistic approach. Gökalp wrote three more essays in the same review (nos. 7–9, 1916) as rejoinders to Sâti's criticisms. These latter essays are not taken into this volume as they were only a theoretical discussion of the individual psychological *v.* collectivistic sociological approaches to education, defended respectively by the two discussants. A similar, and longer, argument took place at the same theoretical level between the two men when Gökalp wrote a series of articles on 'The Problem of Education' in *Yeni Mecmua* (nos. 32, 34, 36, 38, Istanbul, 1918).

15. 'Asrî Aile ve Millî Aile', *Yeni Mecmua* (I, no. 20, Istanbul, 1917).

16. 'Türk Ailesinin Temelleri', *Yeni Mecmua* (I, no. 22, Istanbul, 1917).

17. 'Aile Ahlâkı, Düğün Âdetleri', *Yeni Mecmua* (I, no. 21, Istanbul, 1917). This essay is not included in this volume.

18. Gökalp here gives a description of a rite for *Aisyt*, the goddess of fertility among the Yakuts, on the basis of an article by Sierożewski in *Rèvue de l'Histoire des Réligions*, Vol. 46. His summary and quotations have been omitted while his conclusions are included.

Chapter VIII (p. 259)

1. 'Halka Doğru', *Türkçülüğün Esasları* (Ankara, 1923), pp. 41–5.

2. 'Dehaya Doğru', *Küçük Mecmua* (no. 1, Diyarbekir, 1922).

3. See below, 'Towards Modern Science'.

4. 'İnkilâpçılık ve Muhafazakarlık', *Yeni Gün* (Ankara, May 17, 1923).

TRANSLATOR'S NOTES 321

5. The newspaper *Hâkimiyet-i Milliye* was founded by Mustafa Kemal (Atatürk), and was the organ of the nationalist government of Ankara. Gökalp published five articles in it on political parties (April 17, 19, 23, 29 and June 13, 1923). These articles are reprinted in *Fırka Nedir?* (Zonguldak, 1947), edited by E. B. Şapolyo.

6. Gökalp apparently alludes to the closing of the Straits by Turkey during World War I, which, according to the belief of some, prevented the Western allies from helping Russia and, thus, contributed to the fall of the Tsarist régime.

7. Allusion to the so-called *Ergenekon* captivity of a branch of the Turks. According to an old Turkish myth, the Turks were confined in a valley for four centuries until a blacksmith, by melting iron rocks, opened up a gate, and they were delivered under the leadership of a Grey Wolf. The allusion in the last sentence of this essay is apparently to Mustafa Kemal.

8. 'Medeniyetimiz', *Yeni Mecmua* (no. 68, Istanbul, 1923), reprinted in *Türkçülüğün Esasları* under the title 'Garbe Doğru' ('Towards the West') (Ankara, 1923).

9. 'İlme Doğru', *Küçük Mecmua* (no. 2, Diyarbekir, 1922).

10. 'Hars ve Tehzib', *Türkçülüğün Esasları* (Istanbul, 1923), pp. 89–93. The word 'refinement' is used for 'tehzib' which is derived from Arabic *tahdhîb*, originally meaning shaping a tree by cutting leaves or branches. The German word 'Bildung' is the exact equivalent of this term as used by Gökalp.

11. Cf. p. 168 above and Gökalp's own footnote in the essay entitled 'National Education' (p. 238 above). He seems to modify his opinion about the relation between the meanings of the German *die Kultur* and of his own term *hars*!

Chapter IX (p. 287)

1. 'Türkçülük Nedir?', *Yeni Mecmua* (no. 28, Istanbul, 1917).

2. See Chapter II, 'New Life and New Values'.

3. *İrfan*. In Gökalp's terminology this word should not be translated here as 'culture' because he used it previously in a more general and ambiguous sense covering both 'culture' and 'civilization' (see p. 68) or in the sense of 'lore', the whole body of knowledge possessed by a people, or of 'learning', 'knowledge' possessed by the intellectual élite pertaining to particular subjects (see pp. 170 and 238 above). Here I have felt forced to render it as 'culture'. I draw the reader's attention to the fact that *in this essay* I have put this word in quotation marks only when it is used as an equivalent of *irfan* and have used *Culture*, with capital C, for *hars*.

4. Pera, the Europeanized section of the city of Istanbul, where the Europeans, called *Frenks* by the people, who settled in the Levant, used to live.

5. From 'Hars ve Medeniyet', *Türkçülüğün Esasları* (Istanbul, 1923), pp. 38–40. The earlier and main portion of this essay is found in this volume under 'Culture and Civilization'. See Chapter IV.

6. 'Lisanî Türkçülük', *Türkçülüğün Esasları* (Ankara, 1923), pp. 98–122.

7. 'Edebiyatımızın Tahris ve Tehzibi', *Türkçülüğün Esasları* (Ankara, 1923), pp. 127–9.

8. 'Millî Musiki', *Türkçülüğün Esasları* (Ankara, 1923), pp. 130–1.

9. 'Dinî Türkçülük', *Türkçülüğün Esasları* (Ankara, 1923), pp. 163–4.

10. 'Vatanî Ahlâk', 'Meslekî Ahlâk', 'İstikbalde Aile Ahlâki Nasıl Olmalı?', 'Medenî ve Şahsî Ahlâk', *Türkçülüğün Esasları* (Ankara, 1923), pp. 138–41, 142–4, 155–6, 157–8 respectively.

322 TURKISH NATIONALISM AND WESTERN CIVILIZATION

11. 'Hukukî Türkçülük', *Türkçülüğün Esasları* (Ankara, 1923), pp. 161–2.

12. 'Siyasî Türkçülük', *Türkçülüğün Esasları* (Ankara, 1923), pp. 170–1.

13. 'İktisadî Vatanperverlik', *Küçük Mecmua* (no. 43, Diyarbekir, 1923).

14. 'İktisadî Mûcize', *Küçük Mecmua* (no. 23, Diyarbekir, 1923).

15. From 'İktisada Doğru', *Küçük Mecmua* (no. 7, Diyarbekir, 1923).

16. 'İktisadî İnkilap İçin Nasıl Çalışmalıyız?', *Küçük Mecmua* (no. 33, Diyarbekir, 1923).

17. 'İktisadî Türkçülük', *Türkçülüğün Esasları* (Ankara, 1923), pp. 165–9.

GLOSSARY

THIS glossary contains only those Turkish, Arabic, and Persian words that have passed in the text without being translated or defined. (T. denotes Turkish; A. Arabic; P., Persian.)

abdest, ablution.

Ahl al-Hadīth (A.), those Muslims who adhered strictly to the traditions attributed to Muhammad.

Ahl al-Sunna (A.), the people of prophetic tradition who refrained from deviating from dogma and practice.

Ahliyya courts, the courts handling family affairs.

Ahl al-dhimma (A.), non-Muslims possessing scriptures, such as Christians and Jews, living under Muslim jurisdiction.

Akhlāq-i Nāsirī, Akhlāq-i Jalālī, Akhlāq-i 'Alā'ī, treatises on ethics written by Tūsī, Dawwanī, and Ali Çelebi respectively.

akhī (T. *ahı*), a member of the guilds of the thirteenth century in Anatolia.

aksakal, lit. white-beard; the head of the village community called *oba*.

Alevi (A. *'Alawī*), the followers of Ali, the Prophet's son-in-law, in his claim to succeed the Prophet; they were in opposition to the *Sunni*s (*q.v.*).

aruz (A. *'arūḍ*), Arabic prosody; poetic metres used commonly by Muslim writers of different lands.

avariz (A. *'avāriḍ*), general taxes levied by the Ottoman rulers.

áyan, the local chiefs or dignitaries recognized by the central government whose increased strength in the eighteenth century allowed them to defy the central authorities.

baba, lit. father; the spiritual leaders of the Turkish religious orders; when undifferentiated, usually refers to Bektashi leaders.

Bashkim, 'union' in Albanian; the name of the Albanian nationalist society founded in 1899.

bayn al-'umam (A.), international.

bedüyet, being aesthetic.

bey, the Turkish word originally corresponding to 'lord' which in modern Turkish usage follows the given name to denote 'Mr' as İsmail Hakkı Bey.

boy, Turkic tribe.

boy beyi, tribal lord.

budun, ethnic community or nation.

Burhān-i Qātı', the title of an Arabic dictionary.

çarçūbe (P.); (T. çerçeve), frame.

Dede Korkut, see Chapter V, note 10.

deniz (*tengiz*), sea.

divan, state council.

Divân-ı Lûgat-üt Türk, a dictionary of Turkish-Arabic written by Mahmud of Kashgar during the second part of the eleventh century; see Chapter IV, note 11.

Enderun, the personnel of the household services of the Ottoman rulers.

Ergenekon, see Chapter VIII, note 7.

evkaf (A. *awqāf*), Muslim pious foundations.

324 TURKISH NATIONALISM AND WESTERN CIVILIZATION

fakih (A. *faqīh*), a scholar of Islamic jurisprudence; see *fikh*.
fetva (A. *fatwā*), the responses given by the *mufti*s on religious-juridical questions.
fikh (A. *fiqh*), the knowledge of Islamic jurisprudence.
fikr, idea.
fitra, the alms given at the close of Ramazan, the month of fasting; see *Ramaḍān*.
Frenk, the French; Europeans generally in Ottoman-Turkish usage.
futuwwa, the ethics of generosity and chivalry practised by the Muslim guilds.

gazel (A. *ghazal*), an ode of not more than twelve distiches.
gusül (A. *ghusl*), total ablution of the body.

ḥadīth, tradition recording an act or saying of the Prophet.
ḥāfiz (A.), one who knows the whole text of the Kur'ān by heart.
Hakimiyet-i Milliye, the newspaper founded in January 1920 by Mustafa Kemal (Atatürk) as the organ of the Nationalist Government in Ankara.
halk (A. *khalq*), common people (in Turkish usage).
halkiyat (A. *khalqiyyāt*), folklore (in Turkish usage).
Hanafī, those Muslims who adhere to the religious jurisprudence founded by the jurist Abu Hanīfa. See *Shāfi'ī*.
ḥanīf, one who possesses the real and true religion.
hars (A. *ḥarth*), a word coined by Gökalp from the Arabic *ḥaratha* ('to cultivate') for 'culture'; see Chapter II, note 14.
Hijra (T. *Hicret*), the Prophet's migration from Mecca to Medina; the starting-point for the Islamic, Hijra, calendar.
hulla (A.), a legal but fictitious marriage between a woman divorced three times consecutively by one man and another man in order that she may remarry the first husband; the *hulla* was customarily dissolved by a formal divorce after one day.

iftā, the act of issuing a *fetva* (*q.v.*).
iḥrām, a state of abstention from many ordinary acts for the purpose of making a pilgrimage to Mecca, signified by the wearing of a special dress also called *iḥrām*.
ijtihād, exerting one's self to form an opinion on a rule of law.
imam, the leader of a congregation at prayer; also the head or leader of the Muslim community or state.
irfan, see Chapter II, note 14, and Chapter IX, note 3.

jihād, originally, fight or struggle; later, struggle against heretics and infidel; still later, Holy War.

Ka'ba, the cubical temple at Mecca which is the most sacred place for Muslims.
kalām, Islamic theology.
kanunname (P. *kanūn-nāmah*), the codes of temporal ordinances issued by the Ottoman-Turkish rulers.
kaside (A. *qasīda*), a form of poetry used by Muslim poets containing distiches numbering in the hundreds.
kaza (A. *qaḍā*), judicial function.
khan, old Turkish word for 'prince'.
Khārijī, lit. secessionist; a member of the earliest Muslim sect which ceded over the question of the successorship to the Prophet.
khatīb (T. *hatip*), one who reads the formal sermon on special occasions, especially at Friday prayers.
khutba (T. *hutbe*), the sermon read by the *khatīb*.

GLOSSARY 325

Kızıl Elma, lit. Red Apple; originally referring to Rome as the goal of Ottoman conquests; the original and lost home of the Turks in Central Asia in the Turkist ideology.

Kibla, the direction of the Ka'ba which is faced by Muslims at prayer.

Kölemen, the Turkish word for the Mamluks.

Kutadgu Bilik, a treatise in verse on morality and statecraft regarded as the oldest extant Turkish document written under Islamic influence. Its author, Yūsuf Khass-Hājib, completed it in A.D. 1070.

levend, Ottoman seaman.

Lûgat-ı Çağatay, a dictionary of the Ottoman and Çağatay Turkish dialects written by Shaikh Süleyman al-Buharî and printed in 1882.

ma'rūf, see Chapter VI, note 4.

mashāyikh, pl. of *shaikh* (*q.v.*).

mashīkhat, the office of *Shaikh-ul-Islam* (*q.v.*).

masjid (T. *mesçit*), the Arabic word the corruption of which gave the English word 'mosque'; a small mosque with no minaret (in Turkish usage).

Mawālī, the category of Muslims who were non-Arabs during the Umayyad rule.

Medeniyet-i Islâmiye Tarihi, the Turkish translation of *Ta'rīkh al-Tamaddun al-Islāmī* ('The History of Islamic Civilization'), by Jurji Zaydan (1861–1914).

medrese (A. *madrasa*), medieval Muslim schools of learning.

medresevî, belonging to *medrese* (*q.v.*).

mektep (A. *maktab*), in Turkish usage, the secular school as distinguished from the *medrese* (*q.v.*).

Mevlid (A. *Mawlid*), the Turkish poem composed by Süleyman Çelebi at the end of the fourteenth century as the birth-song of the Prophet.

Mikat (A. *Mīqāt*), a stage on the road to Mecca where *iḥrām* (*q.v.*) is assumed.

millet (A. *milla*), in modern Turkish, 'nation'; in classical Arabic, a community of language or of faith; in medieval Arabic, a sect; in medieval Ottoman-Turkish, a non-Muslim community.

Mu'allaqāt, pre-Islamic Arabic poems hung so as to be read publicly.

mu'azzin (T. *müezzin*), the person who calls the congregation to prayer.

muftī, person who issues a *fetva* (*q.v.*).

mujtahid, person who is authorized to exercise *ijtihād* (*q.v.*).

mutakallimīn (T. *mütekellimin*), theologians.

mutaqaddimūn (T. *mütekaddimin*), the early predecessors.

mutaṣawwif, sufi, mystic.

name (P. *nāmah*), letter or any written statement of document such as *salname* (P. *sālnāmah*), year-book.

nass, a verse of the Kur'ān or a *ḥadīth* (*q.v.*) decisive of any point in Islamic law.

Paşa, pasha, the highest rank in the Ottoman military and, later, also the civil hierarchy.

qaḍā, see *kaza*.

qāḍī (T. *Kadı*), judge.

Qāḍī asker (T. *Kazasker*), the judge occupying the highest judicial rank in the Ottoman system.

Qāmūs, the Arabic dictionary of Fīrūzābādī (1329–1415), translated into Turkish by the Ottoman chronicler Âsim (*d.* 1819).

qiyās, analogical reasoning.

326 GLOSSARY

Ramaḍān (T. *Ramaẓan*), the month of fasting.

Risalah, prophethood.

Rāshidūn, right-guided ones; an adjective applied to the first four Caliphs.

sancakbey, commander or lord of a *sancak* (standard), a unit in the Ottoman military-administrative organization.

Sart, a member of a people of mixed Turkish and Persian origin inhabiting the territory extending from Samarkand to Tashkent. The word is not an ethnological term, as it originally meant merchant.

Selcuk (*Selçuk*), the branch of Turks who ante-dated the Ottoman Turks in establishing Turkish rule in Anatolia.

Servet-i Funûn, a literary review appearing in Turkey from 1896 onwards as an organ of the writers who introduced into Turkish the Western literary forms and ideas.

Shāfi'ī, those Muslims who follow the religious jurisprudence elaborated by the jurist Shafi'ī; see *Hanafī*.

shaikh (T. *şeyh*), in Arabic, the patriarch of the tribe or family; in Turkish, the spiritual head of a mystic order.

Shaikh-ul-Islam, the highest religious authority in the Ottoman system.

Shar', or *shari'ah* (A.), the path; the sum total of the religious-legal rules of Islam.

shar'ī qāḍī, the judges applying the *sharı'a* (*q.v.*).

Shī'ī, the sects recognizing Alī, Muhammad's son-in-law, as the legitimate successor to the Prophet and opposed to *Sunnī* (*q.v.*).

Shu'ūbiyah (A.), those who represented the movement under Abbasi rule the object of which was to inculcate equality among all Muslims as against the discrimination made by Arab against non-Arab Muslims.

shūra, a council.

sipahi, a holder of a benefice in the Ottoman imperial organization.

siyar (A.), a biography or book describing the conduct of the prophets.

Siyasetname (P. -*nāmah*), a treatise on statecraft written by the Selçuk Vizir Nizam al-Mulk in the eleventh century.

sufi, Muslim mystic; see *tasawwuf*.

sultanī, in Arabic, pertaining to a king's authority, or simply authority; imperial, in Turkish.

sunna, the Prophet's tradition.

Sunnī (T. *Sünnī*), the followers of the historical successorship, as established by the first three Caliphs, to the Prophet believed to be the orthodox, as opposed to the *Shī'ī* (*q.v.*), Muslims.

sölen, pre-Islamic tribal feasts of the Turks.

şuur (A. *shu'ūr*), consciousness (in Turkish usage).

tafsīr, a branch of Muslim learning dealing with the exegesis of the Kur'ān.

Tandırname, lit. fireplace book; oral beliefs in magic contained in folk-tales told by old women.

Tanẓimat, reforms initiated in Turkey with the proclamation of a charter in 1839.

tasawwuf, Islamic mysticism.

Tat, or *Tata*, probably a Chinese word from which came the word Tatar or Tartar.

tedbir-i nefs, *tedbir-i menẓil*, *tedbir-i devlet*, medieval Muslim terms for the practical sciences of self, of household, and of government respectively.

tekke, a convent of the Turkish mystic orders.

tengiẓ (*deniẓ*), sea.

teravih (A. *tarawīh*), the prayer performed in congregation only during *Ramaḍān* (*q.v.*).

timar, a benefice allocated to a *sipahi* (*q.v.*).

GLOSSARY

töre, pre-Islamic Turkish customary law.

tuba, a legendary tree believed to have its roots in Paradise and its branches spreading earthwards.

Turan, the country north and east of the River Oxus, believed to be the home of the Turanians or the Ural-Altaic peoples of whom the Turks constituted the majority.

Tüzükât, the ordinances of Timur (Tamerlane, 1336–1405).

'*Ukāz* (A.), a place between Tā'if and Nakhla in Hejaz where a fair was held annually in ancient times.

ulema (A. '*ulamā*), the corps of the Muslim scholars.

ümmet (A. *umma*), see Chapter II, note 7.

'*urf*, see Chapter VI, note 4.

vakf (A. *waqf*), sing. of *evkaf* (*q.v.*).

yasa, pre-Islamic public law of the Turks believed to have been codified by Jengiz.

ziamet, an Ottoman benefice larger in yield than a *timar* (*q.v.*).

zikr (A. *dhikr*), the collective, repetitive chanting of the attributes of God as practised in the *tekke* (*q.v.*) by the *sufis* (*q.v.*).

INDEX

A

Abbasi (*see also* Caliphate), 120, 128, 130, 203, 229, 254
Abdest, 186 f., 323
Abdul Aziz, 66
Abdülhak Hâmid, 146
Abdul Hamid, 181
Abdullah Cevdet, 314
Abdullah Haşim, 39
Abū Bakr (*see also* Caliphate), 225
Abū Hanīfa, 197, 200 f., 203, 301
Abū Yūsuf, 197
Aesthetics (*see also* Architecture, Art, and Music), 108, 271; methods of, 56, 59, 108, 215, 262 ff., 267, 282; Turkish, 108, 263
Ahl al-dhimma, 128, 323
Ahl al-Sunna, 323
Ahlīyya courts, 210, 323
Ahmed Vefik, 66
Albanian, 43, 75, 137; nationalism, 65, 71, 131
Ali Kemal, 314
Âli Paşa, 207
Ali Şefkati, 38 n.
Akçura, Yusuf, 20
Akhī, 302
Akkoyunlu Turks, 43 f.
al-'Arabī, Muhyi'l-dīn Ibn, 50–5
An'ane, *see* Tradition
Anglo-Saxon culture (*see also* Culture), 94, 100, 104, 108, 120–2, 128, 136, 168, 222 f., 244 f., 249, 252, 283, 307
Arab (*see also* Arabic), civilization, 228, 235, 238, 267, 272; culture, 108 f., 130 f., 135, 138 f.; nation, 76, 78, 127 f., 158; nationalism, 65, 71
Arabic, architecture, 272 f.; language forms in Turkish, 36, 43, 74, 77, 83–5, 105, 168, 177 f., 265, 278, 286; 290, 294 f., 297 f., music, 272, 300; sciences, 273; script, 75
Arafāt, 191 f.
Architecture, 107 f., 272, 274
Aristotle, 273 f., 278
Armenian (*see also* Non-Muslims), 59, 207 f., 300; nationalism, 65, 131

Art, 107 f., 262 ff.
Artīkoğulları, 44
Asceticism, Turkish traditions concerning, 29, 108, 254, 303
Aşik Kerem (*Kerem the Lover*), 35, 263, 299
Aşīk Paşa, 95
Atatürk, Mustafa Kemal, 13 f., 63 f., 227, 305, 314, 319, 321
Authority (*see also* Competence, *Mores*, and Sanction), 119 ff., 159 f., 184 f., 195 f., 214 f., 275; of Caliphs, 226 f., 230–3, 304
Azerī Turkish, 43

B

Bacon, Francis, 278
Bâkî, 146
Balkan Wars, 64, 73, 75, 95, 99, 176
Baltacıoğlu, İsmail Hakkı, 239 f.
Bektashi, 65, 263, 317
Benaloğulları, 44
Bergson, Henri, 61, 94, 253
Berkeley, Bishop, 51, 55
Bid'a, 152 f., 211, 234 f.
Binet, Alfred, 61

C

Caesaro-Papism, 218 f.
Caliphate, 120, 203, 205, 207 ff., 220 ff., 225–33; abolition of, 14, 319 f.
Capitalists, 311
Capitulations, 208, 277, 307 f.
Cemaat (*see also* Community), 206 ff., 307 f.
Cevdet, Abdullah, 314
Cevdet Paşa, 202
Charismatic power (*see also* Great Men), 63, 185 f.; Gökalp's, 14; use of term, 316
Chauvinism, 283 f.
Christianity and modern civilization (*see also* Civilization, European, and Civilization, Western), 75, 84, 101 f., 143, 144 f., 214–24, 272–5
'Civilization', carriers of, 259, 262, *see also* Great Men; definition of, 23–6, 89–92, 104 f., 109, 167, 171 f., 254, 266,

269, 282; development of, 68, 74 ff., 95 f., 142, 167 f., 259, 270 f., 309
Civilization, Eastern, 29, 75, 171, 236, 240, 249, 254, 265 ff., 270–5, 277 f., 286, 289 f., 300; European, 167 f., 179, 183, 251, 266 f., 270, 275 ff., 279, 286; Far Eastern, 167, 270 f., 273, 278; Greek, 144, 303; Iranian, 130 f., 133, 238, 249, 303; Islamic (*see also Ümmet*), 28, 167, 172, 183, 222, 265 f., 271 f., 289; Mediterranean, 267, 270, 272; Oriental, 262, 265; Ottoman, 102, 108, 237, 262, 265, 268, 289; Roman, 265, 270, 272; Taoist, 167; Turkish, 60, 269, 271, 284, 298; Western, 13, 23 f., 26, 28, 30 f., 63, 101 f., 104, 250, 262, 266 f., 270, 272–8, 282, 289, 296
Civilization-group, 25, 97–100, 120, 126, 171, 236, 241, 248, 270, 281, 287, 303
Clan, 118–21, 124 f.
Class, social (*see also* Consciousness and Solidarity), 62, 79, 100, 107
Classicism in Europe, 144 f.; in Turkey, 145 f.
Clericalism, 304 f.
Collective, conscience, 22, 158, 163 f., 185; consciousness, 62–5, 158; ideal, 68; representations, 62–5; sentiments, 158, 163; soul, 189
Collectivism (*see also* Culture), 100
Collectivistic education (*see also* Education, national), 320
Collectivity, 184, 189 ff., 242
Commune, 101, 120–5, 138 ff.
Communism, 312
Community (*see also* Cemaat and *Ümmet*), 64 f., 97, 102 f., 113–23, 125–32, 138 ff., 153–6, 225, 227, 287, 289, 317
Competence, authority through, 221, 227
Concordate system, 219 f.
Congregation (*see also* Collectivity), 225
Conscience, 22, 48, 98, 114, 153, 155, 158, 161–4, 165, 167 f., 172, 174 f., 185, 194, 306
Consciousness, 47 f., 51, 61–5, 68, 79, 98 n., 100, 102 f., 121, 125, 135, 150 f., 158, 161 ff., 192, 194, 264, 288, 314 f.
Conservatism, 92–5, 167, 174, 265, 279
Constitutional régime, 39, 40, 41
Constitutional Revolution of 1908 (*Meşrutiyet*), 18, 159, 182, 315
Contract, social, doctrine of, 215

Corporative basis, nations with, 121
Cosmopolitanism, 18, 74, 107, 281, 287, 306 f.
Cult, affairs of, 206 ff., 232
'Culture', 15, 23, 89, 98, 142, 238, 245, 259, 316, 321; definition of, 23 f., 25 f., 128, 104–9, 120 f., 166 f., 172, 224, 235, 254, 269, 280–3; national, 236 ff., 243 f., 245 f., 248 ff., 251 f., 259, 261, 264, 266, 281 ff., 284–9, 303; Turkish, 29, 143, 172 f., 246, 251 f., 265, 284–9, 305
Culture-group, 97, 101, 120, 270, 287
Customs, 116, 152 f.

D

D'Annunzio, 260
Dante, 260
Dede Korkut, 145, 263, 299, 318
Demirtaş, pseudonym of Gökalp, 315
Democracy (*see also* Populism and Constitutional régime), 14, 18, 28, 40 ff., 132, 143, 303
Demolins, Edmond, 98 ff.
Dertli, 263, 299
Descartes, 55, 115, 278
Determinism, 49, 60, 199
Divân-ı Lugât-üt-Türk, 167
Division of labour, social, 62, 64, 66, 119, 124, 157, 159 ff., 182, 266, 269, 274 ff., 282, 310
Diya, 129
Diyarbekir, 20, 43 ff., 130, 141, 314
Durkheim, Émile, 22 n., 60 ff., 64, 95, 97, 99, 115, 159 n., 164, 244

E

Eastern civilization, *see under* Civilization
Ecclesiastical councils, 216–19, 222; absence in Islam, 217
Economic patriotism, 306
Economy, national, 66, 73, 182, 280, 302, 307, 309 f., 313
Education (*see also Medrese* and *Mektep*), 81, 90, 135, 137, 147, 170, 212, 233 ff., 244 f., 259, 277 f., 281, 299, 300; Gökalp's, 35 ff., 38 f.; Islamic, 36, 211, 233–5; national, 235–47, 260, 264
Élan, 36, 156, 250, 253
Enderun, 29, 90, 262, 285, 323
Ergenekon, 268, 321
Étatist, 14, 309 f.

INDEX

Eternal essences, 51–5, 273
Ethics, theory of, 50; science of, 267, 315
Ethnic unity, *see Kavm*
European civilization, *see under* Civilization
Europeanism (*see also* Modernism, *Tanzimat* and Westernism), 27, 180 f., 202
Evkaf (*see also Vakf*), 140, 319, 323; Ministry of, 210 f., 319
Evolution, 24, 49, 113, 195 f., 236, 253, 261, 269, 271, 280, 310

F

Family, Turkish, 73, 251 f., 303
Far Eastern civilization, *see under* Civilization
Fārābī, 106, 272, 299 f.
Fatwā, 205, 208, 217, 221 f., 324
Feminism, 57, 303
Feudalism, 138 f., 140 f., 142 f., 262
Feudalization of the Ottoman Empire, 17
Fichte, 67
Fikh, 23, 103, 172, 180, 193–9, 286, 324; —*ism*, 29, 180
Fikret, Tevfik, 20, 146 f., 281, 316, 318
Finno-Ugrians, 75, 80, 167, 271
Folk, 127; civilization, 89 f.; literature, 35, 95, 236, 263, 271, 291, 298 f.; —lore, 30, 44 f., 89 f., 95, 99, 260, 263, 270, 278; music, 300; organizations, 90 ff., 127
Formalism, 17, 92 ff., 103, 174
'Fossil', social, 29, 172, 178, 182, 237, 293, 297
Fouillé, Alfred, 51, 55, 61
Futuwwa, 302, 324
Fuzulî, 106, 146, 317

G

Genius (*see also* Great Men), 30, 42, 63, 164, 175, 181, 244, 260, 263 f.
Ghazzalî, 55
Goethe, 260, 264
Gökalp, Ziya, biographical, 13, 20, 35–45, 314; influence of, 7, 14 f., 30 f.; intellectual framework of, 13–16, 20–6; and Pan-Turanism, 7 f.; writings of, 7, 13, 314–22
Graeco-Turkish War (1897), 176

Grand National Assembly, 225, 227, 309, 320
Great Men (*see also* Genius, Hero, Inventor, Reformer, and Sage), 30, 121, 152, 156–9, 163 f., 176, 238, 264
Greek(s) (*see also* Non-Muslims), 59, 65, 74, 78, 84, 90, 131, 207, 255, 300
Greek Orthodox Church, 64, 206, 217, 219, 254, 273
Grey Wolf, 268, 321
Guyeau, J. M., 51, 150
Gültekin (Orkhon) inscriptions, 89, 180

H

Hadīth, 52, 196 f.
Hâkimiyet-i Milliye, 265, 321
Halim Sâbit, 318
Halk, see Folk
Halkiyat, see Folklore
Hâmid, Abdülhak, 146
Hanafî, 44, 103, 208, 221, 306
Hanbalı, 221
Hanif, 158, 205
Hars, 168, 280, 284–9, 321
Haşim, Abdullah, 39
Havas, 107, 282
Hayy, 138 f.
Hero (*see also* Great Men), 30, 42, 68, 106, 159, 175, 181, 244
Höffding, Harald, 61
Hulla, 200
Humanities, place in education, 241, 243
Hungarian, 75, 131
Hygiene *versus* ritual, 186, 193 f.

I

'*Ibāda*, 207, 210
İbrahim Temo, 314
Idealism, 40, 242; national, 287; philosophy of, 50–5, 195, 243; sociological, 21, 57–66 *pass.*, 315; Turkish, 89, 242, 312; Turkist, 66, 76, 103, 316
Ideals (*see also* Collective representations), 36, 37, 38 f., 41, 50–5 *pass.*, 76, 79, 98, 185, 193, 287; definition of, 49 f., 57, 63, 67, 69 f., 152, 166, 284; development of, 66–70, 103, 242, 315; of nationalism, 71–5, 79–82, 103, 137, 302, 315
Idées-forces, 49, 51, 56, 288
Ideologist, 14, 164 f.

332 INDEX

Iftā, 199, 203 ff., 208 f., 217, 220 ff., 324
Ijmā, 196, 197
Ijtihād, 103, 196, 209, 217, 220
'Ilm, 210
Imām, 107, 201, 207, 225 f.
Imitationism, 17, 23, 39, 89, 94, 97, 250, 262
Imperialism, 228, 311
Individual, 63, 188–91
Individualism, 100, 312
Individualistic education, 235, 238 f., 241, 243 ff., 320
Institutions, social, 17 f., 64, 79, 81, 89–95, 108, 117, 167 ff., 172, 184, 241, 269, 280, 282, 298, 300, 302
Internationalism, 26, 74, 281 f., 287
Internationality (*see also* Civilization, Ottoman, *Ummet*), 75 f., 316
Inventor (*see also* Great Men), 157, 160 f.
Iranian civilization, *see under* Civilization
Irfan, 68, 168, 170, 174, 238, 284 f., 316, 321
Irk (see also Race), 127
İshak Sükûti, 314
Islam, 13, 20, 27, 63, 67, 74 f., 78, 80, 84, 103, 108, 126 f., 129 f., 143, 180, 191 f., 193–235 *pass.,* 254, 285 f.
Islâm Mecmuası, 317, 318, 319, 320
Islamic civilization, *see under* Civilization
Islamic education, *see under* Education
Islamic state, 205, 208, 210, 221 ff.
Islamism, 19 ff., 27, 76 f., 79, 177–81, 202, 233, 252, 314
Islamization, 71, 75, 84, 108, 130, 222, 279
İsmail Hakkı [Baltacıoğlu], 239 f.
İstihsān, 197
İstikbâl, 38 n.

J

Jāḥiz, 106, 317
James, William, 51, 61
Janet, Pièrre, 61
Janissaries, 16 f., 66, 92, 237, 277
Japan, 67, 69, 76, 270, 277
Jengiz, 180, 327
Jihād, 156, 159, 187, 218, 228, 324
Judiciary, 119 f., 122, 200, 203–10, 215–17, 220 f.
Julien, Camille, 135
Junaid, 54
Jurisprudence (*see also Fikh,* Law, and Judiciary), 193, 200, 204, 208

K

Ka'ba, 63, 187, 191 f., 324
Kalām, 180, 324
Kant, 51, 55, 150, 162, 174
Karacaoğlan, 299
Karagöz, 260, 263, 299
Karakoyunlu, 43 f.
Kavm (ethnic unity), 80, 82, 98 f., 113, 126–35, 317
Kaygusuz, 299
Kemal, Ali, 314
Kemal, Mustafa (Atatürk), 13 f., 64, 227, 305, 314, 319, 321
Kemal, Namık, 18–21, 22 n., 24, 36, 146, 163, 181, 202, 287, 314
Khārijī, 231
Khwārizm, 44
Kızıl Elma, 96, 325
Kızılbaş, 107, 317
Kölemen (Mamluk), 92, 226, 230, 325
Köprülü, Fuad, 29
Korkut Ata, 260
Köroğlu, 263, 299
Kultur, die (see also Hars), 168, 238, 283, 321
Kur'an, 63, 103, 155 f., 183 f., 195 ff., 201 f., 212 f., 230, 233, 301
Kurd, Kurdish, 43 f., 65, 75, 130 f., 136, 140 f., 314
Kutadgu Bilik, 180

L

Labour, social division of, 62, 64, 66, 119, 124, 157, 159 ff., 182, 266, 269, 274 ff., 282, 310
Laicism, 220
Language (*see also* Culture, Turkish language, and Turkist), 104 f., 177 f., 193, 228; and civilization, 82–5, 104 f.; and nationalism, 65, 82, 181; and nationality, 77 f., 80 ff., 129, 137, 228; and religion, 74, 80
Lapouge, de, 127
Latin, neologisms, 74, 84; script, 15, 65
Law, 304 f.; private, 118, 121, 195; public, 119 f., 128, 196, 201, 206–10
Legislative Assembly (*see also* Grand National Assembly), 208 f.
Levend confraternities, 92, 325
List, Friedrich, 66, 307, 313

INDEX

333

Literature, *see under* Classicism, Renaissance, Romanticism, and Turkish literature
Loti, Pièrre, 264

M

Mahmūd of Kashgar, 106, 317
Makruh, 194 n.
Mālikī, 197, 221
Mamluk (*Kölemen*), 92, 226, 230, 325
Manchester School (of political economy), 306 ff., 313
Manchurians, 75, 167
Mandub, 194 n.
'March 31', 176, 181
Ma'rūf, 153, 155 f., 194, 216, 318, 325
Marx, Karl, 60 ff., 98
Mashikhat, 210–13; *Yearbook of*, 209
Masjid, 191, 225 f., 228, 325
Materialism, 48; historical, 60 ff., 215
Maudsley, 61
Maunier, René, 253
Mawālī, 128, 325
Māwerdī, 203
Medeniyet (*see also* Civilization), 68, 316
Mediterranean civilization, *see under* Civilization
Medrese, 29, 36, 66, 90, 173 f., 210, 213 f., 229, 237, 278, 314, 325
Mefkûre (*see* Ideals), 70
Mehmed Bey of Karaman, 90, 131
Meillet, 135
Mejelle-i Ahkâm-ı Adliye, 221
Mektep, 173 f., 237, 325
Meşrutiyet, 18, 159, 182
Metaphysics, 46–9, 96, 149, 174
Mevlid, 108, 145, 172, 301, 325
Mezheb, 207, 212
Millet (*see also* Nation), 24, 76 f., 206, 325
Ministry of Economy, 313; *Evkaf*, 210 f., 319; Justice, 208, 210, 319; Pious Affairs, 201, 210
Modernism, Modernists (*see also* Europeanism and Westernism), 177–81, 233
Modernization, 71, 75 f., 101, 180, 202, 205, 245
Mongolian, 75, 167, 271
Moral density, 274 f.
Morality, 27, 37, 73, 106, 149–52, 205, 267, 302 ff., 310
Mores, 23, 152–6, 171–83, 184 f., 198, 216, 286, 288

Mosque, 191, 212 f.
Mubāh, 194
Muftī, 200 f., 203 f., 217, 220 ff., 228 ff., 232, 325
Muhammad, 63, 227 ff.
Mujtahid, 230, 325
Munkar, 153, 156, 194 f., 216
Music, 29, 268, 272 ff., 289, 299 ff.
Mustafa Kemal Atatürk, 13 f., 64, 227, 305, 314, 319, 321
Mysticism (*see also* Bektashi, *Sufi*, and *Tasawwuf*), 37, 50, 95, 273

N

Namık Kemal, 18–21, 22 n., 24, 36, 146, 163, 181, 202, 287, 314
Nasreddin Hoca, 260, 263, 299
Nass, 194, 196–9, 325
Nation, 38 f., 41, 75, 89, 104, 165, 167, 170, 181, 183, 249, 282 f., 286 ff.; definition of, 24 f., 27, 72, 76 ff., 82, 119–22, 128, 133, 134–8 pass., 143, 184, 223 f., 247 f., 281; rise of, 25, 74, 92, 124 f., 126, 128–34 pass., 163 f., 179 f., 224 f., 238, 240, 243, 280; Turkish, 89, 100, 125, 126, 130 f., 134–8 pass., 225, 246, 260 f., 268, 276 ff., 290, 302, 305 ff.
National arts, 263 f., 268, 273, 300; aspirations, 42; economy, 66, 73, 182, 280, 302, 307, 309 f., 313; education, 235–47, 260; language, 82, 95, 290, 297; life, 58, 166, 284, 308; values, 59, 82, 194, 242 ff. pass., 284, 288, 303
National Assembly, Grand, 225, 227, 309, 320
National Pact, 309
Nationalism, 19 f., 21, 71 f., 74, 100; Albanian, 65, 71, 131; Arab, 65, 71; Kurdish, 65; Non-Muslim (Ottoman), 21, 65, 71, 92, 131; Turkish (*see also* Turkism, and Turkist), 65, 74 f., 176, 234
Nationalism and fine arts, 73; and internationalism, 281 ff.; and language, 129, 131, 145; and morality, 73, 145; and religion, 145
Nationality, 15, 39, 43 f., 65, 70, 71 f., 75 f., 79–82, 131, 134, 136–8, 145, 223 f., 245, 268
Naturvölker (*see also* Primitive societies), 118

334　　　　　　　　INDEX

Nedim, 106, 146, 317
Neologisms, 74, 267, 294
Nevaî, 95, 145
New Life, 55–60, 95, 284, 288, 315
Nietzsche, 51, 164
Nizam al-Mulk, 130, 326
Non-Muslim (*see also* Armenian, Greek, and Ottoman), 56, 58 f., 130, 232, 273; nationalism, 21, 71, 92
Nordau, Max, 155
'Normal', 22, 30, 66, 182, 262, 280, 290

O

Oba, 138 ff., 160
Obligations, 187, 204
Ocak, 316
Oghuz Turks, 136, 236, 245
Oriental civilization, *see under* Civilization
Ottoman (*see also* Non-Muslim, *Tanẓimat*, Turkish), 16–20, 29, 43, 58 f., 72 f., 76, 78 f., 90 ff., 103, 105–8, 142, 171 f., 179, 182 f., 226, 229, 236, 245 f., 260 ff., 282, 285, 289, 290–5, 297, 300, 302, 305; civilization, *see under* Civilization; Commonwealth, 65, 260; Empire, 13, 16, 19 f., 71, 92, 128, 130–3, 142, 181, 226, 261; nation, 72 f., 93, 268
Ottomanism, 19 f., 72, 76, 79, 136, 260 f., 265

P

Pan-Islam (*see also* Islamism), 19, 20, 40, 136, 159
Pan-Turanism, 7 f., 20
Pan-Turkism (*see also* Turkism), 20, 22
Papacy, 143, 217, 218 ff.
'Pathological', 22, 25, 30, 66, 95, 100, 182, 262, 280, 290
Patriotism, 36, 73, 81, 193 f., 302, 306; economic, 306
Paulhan, 61
People's Party, 305
Persian, 36, 43, 74, 83 f., 90, 105 f. 108,, 136, 168, 177, 238, 245 f., 265, 272 f., 286, 290–8
Personality, 152, 190, 241 ff., 249
Peter the Great, 17, 40, 275
Petrarch, 260
Phenomenalism, 51
Philosophy, 46–55, 96, 123 f., 273, 295 f., 310; Gökalp's, 21, 31, 37 f., 312

Piety, 35, 188, 200 f., 204 f., 207–11, 213, 220 f., 228 f.
Pious Affairs, Ministry of, 201, 210
Plato, 273
Polygamy, 29, 200, 251–5 *pass.*
Populism, 22, 224, 259, 303, 306
Positivism, 49
Prayer in Islam, 187 f., 191 f.
Press, role of, 17, 41, 65, 71, 74 f.
'Profane', 186 f., 190, 319
Prohibitions, 187, 190, 194
Protestantism (*see also* Reformation), 222
Psychology, 39, 171, 239, 249
Pushkin, 260

Q

Qaḍā, 199, 203 f., 217, 221 f., 324 f.
Qāḍi, 200 f., 203 f., 209, 220 ff., 325; — *asker*, 203, 210, 325
Qiyās, 197, 325

R

Race, 15, 60, 75, 126 f., 134 f., 271, 314
Racialism, 14
Radicalism (*see also* Revolutionism), 92 f., 95, 266, 279, 293
Ramazan, 192, 301, 326
Rāshidūn Caliphs, 229 ff., 326
Rationalism, 194
Ray, John, 307, 313
Red Apple (*Kızıl Elma*), 96, 325
Refinement, 280–3, 297
Reform policy, effects of earlier (*see also Tanẓimat*), 17 f.
Reformation (*see also* Christianity and modern civilization and Protestantism), 131, 145, 244, 274
Reformer (*see* Great Men), 157 ff., 161, 250
Religion, 59, 63, 73 f., 80 ff., 96, 99, 101 ff., 119 f., 129, 133, 136, 143, 159 f., 182, 184–233 *pass.*, 253 ff., 301, 310; comparative, 267 f.; and education, 199 f., 210–14, 233 ff.; and law, 200 f.; and nationality, 80 f., 192; and state, 202–10, 220–3
Renaissance, 145–7, 263, 274
Revelation, 67, 195, 222
Revolutionism, 265 ff.
Ribot, Theodule, 61
Ritual, 27, 187–92, 193, 301, 303
Romanticism, 22, 145, 147, 244, 274
Rousseau, Jean Jacques, 252, 260, 264

INDEX 335

S

'Sacred', 185–92, 217 f.
Safavids, 245
Sage (*see* Great Men), 175, 181
Şah Ismail, 35, 263, 299
Sammiya, 138 f.
Sanction, power of, 69, 97, 185, 204 f., 216
Şefkati, Ali, 38 n.
Shāfi'ī, 44, 221, 326
Shaikh, 108 f., 201, 211, 326
Shaikh-ul-Islām, 203, 205, 208–10, 214, 228, 326
Shakespeare, 264
Shamanism, 254
Shamanist Tunguz, 75; Yakuts, 80
Shar' (*sharī'a, sheriat*), 18, 21, 27, 31, 103, 194 ff., 198, 203, 208 ff., 319, 326
Shī'ī, 231, 326
Shinasi (Şinasi), 19, 105, 146 f., 317
Shūra, 198, 326
Shu'ūbiyah, 128, 249, 326
Sipahi, 16, 81, 92, 142, 326
Siyasetname, 130, 326
Socialism, 57, 79, 82, 316
Society, 24 f., 63, 123–6, 142 f., 162 f., 166, 173, 181, 184, 195 f., 245, 269, 280, 289, 302 f., 312, 317; democratic, 132 f.; ethnic, 132 f.; feudal, 125, 262; organic, 62, 124 f., 184 ff., 294 f.; primitive, 62, 124 f., 184 f., 269, 303; segmentary, 62, 124 f., 132, 157 ff.
Sociology (Sociologists), 22, 27, 39, 56, 124, 144, 164 f., 169 ff., 171–83 *pass.*, 186, 193, 196–9, 222 f., 239, 253, 260, 269, 274, 280, 288
Solidarism, 15, 312
Solidarity, 59, 73, 102, 124 f., 139, 143, 157, 226, 286, 302, 312.
Soul, 70, 239, 247–50 *pass.*
State, 61, 74, 76 ff., 79, 81 f., 98 f., 103, 117, 127–30, 135, 142 f., 159, 184, 202, 205–8, 214 f., 217, 218 ff., 222 f., 224, 244 f., 248, 280, 310 f.
Sufism (*see* Tasawwuf), 14, 20, 50 f., 326
Süküti, İshak, 314
Süleyman (the Magnificent), 180
Süleyman Chelebi, 145
Süleyman Pasha, 66
Sultanate, 66, 182, 205, 207, 229, 320
Sultanī, 16, 127
Sumner, W. G., 22 n.
Sunna, 103, 184 f., 326

T

Sunnī, 130, 231, 326
'Survival', 29, 172, 179, 182, 260
Symbol-terms, Gökalp's, 15 f.
Symbols, 77, 159, 194, 293
Syndicalism, 15
Syndicates, 302 f.

Ta'āruf, 172, 177, 179, 228
Tanākur, 172, 177, 179, 228
Tandırname, 167, 271, 326
Tanzimat (*see also* Ottomanism), 16, 27, 72, 133, 145, 159, 181 f., 202, 205–8, 223, 234, 237, 245, 249, 254, 260, 262, 270, 276, 285–90, 326
Tarde, Gabriel, 71, 74, 97 f.
Tasawwuf (*see Sufism*), 14, 50 ,52, 145, 205, 326
Tat, 89, 326
Tatar, 237, 292, 326
Technology (*see also* Civilization), 75, 96
Tehzib (*see* Refinement), 280–3
Temo, İbrahim, 314
Terminology (*see also* Neologisms), 74, 77, 84 f., 104 f.; Gökalp's, 15 f., 20
Tevfik Fikret, 20, 146 f., 281, 316, 318
Tevfik Sedat, pseudonym of Gökalp, 314, 315
Theocracy, 24, 27, 119, 121, 305
Theology, 37, 95, 186 n., 306
Timar, 92, 326, 327
Timur, 180
Tönnies, 22 n.
Tore, 62, 82, 180, 236, 254, 260, 327; —ism, 180
Traditions, 23, 91, 94 ff., 171–4, 271, 280, 303 f.; Ottoman, 18, 265
Tunguz, 75, 270, 271, 293
Turan, Turanian, 8, 78 f., 267, 312, 316, 327
Turgut Reis, 92
Türk Yurdu, 8, 71, 316, 317, 318
Turkish-Arab state, 78
Turkish (*see also under subject headings*): arts, 95, 105 ff., 262 f., 272, 299 f.; culture, 29, 62, 143, 179; dialects, 43, 237, 292, 298; education, 66, 90, 236 f., 328; literature, 17, 35, 38, 95, 105 f., 145 f., 236, 262, 268, 281, 295 f., 298 f.; morality, 73, 106, 303; patriotism, 73; traditions, 24 f., 180
Turkish (language), 43 ff., 62, 143; development of, 73, 83 ff., 105, 177 f., 261,

336 INDEX

290; reform policy, 14, 16, 66, 84 f., 95, 143, 267, 290–8

Turkism, 20, 22, 27, 63, 71 f., 76, 79, 134, 177, 180 f., 237, 259, 261, 265 f., 282 f., 287 f., 289, 297, 301–6, 315

Turkist, 64, 77 f., 134 ff., 177 ff., 233, 237, 261, 266, 282, 288, 289, 290–6 *pass.*, 298

Turkoman, 130 f., 141, 245

Tüzük, 89

Tüzükât, 180, 327

U

'Ulamā (Ulema), 106 f., 199, 211, 229, 291, 327

Umayyad, 127, 229

Umma (see also Ümmet), 200, 215, 315, 327

Ümmet (see Umma), 21, 24, 59, 63, 65 f., 73, 76 ff., 79, 84, 95, 98–101, 103, 117, 126–9, 131, 133, 136, 145 ff., 163, 184 ff., 223–6, 227, 245 f., 285 ff., 315, 327

'Urf (see Mores), 152, 156, 183, 184, 194–9, 216, 318

Utilitarianism, 194, 215, 240

Uygur Turks, 90

V

Vakf (see Evkaf), 139, 231, 327

Value judgment, 23, 28, 148 f., 171, 190, 235 f.

Values, 24, 49, 56–9, 99, 117, 160, 162 f., 165, 189, 194, 242–4, 284, 288, 302 f., 305

Vefik, Ahmed, 66

Völkerpsychologie, 243 f.

W

Weber, Alfred, 22 n.

Weber, Max, 316

Weltanschauung, 146, 270

Western civilization, *see under* Civilization

Westernism, Westernists (*see also* Europeanism and Modernism), 14, 19 ff., 24, 27, 178, 252, 285

Wilsonian principles, 261

Womanhood (*see also* Family, Feminism, and Polygamy), 29, 252–5, 273 f., 303, 305

World classics, translation of, 208, 299

Worship, *see 'Ibāda*

Y

Yasa, 89 f., 180, 327

Young Turk Revolution (*see Meşrutiyet*), 176, 315

Yunus Emre, 108, 260, 263, 299, 317

Yusuf Akçura, 20

Z

Zakāt, 187

Zanîm, (*see* 'Profane'), 319

Zaydan, J., 158, 325

Zenbilli Ali, 203, 209 f., 319

Ziamet, 142, 327

Zikr, 301, 327